TITLE II

W9-ATE-470

JAN 1977
RECEIVED
OHIO DOMINICAN
COLLEGE LIBRARY
COLUMBUS, OHIO
43219

1911 OHIO DOMINICAN COLLEGE

LIBRARY

1216 SUNBURY RD.
COLUMBUS, OHIO

BY THE SAME AUTHOR
*The Dialectical Temper: The Rhetorical Art of
Robert Browning,* 1968

Tennyson's Style

Tennyson's Style

W. DAVID SHAW

Cornell University Press

ITHACA AND LONDON

821. 81
7312 Sh
1976

Cornell University Press gratefully acknowledges a grant from the Andrew F. Mellon Foundation that aided in bringing this book to publication.

Copyright © 1976 by Cornell University

All rights reserved. Except for brief quotations in a review, this book, or parts thereof, must not be reproduced in any form without permission in writing from the publisher. For information address Cornell University Press, 124 Roberts Place, Ithaca, New York 14850.

First published 1976 by Cornell University Press.
Published in the United Kingdom by Cornell University Press Ltd., 2–4 Brook Street, London W1Y 1AA.

International Standard Book Number 0–8014–1021–5
Library of Congress Catalog Card Number 76–12814
Printed in the United States of America by York Composition Co., Inc.
Librarians: Library of Congress cataloging information appears on the last page of the book.

For Carol and Cathy

100935

Acknowledgments

My ideas about Tennyson are not the offspring of a sudden interest, but the result of many years of study and thought. Though my subject is style, any study of Tennyson's poetry is also concerned with human experience in its broadest sense, and I have been obliged to draw frequently on the labors and insights of others. I have learned most from my former mentor, F. E. L. Priestley. As the author of a book on Tennyson's language, he has refined my understanding; as a generous counselor, he has given the manuscript an indispensable first reading; as a teacher, he encouraged me almost twenty years ago to look closely at the grammar of poetry and to trace connections between a poet's language and his thought. I am also under special obligation to two scholars who taught me at a later time. Jerome Buckley and Douglas Bush have written on Tennyson with humanity and grace and with easy erudition, and I was privileged to benefit from their rare example. Like everyone writing on Tennyson today, I am also indebted to the scholarship and criticism of Christopher Ricks and to the pioneer work of Alan Sinfield. To these five scholars, I would like to enumerate my debts in detail and in this way express the gratitude I feel, but I doubt if I could accurately recall how much I owe to each.

I have been much influenced by theories and criticism not specifically concerned with Tennyson. Whether in the study, in the classroom, or in conversation with friends and colleagues at Victoria College, University of Toronto, consideration of various critical methods has been seminal. W. K. Wimsatt has influenced

my discussion of puns, rhyme, and metaphor; W. H. Empson has
provided a useful model for the analysis of ambiguity; Northrop
Frye has shaped my views of Tennyson's prosody and use of
myth. To Yvor Winters I owe my conception of the imitative
fallacy, and to Barbara Herrnstein Smith the idea of poetic closure. J. C. Ransom has suggested the scheme of indeterminate
meanings, and Roman Jakobson's theory of metaphor and metonymy has shaped my understanding of syntax in *Maud*. To the
methodology of two studies that propound the doctrines of a neo–
New Criticism—Stephen Booth's *Essay on Shakespeare's Sonnets*
and Helen Vendler's *On Extended Wings: Wallace Stevens'
Longer Poems*—I owe less specific debts. I have adapted Booth's
treatment of formal, phonetic, and other patterns in Shakespeare's sonnets to portions of *In Memoriam;* to Tennyson, I
have applied Vendler's approach to Stevens' grammar. However
greatly transformed these influences have been by my own speculations, I acknowledge them here with gratitude.

For the kind support and expert counsel I have come to identify with the editors at Cornell University Press, I am grateful.
This study would not have been completed without the generous
aid of the Killam Foundation of Canada: a Senior Research
Fellowship enabled me to complete a first draft of the manuscript
during the academic year 1973–1974. I also wish to thank the
staff of the Tennyson Research Centre, The City Library, Lincoln, England, for their friendly assistance.

Quotations from unpublished manuscripts in its possession are
by permission of the Houghton Library, Harvard University.
The quotation from a Walt Whitman manuscript is by permission of the Collection of American Literature, The Beinecke Rare
Book and Manuscript Library, Yale University. The British
Library Board has kindly allowed me to quote from Egerton MS
2825. For permission to use material that I wrote originally for
scholarly journals, I am grateful to the editors. I have used portions of the following articles: "The Aurora: A Spiritual Metaphor in Tennyson," *Victorian Poetry,* III (Autumn, 1965), 213–
222; "The Transcendentalist Problem in Tennyson's Poetry of

Debate," *Philological Quarterly*, XLVI (January, 1967), 79–94; *"In Memoriam* and the Rhetoric of Confession," *Journal of English Literary History*, XXXVIII (March, 1971), 80–103; "Imagination and Intellect in Tennyson's 'Lucretius,' " *Modern Language Quarterly*, XXXIII (June, 1972), 130–139; "Tennyson's 'Tithonus' and the Problem of Mortality," *Philological Quarterly*, LII (April, 1973), 274–285; "Tennyson's Late Elegies," *Victorian Poetry*, XII (Spring, 1974), 1–12; and "Consolation and Catharsis in *In Memoriam,*" *Modern Language Quarterly*, XXXVII (March, 1976), 47–67. Quotations from Tennyson's poems are from *The Poems of Tennyson,* edited by Christopher Ricks (London and Harlow: Longman Group Limited, 1969).

The person who has most freely combined frankness with discernment in her reactions to the book is also the person who has given me most support in writing it. I refer to my wife, Carol, who has been catalyst, critic, and coauthor all in one.

W. DAVID SHAW

Toronto

Contents

Tennyson's Style

Finally, there should grow the most austere of all mental qualities; I mean the sense for style. It is an aesthetic sense, based on admiration for the direct attainment of a foreseen end, simply and without waste. Style in art, style in literature, style in science, style in logic, style in practical execution have fundamentally the same aesthetic qualities, namely, attainment and restraint. . . . Style, in its finest sense, is the last acquirement of the educated mind; it is also the most useful. It pervades the whole being. . . . Style is the ultimate morality of mind.

A. N. WHITEHEAD, *The Aims of Education*

Introduction: The
Victorian Context

An influential critic of our time has found Tennyson deficient in subtlety and surprise. T. S. Eliot writes that "the blank verse of Tennyson . . . is cruder . . . than that of half a dozen contemporaries of Shakespeare; cruder, because less capable of expressing complicated, subtle, and surprising emotions."[1] By tracing through the major poems some of Tennyson's experiments in tone, genre, prosody, rhetoric, and syntax, I hope to refute Eliot's charge. To readers accustomed to the more complicated figures of modern and metaphysical poetry, I hope to demonstrate that Tennyson's acknowledged grandeur is compatible with indirection and his ornament with subtlety.[2] His style, I argue, is "refined," not simply because it is polished, but because it is finely faceted. It calls for a sympathy, not just with a technique of composition, but with a reflective temperament that loves to circle back on its moods in a self-retarding movement. Many of Tennyson's repetitions are, in Hopkins' sense, an "over-and-overing" of ideas in order to map the "inscape" of thought. His use of long vowels to mute the accents and to minimize the sense

1. "Christopher Marlowe," in *Selected Essays* (London, 1932), pp. 118–119.
2. Since I trace connections between Tennyson's style and his thought, I also try to show that Tennyson is not as intellectually deficient as some critics claim. W. H. Auden, for example, praises Tennyson's metrical skills, but complains that he was "the stupidest [English poet]; there was little about melancholia that he didn't know; there was little else that he did" (*A Selection from the Poems of Alfred, Lord Tennyson,* selected and with an introduction by W. H. Auden [Garden City, N.Y., 1944], p. x).

of movement "compels the rhythm," in Northrop Frye's phrase, "to return on itself, and to elaborate what is essentially a *pattern of sound*."[3] The slow unfolding creates a motion of unhurried calm. It displays what Henry James calls "the slow depositing instinct" of his genius. Tennyson steadily moves into their appointed places elements of parallel syntax and repeating sounds till they fall into patterns, "in stillness, in peace, in brooding."[4] His best poems combine directness and indirectness. Tremors of doubt and nuance express inward reserves. The poems tremble always at halfway points, at moments of transition or uncertainty—when Tithonus is suspended between life and death, when Persephone's winter sojourn turns into spring, or when "the speck" that bears King Arthur "pass[es] on and on, and goe[s] / From less to less" before dissolving ("The Passing of Arthur," ll. 465, 467–468).

Though Tennyson's refined manner evolves very rapidly, he patiently experiments with a great variety of ballads, sonnets, visionary fragments, blank-verse monologues, and so on, before he finds the proper modes for his reflective temperament. It is not, for example, until *In Memoriam* that Tennyson finally settles on the tetrameter quatrain with included couplet as the metrical form best suited to organize his thought in long reflective stretches. Composing a poetry of epitaph and inscription, he slows the tempo with vowels of varied quantities that mute the accents. Before he achieves the final technical perfection of "The Lady of Shalott" he eliminates a host of infelicities, and before the fluent originality of "Tithonus" come episodes of faltering and borrowing. The sublime visions of "The Holy Grail" were not achieved without many trials in the visionary mode; parts of "The Poet," in which Shelley's disciple is still too mesmerized by the throb of the Pindaric ode, produce mere strain and pretension. In the classical monologues Tennyson arrives at Ulysses' hard, laconic reticence only by first experimenting with and taming the effusive lamentation of the lotos-eaters and Oenone.

Because his poetry is the result of endless experiments, he is

3. *Anatomy of Criticism* (Princeton, N.J., 1957), p. 256.
4. Quoted by Christopher Ricks in *Tennyson* (New York, 1972), p. 293.

harder to imitate than earlier poets—and also harder to appreciate. Most inimitable is the way Tennyson's style, "his technical accomplishment," in Eliot's phrase, "is intimate with his depths. . . . By looking innocently at the surface we are most likely to come to the depths."[5] All his efforts to create classical deities, heroes, and human beings, all the fantasia of Ida's college or Arthurian romance derive from Tennyson's discernment of a fatal blank or void. Even as Tennyson tries and discards style after style, genre after genre, his response to the void shapes his experiments. It creates a sense of pathos, but also of courage and honesty—a quality that is not separate from the poetic art. The poet who emerges from this study always revised, tested, and questioned the poetic traditions he inherited. By renewing Miltonic, Spenserian, and Romantic styles Tennyson fashioned a Victorian tradition that served successors such as Yeats and Eliot as a support, even though they finally repudiated that support. That he did so without having such support himself, in an age that was predicting the imminent decline of poetry, suggests, as Valerie Pitt has said, "an unusual greatness."[6]

The Poetic Tradition

At the beginning of the Victorian age poets wavered, in their practice, between two traditions, and critics wavered, in their allegiance, between two theories describing these traditions. Alba Warren generalizes that the affinities of the age were "all subjectivist but it long[ed] for objectivity."[7] In an influential essay in the *North British Review* (August, 1852) David Masson dramatizes the conflict as an opposition between the idealizing theories

5. "In Memoriam," in *Selected Essays,* p. 337. Is Eliot's appreciative comment inconsistent with his general indictment of Tennyson in the essay "Christopher Marlowe"? Eliot responds to Tennyson in the same ambivalent way that he responds to Milton—and for comparable reasons. He believes that Milton and Tennyson realize superbly one important element of poetry, grandeur of sound, but that there exists in both cases a division between the philosopher or theologian and the poet.

6. *Tennyson Laureate* (Toronto, 1962), p. 270.

7. *English Poetic Theory, 1825–1865* (Princeton, N.J., 1950), p. 210.

of Francis Bacon and the mimetic theories of Aristotle.[8] According
to Bacon, poetry is "feigned history";[9] the poet creates an idealized world, but in no sense a true one. In the classical theory of
Aristotle, on the other hand, the poet presents, not a more
idealized world than is normally perceived but a more *essential*
world—one in which the final and formal causes are more readily
discernible. Theorists debate to this day what Aristotle means by
his concept of imitation. It seems to be the poetic equivalent of
his doctrine of immanent teleology, his teaching that final and
formal causes do not dwell apart from their material causes, but
dwell within them. Thomas Hobbes, in drawing up an English,
neoclassical poetic whose keystone is the imitation of nature, reduces the idealizing imagination discussed by Bacon to a subordinate office: "Beyond the actual works of nature a poet may . . .
go; but beyond the conceived possibility of nature, never."[10] Dr.
Johnson, who maintains that all predominance of fancy over
reason manifests a degree of insanity, follows Hobbes in relegating
imagination to a subordinate role.[11] It remains for Wordsworth
and Coleridge to reconcile in theory the rival claims of imagination and the imitation of nature.

8. Masson's review of E. S. Dallas' *Poetics: An Essay on Poetry* (London,
1852) and of Alexander Smith's *Poems* (London, 1853) originally ap-
peared as an essay, "Theories of Poetry and a New Poet," *North British
Review,* XIX (August, 1853), 297–344. The essay was republished as the
ninth chapter of Masson's *Essays Biographical and Critical, Chiefly on
English Poets* (Cambridge, Eng., 1856). Tennyson owned a copy of
Masson's *Essays,* which is now in the Tennyson Archives at Lincoln,
England.

9. Poetry "is nothing else but FAINED HISTORIE, which may be stiled as
well in Prose as in Verse. The use of this FAINED HISTORIE hath beene to
giue some shadowe of satisfaction to the minde of Man in those points
wherein the Nature of things doth denie it" (*The Advancement of Learn-
ing,* Book II; quoted in *Critical Essays of the Seventeenth Century,* ed.
J. E. Spingarn [Oxford, 1908], II, 62).

10. "Answer to Davenant's Preface to *Gondibert*"; quoted in *Critical
Essays of the Seventeenth Century,* ed. Spingarn, II, 62.

11. Thomas Hobbes, *Leviathan,* ed. C. B. Macpherson (Harmondsworth,
Eng., 1968), Part I, ch. viii, p. 136: "But without Steddinesse, and
Direction to some Ende, a great Fancy is one kind of Madnesse."

The Romantics claim for the imagination the same degree of autonomy that idealizing theorists such as Bacon, and such eighteenth-century adherents of the Baconian tradition as Joseph Addison and Joseph Warton, had claimed. (In his *Spectator* papers—Numbers 411–421—Addison maintains that the poet "humours the imagination by mending and perfecting nature"; Warton's "Ode to Fancy," which reflects the influence of Addison, ascribes to poetry the power of providing vicarious emotional experience.) But Romantic theory transforms this tradition: it asserts not merely the centrality of the imagination but the truth of its creations. It attributes to poetry the same *degree* (though not, to be sure, the same *kind*) of truth that classical and neoclassical theory had attributed to the imitation of nature. The Romantic imagination, identified with "Reason in her most exalted mood" (Wordsworth, *The Prelude*, XIV, 192), assumes a cognitive dignity inconceivable in either the Baconian tradition (which views imagination as the organ, not of truth, but of mere fiction) or in the neoclassical tradition of Hobbes and Dr. Johnson.

Masson's theory of the opposition between Bacon and Aristotle, between imagination and the imitation of nature, runs deep in Victorian poetics. Common in poetic criticism of the age is the quotation of the lines from Shakespeare's *The Winter's Tale* in which Polixenes tries to resolve the claims of the two traditions:[12]

> Yet nature is made better by no mean
> But nature makes that mean: so, over that art,
> Which you say adds to nature, is an art
> That nature makes.   [IV, iii, 89–92]

Arnold's "imaginative reason," Newman's "illative sense," Browning's "fancy with fact," Ruskin's "naturalist ideal"—all are

12. The quotation from *The Winter's Tale* appears in the following essays devoted to poetics and criticism: David Masson, *Essays Biographical and Critical*, p. 418; John Skelton, "What Are the Functions of the Artist?"—review of John Ruskin's *Modern Painters*, in *Fraser's Magazine*, LV (June, 1857), 631; and John Skelton, review, "Mr. Dallas, *The Gay Science*," in *Fraser's Magazine*, LXXIV (December, 1866), 782. A similar idea, without the supporting quotation, appears in John Eagles, "The Natural in Art," *Blackwood's Magazine*, LI (April, 1842), 435.

evidence of attempts to maintain the great Victorian synthesis, to
keep the revolutionary Romantic and the conservative eighteenth-
century elements in balance. Masson himself, in the article in
which he defines the opposition, identifies with Bacon. In praising
Tennyson's "Vision of Sin" for its "continued phantasmagory of
scene and incident," Masson anticipates the aesthetic theory of
the Symbolists, who banish description so that beautiful, surreal
things may be magically evoked. Though Masson calls his theory
of poetry "dramatic," it is, as Isobel Armstrong observes, "not
dramatic in Arnold's [or Aristotle's] strictly classical sense. . . .
[Masson's] theory of dramatic poetry derives from Keats and the
letters of Keats. . . . With Masson we are back with . . .
Hallam's belief in the poetry of sensation."[13] When such poetry is
not directly lyrical, it is either dramatic in the sense understood by
Masson and E. S. Dallas, the author of the treatise Masson was
reviewing in his *North British* article—that is, it abandons the
poet to the range of moral and imaginative license enjoyed by
Tennyson and Browning in their dramatic monologues—or else
it creates an autonomous world, like the world of Browning's
"Childe Roland" or Tennyson's "The Hesperides." As in Baudelaire and Poe, the dreamlike progression in these last two poems
aspires to the condition of music, which is one of the principal
aims of Symbolism. Half the charm of these poems derives from
the satisfaction of guessing what the poet intimates as he draws
a circle of words around his meaning without directly stating it.

If the lyric, the dramatic lyric, and the dramatic monologue
are the genres in which the autonomous, Baconian tradition in
Victorian poetry finds its most liberated expression, one would
expect that the two major genres, the epic and the drama, would
be the forms in which the Aristotelian, classical tradition of the
age finds its clearest expression. In fact, however, the epic and the
drama are uncongenial to the Victorians. Poems such as Arnold's
Merope, which conform most closely to classical canons of
tragedy or epic, are less successful than hybrid forms such as

13. *Victorian Scrutinies: Reviews of Poetry, 1830–1870* (London, 1972),
p. 38.

Arnold's "Sohrab and Rustum," Browning's *Sordello*, and Tennyson's *The Princess*. Neoclassical poetics bases its theory on the belief that "kinds" of writing exist apart from the poet, and that they correspond to the objective classifications of taxonomy. The dogma of kinds breaks down in the nineteenth century, as poets begin to experiment, in epical autobiographies such as *The Prelude* and in elegiac confessions such as *In Memoriam*, in monologues and in monodramas, with a vast array of hybrid forms that are all more personal than plays and epics but less personal than lyric poems. If we try to read "Sohrab and Rustum" as Homeric epic or Sophoclean tragedy, the way we read *Merope*, we miss its real power. The poem succeeds as an elegiac expansion of "Dover Beach," as an account of confused struggle on "the darkling plain," in which a father kills his son. Despite Arnold's meditative use of epic similes, the sheer velocity of epic would ruin the reflective rallentando, the slowing down of life and tempo, in an elegy. If, on the other hand, we value the confused struggle for its pathos, we cannot at the same time read "Sohrab and Rustum" as a classical tragedy, even though its anagnorisis, or recognition scene, may coincide with its peripeteia, or turning point, in the best Aristotelian fashion. An elegiac narrative cannot disclose a truly tragic event but, at most, a pathetic accident. The one generic type precludes the other: the more tragic irony, the less elegiac pathos, and the more pathos, the less irony. As for Browning's *Sordello*, which, like Arnold's poem, abounds in epic devices, it is a confessional displacement of the epic, in which the subject is less the nominal hero than the speaker's consciousness. It is as if Homer, in displaying his genius for contriving the *Iliad*, were to boast that, as the content of the poet's own consciousness, Achilles' story is more "real" than a story that does not allow us to see into the creative life of the epic poet. The effect of Tennyson's narrative experiments in *The Princess* is less that of epic than of dream vision: logical connections of the narrative carry less of the meaning than does the logic hidden in the transformation of Ida from a royal eagle into a vicious tiger cat or mare. The children in the lyrics serve as proxies for other elements that cluster round them: the parents, marriage, love, and so on. Such clusters, for which any one image may do synecdochic duty as a part that stands for the whole, tend to occur in close proximity to each other, like fragments in a dream.

Since the classical, conservative strain in Victorian poetics is not successfully realized in the major classical genres of epic and tragedy, how is it realized? It is realized, I think, in the revival of a rhetorical tradition—a tradition prominent in ancient, Renaissance, and neoclassical poetics, but out of favor in our own time. An indispensable study of the background of this rhetorical and grammatical tradition in Victorian poetry is P. W. K. Stone's *The Art of Poetry, 1750–1820* (London, 1967). Stone ascribes to the influence of Romantic poetic theory "the renunciation of classical genres," and he blames Romanticism for the deplorable loss of "the tropes and figures of rhetoric, [which], with a few exceptions, fell into disuse" (p. 147). Stone also points out, however, that even in the works of such eighteenth-century rhetoricians as Hugh Blair and George Campbell "the lists of tropes and figures so lovingly elaborated by Renaissance rhetoricians appear in their works (if they appear at all) in a much simplified and rationalized form, as do most of the other traditional sharp divisions and sub-divisions of rhetoric" (p. 13). The truth of Stone's generalization is readily confirmed by consulting any of the handbooks on grammar and rhetoric that were available to Tennyson in his father's library. In analyzing the grammar and rhetoric of Tennyson's poetry I try to show how Tennyson combines the symbolic form characteristic of Romantic poems with grammatical and rhetorical structures of the kind treated in neoclassical theories. One suspects that a great deal of Victorian poetic theory is an attempt to unify the two approaches that Stone distinguishes: on the one hand, a Romantic emphasis on symbol and image (corresponding to Masson's Baconian tradition); and, on the other hand, a neoclassical emphasis on grammar and rhetoric (and hence on literary theory of the rhetorical type). Critical of the Romantic rejection of "even the laws of grammar and syntax" (p. 149), Stone polemically defends the rhetorical emphasis as the only "valid approach to the analysis of literary techniques and, by extension, of literary values" (p. 141). The adaptation by the Victorians of both their neoclassical and Romantic heritage is a chapter in the history of nineteenth-century poetic theory that has still to be written.

So dominant, however, is the classical, rhetorical tradition in Victorian poetry that I have been able to find in Tennyson, the prototypic Victorian, many examples of every rhetorical scheme that John Broadbent discusses in his analysis of the classical epic style of *Paradise Lost*.[14] These schemes range from anadiplosis, repetition of the last word of a given line at the beginning of the next, to *traductio*, repetition of a word in an altered form.[15] It is

14. *Paradise Lost: Introduction* (Cambridge, Eng., 1972), pp. 129–131. Broadbent shows how the repetitive syntax of Milton's speeches in heaven renders the infallibility of God's logic. Similarly, in the syntax of "Demeter and Persephone," which is often highly repetitive and schematic, Tennyson uses the iterative device of starting and ending a line with the same word—"Earth-mother, in the harvest hymns of Earth" (l. 146)—to dramatize the interrelatedness and order of the deity's works. Like Homer and Virgil, Milton also repeats whole sentences of *Paradise Lost* in successive paragraphs. Tennyson uses the same device in "The Passing of Arthur": "And answer made the bold Sir Bedivere: / 'I heard the ripple washing in the reeds, / And the wild water lapping on the crag.' / To whom replied King Arthur" (ll. 237–240). When these three sentences are repeated forty lines later (ll. 283–286), the second and third lines are reversed. The block repetition dramatizes the formality of the ritual, but minor changes in the formula suggest Bedivere is delinquent in performing the rite. Even Tennyson's repetition of a word in an altered form—"and clomb / Even to the highest he could climb, and saw, / . . . Or thought he saw" ("The Passing of Arthur," ll. 462–465)—doubles the syntax back upon itself, as in Milton's "highly they raged / Against the Highest" (*Paradise Lost*, I, 667–668). Similar to the interlocking parallel constructions that Milton's God uses in addressing the Messiah—"be judged and die, / And dying rise, and rising with him raise / His brethren" (*Paradise Lost*, III, 295–297)—is *In Memoriam*'s arrangement of words in a climactic order of sense: "Who trusted God was love indeed / And love Creation's final law" (LVI, 13–14). None of these rhetorical devices is significant by itself. But in Tennyson their cumulative effect is self-retarding. The expansion of the syntax—then the return to its original ground before expanding further—allows Tennyson to trace the motions of his soul as it hesitates in a pause. For a moment his words stay poised and trembling. They circle back on themselves, hovering like insects in mid-air.

15. A study of Sister Miriam Joseph's *Shakespeare's Use of the Arts of*

easy, of course, to argue from either a modern or a Romantic pre-
conception of what poetry should be, to discredit any rhetorical
theory of poetry which loses sight of ambiguity or sight of the affective self, then to offer what remains as true criticism—even when
that truth turns out to be a bundle of discrepancies or a psychological monster. Instead of yielding to such dogmatism, the objective
scholar will remember that the rhetoric of the best Victorian
poems is essentially a means of showing how the mind is moved
to make moral and intellectual distinctions. By determining which
poems still persuade a reader who has only an antiquarian interest
in the logical, scientific, or religious ideas they contain, it is
possible to distinguish between a Victorian sage who simply tells
a reader what to believe and a sage like Tennyson's Tiresias, who
uses "ambushed" meanings, or indirect persuasion, to engage
even a skeptical reader in the issues at stake. Like Mill, Newman,
and Ruskin (writers on such diverse subjects as politics, religion,
and the visual arts), the poet of *In Memoriam* and "The Ancient
Sage" does not persuade his readers by devising logical arguments,
but by projecting a coherent vision of life into which his arguments will fit. By seeing the rhetorical tradition in its proper context, the historian who studies nineteenth-century literature will
be in a better position to understand that tradition. He will also
be in a better position to judge its special importance in the
history of an age whose rhetorical writings rank with its poetry
and fiction as artistic achievements of a high order.

Stylistic Models

   Tennyson's allusions to other poets are easy to identify. But the
pervasive stylistic influences are more elusive. There are few
critical rules for the study of such influences, despite the fact that

---

Language (New York, 1947) discloses that Tennyson uses many of the
schemes found in epic and dramatic poetry and discussed in Renaissance
handbooks on grammar and rhetoric. For a detailed discussion of Tennyson's familiarity with these rhetorical schemes see below, in the Bibliographical Essay, under "Elements of Tennyson's Poetry," the section
"Knowledge of Rhetoric," pp. 310–313.

historical scholarship has made the game necessary and respect-
able.[16] The allusions cited by Christopher Ricks in his edition of
The Poems of Tennyson are the most comprehensive guide.[17] The
greatest number of allusions are to the Bible (a total of 272),
followed, in order, by Milton, 213; Shakespeare, 155; Shelley,
129; Keats, 86; Horace, 57; Malory, 47; Virgil, 44; Lucretius,
38; Homer, 37; Gray, 29; Spenser, 27; Pope, 26; Wordsworth,
25; Ovid, 20. (I have omitted poets with fewer than twenty
references.)

As George Ford[18] and others have demonstrated, the Romantic
poet who exercises the greatest influence on Tennyson is Keats.
Few other poets catch so successfully as Tennyson the distinctive
quality of Keats's synesthetic imagery. When Tennyson compares
the "dark . . . forethought" in Merlin's brain to a "blind wave
feeling round his long sea-hall / In silence" ("Merlin and Vivien,"
ll. 228–231), he is fusing his sense impressions to make sightless
liquidity seem tactile and solid. As Walter Jackson Bate explains,
Keats's "really distinctive quality . . . is less the SUBSTITUTION
than it is the SUBSTANTIATION of one sense by another in order to
give, as it were, additional dimension and depth."[19] In a passage
in *Maud* that echoes Keats's "Ode to Psyche," Tennyson captures
Keats's power of active suggestion through compressed metaphor.
In his description of a strange beloved cedar of Lebanon, whose
"limbs have increased / Upon a pastoral slope," and whose fore-
fathers shadowed "the snow-limbed Eve" (*Maud*, I, 616–617,
626), sensuous and spiritual mystery is conveyed. Like Keats's
"branchèd thoughts, new grown" ("Ode to Psyche," l. 52), the
"merry play" (*Maud*, I, 629) of the erotic stars, as they move
"in and out" among the swaying limbs, exhibits the poet's
organically felt participation in the disparate objects he combines,

16. For a sensible discussion of the problem see Winifred Nowottny,
The Language Poets Use (New York, 1962), pp. 201–202.
17. London, 1969.
18. *Keats and the Victorians* (Hamden, Conn., 1962).
19. "Keats's Style: Evolution toward Qualities of Permanent Value," in
English Romantic Poets: Modern Essays in Criticism, ed. M. H. Abrams
(New York, 1960), p. 345.

a kinesthetic gift that is "comparatively weaker in metaphysical poetry." The suggestive erotic play introduces a stroke of broad parody across the biblical solemnity of the "thornless garden" (I, 625) of Eden. As Bate says of Keats's style, Tennyson's "provides us with an idiom that at its best approximates that of Shakespeare. The combination, at least, is rare since Shakespeare."[20]

Lionel Stevenson,[21] among others, has traced the influence of Shelley, especially on the *young* Tennyson. Characteristic of this influence is Tennyson's description of the "Low voluptuous music" (ll. 16–32) in "The Vision of Sin" (1842). Like one of Shelley's self-woven similes in *Prometheus Unbound,* or Shelley's successive comparisons of the skylark to a poet, a maiden, a glowworm, and a rose, Tennyson's comparisons multiply rapidly. To confuse the senses and create a sense of swooning, Tennyson likens the orgiastic music to more and more exotic and surreal notions of itself—to a storm, "a hundred-throated nightingale," and even an image that is no longer auditory: the gold and purple circles in a rainbow. Tennyson's rustic and domestic idylls —"The Gardener's Daughter," "Dora," "The May Queen," "Lady Clara Vere de Vere," "Aylmer's Field," and *Enoch Arden*—are clearly indebted to the pastoral art of Wordsworth. But a comparison of Tennyson's "Mariana" poems with Wordsworth's treatment of a similar subject in "The Ruined Cottage" (later revised as *The Excursion,* Book I) discloses the difference between Tennyson's artificial and Wordsworth's simple style. Tennyson can be simple as well as ornate, but even when he arranges simple words in prose order—"They sat them down upon the yellow sand / Between the sun and moon upon the shore" ("The Lotos-Eaters," ll. 37–38)—no one would mistake them for the diction of Wordsworth or Frost. Tennyson's most important affinity with Wordsworth is less stylistic than visionary.

20. "Keats's Style," p. 352.
21. "The 'High-Born Maiden' Symbol in Tennyson," in *Critical Essays on the Poetry of Tennyson,* ed. John Killham (London, 1960), pp. 126–136. On the influence of Byron see W. D. Paden, *Tennyson in Egypt: A Study of the Imagery in His Earlier Work* (New York, 1942), pp. 60, 137–138.

In *The Prelude* and *In Memoriam* the poets experience similar doubts. Tennyson is assailed by fears that the nature he has venerated as a "lucid veil" is merely the image of himself, reflected from a nonexistent mirror. The same fear is the source of Wordsworth's dread and exaltation in *The Prelude*. In moments of visionary dreariness the poet who has multiplied himself endlessly through encounters with nature begins to fear that there is nothing behind the mask of nature that is not already in front of it.

Despite the greater number of allusions to Gray, the most important eighteenth-century influence on Tennyson is Pope. Tennyson and Pope are the two absolute masters of English style. Ruskin says of Pope, "you have in English much higher grasp and melody of language from more passionate minds, but you have nothing else, in its range, so perfect."[22] Tennyson's father had insisted that his son master Pope, and the pupil learned his lesson well. Where in English poetry, outside Pope himself, will one find more delicately chiseled irony than in *The Princess,* insinuated with a lighter touch or better conveying the beauty that is in microcosms? Compared to the delicate game of innuendo that Tennyson plays, and that Pope plays with comparable skill in *The Rape of the Lock,* the usual mock-epic tricks seem almost crude. Tennyson is also indebted to Pope for his classical inspiration. His "Ulysses," for example, has passed its Greek original through the same rhetorical crucible through which Pope passed Homer. What has emerged is highly sententious and intellectualized. Though well suited to a Homeric passage that has passion, oratory, or a great crisis for its subject, what impresses us strongly is what also impresses us in reading Pope's translation, not what we remember of the much simpler style of Homer himself.

If we are to judge by the allusions that Ricks cites in his edition of Tennyson, the single most important influence (after the biblical authors) is Milton. Ricks himself has spoken well of the way in which Milton enlivens his metaphors, "without shock and

22. John Ruskin, "Lectures on Art"; reprinted in *The Literary Criticism of John Ruskin,* ed. Harold Bloom (New York, 1965), p. 191.

with the dignity suited to the Grand Style."[23] Like Milton's metaphors, Tennyson's are usually traditional; he makes them original
with a minimum of alteration. The metaphors in *In Memoriam,*
for example, are in keeping with the decorum of elegy, which
encourages the poet to enliven the discreet puns in "far-off
interest" (I, 8) and "fallen leaves which kept their green" (XCV,
23). The second conceit enacts a brief apotheosis, for "green"
invigorates the metaphor in "leaves" and reverses the cycle of fall
and ruin. The pun is dignified because of its association with
"The noble letters of the dead" (XCV, 24), and natural in the
ease with which the perpetual verdure to which it refers provides
for Hallam an unexpected immortality. Ricks shows how Milton
re-establishes the power of metaphors gone dead in words like
"transport" (*Paradise Lost,* III, 81). In order to preserve a
balance between idiosyncrasy of style and observance of decorum,
Tennyson also enlivens faded metaphors, expelling from his
wordplay whatever is conceited or bizarre. In "The Palace of
Art" he discreetly revives forgotten etymologies. The turn on
"stood" and "standing," and the clash of "Rolled" and "fixed,"
draw attention to the fact that language is quickening.

> Joined not, but stood, and standing saw
> The hollow orb of moving Circumstance
> Rolled round by one fixed law.   [ll. 254–256]

The word "Circumstance," which like most abstractions is a
dead metaphor, is set in a context of motion that restores its
etymology of "standing round." The paradox of stationary motion
tightens the whole line, and puts the needed note of mystery into
cosmic law.

A number of commentators have observed that, though Milton's
verse has great momentum, it also pivots on itself, moving backward as well as forward. According to one critic, Milton's "verse
revolves on its axis at every line";[24] another commentator compares Milton's "Grand Style" to "the energy of Satan, who

23. Christopher Ricks, *Milton's Grand Style* (Oxford, 1963), p. 59.
24. Walter Raleigh, *Milton* (London, 1900), p. 192.

'Throws his steep flight in many an Aerie wheele.' "[25] There are
few poets who have reproduced this self-retarding movement
more accurately than Tennyson. His style seems to be going forward when it is actually turning round, like the phrases in *In
Memoriam* which repeat, repeat, and repeat again, though the
last time with some redeeming difference. The circularity was
first recognized by Walt Whitman, who perceived that Tennyson's
"doubts, swervings, doublings upon himself, have been typical of
our age."[26] Resourceful hovering is the feature of Tennyson's
style that Alan Sinfield calls "analogical." Tennyson's syntax, like
Milton's, "lingers over a given idea. . . . A notion is not explored in depth and explained, but approached from various
angles on the same plane, turned round and reformulated."[27]

Among the Elizabethans, the most important stylistic influences
on Tennyson are Spenser and Shakespeare. Northrop Frye has
suggested that "the most remarkable sustained mastery of verbal
OPSIS in English . . . is exhibited in *The Faerie Queene*."[28] The
ability to present the visual through sound is a gift that Tennyson
shares with Spenser. In "The Lotos-Eaters" Tennyson visualizes
the trembling, forward movement of the stream, about to plunge
over the edge, by means of the cautious advance of his alexandrine, which seems hesitant to swell out beyond the nine preceding lines:

> And like a downward smoke, the slender stream
> Along the cliff to fall and pause and fall did seem. [ll. 8–9]

The extra syllables combine with the pattern of advance and retreat to exaggerate the horizontal motion. The use of sound to
visualize the stream is far more intrinsic to Tennyson's adaptation
of Spenser's technique than the mere use of the stanzaic form that

25. *Milton's Grand Style*, p. 36.
26. Whitman's comments appear on unnumbered, disconnected pages of
a manuscript (now in the Beinecke Library at Yale), containing material
for a projected essay on Tennyson.
27. Alan Sinfield, *The Language of Tennyson's "In Memoriam"* (New
York, 1971), p. 100.
28. *Anatomy of Criticism*, p. 259.

bears Spenser's name. The use of sound is comparable to Spenser's in Frye's example of visual OPSIS in *The Faerie Queene*—"The Eugh obedient to the bender's will" (I, i, 76)—where the weak syllables in the middle make the line sag out in a bow shape. Frye goes on to observe that "when Una goes astray the rhythm goes astray with her: 'And Una wandring farre in woods and forrests.' " This Spenserian effect is reproduced in "Oenone." When Paris goes astray, Oenone makes a loose sentence even looser by adding a present participle and carelessly heaping "bunch and berry and flower" in the final phrase (ll. 97–100). When Spenser's subject is harmony in music, we have, as Frye observes, "an identical rhyme on one of the few appropriate words in the language."[29] Similarly, in "Oenone," when the subject is song, Tennyson's blank verse appropriately breaks into repetition and near rhyme:

> . . . and build up all
> My sorrow with my song, as yonder walls
> Rose slowly to a music slowly breathed.   [ll. 38–40]

Though Shakespeare's sonnets and his play *Love's Labour's Lost* are models for *In Memoriam* and *The Princess*, respectively, and though Tennyson calls *Maud* his "little *Hamlet*,"[30] Tennyson is most Shakespearean, not in his actual use of Shakespearean sources, but in his use of metaphor. It is preposterous to judge Tennyson according to the high standards set by Shakespeare, the greatest of all masters of this figure. I suggest that Tennyson's metaphors are seldom as bold as Shakespeare's: they are traditional in Milton's manner. But occasionally, as in the lover's climactic celebration of Maud (Part I, XVIII, 611–626), we may fairly compare Tennyson's metaphors with Shakespeare's— in this case, with the metaphors Cleopatra uses to praise Antony (*Antony and Cleopatra*, V, ii, 82–92). In both passages the boldest and most abrupt transitions are also the most successful: the transformation of Antony, the colossus astride the ocean, into

29. *Anatomy of Criticism,* p. 260.
30. Hallam Tennyson, *Alfred Lord Tennyson: A Memoir* (London, 1897), I, 396.

the rattling thunder that shakes the world, then into the genial
overflowing of nature's bounty; the transformation of Maud's
English garden into the *hortus conclusus* of the Song of Songs,
then into the thornless paradise of Eve. Both Antony and Maud
are impressed upon our minds as immense, generous forces; the
tenors of the metaphors, like their vehicles, literally overflow.

To evoke such elemental qualities neither Shakespeare nor
Tennyson can rely on the exactness of particular comparisons.
Antony's "dolphin-like" delights, for example, which "show'd his
back above / The element they liv'd in," comprise a sunken metaphor that keeps just below full visibility. Cleopatra suggests
Antony's generous reserves without actually defining them. Similarly, in *Maud,* when the reader tries to construct a unified
impression from the psalmlike prayer which plays upon the lover's
pulses with an erotic fullness of the blood, and which uses the
same words to speak simultaneously of a woman, a landscape,
and a biblical idea, he gets lost in the process. Such use of metaphor to convey in Antony a force of nature (some elemental
thing, rather than a normal human attribute) is characteristic
of Shakespeare. When Tennyson writes this way in *Maud,* he
takes what seem to be impossible risks. But by controlling the
changes of his lyric force and tempo, Tennyson never gives the
reader time to ponder the transitions, as he might ponder them in
reading prose. Tennyson, like Shakespeare, is infinitely bolder
than most of his contemporaries. But because his metaphoric resources are also richer and more flexible, his risks are justified. He
wins his gambles with ease.

The classical influences on Tennyson, especially of Homer,
Theocritus, Lucretius, Catullus, Virgil, Horace, and Ovid, are
the subject of an authoritative monograph by W. P. Mustard.[31]
The most just summation of these classical influences comes from
Douglas Bush: "In spite of his fondness for Greek poetry and
Greek subjects, Tennyson was much more of a Roman." As Bush
points out, Tennyson is "in so many ways akin to Virgil that one
cannot, in some of his best writing, mark where Virgilian inspira-

31. *Classical Echoes in Tennyson* (New York, 1904).

tion leaves off and Tennyson begins."[32] Tennyson, for example, has a fondness for Latin word order and for Virgil's self-embedding syntax, which envelops its subject in modifiers that divide it from the main verb. The kernel words in Tennyson's sentences are often qualified by clauses that come after them, as in Virgil, so that in the first eight lines of Section LXXXVI of *In Memoriam,* for example, which is quoted in the next paragraph, the mind has to double back on the sequence. In Tennyson the shift from self-embedding, Latin syntax to more normal "branching" syntax, which sends off modifiers from the main trunk of subject and verb, usually signals a change of tone, as when the involuted rhetoric of Ulysses the orator alternates with the plain Homeric style of the mariner. The many phrases that modify the "idle king" (l. 1) are designed to be read in bits, as a sequence; and phrases in apposition to "My mariners" (l. 45) are so elaborately self-embedded that Ulysses has to repeat the subject "you and I" (l. 49) before introducing the main verb.

> My mariners,
> Souls that have toiled, and wrought, and thought with me—
> That ever with a frolic welcome took
> The thunder and the sunshine, and opposed
> Free hearts, free foreheads—you and I are old.   [ll. 45–49]

Elsewhere in "Ulysses" the syntax branches; and the fading margin glimpsed through the arch, though presented in a less logical sequence, is grasped at once as a sensory whole (ll. 19–21).

Though the language of *In Memoriam* has the severity of a knife that strips away distracting detail and probes eternity, in rare moments of Virgilian opulence, as in Section LXXXVI, the syntax starts to drape itself in veils, tying its modifying clauses and phrases in between adjective and noun, subject and verb, with knots of conjunctions, prepositions, and participles. The kernel of the sentence is "Air, fan my brows." But "air" is heavily qualified by the clauses that come after, so that the mind has to double back on the sequence that advances and returns upon itself in

32. *Mythology and the Romantic Tradition in English Poetry* (Cambridge, Mass., 1937), pp. 226–227.

Virgil's manner. Though less natural than branching syntax, this self-embedding type is closer to the causal series: *showers, rollest from the gloom, breathe bare, fan and blow.* Yet by the time we reach the main verb the veiled subject of the lyric, lost amid the profusion of detail, has all but dropped from view.

> Sweet after showers, ambrosial air,
>   That rollest from the gorgeous gloom
>   Of evening over brake and bloom
> And meadow, slowly breathing bare
>
> The round of space, and rapt below
>   Through all the dewy-tasselled wood,
>   And shadowing down the hornèd flood
> In ripples, fan my brows and blow
>
> The fever from my cheek, and sigh
>   The full new life that feeds thy breath
>   Throughout my frame, till Doubt and Death,
> Ill brethren, let the fancy fly
>
> From belt to belt of crimson seas
>   On leagues of odour streaming far,
>   To where in yonder orient star
> A hundred spirits whisper 'Peace.'

The first line is generated from a conventional phrase, "sweet air," which we recover by removing the first and last words. Viewed in this way, the line is the result of separating adjective from noun— an attempt, by inserting words between them, to open spaces in the mind. In the rest of the section the spaciousness is as much a function of the self-embedding syntax as it is of the sacramental images or of the expanding pattern of alliterating sounds. Grammatical elements that are conventionally joined—the apostrophized "air" and the principal verb, "fan," for example—are disjoined to accommodate effects of marveling interjection. Through godlike sundering of elemental matter, the self-embedding Latin syntax gives extra value to the verb. Though the petition to "fan" comes in the middle of a line, it is so strong compared to the endings of most lines that it escapes its grammatical tie. Enacting a leap of volition, syntax alone affirms the autonomy of prayer.

The verbs "sigh" and "fly" are also stressed by their being syntactically distanced. Because these verbs are also terminal rhymes, Tennyson is able to combine strongly alliterating internal words with elements firmly bonded to the poles. He also combines his self-embedding syntax with a seamless joining of quatrain to quatrain. The syntax of a single sentence has to carry the poet across fearful divides. But as Tennyson severs his grammar to integrate his hopes and his fears, his self-embedding syntax magnificently survives its crossings to dramatize the dangers inherent in all crossings and the precarious move toward finality and "Peace." Tennyson's Latin syntax is most obtrusive, and least successful, in passages like this from *The Princess:* "while / They stood, so rapt, we gazing, came a voice" (II, 296–297). The absolute construction "we gazing," with its present participle operating inside the general pastness, is syntactic shorthand for a carefully subordinated temporal sequence. The crushing together of parts of speech is efficient in Latin, but in English the narrative economy is lost in the abruptness and discomfort.

Even when Tennyson is imitating Homer, the sophisticated syntax of Tennyson is closer to the slower, more involved movement of Virgil than it is to the spontaneity and ease of the Greek poet. One of the most important influences on Tennyson, however, is the use of classical epic similes common to both Homer and Virgil. Like their similes, the impressionistic syntax of *Maud* juxtaposes pictures, not just of the garden and the red-ribbed hollow, but of love and hate, light and dark, heaven and earth, so that each may be viewed in terms of all the others. Each picture opens another window in the speaker's head. John Broadbent believes "there is pleasure in the mere opening of the windows, as with cut-out Advent calendars."[33] The shifting frames of Tennyson's "The Vision of Sin" and "The Holy Grail" seem to satisfy a desire of the Victorians to look through magical windows into a world more real than their own. Like many of the similes in Homer and Virgil, the apertures in Tennyson's story flow operate like backgrounds in surrealist paintings. They satisfy the same

33. *Paradise Lost: Introduction,* p. 142.

desire as do Daguerre's diorama and a host of Victorian inventions like the stereopticon, the panorama, and the magic lantern. Many of Tennyson's short similes are brief associative poems, like Tithonus' comparison of Aurora's whisper to "that strange song I heard Apollo sing, / When Ilion like a mist rose into towers" ("Tithonus," ll. 62–63). "Like a mist" merges the solid towers with the insubstantial and the strange. Psychologically, the enclosure of simile within simile represents a kind of reverie, and the abundance of similes in the proem to "The Lotos-Eaters" has a window-opening or perspective effect appropriate to dreaming. As in Homer and Virgil, the epic similes in *The Princess* have the important and beautiful function of removing the action from the confused human foreground to a pastoral world of "snowy doves athwart the dusk" (IV, 149–151). In the midst of flying scarves and fiery splinters, similes of the "Saint's glory up in heaven" (V, 503) and the "pillar of electric cloud" (V, 513) create a landscape that is decidedly surrealist. By changing the focus like a magic lantern, they beguile us into accepting the muddledom and charm.

The quality that is perhaps most inimitable in Tennyson's style is Virgilian regret treated with Homeric simplicity. We hear it at the end of "Ulysses" and "Tithonus," when the speakers, having reached a center of reflection and knowledge, stand serene, watching their feeling, as it were, from a great distance. Tennyson, like Dante in his most intense moods, has complete command of himself; he can look calmly round, while the barge that bears King Arthur passes on. Though Arnold, in his second lecture on translating Homer, denied that Tennyson was a master of the grand style, the ending of "Tithonus" offers one of the most perfect examples of Arnold's "grand style severe,"[34] the peculiar achievement, Arnold believes, of Dante and Milton.

> Thou seëst all things, thou wilt see my grave:
> Thou wilt renew thy beauty morn by morn. [ll. 73–74]

34. "On Translating Homer: Last Words," *The Complete Prose Works of Matthew Arnold*, ed. R. H. Super (Ann Arbor, Mich., 1960), I, 189.

There is a power of classical restraint here, a power that comes, in
Arnold's phrase, "from saying a thing with a kind of intense compression, or in an illusive, brief, almost haughty way."[35] Tithonus
has to speak in sadness of the earth, but he will not let that sadness falsify what he sees. His acute feeling is equaled only by his
perfect command of what he feels. In "Thou seëst all things, thou
wilt see my grave" and in such lines as "And the new sun rose
bringing the new year" ("The Passing of Arthur," l. 469), there is
that undercurrent of meaning, that Virgilian sense of the abyss in
things, which is the evidence in, and shadow upon, Tennyson's
style of all those deeper places out of which his best poetry has
come. It is as if the poet is saying that these are the facts of the
thing as they stand. Though perfectly severe and accurate, utterly
uninfluenced by the firmly governed emotion of the speaker, such
lines possess the special dignity of the classical style—a style which
limits the expression to the simple facts and leaves the reader to
gather from them what he can.[36]

Bagehot on Ornate Style

Though Walter Bagehot's comments on Tennyson's style,
originally made in 1864, and republished in his *Literary Studies*
in 1879,[37] did little to damage the poet's reputation during his

35. *Ibid.*
36. Ruskin's example of such "calm veracity" in classical style is *Iliad,*
iii, 243: "So she spoke. But them, already, the life-giving earth possessed,
there in Lacedaemon, in the dear fatherland" (quoted in "Of the Pathetic
Fallacy," in *Modern Painters,* III, Part IV, ch. xii; in *Works of John
Ruskin,* ed. E. T. Cook and Alexander Wedderburn, Library Edition
[London, 1904], V, 213).
37. According to Bagehot's most recent editor, Norman St. John-Stevas,
in *The Collected Works of Walter Bagehot* (Cambridge, Mass., 1965),
"after Bagehot's death, Lord Bryce suggested to Richard Hutton in a letter
of October 2 1877, that the essays of Bagehot should be collected and
published and Hutton himself undertook the editing. The result was
Literary Studies, containing a selection of Bagehot's essays in two volumes
which were published by Longmans in 1879. They were followed by
Biographical Studies, which came out in one volume in 1881"
(Editor's Preface, I, 13). Bagehot's literary essays were popular enough to
justify another edition in 1898; my quotations are from a chapter in this

lifetime, the depreciation of Tennyson that accompanied the de-
valuation of patriotism and Victorian values in general after
World War I found in the argument of the Victorian economist a
useful weapon. Just as Victorian poetry has never recovered from
T. S. Eliot's charge that its major poets are merely reflective,[38]
so Tennyson's reputation in the twentieth century has never quite
recovered from Bagehot's criticism. Too often Bagehot's praise of
Tennyson's poetry of illusion is forgotten, and only his unfavor-
able comments recalled. The crux of Bagehot's charge is that
when Tennyson pursues ornateness for its own sake, he chokes on
the kind of lush circumlocution that turns Enoch's fish into
"ocean-spoil / In ocean-smelling osier" (*Enoch Arden,* ll. 93–94).
What Shakespeare's puns were for Dr. Johnson, circumlocutions
are for Bagehot: they are the fatal Cleopatra for which Tennyson
loses a world and is content to lose it. Bagehot rightly objects to
the love of ornament which veils the commonplace in grandiose
words. If we feel Enoch's "ocean-spoil" is ludicrously inflated, it
is because it so easily changes into its flat equivalent: fish in a fish
basket. A poet who describes King Arthur's moustache as "a
knightly growth that fringed his lips" ("The Passing of Arthur,"
l. 388) feigns an interest in the moustache by trying to make it
less commonplace than it is. Equally offensive is the circumlocution that turns the taking of the Eucharist in *In Memoriam* into
the same savoring of the "foaming grape," described with the
same overripeness, as the drinking of champagne at the wedding:
"Or when the kneeling hamlet drains / The chalice of the grapes
of God" (X, 15–16); "My drooping memory will not shun / The
foaming grape of eastern France" ("Epilogue," ll. 79–80). When
Tennyson tries to celebrate luxuriance in an overrefined style,

edition: "Wordworth, Tennyson, and Browning; Or, Pure, Ornate, and
Grotesque Art in English Poetry," in *Literary Studies,* ed. R. H. Hutton,
II (London, 1898), 326–381.
   38. "The Metaphysical Poets," in *Selected Essays,* p. 287: "It is some-
thing which had happened to the mind of England between the time of
Donne or Lord Herbert of Cherbury and the time of Tennyson and
Browning; it is the difference between the intellectual poet and the reflec-
tive poet."

Bagehot justly criticizes him for trying to be something he is not: a poet of animal and vegetable fertility, like Browning and Meredith.

But abuse of an ornate style is no argument against its right use. Not all of Tennyson's circumlocutions are equally pompous and impossible to justify. In *In Memoriam,* "The very source and fount of Day" (XXIV, 3) is not the equivalent of sun: it is the sun as creator, the origin of light. Nor, in the next line, does "wandering isles of night" translate flatly into "sunspots." To say that the spots are wandering isles is to set the darkness in an ocean of light. By projecting a design upon the heavens, the unfamiliar phrase presents creation, literally, in a new light. Whenever an inflated term, instead of the proper one, approaches the inexpressive, it is possible to cite in Tennyson many circumlocutions which, by not employing the proper term, approach the inexpressible. "The sun / Must bear no name," says Wallace Stevens ("Notes toward a Supreme Fiction," I, 19–20). But when Tennyson calls the sun the "very source and fount of Day" (XXIV, 3) he shows how creative his art of the ineffable, his renaming of "something that never could be named" ("Notes toward a Supreme Fiction," I, 17), can be.

Nor does the ornate style pervade Tennyson to the degree Bagehot assumes. Tennyson's long quantities, accumulating sounds, and parallel syntax may all be present, but if their effects were muted the result would still be a poetry of contrived simplicity, like most of *In Memoriam* and the late elegies. Only the obtrusive presence of all three features produces the extreme form of artifice, the style that Bagehot calls "ornate." In discussing such poems, it is necessary to retain the valuable descriptive meaning of "ornate"—embellishment of syntax and sound—and change its damaging emotive meaning—merely pompous or inflated. When Tennyson's style is most gorgeous and ornate—in such a poem as "The Holy Grail"—it is too often assumed that it is *only* gorgeous and ornate. My argument about such poems is not that they are not ornate, but that their ornateness also allows remarkable subtlety and surprise. Readers will want to discriminate be-

tween the occasional flatness of Tennyson's ornate style and its
more frequent liveliness and daring.

Poetry of Illusion and the Naturalist Ideal

The Victorian who comments most intelligently on style, even
though he consigns Tennyson to the second order of poets, is a
critic of genius, John Ruskin. In *Modern Painters,* Ruskin distinguishes among four classes of writers: "the men who feel
nothing, and therefore see truly; the men who feel strongly, think
weakly, and see untruly (second order of poets); the men who
feel strongly, think strongly, and see truly (first order of poets);
and the men who, strong as human creatures can be, are yet sub-
mitted to influences stronger than they, and see in a sort untruly,
because what they see is inconceivably above them." If the first
and lowest order of men happen to be poets, their style is "insin-
cere, deliberately wrought out with chill and studied fancy," like
many of Tennyson's portraits in "The Palace of Art." Ruskin
was the first to identify as characteristic of Tennyson the kind of
poetry written by the second class of men, those "who feel
strongly, think weakly, and see untruly." Such poets use ornament
functionally, to create an atmosphere of indistinct illusion. According to Ruskin, they "are generally themselves subdued by the
feelings under which they write, or at least, write as choosing to
be so; and therefore admit of certain expressions and modes of
thought which are in some sort diseased or false."[39] More typical

---

39. "Of the Pathetic Fallacy," in *Works of John Ruskin,* ed. Cook and
Wedderburn, V, 209, 216, 210. For a Victorian critique of Ruskin's system
of classification see Roden Noel, "Use of Metaphor and 'Pathetic Fallacy'
in Poetry," *Fortnightly Review,* V (August 1, 1866), 670–684. Noel observes
that "the criticism which disposes of a quality that is essential to such
poetry as Tennyson's, by calling it a weakness, and a 'note' of inferiority,
may itself be suspected of shallowness" (p. 671). According to Noel,
Ruskin's mistake is to assume that the poet "only describes things as they
appear to us" (p. 672). "The analogies of natural things to spiritual, and
the beauty of these which the poet discerns" are not, as Ruskin believes,
"fallacies." A more adequate metaphysics would show that they "are as
much facts as the more obvious facts that sea-water is salt and green, and
that foam is white or grey" (p. 672). See note 40, below.

than Tennyson's direct use of artifice—his use of ornament to feign an interest in King Arthur's moustache or in Enoch's fish— is his use of artifice of this second kind to present in "Tithonus" and the proem of "The Lotos-Eaters" the illusions and half beliefs of strong desire.

The wavering impressions of "The Lotos-Eaters" are a good example of how the poetry of illusion can intimate shifting perceptions of its subject, as if presenting its objects through a light haze. But it must not be thought that such poetry necessarily produces "unreal enhancements"—to use Bagehot's term—of ignoble desires like the lotos-eaters'. There are other poems, such as "Tithonus," in which the speaker is also subdued by strong feeling, but in which we see that the desire is noble; in a more perfect world it ought to be fulfilled. Seldom does the poetry of illusion produce subtler constraints, more wishful longing, or more poignant attempts at self-conviction than in the portrayal of Tithonus' yearning. A noble pathetic fallacy transforms the mists at dawn into "tremulous eyes that fill with tears" (l. 26). We are pleased with Tithonus' fallacy of sight, not because he fallaciously describes morning dew, but because he faithfully describes a worthy impulse: a desire to temper beauty with compassion and make its worship permanent. But the poetry of illusion should also be its own intimate critic; and the moment his mind becomes cold, Tithonus, instead of persisting in "unreal enhancements" that lead to mere embellishment—the first and inferior kind of ornament—admits that nature is indifferent, a constellation of mists and vapors, not a compassionate woman who weeps for her lover.

In some of his poetry of illusion, by which I mean a poetry of conditional assertion,[40] it is hard to tell whether Tennyson's shift-

40. According to the most penetrating Idealist work on logic of the Victorian age, F. H. Bradley's *The Principles of Logic* (London, 1883), ordinary judgments, no less than poetic assertions, are conditional. If Tennyson is to be judged, then, by the principles most applicable to his art—the principles of an Idealist aesthetic—his conditional assertions, which advance no truth-claims, are not to be confused with falsehoods, as Ruskin confuses them. The hypothesis that if hedonists or visionaries

ing impressions are a product of willful fancy, caused by an excited
state of feeling in the speaker, or an accurate rendering of
Gareth's perception of what actually exists. When Gareth first
approaches Camelot, the carved figures on the gate dazzle his
senses. Tennyson fills the mind with impressions of fish, wind,
storm, and flowing water. But does the presentation of solid forms
that move and seethe accurately describe the gate? Or does it
render only a marveling reaction in the viewer?

                                          All her dress
    Wept from her sides as water flowing away;
    But like the cross her great and goodly arms
    Stretched under all the cornice and upheld:
    And drops of water fell from either hand;
    And down from one a sword was hung, from one
    A censer, either worn with wind and storm;
    And o'er her breast floated the sacred fish;
    And in the space to left of her, and right,
    Were Arthur's wars in weird devices done,
    New things and old co-twisted, as if Time
    Were nothing, so inveterately, that men
    Were giddy gazing there; and over all
    High on the top were those three Queens, the friends
    Of Arthur, who should help him at his need.
        Then those with Gareth for so long a space
    Stared at the figures, that at last it seemed
    The dragon-boughts and elvish emblemings
    Began to move, seethe, twine and curl: they called
    To Gareth, 'Lord, the gateway is alive.'
                    ["Gareth and Lynette," ll. 212–231]

exist, then there are also lotos lands and Camelots, does not ascribe either
hedonists, lotos land, or their connection to the real; it merely ascribes to
the real an undefinable quality of life, an *X,* which can never be abstracted
from the poems. In a poetry of "hypothetical forms" I do not mean to
include all poetry. For though all literature consists of imaginative hypotheses, one of the problems with a play such as Tennyson's *Becket* is that
it too often substitutes for literature's "suppose this is," history's "this is."
On the distinction between the hypothetical and the real, compare Bradley's
theory of hypothetical judgments with the early Eliot's assertion: "Reality
is a quasi-object: there was an experience as if . . . " (T. S. Eliot,
Knowledge and Experience in the Philosophy of F. H. Bradley [London,
1964], p. 98). For a defense of the hypothetical form of judgment, see
Bradley, *The Principles of Logic,* Book I, ch. ii, pp. 46–47.

This crucial passage consists of a number of past-tense verbs, representing the statuary as a thing devised and made, and a cluster of present participles and infinitives—"water flowing away" (l. 213), "giddy gazing there" (l. 224), "to move, seethe, twine and curl" (l. 230)—which evoke the gate as a living presence. The two acts of Merlin's making the gate and of the viewer's restoring it to life are difficult to distinguish syntactically, but the accounts of both acts use verbs or verblike words, resulting in a powerful strength of motion. Adding to the confused amazement is the alliterative crowding of "giddy gazing there" and the rhythmic compression of "High on the top," followed by the spacious emphasis on "those three Queens, the friends / Of Arthur" (ll. 225–226). The hypothetical conjunction, "as if" (l. 22), which gives prominence to the one subjunctive use of "Were" (l. 223), assimilates to itself the cluster of indicative "were's," qualifying the impression of historical fact that past-tense verbs normally convey. It would be absurd to accuse Tennyson of being visually inaccurate, because he has no desire to be visually convincing. Yet the constant sense of disparity between the gate and its description need not turn Camelot into a mere *trompe l'oeil*. The weird, ethereal city expresses an optative of desire. The grammar is fluid; and if its assertions are assimilated to subjunctive moods, its hypothetical forms—"as water flowing away" (l. 213), "as if Time / Were nothing" (ll. 222–223)—are also ways of obliterating illusion. Tennyson is using his equivocations, not simply to forsake accurate description in favor of presenting Gareth's hallucinations and enchantments, but in order to penetrate beyond illusion, in order to arrive at a vision of Camelot as a timeless creative principle.

Whether the poetry of illusion is veiling the ignoble desires of the lotos-eaters or rendering equivocal the worthy visions of Tithonus, its hovering elusiveness is always natural to speakers who "perceive wrongly," as Ruskin says, "because [they] feel" keenly. Though Ruskin is defining Tennyson's characteristic mode, we must not conclude, as Ruskin does, that Tennyson can never "perceive rightly in spite of his feelings." At inspired moments, in

"Demeter and Persephone," "St. Agnes' Eve," and in parts of *In Memoriam,* Tennyson's artifice carries him beyond qualified belief to a third stage: to a rare union of strong feeling, true vision, and accurate thought—a form of Ruskin's "naturalist ideal."[41]

In "Demeter and Persephone," for instance, the goddess who conjures crocuses at will and closes fissures with her foot may seem more believable as a magician than as a mother. But Persephone's repossession of the "field of Enna" (l. 35) is also the annual return of spring, a conquest of death. The final prophecy may seem a triumph of millennial hope over accurate vision, an example of Ruskin's fourth or prophetic style, in which the poet "see[s] in a sort untruly, because what [he] sees is inconceivably above [him]." Yet the coda's shifting sense of the world is accurate: there is a final beauty beyond harvest in the "dimly-glimmering lawns" (l. 148). And though man is suspended over "hateful fires" (l. 149), his torment is relieved by the quiet dignity of the warrior, gliding lightly over fields. The higher creative state which results from the perseverance of vision that conquers—a state foreseen by Demeter in her concluding prophecy of an eventual victory of heaven over hell—is an imaginative extension of Demeter's reunion with her daughter, which also unites creator and creature, energy and form, restoring life to the world. The classical myth has the great advantage of allowing the poet who feels strongly to "think strongly, and see truly," too.[42]

In other poems the fluctuations of auroral light serve the same function as Tennyson's classic myths. Instead of receding into a prophetic mist, which God himself would not dare penetrate, the hovering light allows Tennyson to be true to the kindred

41. "Of the Pathetic Fallacy," in *Works of John Ruskin,* ed. Cook and Wedderburn, V, 209.

42. *Ibid.* For a comparable Victorian view of the harmonious interaction of reason and imagination see H. G. Hewlett's analysis of historical, physical, poetic, allegorical, and etiological theories of myth in "The Rationale of Mythology," *Cornhill Magazine,* XXXV (April, 1877), 407–423.

points of heaven and home. The nighttime apparition of the
"dragon winged" ship in "The Coming of Arthur" (ll. 372–
376) is a splendid piece of artifice. But because it also describes
the northern lights—because its wings are also the enormous kinks
and folds of a spiraling auroral band—the passage's scientific
precision helps justify the artifice. In "Sea Dreams" the wife's
vision of the "lines of cliffs" that fade with height, then turn into
"huge cathedral fronts" (ll. 210–211), is in danger of becoming
too grand and obvious, like one of the portraits in "The Palace of
Art." But, once again, the auroral description is scientifically
accurate. Its grandeur is refined into wavering impressions of
rayed auroral shapes, which are then transformed into "huge . . .
fronts," homogeneous bands that hide the rays from view.[43] In
"St. Agnes' Eve" (1833) there is a danger that the ritual symbolism of the phrase "Sabbaths of Eternity" will become too obtrusive, and that Tennyson will succumb to the visionary paralysis of
his ode "The Poet." Instead, the auroral blending of Keats's
jeweled colors into nonchromatic shades of white and black produces new and subtle colors for Tennyson to explore. As "The
flashes come and go," the sheets of auroral light seem to burst
from the magnetic zenith, creating a heavenly corona for the nun
(ll. 26–28). The pulsating rays that strew their "lights below"
give the appearance of a gigantic curtain or drapery, falling like
the folds of the bride's wedding gown upon the "floors" of heaven.
At the end of the second stanza, an appositional grammar, without syntactic links (X, Y, Z)—"Draw me, thy bride, a glittering
star" (l. 23)—replaces the analogical grammar $(A$ is to B as X
is to $Y)$:

>As these white robes are soiled and dark,
>   To yonder shining ground;
>As this pale taper's earthly spark,
>   To yonder argent round;

43. For a more complete account of the auroral symbolism see W. David
Shaw and Carl W. Gartlein, "The Aurora: A Spiritual Metaphor in
Tennyson," *Victorian Poetry,* III (1965), 213–222.

So shows my soul before the Lamb,
  My spirit before Thee;
So in mine earthly house I am,
  To that I hope to be.   [ll. 13–20]

As in Revelation, where Christ is the union of all categories, the comparisons of simile (the candle flame is to the moon as the nun's soul is to Christ) yield to the identities of metaphor: nun = bride = star. The absence of verbs in the last four lines of the poem evokes an immediate perception, with no grammatical subordination of the worshiper to God.

The sabbaths of Eternity,
  One sabbath deep and wide—
A light upon the shining sea—
  The Bridegroom with his bride!   [ll. 33–36]

The wavering auroral shapes, fluctuating by virtuoso turns between heaven and earth, assimilate the artifice of witnessing the glorified light of Christ's life and love shining through the marriage feast of the New Jerusalem. Like the conjunctions of science and ecstasy in cloudscapes by Constable and Turner, each element in Tennyson's picture balances and justifies the others.

Artifice is used with comparable skill in *In Memoriam*, where Tennyson hears the Holy Spirit talking in the breeze, and perceives rightly in spite of his feelings. Section XCV is one of the poem's crowning achievements. A perfect example of Ruskin's "naturalist ideal," it culminates in a doctrine of immortality that Tennyson insinuates so indirectly, and with such subtle sleight of hand, that, without producing any strain or dogmatism, it leads us from the equivocations of half belief to the assurances of belief before we realize what has happened.

The visionary scene develops brilliantly by slow accretions, beginning with notations of skeletal whiteness in the sky and in the kine, but qualified by modifiers of that whiteness: the haze and the phosphorescent glimmering. The skeptical reporter must acknowledge the presence of the oracular phenomena, but he refuses to acknowledge any meaning. Trying to soften the weirdness

of the silver sky, he digresses to the innocuous domestic light of
the "tapers." But no sooner has he contrasted the "Unwavering"
candelight with the curious fluttering motions of the "urn" than
the deadly observation of the naturalist resumes. He notes that
the bats have filmy shapes and that the cattle are enveloped in a
ghastly white glow. After Hallam's "living soul" is "flashed on"
Tennyson's, the "breeze" that trembles over the landscape begins
to rock the "full-foliaged" elm trees, as the whole amplitude of
night is consigned to splendor.[44] Bathed in a spectral glow, the
firmament flares, absorbed into a volatile world, startling and
evanescent as the gusts of wind, oracular as its words.[45]

> And sucked from out the distant gloom
>   A breeze began to tremble o'er
>   The large leaves of the sycamore,
> And fluctuate all the still perfume,
>
> And gathering freshlier overhead,
>   Rocked the full-foliaged elms, and swung
>   The heavy-folded rose, and flung
> The lilies to and fro, and said
>
> 'The dawn, the dawn,' and died away;
>   And East and West, without a breath,
>   Mixt their dim lights, like life and death,
> To broaden into boundless day.   [ll. 53–64]

The departures from expected tense and mood are unobtrusive, as when the timeless infinitives "to tremble," "To broaden,"
interrupt the succession of past tenses—"Laid" (l. 52), "sucked,"
"Rocked." The transitions are eased through the diplomatic
mediation of the participle "gathering" and the verb "fluctuate."
This intransitive verb, which Tennyson uses transitively, hovers,

44. For an excellent discussion of the sacramental significance of the
breeze see M. H. Abrams, "The Correspondent Breeze: A Romantic
Metaphor," in *English Romantic Poets,* pp. 37–52.
45. The spectacle of the fusing lights is not, in Yeats's phrase, "out of
nature"; it is Tennyson's middle term, and serves to connect the natural
setting with his apocalypse of the talking breeze. The midsummer lights are
not, as I once thought, a vivid piece of Arctic surrealism; at Lincoln's
latitude of 53 degrees, 15 minutes, north, Tennyson could have seen them
in an actual English garden.

like its meaning, halfway between an infinitive and a finite form. In the climactic vision, in the same kind of simple declarative sentences used for the eye's earlier notations, Tennyson unites the white lily to the white lights of the northern midsummer night, joined now in a surrealistic atmosphere dominated by the talking wind, in which the totality of whiteness is at last wholly admitted. As the flaring lights of East and West join together to form a radiant center, Tennyson moves from natural observation to prophetic vision, but so unobtrusively that we scarcely notice what has happened. So obliquely does he introduce the concluding prophecy about life and death, and so firmly does he bind the simile in which it appears to the rest of the quatrain, that tenor and vehicle have already reversed themselves before we register the change. Immortality seems just as certain—just as much a natural fact—as the exhilarating midsummer phenomena that Tennyson describes. The life-and-death simile is followed, quite oddly, by a timeless infinitive, deliberately forcing the section to end with a continuing event. The merging of life and death, at first clearly metaphorical, becomes strangely real as the infinitive hovers over an argument for immortality without actually making it.

To separate out the inferences would be to insist on demarcations between East and West, life and death, that run counter to the meaning of the episode. If Tennyson has a doctrine to expound, it is the doctrine of the half-glimpsed, the half-seen, the barely perceived merging of death and life, of the evening twilight and the first glow of dawn. Only these shifting half lights, the merging of the shadowy and iridescent, can release thoughts about immortality that become, not reflections on the scene, but actors in it. The transformations come as an immense relief, for they allow Tennyson to pass from a midnight atmosphere of false precision to a landscape in which all the analogies are in soft focus—in which the ideas are discovered, not imposed, and readily flow into each other. Contrary but inseparable reactions easily coexist; but they do not give the impression of pseudoethereal haziness—the kind of imprecision that often mars the visionary

passages in Shelley's and Swinburne's poetry. The changes are
from one clear impression to another, and the fusions do not confuse the reader, nor do they seem confused. The poet's metaphors
are less than the voice that speaks to him from the wind; but
more can be expressed in metaphors than in any voice he can
yet hear.

It is against the background of such richly elusive language, in
which Tennyson is most eloquently himself, in which he allows
himself no forced feelings, that we must study the individual
variations and developments in major poems. The evasion of
direct statement and the preference for visions veiled by hints and
shades first appear in "Timbuctoo," "The Lady of Shalott," and
"The Lotos-Eaters." To study the perfection of Tennyson's art,
which is always in danger of becoming too self-conscious and
predictable, we must study how he combines directness with indirectness. How, during sixty years of writing, does Tennyson
learn to release his full predilection for grandeur while gaining
all the advantages of being subtle and oblique?

1

Rites of Passage:
The Poet of Sensation

The qualities that Sir Henry Taylor[1] criticizes in Romantic poetry are exactly the qualities that Arthur Hallam praises in his review of Tennyson's *Poems, Chiefly Lyrical* of 1830.[2] In poets of "sensation" like Tennyson and Keats, as distinguished from a "reflective" poet like Wordsworth, Hallam praises the ability to live "in a world of images" and to make poetry a means of escape from the impermanence of life. Hallam fails to observe that even in these early poems Tennyson seldom records his sensations without refracting and refining them or without expressing, like Keats himself and Tennyson's Victorian contemporary Taylor, an inability to disengage himself completely from the "agonies, the strife / Of human hearts" ("Sleep and Poetry," ll. 124–125). Just as the early Victorian age is torn between a Philistine worship of facts and a Romantic pursuit of beauty, so Tennyson wavers between his impulse to write poems of pure sensation, such as "Recollections of the Arabian Nights," and his impulse to test and enlarge his poetry. He writes his way out of the Romantic into the new Victorian age, just as Yeats, sixty years later, writes his way

1. Preface to *Philip Van Artevelde* (London, 1834). This important document of literary history is reprinted in *Victorian Poetry and Poetics,* ed. W. E. Houghton and Robert Stange (Boston, 1968), pp. 861–865.
2. "On Some of the Characteristics of Modern Poetry and on the Lyrical Poems of Alfred Tennyson," *Englishman's Magazine* (August, 1831); reprinted in *Victorian Poetry and Poetics,* ed. Houghton and Stange, pp. 848–860. The distinction between ideas of sensation and ideas of reflection originates in Book II, chapter vii, of John Locke's *Essay Concerning Human Understanding* (1690).

out of the nineteenth into the twentieth century. Even as a poet
of sensation the young Tennyson anticipates, like Yeats, a return
from the autonomous Romantic "world of images" to a world of
quick, unpredictable decay or change and the claims of the
human heart.

The fear that poetry will yield to empiricism and technology is
typically Victorian. The idea appears in Thomas Love Peacock's
anti-Romantic manifesto, *The Four Ages of Poetry* (1820), and,
most notably, in Macaulay's *Essay on Milton* (1825). For
Macaulay the conflict between poetry and science raises the question, not merely of poetic decline, but of poetic survival. Tennyson
knows that every transition of the spirit of poetry into a new age
and place may also mean the death of poetry. As a poet of transition he succeeds in adapting his Romantic heritage only when
he presents his sensations as half-seen shapes and wavering forms.
Tennyson is a poet of the not-quite-living and the not-yet-perished.
He leaves many of his speakers poised at transitional moments,
suspended like Tithonus between heaven and earth. Ulysses is
about to sail to his death; Menoeceus, in "Tiresias," is to be fed
to the dragons; and the souls of saints and suicides—St. Simeon,
St. Agnes, and the crazed Lucretius—are about to rise into
heaven, or alternatively, "fly out . . . in the air" ("Lucretius,"
l. 273) and perish there. Transition is a recurrent fascination of
Tennyson. Cultural transition is also what the *Poems, Chiefly
Lyrical* of 1830 and the *Poems* of 1832 typify in the literary history of the age. They mark the same type of transition at the
beginning of the period that Yeats's volumes of 1899 and 1904
mark at its end.

The subject of transition is most explicit in Tennyson's Cambridge prize poem, "Timbuctoo" (1829), which presents a rite of
passage, a moment of cultural change, in which the youthful
visionary is asked to channel his Romantic and Miltonic heritage,
the whole burden of the past, through the narrow passage of his
mind.[3] More generally, early poems such as "The Hesperides,"

3. The problem of adapting a literary heritage is the subject of a full-
length study by W. J. Bate, *The Burden of the Past and the English Poet*

"The Palace of Art," "The Lady of Shalott," and "The Lotos-Eaters" explore the kinds of transition, sometimes failed or aborted, that every man must attempt if he is to escape the despair and apathy of isolated living. Their subject is the youthful fall or progress from the re-creative paradise, which is the enigmatic subject of Blake's "Book of Thel." All these poems of Tennyson are begun, so to speak, by the Romantic poet of sensuous luxury, but they are taken over by the Victorian poet who is critical of escape and who must descend down the ladder to the human condition, to the desires that disturb Yeats's dying animal, from which "all ladders start" ("The Circus Animals' Desertion," l. 39).

Oblique Vision

At the beginning of "Timbuctoo" it seems as if the poet of sensation will fail his initiation. The visionary traditions—Romantic and Miltonic—that once nourished great poetry are no more available to Tennyson than are the lost worlds of Eldorado and Atlantis to his speaker. The account of the transformation of thoughts into "starlit wings" (l. 152) that "Winnow the purple" is written with a forced breathlessness, and shows the danger of being too direct. The starlit Shelleyan vision (ll. 149–157) exceeds the poet's vocal range, and the strain shows in the overpitch of his rhetoric. More successful than the first superlatives, which represent merely the ecstasy of the moment, is the epic simile of the lake, which defines a complex mental state (ll. 119–130).

> as when in some large lake
> From pressure of descendant crags, which lapse
> Disjointed, crumbling from their parent slope
> At slender interval, the level calm
> Is ridged with restless and increasing spheres
> Which break upon each other, each the effect
> Of separate impulse, but more fleet and strong
> Than its precursor, till the eye in vain

(Cambridge, Mass., 1970). As a source of poetic anxiety, it is also a subject of Harold Bloom's studies *The Anxiety of Influence: A Theory of Poetry* (New York, 1973) and *A Map of Misreading* (New York, 1975).

Amid the wild unrest of swimming shade
Dappled with hollow and alternate rise
Of interpenetrated arc, would scan
Definite round.

The syntax is self-embedding: the kernel of the simile, "the level calm," in addition to being followed by increasing spheres of concentric waves, is heavily qualified by the adverbial phrases and clauses that come before it. The bits of syntax are long and complicated. By the time we reach the end of the simile we may even have to double back on the sequence to recall what the beginning was. Yet the normal word order—lake, waves, falling rock—would be less logical. The self-embedding syntax is closest to the causal sequence: pressure on the crags, descending rock, ripples on the lake, advancing waves. The syntax moves all the elements at once, tying its complications economically into the middle of the simile with conjunctions and prepositions, and with a density of participles, active as well as passive. A disciplined movement of phrases and clauses, all expanded and vivified, gives the impression of pictorical truth, which Tennyson uses to define extremely subtle states in the perceiving mind.

Elsewhere in "Timbuctoo" Tennyson refracts his sensations by placing barely perceived presences between himself and his visions. He tames the unnamable ecstasy by delineating forms half-glimpsed and half-seen—"The indistinctest atom" or "white cities" on the moon (ll. 98–99). "The soft inversion" of the City's "tremulous Domes" (l. 228) hovers in the water, half-substantial and half-fantasy. The domes resemble the word "tremulous" itself, which hovers in the scansion between two and three syllables, in an uncertain union of both. The hypothetical grammar also anticipates a form of wavering vision that Tennyson puts to exquisite use in major poems. The indicatives of stable seeing— "Stood out . . . of burnished gold" (l. 171)—are carefully qualified by subjunctive verbs—"if gold it were" (l. 172)—anticipating the flicker of hesitation in Percivale's grammar: "ran the boat, / If boat it were" ("The Holy Grail," ll. 514–515).

When Tennyson writes as a poet of trancelike devotion to the ceremonial and the exotic, his sensations are likely to be too solid and stable. He is much better at expressing the frail tentatives of vision, as Coleridge is at the end of "Kubla Khan," when he relates the vision of the damsel to the hampered, self-critical voice of the speaker, who longs in vain to revive her song. The best parts of "Timbuctoo" are superior to anything in "Recollections" because they view the opulent forms through their shimmering reflection from the water's surface. Tennyson also sees the visionary world through the wavering light cast upon it by his mind and memory. As a poet of sensation, Tennyson disappoints and is false only when he refuses to acknowledge the half-seen forms that brighten the human world without eclipsing the visionary one. Unless his syntax can refract his sensations, they either become too solid and stable or else threaten to dodge expression entirely, bursting like bubbles at the dome of Shelley's starlit heaven.

Dangers of Directness

Though Tennyson, as a poet of refracted and refined sensation, is increasingly critical of any indulgence in what Sir Henry Taylor calls "the mere luxuries of poetry,"[4] some of the lyrics in his volumes of 1830 and 1832 are the product of an art in which events leave little trace. The lyrics illustrate the dangers that attend any escapist poetry of fervid feeling, of images that "grow in beauty as they grow in sterility"—to use Yeats's phrase for the aesthetes of "the tragic generation."[5] Many such excesses, to which Taylor objects in Shelley's poetry, are apparent in Tennyson's rhapsodic ode "The Poet" (1830). While a frankly didactic spirit is upholding an optimistic Victorian view of man, the ode's detachable form of ornament—"fanciful" in Coleridge's sense—is producing merely decorative effects like these:

> And Freedom reared in that august sunrise
> Her beautiful bold brow,
> When rites and forms before his burning eyes
> Melted like snow.

4. Preface to *Philip Van Artevelde*, in *Victorian Poetry and Poetics*, ed. Houghton and Stange, p. 862.
5. "The Tragic Generation," in *The Autobiography of William Butler Yeats* (New York, 1965), p. 209.

> There was no blood upon her maiden robes
>   Sunned by those orient skies;
> But round about the circles of the globes
>   Of her keen eyes
>
> And in her raiment's hem was traced in flame
>   WISDOM, a name to shake
> All evil dreams of power—a sacred name.   [ll. 37–47]

Simple units—the eyes, the garment, the sunrise—are hammered into place, and given a superficial complexity by the varying phrases. But "keen eyes" adds nothing to "burning eyes." And "Sunned by those orient skies" simply repeats "august sunrise" and "Rare sunrise" (l. 36). With an emphatic obviousness of description, Tennyson piles "a sacred name" onto "a name to shake / All evil dreams," and "globes" onto "circles." Like many young poets, he delights in tautology, decoration, emphasis. The majestic motion with which Freedom shakes the world with "one poor poet's scroll" (l. 55) is executed with an intense degree of energy. But there is something damaged, neurotic, about this rhapsody. The ode seems less a celebration of the Shelleyan poet's power of universal sympathy than of Tennyson's own virtuosity. It is hard not to think that the "one poor poet" is the same poet who writes the triumphant tribute. The ode's conclusion is the literary equivalent of declamation; it is the effusion of one who says everything twice, and insistently repeats the obvious.

The danger that attends a poetry of pure sensation is also illustrated by the stanzaic pictures in "The Palace of Art" (written by 1832), among the most decorative of Tennyson's early poems. There is an overriding excess in most of these portraits—a kind of Gothic loftiness—which begins to oppress as soon as the nominal theme of the poem, aesthetic surfeit, becomes a quality of its language as well.

> One seemed all dark and red—a tract of sand,
>   And some one pacing there alone,
> Who paced for ever in a glimmering land,
>   Lit with a low large moon.   [ll. 65–68]

> And one a foreground black with stones and slags,
>> Beyond, a line of heights, and higher
> All barred with long white cloud the scornful crags,
>> And highest, snow and fire.   [ll. 81–84]

As the descriptions of Gothic sublimity go on, it is the quantity of glimmering and gloom that oppresses, rather than anything distinctive about them. The pictures are memorable enough by themselves, but they blur into uniformity. Each element of sublimity—the darkness, the largeness, and the light—is given so much elaboration that instead of being finely faceted (refracted into different kinds of gloom), it congeals into one general lump. Thus we have gloom ("all dark," "iron" and "angry" [l. 69], "thunder brooding low" [l. 75]) and glimmering ("low large moon," "shadow-streaks" [l. 76], "barred with . . . fire"). It is not merely that the fire-capped crags set against the black foreground make no real addition to the earlier contrast of "dark and red," but that they use the colors quite differently. The fire is no longer that of "a low large moon," but of the sun. Pictures are switched on for a few seconds, then switched off. When they are indiscriminately changed in this way, not in order to create new meaning but in order to impress us with their grandeur, they cease to form a living tissue. An ornamental effect that has been shifted in can just as easily be shifted out. Indeed, when Tennyson was revising the poem he often substituted one stanzaic picture for another; yet the lines around each picture were seldom altered. All poetic effects draw life from their context. In an ornamental poetry so detachable from its context, this life is continually being lost, and the verse suffers as a result.

Generically, "The Palace of Art" belongs to the tradition of "progress" poems popular in the Renaissance and eighteenth century; its panels recall Milton's masque "Arcades" or Gray's "Progress of Poesy." But the pictures are lavish and decorative, and though the poem is literally a "progress," a moving forward from panel to panel, any "progress," in the sense of development, is difficult to discern. The "white roses" and "gilded organ pipes" (ll. 98–99) might be perfectly appropriate in a Pre-Raphaelite

painting of St. Cecily. But the speaker elaborates them with the
chill and studied fancy that produces the first and inferior type of
ornament criticized by Ruskin. The "scornful crags," barred with
cloud, "snow and fire" (ll. 83–84), could be the kind of sublime
prospect presented by Pope or Wordsworth. But the bright chill
of the mountain portrait, painted with cold ease, is an unfeeling
embellishment. The soul simulates a dread and awe that its facile
depiction of a panorama of many scenes cannot support. The picture of the "English home—gray twilight poured / On dewy
pastures" (ll. 85–86) might be of rural a setting by Constable
faithfully describing the painter's mood. But the perceiving mind
is cold; when the soul tries to appropriate the landscape's gentle
vibrations of light and atmosphere it turns the pastoral emana-
tions into what one critic aptly calls "soporific calendar art,"[6]
"Softer than sleep" (l. 87). The purifying of the tragic into the
visual, with no overtones of suffering except for Dante's grim
smile or the dozing of the "deeply-wounded" Arthur (l. 105) "in
the vale of Avalon" (l. 107), composes a poetry of surfaces only.
The eye sees no reflections, only Shakespeare's glassy stare, "bland
and mild" (l. 134), or the "godlike faces" (l. 162) of Plato and
Bacon, ethereal and detached. If the soul were to become as immaculate and remote as these portraits, it would be dead; and a
chill descends whenever we feel behind the poem Tennyson's
desolate truth, that for the soul art has become, not an affair of
life and people, but a tomb.

   In view of the poem's conclusion, a reader would like to think
that the overriding artifice is being offered as oblique self-criticism.
At the outset the odd use of pronouns alerts us to the soul's
neglected community with its fellows: "I said, 'O Soul'" (l. 3);
"My soul would live alone unto herself" (l. 11). Union is replaced by a private self set up as substantive, as a third-person
pronoun independent of the "I" and the world. Does not Tennyson's criticism of the soul present the last seventy-five lines as a
self-justifying surprise? As the "great wild beasts" (l. 283) turn
loose on their victim, like the reveling satyrs in "Lucretius," the

6. John Pettigrew, *Tennyson: The Early Poems* (London, 1970), p. 32.

"progress" poem that begins as a frozen masque turns near the end into a riotous antimasque. What better way of indicating that the presentation is ironic?

In theory, "The Palace of Art" should succeed. But no poem can be justified merely in retrospect. And though we may be armed with expectations of irony, each successive reading continues to disappoint. We review the portraits, and instead of admiring a controlled statement about surfeit, we are cumulatively oppressed by it. The suppression of the tragic and the human produces the least defensible use of ornament, the decadent embellishing of a subject like Enoch's fish or Arthur's moustache—subjects about which the poet of sensation obviously feels nothing. On one of the rare occasions when language quickens, and the soul is compared to a lighthouse that "Changeth athwart the gleaming main, / From red to yellow, yellow to pale white, / Then back to red again" (ll. 138–140), Tennyson is forced to discard the comparison. His theory of mind requires a more conventional analogy, a comparison of the soul to the "manyfacèd glass" of neoclassical epistemology (l. 132). Even the concluding picture of the valley cottage is disappointingly conventional, one more ornament on the palace wall. A vigilant reading may make us more sympathetic with the problem of illustrating the defects of decoration without being merely decorative. But the main ironies are delayed too long. Because the poet of sensation is rarely critical of his own excess, his "Palace of Art" anticipates a Pre-Raphaelite interest in single pictures, and an effort to string together a poem about a set of hangings or tapestries, to the neglect of overall design. The soul may return to life in the valley, but the return of the poetry to real life among justifying ironies has been cut off forever. That is the genuine misfortune of the poem.

Refined Sensation

Usually Tennyson refines his sensations by deflecting them into half-lights and shades, producing, as Bagehot and Ruskin perceived, a poetry of illusion. An alternative method, which Bagehot rightly associates with the grotesque art of Browning, is to juxtapose incongruous sensations until their interaction achieves in the sphere of sensory objects what metaphor achieves in speech. In "The Hesperides" (published in 1832), Tennyson presents such objects as a dragon, sisters, and a golden tree. Without allowing these objects to stand for concepts, he presents them so that they stand for something more than themselves. Yet in contrast to the analogical elements that are present in most metaphor (the "pale taper's earthly spark" is to the moon's "argent round" what the nun's "soul" is to "the Lamb" [St. Agnes' Eve," ll. 15–17]), their meaning cannot be conveyed through any other words than the five autonomous "links" of Tennyson's "chain."

> Five links, a golden chain, are we,
> Hesper, the dragon, and sisters three,
> Bound about the golden tree.   [ll. 65–67]

The "Five links" modify each other, but none can be explained analogically by concepts like art, greed, or evil. Freed of all such content, each sensory element is magical, a mystery.

Like Browning's "Childe Roland," "The Hesperides" is a grotesque vision, a dream which does not resolve the contradictions it contains. In Ruskin's view, the key to the grotesque in art is its parataxis, its placement of components one after another without explicit connecting links.[7] A grotesque style associates ideas and images in the way J. S. Mill (in his two essays "What Is Poetry?" and "The Two Kinds of Poetry") says the poet of sensation associates them.[8] But in grotesque art the laws of associ-

7. "Of the True Ideal:—Thirdly, Grotesque," *Modern Painters*, III, ch. viii, in *The Works of John Ruskin*, ed. E. T. Cook and Alexander Wedderburn (London, 1904), V, 132: "A fine grotesque is the expression, in a moment, by a series of symbols thrown together in bold and fearless connection, of truths which it would have taken a long time to express in any verbal way, and of which the connection is left for the beholder to work out for himself; the gaps, left or overleaped by the haste of the imagination, forming the grotesque character."

8. The two essays, originally published in the *Monthly Repository*, VII (January and October, 1833), 60–70, 714–724, are reprinted as "Thoughts on Poetry and Its Varieties," in Mill's *Dissertations and Discussions*

ation are more incongruous than usual; as in the Symbolist aesthetic of Swinburne and Baudelaire, the viewer is forced to discover most of the connections for himself. In "The Hesperides," instead of blending his pictures in the best light, using the most appealing colors he can find, Tennyson works by disjunction. His disjoining is apparent from the opening sentence. The first phrase, "The North wind fallen," is a nominative absolute, with no syntactic link to the rest of the poem. The proem itself is detached from the song that follows; its value is in its perspective effect, in its serving as another "frame" to which the song adds a series of discrete pictures. Each picture drifts into the mind like "the voices in a dream" (l. 12), and keeps opening another window in the dreamer's head. An appositional grammar of discrete nouns—"Hesper, the dragon, and sisters three" (l. 66)—distills Milton's fable into a twilight piece. Each link of the chain is grammatically autonomous like the elements of syntax in Symbolist poetry. Unfortunately, the links of this chain are partly cartoon characters and partly oracles. Though there is precedent for caricature in Turner's painting the *Garden of the Hesperides* (1806), which Ruskin interprets ironically as a garden of Mammon, it would be an abuse of the principle of illustrative failure, the intentional breakdown of form for dramatic purpose, to argue that Tennyson is deliberately presenting the image-making faculty of the visionary poet in its most absorbed, and therefore, quite consciously, in its least compelling state.

Even if Tennyson's incongruities are illustrative incongruities, their mock solemnity and bathos commit the imitative fallacy; instead of dramatically rendering bathos, they *become* bathetic. No less an admirer than T. S. Eliot praises the poem's masterful

---

(London, 1859), I, 63–94. Mill's example of the poet of vivid emotion and sensation is Shelley; Wordsworth is his example of the poet of culture, in whom sensation is the mere setting of thought. In contrast to these 1833 essays, Mill's later review of Tennyson's *Poems, Chiefly Lyrical* (1830) and *Poems* (1833) in the *London Review*, I (July 1835), 402–424, argues that there is no antipathy between poetry of sensation like "Mariana" and reflective poetry.

meter, the subtle incantation of its rhythmic norm.[9] But what are we to make of the heavy repetitions, the faltering meter, and the parody of vatic utterance in inane rhymes like "yellowly," "mellowly" (ll. 99, 101)? Though generically they are charms, designed to keep the sap flowing and the guardians awake, sprawling jingles like "singing airily, / Looking warily" (ll. 39–40) are also soporific. Is Tennyson conscious of the irony? Is he devising rhythmic jokes to mock the daughters' efforts? Divided critical opinion suggests there is no simple answer. I suspect Tennyson wishes to imply that the Garden of Hesperus must become a garden of Adonis. As a place of shades, where the forms of life wait in disconsolate exile, it must become a genuine paradise of generative principles, of Aristotle's formal causes, on which the cycle of nature depends. But it is difficult to appreciate the irony in a poem whose main direction is unclear. Because the grammatical elements are discrete, with few syntactic links, the poem becomes an exchange center to which the poet brings some magical objects and the reader brings some meanings. Like most Symbolists, Tennyson tries to do with sensory objects what metaphor does with verbal comparison. In subsequent editions of his poems he suppressed "The Hesperides." Tennyson was always more than a poet of sensation, and never trusted objects enough to be a real Symbolist.

The young poet is more successful in making objects stand for something more than themselves when he elliptically conceals their meaning in a narrative. In turning now to "The Lady of Shalott" and "The Lotos-Eaters" (both originally published in 1832 and revised in 1842), I am deliberately getting ahead of the chronological story; but I shall return to the poems of 1830 in the next chapter. "The Lady of Shalott" may be analyzed, like many popular ballads, as a metaphor without a tenor, as a symbol which speaks for itself. The poem tells a story: a lady grown tired

9. "In Memoriam," in *Selected Essays* (London, 1932), p. 330: "A young man who can write like that has not much to learn about metric; and the young man who wrote these lines somewhere between 1828 and 1830 was doing something new."

of shadows leaves her tower, but on entering the world she is destroyed. At a more abstract level, the poem is about thwarted transition: the failure to develop a merely potential existence into an actual one. It sings of the irreversible departure from the mysterious lure of beauty and shadows, and the process of becoming vulnerable and human. Each reader will experience the poem at his own level of experience or at several levels. The poem is like a stone thrown into a pond, causing ever widening circles of meaning to go out from the center.

How does Tennyson hint of significance and make his narrative mean more than it says? Answers can be found in a study of his revisions. In the 1832 version the poet of sensation could not resist a complete account of the Lady's wardrobe. She wears a "cloudwhite crown of pearl" (l. 126), and after her death she is described, starkly, as a "corpse" (l. 156). The scenario is bizarre. In revising his poem Tennyson never allows the Lady to assume an individualized form. As James Spedding notes in a contemporary review, she is "stript of all her finery."[10] She moves into the background and becomes a figure of mystery—both a spirit and a human being, but not quite either. Also, in the 1842 version, the strict separation of the sensuous world of Sir Lancelot from the wan world of the Lady gives symbolic force to their final, fatal commingling. In revising, the poet of sensation gains a compression of substance that amounts to a fact of form. In his new form he discovers a tenor for his metaphor. He still speaks through a concrete representation, but he speaks also to and for our common humanity, and for something universal.

A popular ballad like "Sir Patrick Spens" commemorates a public event. But the values of Tennyson's heroine are too intrinsic for publicity. A source of major pathos in the poem is that its significant truths are all private truths. In the end the Lady is alone; and her poem, like her life, never tells more than half. The poem's mixture of lyric and ballad forms has therefore less in common with a popular ballad, or even with Wordsworth's

10. *Edinburgh Review* (April, 1843); quoted by Hallam Tennyson, in *Tennyson: A Memoir*, I (London, 1897), 191.

Lyrical Ballads, than it has with Blake's parable "The Book of Thel." Working in harmony with this parabolic form, with this metaphor without a tenor, is the mystery of the mirror. In the 1832 version the mirror was an incidental feature of the Lady's surroundings, no more important than the tinkling sheep bell. In the 1842 version the mirror moves to the head of the stanza, and a long, colorful procession of churls and abbots is reflected from its surface. The tapestry the Lady weaves is a reflection of reflections; if the Lady is at one remove from the world, her art is at two removes. The Lady's mirror also reflects the knight's reflection in another mirror—the river (ll. 105–106).

The unstable world of mirrors, which breaks apart solid sensation, is rendered even more unstable by the wavering grammar. The fifth stanza abounds in hypothetical clauses and subjunctives: "If she stay," "the curse may be"; and in syntactic uncertainty: "if she stay / To look down to Camelot" (ll. 40–41). Does "stay" mean "remain" or "refrain from?" From certainty to probability, from past to present tense, the fluidity of mood in Part II commits Tennyson to nothing but hypotheses. If Tennyson were to keep to the past tense, such a construction would imply that the actions had been completed and their results known. But the pervasive mingling of tenses implies that the results of past events are not yet known. The pathos of the questions—"But who hath seen her wave her hand? / Or at the casement seen her stand? / Or is she known in all the land?" (ll. 24–26) and "Who is this? and what is here?" (l. 163)—comes not only from the constraint and wishful yearning but also from the incongruity between the phrases "known in all the land" and the harshly empirical "what is here?" W. H. Empson analyzes the first set of questions as an example of sixth-order ambiguity: "The poet poses questions whose answers are both yes and no. . . . [The Lady] is not known personally to anybody in the land, but everybody knows she is a legend."[11] The Lady's personal history and meaning, even though they imply obligations and fates of an

11. *Seven Types of Ambiguity* (London, 1932), p. 182.

interior kind, are never safe from questions. The inquisition of innocence makes the whole poem tend toward incongruity and pathos.

Though Tennyson's form is enigmatic, the conclusiveness of the poem's conclusion seems predetermined. "The Lady of Shalott" is a fated and, in a sense, a suicidal poem. The self-imposed poverty of its rhyme words ("lie," "rye," "sky," "by," for example [ll. 1–4]), their diminution in number from four to three ("go," "blow," "below" [ll. 6–8]), to two ("Camelot," "Shalott" [ll. 5, 9]); the quick descent of each stanza to the stability of the refrain—all these features are designed to secure the conclusiveness of the outcome. The separation of private and public worlds in the first three parts seems fated to will, in a destructive commingling of these worlds in Part IV, the suicidal completion of the poem's design. All the energy of Tennyson's parable is directed toward its own termination. The Lady's cry "The curse is come upon me" (ll. 116) echoes the shriek of Blake's Thel. The Lady's shriek is that of "the disappearing ghost or the uprooted mandrake," as Northrop Frye observes of Blake's heroine; "and her tragedy could be anything from a miscarriage to a lost vision."[12] By concealing his meaning elliptically in a narrative form, Tennyson the poet of sensation is able, not merely to describe a special fate, not merely to tell a story of unrequited love like "Lancelot and Elaine," but to give a general representation of the process of dying into nature, of trying to acquire a stable human form. Tennyson is engaged in a lifelong search for stable identity. Renouncing the mysterious lure of a beautiful realm, a shadow world of "negative capability," Tennyson is fully aware that a death of the imagination such as Wordsworth suffered is the price the poet may have to pay for trying, like the Lady of Shalott, to make his world human. The memorial of Tennyson's poet might well be the epitaph of Wordsworth's "Elegiac Stanzas": "A power is gone, which nothing can restore; / A deep distress hath humanized my Soul" (ll. 35–36).

12. *Fearful Symmetry: A Study of William Blake* (Princeton, 1947), p. 233.

Nowhere is the young Tennyson's ability to refine sensation, refracting it through thought, better demonstrated than in "The Lotos-Eaters." Whereas "The Lady of Shalott" presents the failure to carry alive the imagination of innocence into the stable forms of nature, "The Lotos-Eaters" illustrates the opposite problem: the failure to take the lessons of the wavering world outside, the world of quick decay and change, back into the timeless land of lotos. There are two rites of passage in the poem: one explicit, and the other merely proleptic, or ironically foreshadowed. The first rite occurs when Ulysses' men discover the essential anguish of being in time—the torment of "ever climbing up the climbing wave" (l. 95)—and they decide to escape into a changeless world. But lotos land is not paradise. It is to the garden in *Maud* what Blake's Ulro is to Beulah: its satisfactions are enervating and narcotic. The mariners will have to undergo a second rite of passage by returning to their oars; there is no refuge from what Yeats calls the "murderous innocence of the sea" ("A Prayer for My Daughter," l. 16).

In the proem of "The Lotos-Eaters," as mid-morning aspects of the world deepen into half-lights and shades, Tennyson dwells on forms that are tremulous and enigmatic. He qualifies his assertions by repeating "seemed," the verb of illusion, six times— twice in its emphatic form, "did seem" (ll. 9, 32). He also stresses the qualifications by once shifting the accent to the second syllable—"seemèd" (l. 4)—and by once using the verb at the end of the alexandrine, the position of greatest prominence (l. 9). Most of the other verbs are in the past tense, as if to consign the mariners to legendary time. When infinitives such as "fall and pause and fall," or "mourn and rave," momentarily replace these verbs, any impression of timelessness is carefully qualified by the use of the illusory "seemed." Though the drift is from the less certain to the more certain, Tennyson blunts the force of the concluding "will," in both the proem and the song—"we will no longer roam" (l. 45); "we will not wander more" (l. 173)—by playing off these volitional forms against Ulysses' opening use of the simple future tense: "will roll us shoreward soon" (l. 2).

Ulysses' commanding future, ringing through the rest of the poem, presents the beauties of lotos land as of unreal duration, as a fracture in the midst of normal life. As Bagehot notes, "Illusion, half belief . . . are as much the proper sphere of ornate art, as an inferior landscape is the proper sphere for the true efficacy of moonlight." The half-lights of lotos land are a great "equaliser of beauties."[13] They win temporary credence for premises and moods that could not survive severer light.

One of the marvels of "The Lotos-Eaters" is the way the chorus, no less than the proem, foreshadows the mariners' return to sea even as it celebrates their life on land. To show that the mariners are temperamentally unsuited to a life of ease the poem presents a paradox: if inhabitants of lotos land are incapable of action, how can they be roused to sing their hymn? How can they muster enough energy to celebrate even their own lack of energy in a choric song? The mariners' analytic intelligence is constantly at work; their rhetorical skill denotes an intellectual power that could never be exercised if the "land of streams" had already been possessed as their rightful home. Since the mariners know they must return to sea, where they will be torn to pieces by the gods they are indicting, their torment turns their blasphemy into a heroic enterprise, combining the grand cosmology of Lucretius' *De rerum natura* with the introspective "heresies" of the Book of Job. In their cosmological vision of the "Gods together, careless of mankind" (1. 155) the lotos-eaters pervert the traditional religious yearning for divine union. Their oath of renunciation is a parody of religious ritual, substituting for a community of believers a conspiracy of hedonists. And what begins as a prayer of praise and thanksgiving for the pleasures of mankind ends as a denunciation of man's "endless anguish" (1. 169).

The irony of an argument that loses direction reminds the reader that there is no refuge in lotos land from the fear of welter, from the fear of quick, unpredictable decay and change. Because the Choric Song is polemical as well as lyric, it reinstates the rational imagination, and it reaffirms the assertive, unstilled de-

13. *Literary Studies,* ed. R. H. Hutton, II (London, 1898), 374–375.

sires of the human heart, in ways that a pure lyric could never do. The even-numbered stanzas refract through thought the very sensations that the odd-numbered stanzas celebrate. Dislodged accents and explosive consonants stumble over strongly marked caesuras; the tone of the even-numbered stanzas is fretful and agitated. A syntax of passive participles and of impersonal constructions creates a sense of being weighed upon and oppressed. But there is also an active, more personal syntax in the poem. Unlike the verbs of the proem—the intransitive "came," "did go," and the reflexive "sat them down"—the verbs of the chorus call for active human subjects—"toil," "ever climbing," "cleave"— and for value words—"let us swear." Qualifying the general passivity are transitive verbs like "give" and "lend," which demote lotos land's narcotics, the subject of most of the sentences in the proem, to the tertiary status of indirect objects. The succession of adjectives—"mild-eyed melancholy Lotos-eaters" (l. 27)— which originally muffle a human subject in a blanket of alliterating sounds turns in the chorus into the phrase "of mild-minded melancholy," which modifies the indirect object of an infinitive of active choice: "To lend our hearts and spirits wholly '/ To the influence of mild-minded melancholy" (ll. 108–109). The effect is not to drug the lotos-eaters, as it is in the proem, but to intensify their action. This syntax gives the impression of assertiveness and force. The actors are not weak, as the original grammar affirms, but strong for the struggle.

Ironically, just as the mariners are drifting back to dreamy meditation, their rhetorical energy begins to contradict their stated goal of withdrawing into an artificial paradise. To relieve the horror of existing in a present without duration, the lotos-eaters develop the coda's long epic simile, in which they continue to acquire divinity (ll. 155–170). For the gods there is also, traditionally, no past or future. But as the analogy carries them away, it gradually changes direction. The illusion of the mariners' union with the gods becomes the certainty of separation; and the simile ends, not with a reassuring analogy between the lotos-eaters and the gods, but with a disturbing contrast. The simile finally opposes the cruel indifference of the gods to the struggles, not just of the lotos-eaters, but of all mankind. The logical reversal is signaled, not simply by the initiation of a pattern of triple rhymes: "we," "free," "sea" (ll. 150–152), but also by the syntactic device of starting and ending line 150 with the same word. For the first time in the chorus the passivity of undirected "motion" is "framed" and controlled by active subjects: *"We* have had enough of action, and of motion *we"* (l. 150—my italics). What begins in comfortable complacency, like Browning's "Johannes Agricola in Meditation," ends with the angry protest of his Caliban or the biblical Job. For mariners who have had "enough . . . of motion" the heroic blasphemies of the final version are deftly ironic; and to my mind, the blandness of the gods at the beginning of the simile provides the "subtly apt" counterpoint to rant that Christopher Ricks finds lacking.[14] Instead of being crudely anticlimactic, the weakly repetitive "Surely, surely" (l. 171) points the reader beyond the poem. It dramatizes a desperate effort to create certainty where only uncertainty exists.

The long epic simile combines with a striking shift in rhythm to dramatize the main irony in the poem: "like Gods together . . . / Till they perish and they suffer—some, 'tis whispered—down in hell" (ll. 155, 168). In their simile the mariners do not come out where they have planned, and it is clear from the beginning that they will not remain in lotos land, as they have planned. Because of this reversal the outcome of the poem, though predestined from Ulysses' first staccato words—" 'Courage!' he said, . . . / This mounting wave will roll us shoreward soon' " (ll. 1–2)—is also unforeseen. The poem is not a trick poem that saves its best thought for the end. As Robert Frost would say, it is "a series of revelations, as much for the poet as for the reader."[15] Step by step, as the wonder of unexpected discovery keeps growing, the mariners come to realize that their impulse to emulate the gods is servile and self-hypnotic. The sensitivity of the soul is

14. *Tennyson* (New York, 1972), p. 91.
15. "The Figure a Poem Makes," in *Selected Prose of Robert Frost,* ed. H. Cox and E. Lathem (New York, 1968), p. 19.

an unpardonable blot upon the hedonists' scheme, and for their philosophy an unexplained enigma. Like disappointed and rebellious children, the lotos-eaters are critics of their parent, Nature. Because they see, like T. H. Huxley, that cosmic nature is "no school of virtue, but the headquarters of the enemy,"[16] they judge the morals of its gods to be detestable. Their thrill of discovery is the surprise of remembering something they are not aware they know. Like the poem which is "a series of revelations," the Choric Song is always hurling insight ahead of the lotos-eaters so that they may strike new lines of purpose across it. Ironically, the last verb of a poem that renounces all volition is introduced by an auxiliary of volition: "we *will* not wander more" (my italics). The lotos-eaters will leave lotos land, not because they are too weak to keep their oath, but because they are too strong. The desire to become gods is unworthy of them.

In general, Tennyson's most authentic freedom in his early transitional lyrics comes from two sources: imitation and irony. His imitation of English models from Spenser to Keats, and his adaptation of Homer, create a great deal of free and genuine lyric expression, especially in "The Lotos-Eaters." Later, Tennyson's dialect poems and his Anglo-Saxon imitations will provide him with a new kind of freedom. In "The Battle of Brunanburg" (1880) he combines contemporary English with certain freely mingled features of his Old English original; and in his two monologues "Northern Farmer, New Style" (1869) and "Northern Farmer, Old Style" (1864), the Lincolnshire dialect allows him to escape Victorian norms of refinement and decorum. Tennyson can enjoy the raciness and vigor without being held responsible for the harshness or uncouthness of a dialect that is largely intelligible to the educated reader.

A second source of Tennyson's lyric freedom is his irony and indirection. There is always a danger that in trying to create an

16. T. H. Huxley, "Evolution and Ethics," in *"Evolution and Ethics" and Other Essays,* ch. ii (New York, 1897), p. 75: "The pertinacious optimism of our philosophers hid from them the actual state of the case. It prevented them from seeing that cosmic nature is no school of virtue, but the headquarters of the enemy of ethical nature."

autonomous world, the imitator of the Romantics will create only a remote or irrelevant one. Tennyson's playful treatment of the Hesperides provides a valuable antidote to Romantic solemnity; it gives Tennyson the kind of freedom available in satire or burlesque—a discovery he will turn to advantage in a poem such as "New Timon, and the Poets" (1846), a small masterpiece, dancing with animus and wit. The same freedom is more or less available in all dramatic monologues, in the Choric Song of "The Lotos-Eaters," for example, which is a form of simultaneous connivance against the speakers and participation with them, and hence of originality and freedom. An example of indirection is "Timbuctoo's" refraction of vision into the simile of the lake, which achieves more range and freedom than unmediated accounts elsewhere in that poem. The comparison allows the poet to break apart his sensations, making them as exact as he can, even when his subject is beyond the power of words to reproduce completely. To be sure, Tennyson is more original than most young poets, but this is because he is also more traditional. He writes with more awareness of Romantic, Miltonic, and Spenserian tradition, and hence with more conscious deviation.

Though Tennyson knows that the poet who tries to humanize his imagination may also destroy it, neither the self-isolated intellectual in the palace of art, the Lady of Shalott, nor the lotos-eaters are capable of resting in self-sufficiency. If they are to survive and grow, all must submit to the unpredictable decay or change of life, to the unstilled desires of Yeats's dying animal ("Sailing to Byzantium," ll. 21–22). Yet Tennyson's knowledge still remains uncertain and derivative. He is uncertain, for example, whether the mariners' gestures of volition, which are determined, it seems, by malevolent gods, are puppet-like or genuine; and whether the soul's efforts to engage a world beyond its private ecstasies will destroy or redeem the soul. Despite their many felicities, the transitional lyrics are sometimes too embellished. The grotesqueries of "The Hesperides," bordering on caricature, and the ceaseless decorative effects of "The Palace of Art," though clearly antidotes to Tennyson's terror of quick decay

and death, are too elaborately contrived, and too possessed by
rapturous memories of Greek and medieval myth, for the poet's
intimations of ruin to be convincing. After composing the choiring
verses of "The Lotos-Eaters," derived from the ravishing harmonies of Spenser, Tennyson fashions a new spareness of language. Without abjuring the sensuous refinement that is natural
to him, Tennyson experiments in "Mariana," "Ulysses," and
"Tithonus" with elegiac plainness. "The Lotos-Eaters" is beautiful
and satisfying: Tennyson's style is as perfect as it can be for that
poem. But there is a sudden access of energy in its coda. Such
energy is prophetic. It suggests what the transition from a pastoral
to a tragic vision means. It also allows us to foresee that as a poet
of sensation Tennyson will be increasingly responsive to the
"sensual music" of Yeats's "dying generations" ("Sailing to
Byzantium," ll. 3, 7) and the claims of the human heart. Not
until he contracts his inherited harmonies into more austere, more
fastidious music, simple and dramatic in conception, will Tennyson produce, in "Ulysses" and "Tithonus," his first great poems
of enlarged and nuanced meaning.

2

The Elegiac Mode: Enlarged
and Nuanced Meanings

Except for his marriage in 1850, the most important event in Tennyson's life was the death in September, 1833, of Arthur Hallam. The sudden death of a friend is always a brutal affront. But about the death of Hallam, the person Tennyson most loved, there was something deceitful and harshly malicious. In the month of his death Hallam sent Tennyson an exuberant letter expressing his excitement over a gallery of pictures in Vienna. Hallam was "Our Sidney and our perfect man" ("In Memory of Major Robert Gregory," l. 47). He should have shared in the discourtesy of death only after his life had faded and lost its glow and energy. There will always be something unexplained about the friendship of Tennyson and Hallam. Though the mystery is deepened by the fact that Hallam's father destroyed Tennyson's letters to his son and Tennyson's son destroyed Hallam's letters to Tennyson, the mystery arises less from what is unknown and unknowable about the friendship than from something unlimited in it. There were similarities between the two men that were always recognized but not admitted. Hallam's admissions to Milnes about his fears of going mad suggest that the old view of Tennyson, the melancholy introvert, and of Hallam, his sturdy complement, is seriously distorted. One may just as easily reverse the proposition and see in Hallam a young man of restless, encompassing enthusiasms, intermittently buoyant but subject to dark feelings like Tennyson's. Hallam, as Christopher Ricks suggests, was someone "whom the Somersby Tennysons—so in-

cessantly in need of support—could support" themselves.[1] The
suicidal drunkenness and violence of Tennyson's father had already produced doubts and morbidities, reflected in Tennyson's
melancholy, Byronic verses in *Poems by Two Brothers* (1827)
and in many poems of 1830 and 1832, written prior to Hallam's
death. The latter poems are works of a supple mind that has
brooded on change, of a poet whose writing is essentially elegiac,
a *meditatio mortis*. From the youthful elegy "The Dying Swan"
(1830) to the somber valediction "Crossing the Bar" (1889)
Tennyson is a poet of solemn requiems. Hallam's death, then,
reinforces dark feelings with which the young Tennyson was already painfully familiar. In masterpieces such as "Ulysses" and
"Tithonus" the poet's reflections on the death of a friend who
could have shared, ennobled, and humanized these feelings gives
enlarged and nuanced meaning to elegiac reflections in the earlier
"Oenone" and "Mariana," poems which Tennyson had already
written and published before Hallam died. There may be an
appeal in some of these earlier poems to prophecies and visions
that disengage the elegist from the world of process and the claims
of the human heart. But after Hallam's death the drama lies in
the return—the descent down the ladder, as in "The Circus Animals' Desertion"—to the fear of quick, unpredictable decay or
change that has so intimidated the imagination of lesser writers.
Tennyson's greatest elegies cannot be considered apart from this
drama.

Epitaphs and Prophecies

Even in *Poems, Chiefly Lyrical* of 1830, Tennyson's inquisi-
tions of change are more than rehearsal exercises. They are reflections of a poet who has brooded on ruin, who echoes the protest-
ing cry of Heraclitus, heard down the ages: "All things give way:
nothing remains."[2] In elegies such as "The Lintwhite" and the
sonnet "Love and Death," Tennyson changes his generic form in

1. *Tennyson* (New York, 1972), p. 115.
2. Quoted by Walter Pater, as an epigraph in his Conclusion to *The
Renaissance: Studies in Art and Poetry* (London, 1888), p. 246.

mid-course, with the result that the poem we are reading fulfills our expectations in a novel way. "The Lintwhite" (1830) begins as a lyric of surmise. It imagines the bird's pleading with the year to pause and heed its song. Each stanza ends with an unsuccessful appeal to the year: "And stay," "Oh! stay." But the two-syllable lines represent the penultimate moments before the end of each stanza, not the end itself.

> Oh! stay.
> Alas! that lips so cruel-dumb
> Should have so sweet a breath!   [ll. 16–18]

> Yet stay.
> Alas! that eyes so full of light
> Should be so wandering!   [ll. 25–27]

> Oh! stay.
> Thou art the fairest of thy feres,
> We prithee pass not on.   [ll. 34–36]

Each stanza ends with a lament, as time, like the stanzaic form, sweeps ahead. With the frustration of its efforts, the lyric of surmise and complaint changes into an epitaph inscription, a gravestone for the nature time destroys. When poetry tries to impose on unexpected or unstable materials the finality of an epitaph, the result is usually wit or surprise, as in Shakespeare's defiant paradox: "And death once dead, there's no more dying then" (Sonnet 146, l. 14). Here, with a gradual and relaxed movement rather than a quick turn, with a cadence so gentle we may even miss the irony, the images of a Chaucerian spring under sentence of death—the king with "locks . . . of sunny sheen" (l. 28) who soon is gone—point like a gravestone to the passer-by's own death. If the year, the young king munificent in his bounty, is "deaf as death" (l. 11), it is because the cycle of the year *is* death. Because an epitaph offers maximal finality, it not only fulfills the expectation of closure set up in the lyric of surmise, but greatly exceeds that expectation. This excess, combined with the economy of means, accounts for the surprise and pointedness of the reversal. We are arrested by the irony that time—the year—the gold-haired king himself, will soon have to contemplate his own passing.

A similar irony fixes attention in the sonnet "Love and Death" (1830). The formal rhymes and symmetries of epitaph decorum— "these walks are mine"; "This hour is thine" (ll. 7, 9)—suggest an ultimate justice operating in the grave. The dispassionate economy of a tombstone inscription checks the drift into Keatsian artifice evident in "thymy plots" and "sheeny vans" (ll. 2, 8); the tone is one of oracular or supernatural utterance. By defining the subject for eternity, the detached attitude of the form also allows everlasting day, the "light of great eternity" (l. 12), to flow back into nature. Here the reversal of the epitaph no longer works with the gentle wit of "The Lintwhite." Though the optical metaphors are accurate notations of a scientific observer, they also belong to Platonic and biblical traditions. The force of the reversal is not witty, as in Donne's "Death thou shalt die." The vision of endless light grows effortlessly out of the sepulchral setting, like the vivid whorls of northern midsummer and auroral light that crown similar scenes of desolate splendor in *In Memoriam* and *Maud*. The epitaph tradition, working with quiet indirection beneath the allegorical decor, allows Tennyson to contract the sepulchral setting of Milton into more attenuated forms. The epitaph gives a stamp of special validity to a reversal which Platonic and biblical traditions also help authenticate. The result is sententiousness. The reversal of death's epitaph on love is more oracular than ironic; it is prophetic and sacred rather than witty.

The modulation from elegiac statement to apocalypse in "The Kraken," another poem in the 1830 volume, is less plaintive than prophetic. After an oracular opening, "The Kraken" develops a countervailing movement of slow, millennial growth. The weakening of poetic shape, produced by the drift of adjectives— "His ancient, dreamless, uninvaded sleep" (l. 3)—arrests the flow of time. The "thunders of the upper deep" (l. 1) are all but forgotten as the illusion of immunity to time's ravages takes over. In the second half of the poem this immunity becomes less certain.

The caesuras start to waver, then fall with increasing regularity after the seventh syllable, which is as close to the end of the line as they come in Tennyson.

> Unnumbered and enormous / polypi   [l. 9]
>
> There hath he lain for ages / and will lie   [l. 11]
>
> Battening upon huge seaworms / in his sleep   [l. 12]

The seventh-syllable breaks point toward termination. Like the persistence of the dominant (and particularly the dominant seventh) in music, they anticipate the cataclysm of line 13, when "the latter fire shall heat the deep." Even the last word, "die," yields what Barbara Herrnstein Smith would call a "closural allusion."[3] As in the Spenserian stanza, the concluding alexandrine increases the sense of closure by disturbing the reader's expectation of a simple continuance of the blank-verse line. Together, these formal devices signal, not merely the end of the poem, but the end of time and the world.

Elegiac Reflections

In order to escape morbidity, the elegiac poet must deflect his melancholy moods into what Eliot calls the "third voice" of poetry, "the voice of the poet when he attempts to create a dramatic character speaking in verse."[4] Instead of allowing his readers to overhear directly his own laments, as he does in his "Supposed Confessions," which is written in the "first," or lyric, voice of poetry, Tennyson must experiment with a wide variety of elegiac masks, as he does in the more successful "Mariana" poems. Whereas the "first voice" of poetry is too confessional, the "third voice" is too impersonal. Before Tennyson can find the voice he wants, he has to experiment in "Oenone" with an unstable union of the speaker's voice and his own voice; he has to talk like a ventriloquist through Pallas Athene, a second character in the poem. Though the attempt in "Oenone" is not wholly

3. *Poetic Closure: A Study of How Poems End* (Chicago, 1968), p. 61.
4. T. S. Eliot, "The Three Voices of Poetry," in *On Poetry and Poets* (New York, 1961), p. 96.

successful, it is his closest approach, before "Ulysses" and "Tithonus," to a realization of the full potential of the monologue form. Only by finding a form in which the elegist can speak in unison with his characters is Tennyson finally in a position to write, in "Ulysses" and "Tithonus," the first great monologues in which he rises from and through his grief, returning to it with an enlarged sense of its dimensions and meaning.

Despite their elegiac simplicity, the "Mariana" poems are highly contrived. Without subtle variations, their laments would soon begin to pall. Indeed, in the "Mariana" of 1830, the poem which is set in an English landscape, the monotony seems at first to be relieved by few subtleties; the same phrases reappear predictably in the downbeat of the refrain and the steady resurgence of despair. Mariana is compelled into the dreary rhythm of things, swaying with the poplar tree and beating time to the monotonous continuo of the clock. The paralyzing sameness prevents any rejuvenating lift of the mind; the everyday details create a scene of nightmare, evoking what T. S. Eliot calls "the boredom and the horror."[5]

Surprisingly, instead of committing the imitative fallacy, Tennyson evokes the boredom without inducing it. Despite the monotony, the interplay of thin and full vowels—"The blue fly sung" (instead of "sang" [l. 63]), "from the crevice peered" (l. 65), "Old faces glimmered" (l. 66)—composes an intricate music. It is unexpectedly varied, piercing, and dissonant. The English "Mariana" succeeds, completely and powerfully, because it is also a poem of sustained implication—Tennyson's version of Wallace Stevens' paradox that "the absence of imagination had / Itself to be imagined."[6] The most potent of the imagined omissions are the absent visitors who lift the latch, people never mentioned but implied—the absent lover who sighs like the wind, the absent Angelo, with whom, strange to say, Mariana will later be united, as is hinted in the epigraph. Indirection is also apparent

5. "Matthew Arnold," in *The Use of Poetry and the Use of Criticism* (London, 1933), p. 106.
6. "The Plain Sense of Things," ll. 13–14.

in the negative grammar, in the latch never lifted and the heaven never seen. Images of "thickest dark" (l. 18) are always more real to Mariana than light, just as absence is more real than presence. But because she is actively engaged in imagining her annihilation, Mariana must defy the nothingness by filling it with images she knows—with "night-fowl" crows (l. 26) and flitting bats. Even the nothingness of her dreams powerfully asserts a countervalue to the void by making absent things predominate over the present, just as the variety of the poem's sound, rhythm, and imagery subtly relieves its oppressiveness. Though Mariana perceives her world as a wreckage of life and mind, a power to transform that world is already present. That power resides in Mariana's ability to imagine enlarged and nuanced meanings, and to prize as a prerogative of the human mind its ability to withdraw from the tyranny of the senses and make even absent things more real than immediate impressions.

To avoid the imitative fallacy when portraying the dreary landscape of his companion poem, "Mariana in the South" (1832), Tennyson varies the grammar of his refrain. To relieve the visionary directness of his coda he also introduces two-way imagery and syntax, phrases like "rosy-bright," which can either reach back to modify "spaces" or reach forward to qualify, more ambiguously, the grief of Hesper.

> There all in spaces rosy-bright
>   Large Hesper glittered on her tears. . . .   [ll. 89–90]

In their untensed eternity, the infinitives of the refrain—"to be all alone, / To live forgotten, and love forlorn"—imply at first a bondage for the speaker. But the endless bondage implied in the first two stanzas by the tenseless infinitives turns in the third and fourth stanzas into a merely temporal lament, and then in stanza 5 into the optatives of prayer. After an interrogative use of the refrain in the next stanza, the return of the simple infinitive in the penultimate stanza evokes an untensed eternity: a paradise of changelessness, frozen into one attitude forever. The change in grammar relieves the monotony of the refrain and prepares for

the qualified vision of a genuine apocalypse—a paradise of endless love—in the final stanza. To set in perspective the elegiac
world, scaled to man alone, Tennyson makes the humdrum space
of the "stony drought and steaming salt" (l. 40) open on cosmic
space. As "The night comes on that knows not morn" (l. 94),
suffering and loneliness are distanced in the sad elations of the
glittering Hesper, who seems to grieve for all the pains of earth.
But Hesper, we remember, is the evening star. Though he is no
longer a jealous father who guards apples in a garden, he is still
the funereal being who will later preside over death in *In
Memoriam:* "Sad Hesper o'er the buried sun" (CXXI, l. 1).
Hesper's consolation is more than release from life, and the coda
is more than a death wish. But its double meaning makes clear
that Tennyson is still wavering in his mind between an intimation
of changeless love and the more desperate type of consolation
Hopkins was later to provide: "Here! creep, / Wretch, under a
comfort serves in a whirlwind: all / Life death does end and
each day dies with sleep" ("No worst, there is none," ll. 12–14).

By repeating the same elements in reverse, the iterative syntax
begins to mirror the reversal it describes: "But day increased
from heat to heat" (l. 39); "From heat to heat the day de-
creased" (l. 78). Reversing syntax turns on the hinge word
"night": "The day to night, the night to morn" (l. 82). An odd
trick of Tennyson's consists of ending successive lines with like-
sounding words of different sense: "moan" and "morn." By
pushing parallel phrases—"And deepening" (l. 91); "And
weeping" (l. 93)—to the beginning of their respective clauses, at
the head of lines, the grammar also invites the reader to relate
the participles. The parallelism adds to the despair of weeping
the cathartic possibility of being transformed—deepened like
night through "silent spheres."

> And deepening through the silent spheres
> Heaven over Heaven rose the night.
> And weeping then she made her moan,
> 'The night comes on that knows not morn. . . .'
>
>   [ll. 91–94]

Even the syntax looks two ways at once. Framed elliptically between "the silent spheres" and rising "night," the adverbial phrase "Heaven over Heaven" may extend the gloom by attaching itself grammatically to night. But it may just as readily achieve the opposite effect by reaching back to modify—and elevate—the shining "spheres." Accompanied like the death ship of Ulysses, or like Tennyson's own crossing of the bar, by a "sound as of the sea" (l. 86), the two-way syntax wavers between elation and grief. We might ask, with T. S. Eliot's Magi: "Birth or Death? . . . / . . . I had seen birth and death, / But had thought they were different."[7] Is this a vision, or only an illusion, of changeless love? And if it is a genuine vision, can it ever be realized on earth? Or is it necessary to die into such love?

"Oenone" (1832) carries the uncertainties of a dramatic presentation one stage further. In this poem, a cross between a Theocritean idyll and a dramatic monologue, we find Tennyson making mistakes that he will not repeat in his major poems. In Athene's sermon about self-control, for example, which occurs in the middle of the poem, Tennyson is trying to introduce something appropriate to the goddess, but also something that he could say for himself, even though the words may not have exactly the same meaning for both. Unfortunately, Athene becomes a puppet in the hands of a ventriloquist, a mere mouthpiece for Tennyson's Victorian attitudes. To be offended by the naked goddess as she mouths her moral doctrine it is not necessary to be one of those Victorians who so dislike the nude that they find something indecent in the naked truth. The problem is that Oenone, the speaker of the monologue, can embody and live her deepest truths but can never generalize them. Athene, on the other hand, a mere character in the poem, can generalize her truths, but Tennyson does not convince us that she has ever experienced them. This severing of voices is a mistake Tennyson does not repeat when he comes to write "Ulysses." In that poem Tennyson unites in a single speaker, through whom he can express himself with dramatic propriety, the reflective powers of a Pallas Athene and the sad

7. "Journey of the Magi," ll. 36–38.

elations of an elegist. Are not the perpetual power and surprise of
the familiar closing lines of "Ulysses" evidence that Tennyson and
his speaker are uttering heroic words in unison, though admittedly
with somewhat different meanings for each?

More successful than Athene's sermon are Tennyson's combining of self-indulgence and strength in his portrayal of Oenone.
Though her dovelike lamentations are far removed from Ulysses'
manly reticence, she is not to be mistaken for another Andrea
del Sarto. Her defense may be evasive, but it never washes away
the moral issues in an enchanting vagueness, like the beautiful
"twilight-piece" created by Andrea. Oenone's language may keep
covering what is naked, doubling back into repression and skipping out diagonally into scene-painting and masks. Redundance
may even commit her language to a decorative veiling of ruin.
But far from indicating moral weakness, her circling syntax is
necessary as a psychological defense, a stay against confusion. Her
feminine caesuras, with their breaks following unacccented syllables, linger nostalgically after words like "vapour" (l. 3),
"morning" (l. 11), "flowers" (l. 7). There is often internal
acceleration, as Oenone quickens to a sense of her loss. Yet after
an overflow line, when the enjambement of "With down-dropt
eyes / I sat alone" (ll. 55–56) seems to be building toward crisis,
she deftly avoids the feeling of trauma. She usually introduces
either a late subsiding of the overflow—after the seventh syllable
in line 11, for example—or else an early breaking after the third
syllable, as in the next line. Syntax doubles back on itself: "My
eyes are full of tears, my heart of love, / My heart is breaking, and
my eyes are dim" (ll. 30–31). By repeating the words in reverse
($X\ Y\ Y\ X$), the language keeps hovering round a few painful
topics. Though one could argue that nostalgia contributes to
Oenone's unhappiness, since Paris, despite his love, has always
been unworthy of her fond remembrance of him, the elaborate
embroidery of her language successfully covers these truths: its
amplitude is part of her evasiveness. At times Oenone even seems
to lose and bury her grief in the folds of her similes and self-
embedding phrases. When Hera offers Paris the gift of omnipo-

tence (ll. 109–113), her syntax is made to imitate her amplitude, engulfing itself in appositions whose phrasal parts begin to lose themselves in a tangle of other phrases and participles, all depending on the same noun. Finally, in the coda, as the victim of Aphrodite's vanity turns into an avenging voice for Troy, Oenone's prophecy seems genuinely cathartic. But even here, where her victory seems most assured, Tennyson incorporates once again those wavering attitudes—stoic and self-indulgent, heroic and evasive—of whose subtle blend the psychology of his heroine consists.

> Hear me, O earth. I will not die alone,
> Lest their shrill happy laughter come to me
> Walking the cold and starless road of Death
> Uncomforted, leaving my ancient love
> With the Greek woman. I will rise and go
> Down into Troy, and ere the stars come forth
> Talk with the wild Cassandra, for she says
> A fire dances before her, and a sound
> Rings ever in her ears of armèd men.
> What this may be I know not, but I know
> That, wheresoe'er I am by night and day,
> All earth and air seem only burning fire.   [ll. 253–264]

Oenone's fatal fixation gives her prophecy an apocalyptic thrill, but its childlike tautology—"only burning fire"—does not convey what an apocalypse should be. The poem leaves us at the end with a sad, pathetic spectacle: a woman whose memory is the source of her unhappiness, but who continues to live in the memory of a past that stares back at her, not as the paradise that she remembers, but as a "cold and starless" ruin.

As assured as Tennyson's shifting perspectives on his speaker is his use of a Theocritean frame. The impersonal descriptive poet of the proem does not know how the more personal sequel will develop. But its structure and conclusion are already limited by Oenone's arrival in the valley at noon. The pretense is that the detached poet of the introductory frame does not know what turn the psychological drama will take. But while the changing flow of sensations pours life into the frame, the frame controls what is destructive in the flow. The turbulence of the interior monologue, which moves irregularly through bitterness, nostalgia, and revenge, is thereby set in a larger context. The monologue may end in "burning fire," but the historical present of the proem— "There lies a vale in Ida, lovelier / Than all the valleys of Ionian hills" (ll. 1–2)—expresses its vision in ultimates and absolutes, exalted even now to permanent value. With the conclusive force of cataclysm, the prophecy of Oenone ends her monologue. Nevertheless, upon this finality of death and termination, the swimming vapor of the proem will, we know, once more arise. "Burning fire" may mark the end of the Trojan war—and the end of Oenone's monologue—but, even if we do not remember Tennyson's sequel to the poem, we know it is not the end of the story. The proem's assurance that more will follow the end of the monologue is the massive assurance of pastoral continuity that our own experience of the proem's abiding value gives.

Enlarged and Nuanced Meanings

Tennyson's first great monologues, "Ulysses" and "Tithonus," are a response to the brutal shock of Hallam's death. In each elegy Tennyson is dealing with a miniature drama. The speaker seeks to identify himself with a pursuit that can lift him beyond a world of flux. In each monologue there is an inability to accept uncritically a total absorption in the speaker's quest. With courage and openness to the "agonies, the strife / Of human hearts" (Keats, "Sleep and Poetry," ll. 24–25), there is a return to the world of process and the claims of Yeats's "dying generations." There is courage here, in the welcome of amplitude and risk. And the quest that finally composes and transcends the bereaved poet's inner turmoil cannot be considered apart from his embrace of unpredictable decay and change, apart from the honesty and openness.

In "Ulysses" and "Tithonus" the speakers find it difficult to choose decisively among different attitudes toward life and death. Instead, they hold them all, with agony, in the mind. Both monologues are stronger for the honesty with which they confront this conflict. They are also more affecting for the authority with which Tennyson's style portrays it; for the integrity with which his dramatic speech reaches out and assimilates it; for the poised repose with which each speaker, having gone through great disorder, comes out again on the other side, not destroyed by his experience, but enlarged and renewed by it.

In "Ulysses" (October 20, 1833) the division in the speaker's mind between regressive impulse and heroic yearning might, if portrayed in a lesser poem, have been confusing. To some extent "Ulysses" has confused readers who respond to the force of its heroic style while ignoring its disturbing implications. Even more, it has confused those readers who seize upon the speaker's elegiac tone and mistake a suicidal indirection in his style for the main meaning. Ulysses holds both the regressive impulse and heroic yearning in balance. He masters death, partly through his rhetoric, but mainly through a succcessful blending of heroic and elegiac styles. There is rhetorical skill in his redefining death as his momentary pause in Ithaca (l. 22), and life as the ship of death about to sail (l. 62). As Christopher Ricks has noted, Ulysses uses "pause" and "end" almost as synonyms. He also associates the "old days" of youth with age, and age itself with youthful adventure. Ulysses, the rhetorician, has known from the beginning that his own virtues must be paired with the domestic virtues of the Ithacans and of his son, Telemachus, if either are to be understood or valued. With a skill so unobtrusive we may even miss the irony, his opening indictment of the Ithacans has served, chiefly, a rhetorical purpose: justifying his neglect of Ithaca during years of "roaming with a hungry heart" (l. 12). Yet in the second half of the monologue we discover that the rhetoric has also filled a deep human need. For even in tribute to Telemachus, magnanimity and self-consciousness cannot quite disguise the superior tone. No sooner has Ulysses established a loving, paternal feeling (ll. 35–42) than he breaks it with a contrasting tone, contemptuous and dismissive: "He works his work, I mine" (l. 43). There is a touch of sententious moralizing in Ulysses' summation. The

verdict is edged with condescension, and composes a kind of elegy
for the Ithacans.

More important than Ulysses' rhetoric is his ability to master
death by dramatically integrating elegiac and heroic styles. We
are first aware of the elegiac undertone in the spacious line "Far
on the ringing plains of windy Troy" (l. 17), which seems to
condense whole books of fighting in the *Iliad*. The spaciousness is
created by a separating out of the elements that alliteration joins:
"Far," "ringing," "Troy"; the verbal space between the alliterating words prevents their converging too soon. "Ringing" is divided from "Troy" and assigned to "plains," while "windy," as
it were, gives up "plains" and is assigned to "Troy" by syntactical
transfer. "Ringing plain" stands for the clamor of war by a
metonymic transfer from the agents to their setting. "Windy
Troy" illustrates the opposite process: a transfer from the setting
to a civilization fashioned out of setting; but it also contains a
metonymy which suggests the ruinous, windswept result of war
instead of the city itself at its "ringing" zenith. By presenting
separate pictures of the turbulence of war and of Troy as the bare,
ruined choir of wasting winds, the distance between cause and
effect in an ordinary chain of events is significantly increased.
Because the termini of the chain—the windswept ruin and the
ring of a proud and boisterous (a "windy") people—are over-
specified, they free the mind from overelaboration of the intermediate stages. The space filled by years of war is collapsed into a
direct confrontation of pride and ruin. By eliding the chain of
mythic events, the multiple metonymies speed the mind. They
allow it to cross in an instant enormous intervals of space and
time.

We are next aware of Ulysses' elegiac undertone in three lines
of melodiously pensive song (ll. 19–21), as the "untravelled
world" that gleams through the arch slowly expands to fill up the
whole space of the horizon.

> Yet all experience is an arch wherethrough
> Gleams that untravelled world, whose margin fades
> For ever and for ever when I move.

The long vowels and assonance, with the extra syllable in the first line and the repetition of "for ever" in the last, create an impression of spaciousness so vast that Matthew Arnold felt "these three lines by themselves take up nearly as much time as a whole book of the *Iliad*."[8] Ulysses creates an illusion of infinite regress by making the margins gleam, fade, and then retreat from view. The shimmering, mobile words of the elegiac mode—"Gleams," "fades," and "move"—add an unsettling evanescence to the solid arch. As the "untravelled" worlds begin to stream away from Ulysses at alarming speeds, the very expansiveness produces a feeling of vertigo. Finally, as the ambiguous simile of following "knowledge like a sinking star" (l. 31) flashes its splendor through the sky, plotting the curve of either the quester or of his goal plummeting through space, it is as if the sheer energy with which the heroic elegist wants to pass beyond the arch, in an avalanche of experience, makes him slip off the edge, wrecked like Dante's Ulysses at the limits of the world. Elegiac in its glimpse of ruin, the style is vigorously heroic. It presents Ulysses engaged in the most strenuous activity of all—spectacularly envisioning his own decline.

Elegiac and heroic styles reach a climax in the last verse paragraph. As Ulysses is possessed by the magic of repose, the slow, long-vowel movement produces a round-and-round hypnotic rhythm that enchants and beguiles him. The apt use of assonance and alliteration creates soporific effects: "The lights begin to twinkle from the rocks: The long day wanes" (ll. 54–55). The fine harmonizing of image and rhythm is beautifully illustrated in the coordinate syntax: "the slow moon climbs: the deep / Moans round with many voices" (ll. 55–56). As the elegiac rhythm becomes more and more languorous, pauses increase and the pace slows down to the expected full stop. In his next breath Ulysses masters the regressive impulse. Without losing his dignity, he conveys his edginess through the imbalance of the rhythm and the

8. "On Translating Homer: Last Words," in *The Complete Prose Works of Matthew Arnold*, ed. R. H. Super (Ann Arbor, Mich., 1960), I, 147.

strong pauses at the end of each short clause. Now that the trance-like mood is broken Ulysses can combine his old heroic energy with the elegist's renewed responsiveness to mystery. We can still feel the heroic thrust of his sentence patterns, as they push against the regularity of the meter, riding across lines. But by the end of the poem the line ends and the pauses for stress fully coincide, and there is more elegiac balance in the phrasing. The final voyage "beyond the sunset" (l. 60) expresses a perfect fusion of action and repose, even though Ulysses' goal remains unspecified, since he wants to seek an infinite goal so that he can seek eternally. The end develops from the double course the poem has been following, heroic and elegiac, and there is no escaping its finality. Ulysses uses isocolon, or parison, the figure primarily concerned with sententious rhythm. The grand fatality of this figure, with its use of clauses of equal length and of corresponding structure, is distinctly declamatory: "It may be that the gulfs will wash us down: / It may be we shall touch the Happy Isles"; "Though much is taken, much abides" (ll. 62, 63, 65). Like Pope in his translation of Homer, Tennyson creates a passage of strong emotion and oratorical movement well suited to a classical imitation that has passion, speech-making, and a great turning point for its subject. We can hear both sadness and stoicism in the telling climaxes and apostrophes of the orator. The nostalgic comparing of the present with the past—"We are not now that strength which in old days / Moved earth and heaven" (ll. 66–67)—is a notable feature of the elegiac style. But in the last five lines the grieving comparisons of elegy are finally abandoned. Ulysses retains the resonant expansions characteristic of the majestic threnodies that reverberate like muffled drum rolls throughout Tennyson's greatest poetry. But he confronts the future with no overtones of misery. His integration of the elegiac undertone into his dominant heroic style enables him to master death. But it also registers the truth that every attainment of power is a loss of power. The bath of stars, linked with the heroic pursuit of knowledge, is also the gulf that will wash Ulysses down. These ironies make "Ulysses" Tennyson's most perfect rendering of the gran-

deurs of threnody that contend in his poetry with the severe refinements of the stoic. Tennyson subdues nostalgia; and by mastering the rich Virgilian sadness that contends with the heroic
impulse to be reticent—to be manly and press on—he leaves the
pathos of his subtext (the emotion of the words behind his words)
to be inferred.

In "Tithonus" (written in 1833, published in 1860) the
speaker's attitudes toward life and death are different from
Ulysses' and reveal a more complicated state of mind. If the
speaker wants to die, it is because he loves life too well to submit
to death in life. The poem expresses anything but a simple death
wish. Though the speaker's main craving has been for immortality, it has always been qualified by a contradictory desire for
immediacy and warmth, which carry with them the penalty of
death. The integration of the two attitudes, instead of providing
a satisfactory resolution of the problem, as it does in "Ulysses,"
produces one of Tennyson's noblest pathetic fallacies. From the
union of permanence and immediacy so ecstatically contemplated
in the goddess, Tithonus must recoil, as Keats does from the
values he has falsely ascribed to the urn's "Cold Pastoral."
Tithonus gains insight into the trap of permanence reflected in
immortality; Keats gains insight into the trap of permanence reflected in works of art. At the end of his "Ode on a Grecian Urn,"
distrusting the profoundly valid truth implied, Keats substitutes
an aphorism for an insight. But Tennyson trusts his indirection.
He prefers, as Robert Frost would say, "the straight crookedness
of a good walking stick." His poem "inclines to the impulse,"
"runs a course of lucky events,"[9] and ends, not perhaps with a
great clarification, but with a resolving conclusion that his poem
as a whole can justify.

We are aware from the beginning of two conflicting attitudes
in Tithonus' mind and of his inability to choose decisively between them. If sensuous immediacy without permanence is horrifying to contemplate, permanence without immediacy is just as

9. "The Figure a Poem Makes," in *Selected Prose of Robert Frost,* ed.
H. Cox and E. C. Lathem (New York, 1968), pp. 18–19.

intolerable. The polysyndeton, or emphatic repetition of the conjunction, at the opening is solemn and relentless: "Man comes
and tills the field and lies beneath" (1. 3); the slow, deathward
movement carries us down to the expiring swan, and composes a
kind of epitaph for creation. The abrupt inversion of the Latin
syntax, which isolates the accusative at the beginning of the
lines—"Me only cruel immortality / Consumes" (ll. 5–6)—introduces the terrifying consequences of the contrary state. Tennyson
gives "cruel immortality" tremendous emphasis by the series of
stresses, the harsh alliteration of "cruel" and "Consumes," and
the portentous Latin diction, which advertises its importance by
taking up so many syllables in the line. The pervasive sense of
ennui, of permanence without immediacy, is given explicitly in
the next lines, where accents and quantities are played off against
each other to produce a heavy rallentando: "I wither slowly in
thine arms" (1. 6); "A white-haired shadow roaming like a
dream" (1. 8). The sinister "shadow" suggests the very opposite
of soft decay; and in horrified reaction Tithonus reverts nostalgically to the sensuous delights of the young worshiper, "So glorious in his beauty" (1. 12). The marveling turn upon "thy choice,"
"thy chosen" swells his sense of wonder, till he seems in his
ecstasy "none other than a God" (ll. 12–14). Tithonus believes
that he can transmute his sensuous delight in the goddess into an
eternal pleasure, and his belief takes the form of a request for
immortality.

But Tennyson introduces an uneasy indirection. The images
and rhythm are unsettling; and what should be the climax of the
poem becomes instead a turning point. Aurora confers her gift
with disturbing facility, with the mindless profusion typical of
"wealthy men who care not how they give" (1. 17). And the
smile of the goddess flickers with sinister implication. The
Miltonic phrasing of "thy strong Hours indignant" (1. 18), which
is threatening and judgmental, prepares for the hammering
polysyndeton, which levels Tithonus with a series of blows:
"And beat me down and marred and wasted me" (1. 19). The
appearance of "Immortal age" between the fixed phrase "immortal youth," which Tennyson repeats in successive lines without

changing its position, stresses the ghastly transformation of the one element that does change: "left me maimed / To dwell in presence of immortal youth, / Immortal age beside immortal youth, / And all I was, in ashes" (ll. 20–23). "Ashes" is the key word, suggesting the waste of Tithonus' ardor and the ruin of the disintoxicated moment. Tithonus' only compensation is to point to the sensual satisfaction, concretely realized, by "the kindly race of men" (l. 29). There is awareness that life is change, growth, and diversity, the fruit of growing into death, that "goal of ordinance / Where all should pause, as is most meet for all" (ll. 30–31).

Elegiac consolation is enriched and complicated by a reluctance to accept the growth into death without realizing at the same time some imperishable bliss. The conflicting attitudes in Tithonus' mind raise the central question of Keats's odes: if what endures is inhuman and what is human dies, is it ever possible to combine sensuous immediacy with permanence? Is it ever possible for all that is valuable in life to triumph over time? "Tithonus" is a stronger poem for the honesty with which it confronts these questions. By trusting the swervings of his speaker's moods and following their lead, Tennyson charts the rift that opens between Tithonus and Aurora, just as "Ode to a Nightingale" charts the rift that opens between Keats, racked by "The weariness, the fever, and the fret," and the bird that soars beyond him into a timeless world: "Lo! ever thus thou growest beautiful / In silence, then before thine answer given / Departest, and thy tears are on my cheek" ("Tithonus," ll. 43–45). The economy of the ellipsis—Tennyson's omission of "is" before "given" and of "thou" before "Departest"—adds to our discomfort; the syntax jostles, and the huddling together of "given" and "Departest" appropriately clogs the action it should speed. Even the loose parataxis, linked by an illogical "and" (l. 45), betrays Tithonus' error. If the goddess is as empty of compassion as her silence and departure suggest, she is also incapable of weeping. The surmise that the dew on his cheek is Aurora's tears is only a pathetic fallacy.

With the reiterated "Ay me! ay me!" (l. 50) Tithonus initi-

ates once again the movement toward vernal air and sun. To
lighten the style, which hovers on the edge of lushness and over-
sweetness, Tennyson introduces the reticence of "half-opening
buds" (l. 59) and the wavering towers of Ilion, as if glimpsed
through a mist. By the last verse paragraph, however, Tithonus
has lapsed altogether from his inspired vision. The crimson glow
that had kindled him to ecstasy now bathes him "Coldly" in its
"rosy shadows" (l. 66). The oxymorons balance the desire for
sensuous fulfillment, unattended by the disadvantages of cooling
blood and "wrinkled feet" (l. 67), with a complementary but
regressive desire for oblivion, which is now put positively as "the
power to die" (l. 70). The iterative syntax is very schematic, as if
the repetition of a word in an altered form—"Coldly . . .
cold . . . cold" (ll. 66–67)—and the framing device of starting
and ending a line with the same word were trying to stave off
terror. Human life comes to fruition and passes into nothingness.
All the equivocations and shifts of mood in the poem converge
toward the suggestion that peace comes only with mature recognition of impermanence. But they do so only through reticences of
mood, through a shimmer of hints that exclude direct assertion.
Our disturbing knowledge that in classical myth Tithonus is
changed, not into a man but into a grasshopper, creates the same
unsettling effect that Tennyson arranges by other means at the
end of "The Lotos-Eaters." Yet even when Tithonus would
blasphemously "forget" the ritual of Aurora's renewing her
"beauty morn by morn" (l. 74), the irony of his muted protest
is perfectly controlled by the resignation implicit in the restraint
and decorum of his tone. Against images that recall the mellow
richness and decline of the human cycle, the triumphal progress
of the goddess begins. The concluding picture conveys the sense
of tremendous rallentando, the great pause, the slowing down of
Aurora's triumphal progress. Though she orbits heaven in a
perfect circular motion, which is the emblem of the divine, her
triumphal pageant is qualified by the pathos inherent in the other
cycle. This is the linking that counts most as metaphor in the last
lines of the poem. To the majestic auroral cycle Tennyson adds

the poignant human cycle of "earth in earth" (l. 75), a cycle which the reader, like Tithonus, can now value and accept, and for which the autumnal richness and slowing down of the opening lines have subtly and beautifully prepared him.

What disturbs a reader at the end of "Ode on a Grecian Urn" is the oracular motto, which is more resolutely conclusive than the poem as a whole can justify. Tennyson's speaker, in contrast, refuses to force belief or falsify results. By trusting the sufficiency of the insight implied, and by recognizing how central the trap of permanence has become to the structure of his poem, Tennyson can afford to be restrained. Charting the swervings of the speaker's moods allows the poet to redirect anxieties, instead of simply throttling or suppressing them. Honestly recording what he finds, Tennyson can leave Tithonus—and the reader, too—to discover for themselves the harsh but consoling truth that whoever rightly understands and celebrates death, at the same time magnifies life. Such thoughts—the poem's deepest truths—are more affecting because they are only half-expressed. Understatement is a tribute to their genuineness.

The elegist's "horror of the last," which Dr. Johnson says "is inseparable from a thinking being whose life is limited, and to whom death is dreadful,"[10] requires a few concluding comments. "Ulysses" and "Tithonus" both achieve strong effects of closure; yet few poems end more reluctantly. The idea of concluding suggests both dread and satisfaction. In the last line of "Ulysses" the regular meter, reinforced by monosyllabic diction, produces a secure sense of ending: "To strive, to seek, to find, and not to yield" (l. 70). Syntactic parallels, formal repetitions, closural allusions to the Homeric underworld—all are familiar terminal devices, and all appear in the last few lines. Even large symmetries in the poem, which extend to the pauses and the syntax, have closing force. The indictment of those Ithacans "That hoard, and sleep, and feed, and know not me" (l. 5) anticipates by parody the lofty close. The concessional clauses—"Though much

10. Samuel Johnson, *The Idler and the Adventurer*, ed. W. J. Bate, John M. Bullitt, and L. F. Powell (New York, 1963), pp. 314–315.

is taken"; "though / We are not now" (ll. 65–66)—draw
Ulysses' life to an end. That these forces of closure should be
honestly acknowledged, and presented with the same authority as
the forces suspending closure, is itself a proof of heroic character.
But grammar also mutes these concessions, and few poetic endings
are more impeded.

"Ulysses" uses a host of devices to keep its outcome poised.
Most important, there is more correspondence between line ends
and major syntactic breaks than in any other of Tennyson's
blank-verse codas. Semicolons and commas fall at the end of
lines, so that, instead of being propelled forward, we keep pausing
to rest. As in "The Holy Grail" ("I saw / That which I saw"
[ll. 847–848]; "ye have seen what ye have seen" [l. 915]), Tennyson's formula for the numbness induced by vision is tautology:
"that which we are, we are" (l. 67). The visionary formula
sweeps the speaker up from finitude into an eternity of present
tenses. There are no past or future verbs at the end of "Ulysses."
Instead, Ulysses is absorbed into a cluster of timeless infinitives,
poised between verb and substantive, between finite acts and endless questing. Is Ulysses active enough to be independently
"strong"? Is this adjective in apposition to "heroic hearts," or is
it preceded by an ellipsis of the passive participle? If the latter,
then Ulysses has been "made" strong, as he has been "Made
weak," "by time and fate" (l. 69). The passive grammar and repeating syntax sweep to their heroic climax with a self-retarding
movement. As if to mute its finitude, the appositional grammar
circles back on itself. To borrow Robert Frost's phrase ("Direc-
tive," l. 49), the poem has a "destiny" but no "destination." It
foresees but impedes its end. Its final phrases drift down, one by
one, with as steady but unhurried a conclusion as any poem can
have.

> that which we are,
>   we are:
>   One equal temper of heroic hearts,
>   Made weak by time and fate,
>   but strong in will

> To strive,
>   to seek,
>   to find,
>   and not to yield.   [ll. 67–70]

It is as if Ulysses, like Tennyson, were as reluctant to end his life as those final, tenseless infinitives—staring off into space and time—are reluctant to end the poem. If morality is the perfect use of an imperfect medium, then the end of the poem, like the end of Ulysses' life, is moral. The poem seems to redress the brutal affront of Hallam's sudden death, the tragedy of his unfulfilled promise, by spending itself without remainder. In Yeats's great phrase, it burns "The entire combustible world in one small room." The end of the poem, so perfectly foreseen and yet delayed, consumes all its forces, as if "the work," like Ulysses' life, "had finished in that flare."[11]

At the end of "Tithonus" the formal repetition of "morn by morn" (l. 74), the syntactical parallels—"Thou seëst all things, thou wilt see my grave" (l. 73)—and the terminal allusion to "earth in earth" (l. 75), are all effective closing devices. But the slow, steady beat that represents repose and stability for the speaker represents renewal of life for Aurora. And his desire for closure is happily contradicted by the expansive evocation of the final line, "And thee returning on thy silver wheels" (l. 76), whose present participle "returning" is indefinitely protracted, stretched across the whole space of the horizon. The desire to live and the desire to die are superbly compressed, without incongruity, in a final indirection. Even the grammar is unstable. To blot Aurora from his mind Tithonus has made the pronoun "thee" the object of forgetting. We are reminded by the more logical possessive form, in the final change rung upon "Thou," "thee," "thy" (l. 73, l. 75), that the pronoun should modify the verbal form, and not the other way round. If "returning" is seen, for a moment, as a gerund, instead of as a participle, then the restoration in our mind of the more logical grammar mutes even further

11. William Butler Yeats, "In Memory of Major Robert Gregory," ll. 82, 85.

the finite verbal force of "returning." As pronouns shift, closure is suspended on the fulcrum of a verbal noun—on a gerund that wavers, like one of Tennyson's timeless-temporal infinitives, between substantive and verbal forms, just as Aurora wavers ambiguously between eternity and time.

What keeps the language vibrant, delaying finality even for the speaker, is not only the worshiper's blasphemy ("forget . . . thee" [ll. 75–76]), or his use of similar repetitions for very different forms of permanence ("morn by morn," "earth in earth" [ll. 74–75]), but also the endless capacity of his mind, given the outcome of his story, to deceive itself. Half consciously, but infallibly, the mind subdues nature to its hopes, converting the future it desires—"wilt see," "wilt renew" (ll. 73–74)—into a simple present tense. Finally, as oblivion crystallizes with terrifying literalness into "earth in earth," there follows a touching change of focus, comparable to the sudden thought of becoming "sod" to the nightingale's "high requiem" in Keats's ode. If the opening of "Tithonus" is artificially simple, the ending of the poem is naturally so. "Thou wilt renew thy beauty morn by morn" (l. 74) has a charged subtext: it sounds like the final compromise Tennyson is offering for a dozen more elaborate endings. The achievement of closure in this poem is also an achievement of personal catharsis. To evoke the end is to accept the end, to surrender the personality to the object evoked, the object for whom there is no end. The objectivity of the closure is therefore moral. It consists of an obliteration of the mind's pathetic fallacies, in a conquest of sentimental attachment to the object defined.

After experimenting with elegiac simplicity in the "Mariana" poems, and with a memorable rhetoric of nostalgia in "Oenone," Tennyson has combined the two styles in "Ulysses." Though the end of "Ulysses," with its first-person plurals, seems to sweep the poet himself into the fellowship of the dead, the elegist uses various devices to blunt death's sting. The ending of "Ulysses" is neither ingenious nor witty, yet it may certainly be regarded as sententious. Its power is evidence that Tennyson and Ulysses are uttering their words in unison, though with somewhat different meanings. This union of voices is a very different thing from the ventriloquism which turns the naked goddess in "Oenone" into a mouthpiece for Tennyson's Victorian attitudes. Though Tennyson told his son that "Ulysses" "gave [his] feeling about [Hallam's death], perhaps more simply than anything in *In Memoriam*,"[12] the use of a mask, instead of turning loose the poet's grief, helps control it. Finally, there are the lines at the end of "Tithonus," which are among Tennyson's supreme poetic utterances; they control grief through the morally interesting device of dramatic understatement. As in Shakespeare's "Ripeness is all" (*King Lear*, V, ii, 9), we seem to hear a still more impersonal voice than that of the character or the poet. "Earth in earth" masters the horror of leave-taking by defining, with restraint, its farewell forever—a farewell that will not, and need not, be spoken again. Accommodations of the human and divine, of the sensuous and the permanent, allow the elegiac poet to amend the flaws of our mortality without seeming to concoct his visions falsely and without producing cosmic strain. The traditional language and ancient symbols have the further advantage of giving the elegist detachment from his pain. By composing a kind of liturgy, the charged subtext sets the poet's grief in the distant but still vibrant pathos of the past, where loss tells chiefly as a consecration of remembering and an enriched autumnal tone. In "Tithonus" the elegist has tamed his love of grandeur to a new mood of reticence, and written a poetry of "earth in earth"—"simple," "severe," and truly grand.

12. Hallam Tennyson, *Tennyson: A Memoir*, I (London, 1897), 196.

3
Dramatic and Narrative
Indirection

Ever since Harold Nicolson praised Tennyson's lyric poems and condemned him for attempting anything else,[1] readers have often assumed that any effort by Tennyson to combine the lyric element of his genius with the reflective and dramatic elements is a damaging concession to moral and social pressures of the Victorian age. Nicolson is right to praise Tennyson's lyric poems for their aesthetic success. Nothing Tennyson writes is as beautiful and seemingly perfect, as hauntingly suggestive and complex, as are many of his lyric poems. Still, Tennyson the lyric poet, the elegist of dissolving forms, yearns for the stable identity of a Victorian sage. His desire, as a poet of sensation, to write reflective poems is part of a Victorian desire for the harmonious development of all the faculties. It comes from a conviction, shared by Ruskin, Morris, and Matthew Arnold, that aesthetic judgments are inextricably related to moral and social judgments. A poet's convictions and his efforts to realize these convictions are no guarantee of his success. But it would be strange if an experimenter so relentless as Tennyson, and a stylist so gifted, could never find poetic forms that manage to hold all the elements together. Though Tennyson's most notable achievements are his lyric poems (as Nicolson rightly insists), his most intellectually

1. Harold Nicolson, *Tennyson: Aspects of his Life, Character and Poetry* (London, 1925). See especially pp. 5–6: "For whereas Tennyson was an extremely good emotional poet, he was, unfortunately, but a very second-rate instructional bard. His gift of emotion, had he indulged it less reservedly, was powerful and immense; his capacity for thought, which he indulged effusively, was of a quite different quality."

and aesthetically ambitious works are monologues such as "Lucretius," the fragmented and hallucinatory *Maud,* the incomparable *In Memoriam*—all poems which combine genres and mix techniques. These major works unite the elegiac, visionary qualities of the lyric style with the narrative and dramatic structure of the plays and idylls. Tennyson, like Browning, must experiment with a great variety of monologues and narrative genres before he can find an intermediate form that allows him to speak more directly than he can as a playwright or a conventional narrative poet but more indirectly than he can as an elegist or a seer.

In turning now—and in the following chapters—to some of Tennyson's long narrative and dramatic poems, I shall be making judgments that cannot be fully demonstrated in a study that concentrates on style. I do not consider my approach exclusive; but sustaining a consistent thesis about style requires a certain purity in exposition. In order to demonstrate the effects of Tennyson's major poems, detailed analysis of larger structural devices by other critics will have to supplement my approach, which is through the microcosm of language and through its relatively minute adjustments.

Dramatic Indirection: The Monologues

The most accurate generalization applicable to Tennyson's dramatic forms is Browning's declaration in the preface to his own *Strafford* that the life of his play is "Action in Character, rather than Character in Action." Such a reversal of the priorities ascribed to Sophocles by Aristotle, for whom action rather than character is the soul of tragedy, is the dramatic equivalent of Wordsworth's reversal two generations earlier of the priority ascribed to "situation" over "feeling" in the ballad form.[2] A dramatic poet who shares the nineteenth-century attitude of Browning and Wordsworth, which is reflected in the Shakespearean criticism of Coleridge and A. C. Bradley, must experiment with genres that allow him to hold action to a minimum.

2. William Wordsworth, "Preface to the Second Edition of 'Lyrical Ballads,' 1800," in *Selected Poetry,* ed. Mark Van Doren (New York, 1950), p. 679.

Tennyson's earliest success in dramatic writing is *The Devil and the Lady* (1823). A revel of paradox and debate, the play opens with a contest in hyperbole between Magus and the devil. Without requiring the young playwright to develop a complicated action, the dramatic exchange has the advantage of containing the verbal overflow that a lyric form might simply turn loose. The ironic distance maintained between Tennyson and his characters finds a parallel within the play in the irony that allows Magus to make fun of his own verbal excess when he sees it reproduced—and unconsciously parodied—in the devil's rhetoric. A poet such as Tennyson who shares Browning's interest in "Action in Character" is entering into a range of psychological and moral experience that is less and less translatable into conventional dramatic forms. Tennyson is drawn to tell Becket's story in the historical play of that name because it raises a complex issue: the nature of martyrdom-suicide. But the complexities are better explored in a dramatic monologue such as "St. Simeon Stylites," where Tennyson can leave his speaker poised, without having to chart the action to a known outcome. Tennyson confronts in the historical play *Queen Mary* many of the same problems that he confronts in *Becket*. Because Queen Mary's last speech adds nothing to her character that we did not grasp intuitively in the first act, it seems defective in a play. Yet her bizarre blend of pathos and vindictiveness, reminiscent of Browning's court lady in "The Laboratory," would make a powerful dramatic monologue, a genre in which no character development need occur. Too often in the plays the psychological conflicts are still in search of dramatic situations. Tennyson hints that Becket's opposition to the state springs obscurely from his love for Henry, and that Mary's fanaticism and her obsession with Philip are rooted in hatred for her father and loyalty to her Spanish mother. But the action of a historical play forces Tennyson to attempt a direct presentation of what he can only imply, what he can dramatize only indirectly. Tennyson must experiment with dramatic forms that use more indirection. Only in this way can he avoid problems that are most acute in attempts at direct expression.

The form that most consistently provides Tennyson with the right kind of indirection is the dramatic monologue. Instead of having to chart the action to a known outcome, the monologue serves as a pause, like the brief aside or soliloquy in a play, in which the human action breaks out into reflection and self-knowledge. Because the characteristic voice of this genre is T. S. Eliot's "second voice"[3] of poetry, the voice of the poet addressing an audience, the monologue provides Tennyson with a rich rhetorical resource. By hiding behind a dramatic mask such as Lucretius, Tennyson can persuade his readers of the defects of positivism without appearing to address them at all. Tennyson is a poet of transitional moments, wavering between stability and dissolution. The dramatic indirection of a monologue allows him to leave many of his speakers poised at crucial moments, suspended like Tithonus between different worlds. Because, as W. E. Fredeman observes, most monologues present "not the end, but . . . the penultimate moment before the end,"[4] they allow Tennyson to play off the final outcome of an action against those pauses in human life which give dramatic expression and even dignity to widely different motives and hopes. That these motives and hopes are not cut to order, and seldom fit the final outcome, is a tribute to their genuineness. It is also a source of irony, for despite his heroism Ulysses is about to sail to his death; and despite her lament Mariana is soon to be united with her lover. The drama is that of life itself, which is rarely conclusive in the answers it provides.

The two most influential theories of the monologue, those of T. S. Eliot[5] and Robert Langbaum,[6] present very different ver-

3. "The Three Voices of Poetry," in *On Poetry and Poets* (New York, 1961), p. 96.
4. " 'A Sign betwixt the Meadow and the Cloud': The Ironic Apotheosis of Tennyson's *St. Simeon Stylites*," *University of Toronto Quarterly*, XXXVIII (1969), 71.
5. "The Three Voices of Poetry," pp. 102–105. For a more detailed analysis of the dramatic monologue as a rhetorical genre see my earlier study, *The Dialectical Temper: The Rhetorical Art of Robert Browning* (Ithaca, 1968), especially pp. 60–64.
6. "The Dramatic Monologue: Sympathy versus Judgment," in *The*

sions of the form. According to Eliot the monologue is a rhetorical genre in which the poet, by speaking through a mask, is able to persuade an audience indirectly. Langbaum sees a much more dramatic and lyric genre, not far removed from that described in Wordsworth's account of his own *Lyrical Ballads*—poems in which "feeling . . . gives importance to the action and situation, and not the action and situation to the feeling."[7] The monologues that Langbaum finds normative present a "flat" speaker, whose deficient point of view, not to be mistaken for the author's, undergoes no notable development. Though a *via media* between rhetorical and dramatic monologues is neither possible nor desirable, it is instructive to see how monologues like Browning's "My Last Duchess" and Tennyson's "St. Simeon Stylites" conform to the dramatic norm. A rhetorical model works better for monologues like Browning's "A Toccata of Galuppi's" or for Tennyson's "Tithonus" and "Tiresias." These poems present a more "rounded" character, whose point of view changes, until he and the poet seem to speak for a moment in unison. Few Victorian monologues present Nietzschean supermen, beyond moral good and evil; and few good monologues present classical rhetoricians expounding doctrine. Most Victorian monologues present a subtle adjustment of the dramatic and rhetorical elements. Monologues such as "Tiresias" that conform too closely to the rhetorical model are in danger of turning into exercises in ventriloquism. Monologues such as "St. Simeon Stylites" that conform too closely to the dramatic model are in danger of so dissolving the poet's ideas in the abnormal psychology of the characters that the author's voice is barely audible. In Tennyson's case, more successful than a poem at either extreme is a monologue such as "Lucretius," which holds psychology and rhetoric in balance. Without addressing the reader directly, the rhetorical poet in his psychological study of the speaker's mental breakdown

---

Poetry of Experience: The Dramatic Monologue in Modern Literary Tradition (New York, 1957), pp. 75–108.

   7. William Wordsworth, Preface, in *Selected Poetry*, p. 679.

is able to strengthen his argument against positivism, providing at the same time a fair and comprehensive picture of the Lucretian system.

Grotesquely, in the early "St. Simeon Stylites" (1833), Tennyson uses dramatic indirection to discredit a humorless fanatic, always teetering on the edge of absurdity. The near obscenity of Simeon's lust for sainthood derives from a typically Freudian linkage between anality and power. Words like "superhuman pangs" (l. 11) veer between two meanings: exaltation of the spirit and "throes and cramps" (l. 13). The downward turn comes with the indecent suggestion that the "lower voices," which "saint" him "from above" (l. 152), are voices of flatulence, like the eructation of Swift's Aeolists. Simeon describes the advent of vision as a cathartic; with a "sting of shrewdest pain" it at last evacuates all his "mortal archives" (l. 157). In being left "blank of crimeful record" (l. 156) is Simeon merely being relieved of his "aches" and "cramps," or has he experienced a genuine catharsis of the spirit? Even if the first alternative is a genetic fallacy, and saintly power transcends its "anal" origins, what assurance has the "saint" that he is not leaving one excremental form for a corruption more subtle? Tennyson reinforces the indirection by introducing various metaphoric and verbal ironies. Simeon pictures "the dull chrysalis" of his body cracking into "shining wings" (ll. 153–154), like a genie released from Aladdin's lamp. The metaphor implies a Gnostic view of resurrection. For the author of "The Higher Pantheism," the physical nausea so painfully developed in St. Simeon is clearly tainted with heresy. The soul is not a ghost in a machine, nor is the body as foul as Simeon imagines. Two-way meaning extends to words like "saint," an elusive and unstable term, as Martin Dodsworth has shown; sometimes Simeon "hopes for exalted rank in Heaven, sometimes he merely wants to be saved (to be a *saint* in the sense of 'member of the elect')."[8]

8. "Patterns of Morbidity: Repetition in Tennyson's Poetry," in *The Major Victorian Poets: Reconsiderations,* ed. Isobel Armstrong (Lincoln, Neb., 1969), p. 16.

But the poem's main indirection is a systematic substitution of the fantasies of childhood for theology. Reading the monologue is like walking down a hall, with doors suddenly flinging open, revealing unexpected recesses, secret corridors filled with harsh ironic light. Simeon's desire to be "whole, and clean, and meet for Heaven" (l. 210) is an infantile regression. The "saint" experiences a child's distress, waking after being unclean, covered with sores "From scalp to sole" (l. 2). He wails and sobs, drowning with his cries the hooting of the owl (l. 32). Though always opening on a saintly motive, new regressions are revealed which present Simeon as a child at its mother's breast, "Suck[ing] the damps for drink" (l. 76). The doors flung open on secret places disclose a prenatal orgy of sensual excess, a fantastic riot of apes and monsters, in the course of which the saint's embryo is presumably conceived. The apes, pigs, and horses are sheerly physical—burlesque replicas of the supernatural powers that await the saint: the trinity of Christ, the angel, and the Holy Ghost. Even Simeon's penitential tone is strident and clamorous, verging on hysteria. If the epithets of his invocation are felicitous, God, like a lax parent, is expected to indulge his child. Concealed directives to God impart to Simeon's names for God the kind of disguised ritual John Austin has exposed in his classic study of "performative verbs."[9] Such words are not neutral definitions: they are performances, designed to bring into being the conditions they describe. When Simeon turns his "storms of prayer" into formulaic assaults, or battering rams, against "the gates of heaven" (l. 7), his invocation to "just, dreadful, mighty God" (l. 9) turns out to be an order to God in disguise.

The strong sense of closure in most of Tennyson's monologues is not authoritatively conclusive. Though Browning's *Dramatic Idyls* reveal comparable uncertainty, most of Browning's dramatic monologues imply a single judgment on their speakers. In contrast, the codas of "St. Simeon Stylites," "Tiresias," and "Lucretius," despite their apparent certitude, convey doubt, tenta-

9. *How to Do Things with Words,* ed. J. O. Urmson (Cambridge, Mass., 1967).

tiveness, and a refusal to make unqualified assertions. In each case the codas are carefully qualified by a tentative grammar and by a steadfast refusal to cut off any impulse that is unforeseen or not made to order. This technique is most integral to "St. Simeon Stylites," where Tennyson turns the conflict between the forces working toward closure and the forces suspending it into a major irony. Toward the end of the poem the syntactic triads seem to be mounting to crescendo and climax: "What's here? a shape, a shade / A flash of light" (ll. 199–200). The strong alliteration and formal repetitions have terminal force independently; and Simeon increases the sense of closure by prophesying his death will occur at a quarter to twelve. He also uses the least subtle way of forcing closure: he announces it is coming: "The end! the end! / Surely the end!" (ll. 198–199). Yet the more urgently Simeon wills closure, the more stubbornly Tennyson resists it. Instead of using stable language, he brings the main indirections more into play than ever. The ambiguous "shape" and "shade" may also be the same lewd forms that assail Lucretius, the faces that burst earlier, "With colt-like whinny and with hoggish whine" (l. 174), upon the speaker's prayers. The extraordinary stress, the successive blows with sharp breaks and repetitions, are the equivalent in sound for the saint's commotion and his irrational surge of hope. Simeon's closest approach to genuine climax is the interlocking syntax of his catalogue of pains, which computes his sufferings arithmetically, as though he were a kind of Bentham among the saints: "Three years," "twice three years," "Twenty," "Twice ten" (ll. 85–89). Later his effort to initiate a climactic order of meaning breaks down in a frantic repetition of single words: "now, / Now, now" (ll. 187–188); "Nay, draw, draw, draw nigh" (l. 204). It is as if Simeon were physically assisting at the miracle, straining to comprehend a mystery, striving to will it into being by hysterical fiat.

Tennyson's suspension of the ending that Simeon wills is mainly a humorous device. But humor is also a means of compelling examination. Its ironic glints dissipate pretension, and reveal new problems that are just as perplexing and important to Tennyson as they are to his speaker. If Simeon cannot conclude, it is also because Tennyson cannot: for what has his poem concluded about sainthood that there is anything to conclude about? Even if spuriously motivated, Simeon's vigil may still be miraculous, at least in the Shavian sense that a miracle is an "event which creates faith."[10] Simeon may inspire, not just belief in his own power to perform miracles, but also—and more importantly— a belief in God himself. The passionate repetitions—"but what of that?"; "but what of that?" (ll. 135, 137)—reflect the most solemn irony in the poem: an impulse to believe and disbelieve at the same time. Sainthood is elusive: the craving to understand it, like the craving to possess it, seems incompatible with either the knowledge or attainment of that state. In the *Idylls*, the sacred is meant to be beyond all conclusions, an elusive ecstasy—or ravishing desolation, engulfing Galahad in gusts of light that hide his end, both his goal and his death, from view. In "St. Simeon Stylites," Tennyson finally suspends closure while seeming to achieve it. He arrests the reader's expectation of the poem's reaching conclusions about sainthood by introducing another subject: "But thou, O Lord, / Aid all this foolish people; let them take / Example, pattern: lead them to thy light" (ll. 218–220). Like the last line in "The Passing of Arthur," the end is a "frame": it separates itself from the thematic structure of the rest of the poem and makes a generalized comment from outside. The prayer is neither sententious nor witty, but it has the terminal effect of an epigram. It achieves finality by yielding the human desire for closure, which is unstable, over to God, who *is* stable.

At the climax of "Tiresias," another dramatic monologue of the year 1833, the rhetoric's very nobility comes from a Victorian sense of responsibility: "Nobly . . . do" and "nobly . . . die" (l. 117). Like Pallas Athene's speech in "Oenone," the appeal to clear-eyed, vigorous action comes close to ventriloquism. For a moment we seem to hear, not the antique prophet, but the Vic-

10. G. B. Shaw, *St. Joan,* scene ii.

torian patriot who wrote "The Charge of the Light Brigade."
The tendency to congeal love in duty has to be set against the
unhindered verve of the closing lines of "Tiresias." Here Tennyson makes his doctrine compelling even to reluctant sympathizers.
In a passage that he liked to quote as "a sample of his blank
verse,"[11] there is no point before the last two lines where a line
end corresponds to a full stop. The major syntactic breaks—all
the dashes and all but one of the commas in the last eleven lines—
fall in the middle of lines. When the syntactic and formal patterns
finally coincide—"On one far height in one-far shining fire" (l.
177)—they satisfy an expectation that has been building up for
some time. When combined with a complex pattern of alliteration
and assonance—"glory," "golden," "grateful," "God"—the closural force of formal repetition—"heroic ears / Heroic hymns" (ll.
173–174)—and of parallel phrasing—"one far height," "one
far-shining fire" (l. 177)—is particularly strong. Even the allusion to the Homeric underworld, to the repose of mingling "with
the famous kings of old" (l. 163), introduces a finality appropriate to terminal events.

> But for me,
> I would that I were gathered to my rest,
> And mingled with the famous kings of old,
> On whom about their ocean-islets flash
> The faces of the Gods—the wise man's word,
> Here trampled by the populace underfoot,
> There crowned with worship—and these eyes will find
> The men I knew, and watch the chariot whirl
> About the goal again, and hunters race
> The shadowy lion, and the warrior-kings,
> In height and prowess more than human, strive
> Again for glory, while the golden lyre
> Is ever sounding in heroic ears
> Heroic hymns, and every way the vales
> Wind, clouded with the grateful incense-fume
> Of those who mix all odour to the Gods
> On one far height in one far-shining fire.   [ll. 161–177]

11. Hallam Tennyson, *Tennyson: A Memoir,* II (London, 1897), 318.

How, then, does Tennyson qualify the coda? How does he modify its stable conclusion, registering the tremors of nuance— the filaments of irony that enlarge and complicate his attitude toward death? To blunt the great horror of concluding, the dread of anything implying a definite termination, the grammar first qualifies its verbs. The phrase "to plunge" (l. 153) transforms the instant of death into a timeless infinitive. To prolong further the conquest of death Tennyson poises the infinitive phrase, suspended between substantive and verb, eternity and time, on a present participle—"fearing not"—the adjectival form that lends itself most readily to indefinite protraction. He also qualifies the coda's oracular verbs by introducing them in an optative mood: "I would that I were gathered" (l. 162). The speaker compels the reader to participate in his own uncertainty by shifting next to a simple future tense. He mutes what seem at first to be a series of active verbs—"whirl," "race," and "strive" (ll. 168–169, 171)— by turning them all into infinitive phrases, doubly removed from present time by being made to depend upon the future verb: "[will] watch" (l. 168). Even though the conclusion is stable, its finality predetermined in syntax and form, Tiresias still manages to postpone its arrival. The last lines float down in their own equilibrium, phrase by phrase. Tiresias never hastens the drift. He combines the dignity of blank verse with the plainness and restraint of classic prose. Guiding the grammar, reluctantly and with what seem endless postponements, to its final phrasal suspensions, Tiresias bides his time in the Homeric twilight, living, like his syntax, in suspended animation.

The monologue that holds the elements of rhetoric and psychology in subtlest balance is the incomparable "Lucretius," written between October, 1865 and January, 1868, more than three decades after the monologues we have just considered. The hallucinations of Lucretius produce a wholeness of form that Tennyson is unable to achieve in dramatic and narrative poems that simply juxtapose dream vision and social commentary, or symbolic and narrative elements. Trapped into a conflict between thought and feeling, facts and values, many Victorian thinkers search like Matthew Arnold for some form of "imaginative reason,"[12] for the synthesizing power Santayana had in mind when he envisaged reason itself as an imagination that succeeds, an intuition that guesses the principle of experience.[13] Refusing to choose either the facts his readers believe in or the values they imagine and desire, Browning claims that "Fancy with fact is just one fact the more" (*The Ring and the Book,* I, 464); he writes *The Ring and the Book* to find some new adjustment of their claims. The same problem is the explicit subject of "Lucretius," in which the speaker makes a brilliant, though unsuccessful, attempt to hold facts and values in unison. Because Tennyson's double role as rhetorician and psychologist allows him, as a critic of positivism, to be comfortably above the positivists' mental aberrations, he is able to write a poem about mental breakdown that does not itself disintegrate.

Most of "Lucretius" portrays a sundering of thought and feeling, as logician and poet wage their deadly conflict. Two-way syntax alerts the mind to its own disintegration: "And here an Oread . . . / . . . A satyr, a satyr, see, / Follows" (ll. 188, 192–193). Is "Oread" or "satyr" the subject of the verb? In a world of dissolving grammatical parts, in which the pursued is also the pursuer, the object also the subject, meanings are likely to reverse themselves at any moment. Syntax dissolves into atomic parts, leaving a subject like "The Gods" (l. 104) suspended for seven lines, without a principal verb. As if to fix attention, and prevent the mind from disintegrating further, Lucretius keeps repeating the last word of one verse paragraph at the beginning of the next.

12. "Pagan and Medieval Religious Sentiment," in *The Complete Prose Works of Matthew Arnold,* ed. R. H. Super (Ann Arbor, Mich., 1960), III, 230.
13. See, for example, George Santayana, *The Life of Reason* (New York, 1954), pp. 60–61: "The naturalist . . . welcomes criticism because his constructions, though no less hypothetical and speculative than the idealist's dreams, are such legitimate and fruitful fictions that they are obvious truths. For truth, at the intelligible level where it arises, means not sensible fact, but valid ideation, verified hypothesis, and inevitable, stable inference."

In lays that will outlast thy Deity?

'Deity? nay, thy worshippers. . . .'   [ll. 72–73]

Which things appear the work of mighty Gods.

'The Gods! and if I go *my* work is left
Unfinished—*if* I go. . . .'   [ll. 102–104]

The kernel subject words "Deity" and "Gods" are the least destructible. But words endowed with purely syntactical function, such as conjunctions, pronouns, prepositions, start to disappear, dissolving the ties of grammatical subordination. In an effort to bind together the disintegrating parts, the repetitions of "meant" (ll. 118, 121–122) and "little life" (ll. 226–228) are modulated in a restless zigzag throughout the poem. When syntax is held together mainly by dashes, and grammatical rules organizing words into higher units are lost, even the turn on unstable verbs like "break" and "breaking" (ll. 241–242) helps stabilize the grammar, before dissolving words again in the chaotic flow.

The opening words are a blend of crashing sounds and stormy lights: "Storm in the night! for thrice I heard the rain / Rushing; and once the flash of a thunderbolt!" (ll. 26–27). A maddened world of tempest, broken down into grammatical fragments, is the objective counterpoint of madness in the mind. The stormy alliteration helps maintain a measured swing in the rhythm, while the tumbling sound and the confusion of the meter fit exactly the commotion of the "streaming mountain-side" and "riotous confluence" of waters (ll. 29–30). In keeping with the grand epic tone of *De rerum natura*, there is a majestic balancing of phrases and clauses. But its grandeur is of a peculiar kind, consonant with Hegel's understanding of sublimity: a spirit exalted beyond all natural forms, but which seeks "to intoxicate itself in them, to seethe and ferment in them."[14] The meter begins to disintegrate in the fourfold repetition of "dreams" and in a series of sharp pauses and continuous stresses: "terrible! for it seemed / A void

14. G. W. F. Hegel, *Lectures on Aesthetics,* in *Hegel on Art, Religion, Philosophy,* ed. J. Glenn Gray (New York, 1970), p. 111.

was made in Nature; all her bonds / Cracked" (ll. 36–38). To create a cosmology consistently dark and chaotic, the philosopher is compelled to imitate its disorder in himself. The Lucretian doctrines are felt, not simply as propositions, but as a blend of experiences of the eye and ear.

Though the poem has many of the characteristics of a psalm or hymn, its logic begins to move in one direction and its religious visions in another. This pulling apart produces a confusion of grandly cosmological, incisively analytic, and coarsely sensual tones. The invocation to the "myriad universe" (l. 39) is a kind of litany; and in celebrating the ascendancy and omnipotence of "holy Venus" (l. 67), Lucretius uses the language of prayer. But this is prayer with a difference, for we are spectators at a religious ceremony that challenges the imaginative adequacy of religion. Lucretius replaces the worshiper's conventional profession of unworthiness with a blasphemous prediction. He boasts that his own epic, *De rerum natura*, will outlast the deity, then immediately corrects his blasphemy: "My tongue / Trips, or I speak profanely" (ll. 73–74). Afraid that Venus may be angered by his boast, Lucretius ponders whether the gods are capable of anger and speculates about their incapacity for pity even as he appeals to them to pity him. As a fine example of what Arnold calls religion of the mind,[15] his prayer resembles Euripides' magnificent invocation in *The Troades:* "O Zeus, whether thou be intelligence of mankind or compulsion of nature, to thee I prayed." Lucretius' invocations replace the conventional epithets of praise with searching speculations about the divine nature, and he tries to work out a definition of the gods in the very act of praying to them.

But as Lucretius continues, logic and religion pull further apart, until the soul's elements are sundered beyond hope of integration. Though there is a close parallel between Lucretius' prayer and the intellectual wrestling of the Psalmist with his God,

15. See Matthew Arnold's distinction between religion of the understanding and religion of the heart in his "Pagan and Medieval Religious Sentiment," *Cornhill Magazine* (April, 1864).

Lucretius' theology is marked by an analytic habit of posing questions and proceeding disjunctively, which is not a feature of biblical rhetoric. The finger of the pedant wags at each word—"Ay, but I meant not thee; I meant not her" (l. 85)—as he tries to make clear that he is worshiping Venus, not in her role as a sensual appetite, but as a metaphysical principle. As his reason runs loose, the logician tries to separate religious myths from the truths they represent. Since the sun "knows" not "what he sees" (l. 132), the fable of Apollo is absurd as scientific fact. But because the analytic intelligence that desires the consoling myths of religion cannot accept what it desires, its speculations are more often points of departure for irony than for rapture. And if the modulation from desire to belief, from cosmology to logic, is marked by irony, the dissolution of logic itself, when it is no longer sustained by visions it desires, is marked by a series of stutters. Syntax keeps stumbling over repeated words, with deliberate grinding of the gears of language: "Meant? I meant? / I have forgotten what I meant: my mind / Stumbles, and all my faculties are lamed" (ll. 121–123).

This disintegration of reason is the psychological correlative of Lucretius' philosophy of the time atom, of the sensory moment. When logic sunders itself from the rest of life, it is no longer even logical, for it ceases to relate. With ironic indirection Tennyson shows that in trying to judge religion by scientific laws, Lucretius is dissolving an imaginative form back into the chaos of the physical world; he is destroying whatever imaginative adequacy religion may have. Nor is Lucretius simply torn between his poetic and scientific natures. He also illustrates what Freud calls the "dissociation" of erotic life. When such men love, they have no desire; hence Lucilia's love philter. And when they desire, they cannot love; hence Lucretius' orgiastic obsessions. The rationalist is never less rational than when, with the intellectual exhilaration of a David Friedrich Strauss, resolving the Bible into myth, he tries to be only rational. Lucretius' translation of mythology into its rational equivalent displays the same defect of positivism that Arnold deplores in Victorian theology: "Our religion has ma-

terialized itself in the fact, in the supposed fact; it has attached its
emotion to the fact, and now the fact is failing it."[16] The scientific
residue of theology—the "natural laws" Lucretius is left with—
turns out to be just as capricious as the gods, and a good deal less
consoling. Nature at "random ravage" (1. 176) is as terrifying as
the capricious god of Browning's Caliban. In mocking mythology
and making fun of Ovid's tale of turning aside god's lightning,
Lucretius commits the kind of blasphemy against religion that
Caliban commits, and he fears the same evidence of divine dis-
pleasure in the coming storm. The rationalist who has been comfortably above the ironies of pagan myth is now painfully involved
in the many contradictions of its scientific version. Hume argues
that life cannot be lived without the persuasion that the past does
in fact repeat itself in the future. But Lucretius will not accept
Hume's premise: he believes that the atoms of "Great Nature's"
tomb, like the void itself, will eventually disappear "Into the
unseen for ever" (1. 258). Up to the end the sentence patterns
have been pushing against the regularity of the meter. Now the
succession of eleven monosyllables achieves the most stable sense
of changelessness: "Thus—thus: the soul flies out and dies in the
air" (1. 273). Lucretius, the hallucinating rationalist, the poet
whose passion is his torment, is completely unmoved by his wife's
appeal (1. 280). The bloodless categories of the atomic philosophy
reveal themselves only to a mind at war with itself. Hung across
the void of nihilism, the huge fabric of the atomic system inspires
Lucretius' darkest fears. Suicide affords such a mind its only release: only through annihilation can its longing for stability be
ironically fulfilled.

After the disintegration of language elsewhere in the monologue, the close of "Lucretius" is unexpectedly secure. Significantly,
the last word of the poem is "Farewell," a terminal feature which
strengthens closure. There is maximal stability, too, in the sen-

16. The statement, which appears at the beginning of Arnold's essay
"The Study of Poetry," is a revision of a passage from Arnold's introduction to a work called *The Hundred Greatest Men* (London, 1879).

tentious questions: "Thy duty? What is duty?" (l. 280). But as in
the earlier monologues, "St. Simeon Stylites" and "Tiresias," the
authoritative form is also betrayed by the doubt and tentativeness
of these questions, and by the denial of moral absolutes, which
makes the conclusion unstable—as we expected. It is the combination of formal surprise and thematic fulfillment that gives the
end its indirection and the sententiousness its point.

Narrative Indirection: *The Princess*

Tennyson takes a much longer time to achieve forms of narrative indirection than to achieve the comparable indirection of
his dramatic monologues. An early experiment in narrative indirection is "Locksley Hall" (1837–1838), a narrative about
storytelling. But it is not clear until Tennyson writes a sequel in
1886 that the two poems are meant to take the reader through
the complex process of adjusting and rejecting untrue stories. The
process is greatly aided by the indirect comment of the second
poem upon the first. Tennyson's generic innovation allows him
to combine a narrative of what happens with the more interesting
narrative of what a lover tells himself is happening. If we take
"Locksley Hall" alone, we can read it as a study in adolescent
psychology. Yet when we read "Locksley Hall Sixty Years After"
and learn the outcome of the story told in the earlier poem, we
realize that Tennyson is interested, not in the story itself, but in
the shifts from one version of the story to another. Amy, the girl
who has refused the speaker, has died in childbirth; and her
husband has never remarried. Instead of being the coarse brute
the speaker imagines, the rival has behaved generously. In old age
the speaker even acknowledges that Amy married his rival because she loved him. But since he is still committed to the fiction
that his own loss was unique, the speaker is quick to take offense
when his grandson, who also has been disappointed in love, draws
a parallel between them. Like several poems by Browning—*A
Soul's Tragedy,* for example, and *The Ring and the Book*—the
sequence is not primarily about events or even about character,
but about the changing relation of the narrator to the events he
describes.

The narrative experiments in Tennyson's English idylls have produced a sharp division of critical opinion. Some readers feel that *Enoch Arden* and "Aylmer's Field" are not, like the two "Locksley Hall" poems, narratives *about* play-acting; rather, the heroics of Enoch's martyrdom and the heroics of Averill's sermon unwittingly betray Tennyson's own heroic posturing. A case can be made, I think, for effective indirection in the narrative art of both poems. The irony of Annie's looking at the departing Enoch through a telescope, and not being able to see anything (ll. 239–242), confirms the instability of vision. Her linguistic trick of twisting an ambiguous biblical phrase, "Under the palm-tree" (l. 494), until it means what she wants it to mean, and then the narrator's trick of turning the palm into a literal South Sea tree that shelters beneath it a living husband, are techniques that allow the narrative poet to shift the several frames in which any given object or event is to be seen and interpreted. Fragments in the Harvard Manuscript in the Houghton Rare Book Library (loose paper 52)—"Fair ship"; "Thou comest"; "It draweth near"; and even a note comparing Enoch to a resurrected Lazarus—all suggest a melodramatic account of Enoch's rescue. When Tennyson revises, he wisely discards the heroics in favor of an early disclosure of the rescue. The bald statement "his lonely doom / Came suddenly to an end" (ll. 622–623) gains in irony what it loses in dramatic impact. If narrative indirection fails at the end, it is only because the narrative form traps Tennyson into charting events to their depressing close, instead of leaving the reader suspended, as in most dramatic monologues. "The real objection," as Martin Dodsworth says, "is a moral one—Enoch is neither strong nor heroic."[17] Even if the poem discloses "a genuinely equivocal moral matter," as Christopher Ricks has argued,[18] Tennyson is unwilling to suspend the outcome. Instead, he invites the reader to interpret Enoch's death as martyrdom, and to approve of the costly funeral. There is no reason why narrative poetry should aspire to the condition of the dramatic

17. "Patterns of Morbidity," p. 14.
18. *Tennyson* (New York, 1972), p. 282.

monologue. But in such a narrative genre it is hard for Enoch and the poet to stop telling themselves stories about heroism.

Tennyson is more resourceful in "Aylmer's Field," where the cruel sermon of the second part comments with savage irony on the pastoral romance of the first part. Yet, as Wayne Booth observes, "there has been too little criticism based on recognizing incompatibilities of different effects."[19] In "Aylmer's Field," Tennyson wants maximum innocence and maximum bitterness. In crossing "Gareth and Lynette" with "Pelleas and Ettarre," he forgets that such qualities exist together in inverse ratios.

In mature narratives like *Idylls of the King*, Tennyson achieves indirection by rapidly shifting his internal frames. "The Holy Grail" opens a series of windows in Sir Percivale's head. And by shifting its slides like a magic lantern "The Coming of Arthur" achieves what Kenneth Burke calls, in metaphor, "perspective by incongruity." The window-opening or perspective effect satisfies a Victorian desire to look through magic windows, through stereoscopes and dioramas. Most revealing are the shifts of Merlin's riddle, the shifts of confused lucidity, of the order that lies in disorder, of the sanity that lies in madness. Like the operator of a stereopticon, Tennyson keeps shifting the slides from physical, to psychological, to metaphysical explanations of Arthur's kingship —from all that is included in the dark historic moment to all that is beyond it in space and time; from the story flow of the battles we pass to the static picture window of Leodogran's dream; and inside the dream, from the dimmer flux of haze and smoke to the vivid still of Arthur, crowned in heaven, then back again to earth. Each idyll, like each frame, is an aperture in the story flow. Even an overtly narrative structure like *The Princess* is often best approached as a series of lyric utterances or frames. Tennyson has little gift for conventional narrative. But a still frame that can utilize his dramatic and lyric gifts, and emphasize the cinematic quality of the flow without forcing him to narrate the action directly, is obviously a generic form that minimizes his deficiencies.[20]

19. *The Rhetoric of Fiction* (Chicago, 1961), p. 48, n. 39.
20. One of Tennyson's narrative poems, *Enoch Arden,* occupies a place

This kind of narrative indirection is used with greatest success in *Maud,* where changing phases of passion in a single speaker have the same window-opening or perspective effect as the shifting frames in the *Idylls.* Since the action in *Maud* is psychological, any still frame that punctuates the narrative flow, by opening another window in the speaker's head, has the effect of validating the sequence. The apertures in the story flow, instead of impeding the action, as they would in most narrative poems, make a virtue of Tennyson's narrative deficiencies by emphasizing the cinema quality of his poem; they remind us, indirectly, that his story is moving.

Before Tennyson can achieve the technical perfection of *Maud,* he must experiment in his first long narrative poem, *The Princess* (published December 25, 1847), with an ingenious combination of generic elements. Psychological truths that cannot be expressed directly in a narrative form may be presented indirectly. As *The Princess* moves from its contemporary Prologue to the dream romance of its main narrative, then from the narrative to each of the inserted songs and lyrics, and finally from the dream romance back to a contemporary epilogue, each shift in the sequence opens another window in the reader's mind. As in Symbolist poetry, meanings that defy translation can be left for the reader to supply for himself. Like the art of Browning's "Maker-see" in *Sordello,* the poem's appositional technique preserves intact the untranslatable nature of its elements by placing them side by side with few connecting links. Tennyson imparts the gift of vision to the reader. But by resisting "the intelligence / Almost successfully,"[21]

---

in film history. The poem was adapted by D. W. Griffith in 1908 as *After Many Years.* The film is associated with several technical advances: the first intelligent use of the full close-up, and what could be termed the first example of editing; after his close-up of Annie Lee's face as she sits musing, Griffith cuts to Enoch, the object of her thoughts, as he sits under the palm tree on his desert island. See Sergei Eisenstein, "Dickens, Griffith, and the Film Today," in *Film Form: Essays in Film Theory,* ed. and tr. Jay Leyda (New York, 1949), p. 225.

21. Wallace Stevens, "Man Carrying Thing," ll. 1–2.

the shifting frames prevent the reader from being aware of more significance than he can handle at any given time.

Whatever we may think of Tennyson's narrative gifts, his use of a contemporary Prologue to frame his medieval romance allows him to fashion many indirect links between the real and legendary worlds. He develops in his romance the characters and themes of the Prologue, as if he were modeling his invention on a dream vision by Chaucer. The Prologue also introduces characters who serve as lightning rods to ground satiric bolts before they strike his heroine. By gently ridiculing Sir Walter for his eclectic tastes Tennyson can encourage the reader to overlook as harmless luxuries the more grotesque adornments of the college. We have already laughed at the excesses in Sir Walter, a patron who is praised in the Prologue for his vision, and who is certainly more than a parody of the medieval host. Finally, by separating itself from the thematic structure of the main romance, the Prologue allows the ironist to make oblique comments upon it. By the time Tennyson has repeated the Spenserian invocation "O miracle of women" (ll. 35, 48), its truth has begun to effervesce. We can hardly apply the nobility and miracle of Britomart to brutal Amazons who push men from rocks and drown them in whirling brooks (ll. 46–47). And the reversal of sexual roles in the draping of Sir Ralph in female silks alerts us to caricature in Psyche's later discourse on heroic women, which according to Homeric standards is also preposterous.

The poem's main indirections are mock-heroic. They preserve intact the grandeur that they criticize, subduing its refinement to more human language. Tennyson laughs at star-gazing virgins with souls above their social spheres, but pities their embitterment. Though he makes fun of frantic theory and mocks false sentiment, he refines romance by turning its frenzied apotheosis of unsatisfied desire into some of the purest love lyrics ever written. The perversely arch and sexually ambiguous heroine is a familiar character in Victorian fiction, where she appears in *The Portrait of a Lady* and in *Middlemarch* as an Isabel Archer or a Dorothea Brooke—as a woman who is married to an ideology, not to a man. Drawn "into the sexless sphere of disinterested intelligence," as G. M. Young observes, Ida illustrates a "process which may be truly named Victorian if only for the horror with which Victoria regarded it."[22] Tennyson dextrously balances each absurdity in the Princess with qualities that are immensely appealing. While the "lucid marbles" and "ample awnings gay" (II, 10–11) compose a poetry of luxury and well-made objects, the simile comparing the brightly dressed intruders to "rich . . . moths" emerging from "dusk cocoons" (II, 5) gives the reader an exquisite sense of the precious slightness of the ritual. Tennyson preserves the splendor of the "Academic silks" (II, 2), but the essence of his wit lies in the beautiful diminution. Ida is a kind of marvelous sophomore; man's role is to be docile; and the innate foolishness of that teaching, though no more foolish than the opposite doctrine of male superiority, provokes the Prince's unremitting irony. Beyond absurdity, Ida also expresses the values of a world where greatness and ceremony are serious matters. The mock-heroic style is fertile with illustrations of that world's grandeur, often expressed lightly and humorously, but with a delicacy of feeling in which the reasons for admiration are clearly urged.

Another generic innovation is Tennyson's use of a contemporary epilogue, a marvel of indirection that leaves the reader with impressions that are far from serene. The irony at the expense of the genial Sir Walter, the "lord of fat prize-oxen and of sheep" (1. 86), is coolly remote and finally ambiguous. There is a schoolgirl vagueness about Lilia, who yearns for something larger than herself, something bigger than people or society. Yet Lilia deepens, in the epilogue, to a new seriousness. She will not enter into marriage any more lightly than Ida, or with any fewer expectations of the kind of personal fulfillment it should bring. If she and the other women are deluded in trying to convert life and people into works of art, they are also betrayed by their materials. By reminding the reader that the dream romance holds up to the ordinary world of Vivian-place not just a mirror, but a distort-

22. *Victorian England: Portrait of an Age* (London, 1936), p. 91.

ing mirror, the concluding frame perpetuates the genius of the mock-heroic form. Recalling that everything in the poem has more than one aspect, the epilogue helps the reader dispel illusion, too.

In the psychological life of *The Princess* fears and anxieties double back into repression, then skip out obliquely into a bewildering variety of masks, which disguise these fears like displacements of traumatic experience in a dream. Ida's repressed sexuality, and the timidities and seizures of the Prince, tap the poem's deepest psychic life. Its sexual puns, like its dream conventions, are an escape of impulse from the control of the censor. Ida, struggling in the stream, for example, is first compared to a "blossomed branch / Rapt to the . . . fall" (IV, 161–162); then the figurative branch becomes the literal boughs of a tree, which the Prince catches and pulls down (IV, 170–171). The sexual fantasy that the simile opens in the Prince's mind is confirmed a moment later in the description of the gates, those "valves / Of open-work," on which is inscribed the picture of the "rash intrusion, manlike" of the hunter (IV, 184–186). Now the branches of the tree, the limbs of Ida struggling in the stream, reappear as the horns of Actaeon, transfixed into a stag, "grimly spiked"—his punishment for gazing on Diana (IV, 188). Like the multiple meanings of a dream, the sexual puns have a way of dissipating tensions. Often the light is harsh and ironic. But unlike the doors flung open on secret places in "St. Simeon," the innuendoes in *The Princess* tremble into life along a fragile threadwork of suggestion. With little tremors of nuance they feel at each thread; the "touch" is, in Pope's phrase, "exquisitely fine" (*An Essay on Man,* I, 217). Only slowly do the suppressed psychic forces, the assertive, unstilled desires of the human heart, start to surface in the ten inserted songs and lyrics. In these poems *The Princess* charts the deepest motions, grieving and elated, of the human soul.

Psychological forces operate most simply in the second song, "Sweet and Low" (II, 456 ff.), a mother's plea to her child to be calm. The original version of the first stanza contains no sinister elements for the second stanza to control.[23] But the final form achieves on a miniature scale what many of Tennyson's subtlest and most powerful poems achieve: it binds the void in safe grandeur. While the murderous innocence of the sea, as sinister as it is protective, frees the lullaby from easy consolations, the night-time splendor of "Silver sails" controls the terror of the "rolling waters," turning the "dying moon" into a "silver light" guiding the father home. Starting and ending the final line with the same word, "sleep," puts a "frame" around the child. Like the device of repeating the last word of the first stanza at the beginning of the next stanza, the frame helps contain despair. By transferring her fears to the child, the mother subdues them. Her confiding tone becomes a fulfilled trust, not just a lisping statement of the innocence of events.

In the next song, "The Splendour falls on castle walls" (III, 348 ff.), analogies between the snowy summits and the isolated heroine, between the transforming power of love and Ida's thwarted needs, are always latent, though never made explicit. The progression from the wild cataract to the horns of Elfland to the lovers' echoing souls is unobtrusive, as if the speaker were shying away from his own design.[24] This indirection makes it easier to accept a general benefaction, reflected in the final harmony of souls: "echoes" that "roll from soul to soul, / And grow for ever and for ever" (ll. 15–16). The harmony is made plausible by the way each thin and clear reply to the bugle is also an enlargement, richer and more mountainous, even in its prolonged "dying," than the music which precedes it. The solidity of the world is always being dissolved by animate verbs like "shaking," "leaping," "flying," or "fainting." At the same time insubstantial states are

23. The first version is preserved in Harvard loosepaper 26. Hallam Tennyson reprints it in his *Tennyson: A Memoir*, I, 255.

24. The most complete study of Tennyson's metaphorical design is Thomas J. Assad's meticulous essay, "Tennyson's Use of the Tripartite View of Man in Three Songs from *The Princess*," *Tulane Studies in English*, XV (1967), 35–54. Corresponding to Tennyson's "tripartite view" are "three kinds of echoes, the physical, the imaginary, and the spiritual" (p. 39).

allowed to take on the satisfying solidity of objects by the turning of verbs into present participles and by the use of pauses and repetition to protract the flow of sound.

Generally, remembered experience brings enriched understanding with a loss of immediacy. But in "Tears, idle tears" the memory of the past does nothing to displace the aesthetic richness or the psychological depth of the landscapes. The speaker is moved by a double sense of cosmic setting and human littleness. If he is awed by the vastness of "the underworld" (l. 27) and the strangeness of "dark summer dawns" (l. 31), he is also stirred, like Virgil and Pope, by an exquisite sense of the beauty in microcosms, by the charm of the "first beam glittering on a sail" (l. 26) or "The earliest pipe of half-awakened birds" (l. 32). Though the only concrete image besides the tears and the eyes to appear in the first stanza is the rich impression of the "Autumn-fields" (l. 24), which qualify—though in an unexpected way—the vague word "happy," the rest of the lyric is a sustained exercise in immediacy. It is a methodical definition of the apparently contradictory attributes of "the days that are no more" (l. 30): their freshness and sadness, their strangeness, sweetness, and depth. The final attribute of "depth" is also the first attribute treated in stanza 1—"the depth of some divine despair" (l. 22); it seems to justify the detour through the intervening attributes by drawing a complete circle. Tennyson is painting a cycle of scenes; and instead of allowing the haziness of the past to distance him from the present, he places his speaker firmly in a harvest landscape. The chill that falls across the "happy Autumn-fields" comes from an austerity of mind not far removed from Tithonus' when he sees that Aurora's rosy shadows bathe him coldly. The pastoral oxymorons of inner weather—"So sad, so fresh" (l. 30), "So sad, so strange" (l. 35)—prepare for the later accommodations of death and life, of everything included in the present internal moment and of everything beyond it in space or time.

In the two middle stanzas the speaker strays in imagination from the autumn landscapes, but his eye is never allowed to stray. Tennyson's naturally elegiac style is forced into a minute, topographical mode, represented by an insistence on microscopic detail, where nostalgia and notation are kept in balance. Tennyson fixes attention, not just on the present, but on vanishing objects in the present: objects such as the ship and the casement, which he grasps and anatomizes with painful scrutiny. "The poem is about the most potent of absences," as Christopher Ricks has finely said;[25] and in a blank-verse lyric the "most potent absence of all" is the "absence of rhyme." As the here and the now diminish, Tennyson returns to the chill austerity of the opening stanza, now viewed at an inhuman distance from its harvest plenitude. In the first stanza the speaker seeks a tenuous identity with present objects. In the two middle stanzas he precariously sustains the effort, then discovers that in the Persephone-like return of "all we love below the verge" (l. 29), the elusive present must always avoid his embrace, and can be grasped, only fitfully, in unstable relation to dissolving forms, to things "that are no more."

At the end of the poem there is neither the joy of autumn retrospects nor the sorrow of summer dawns, but an access of feeling more fundamental than either. Grammatically, the poem is a series of similes—"Fresh as, . . . Sad as" (ll. 26, 28); "sad and strange as" (l. 31)—yet its most important comparisons are not translatable. A and B may be as X, and B and C may be as Y; but X and Y themselves are ineffable presences: they are mysteries, of which the poet can only say in awe: "I know not what they mean." The overt despair of the similes acquires through these metaphors, for which there are no descriptive labels such as "sad and strange," and no ready equivalents, a providential quality. They resist the sadness, keeping the elation vibrant but subdued. Yet the poem's most desolating thoughts are only intimated. Like the poem's most private ecstasies, they are barely hinted. Distance may lend charm to a landscape, and remembered kisses may be dearer after death. But what can death or distance add to love that is "Deep as first love" (l. 39), to love that is already "wild with all regret" (l. 39), like Tennyson's love for Hallam? The

25. *Tennyson*, p. 199.

love that absence does not lessen or modify, dissolving its very form and image, may be a romantic commonplace, but as *In Memoriam* shows, it can hardly be genuine. We are never allowed to forget that what is most worth saying in the lyric can never be said. The defining attributes of "the days that are no more" are extraordinarily accurate. But they never tell more than half, and in the end perhaps they cannot. In its greatest elations, as in its deepest griefs, the soul in the end is alone.

In the later songs and lyrics the adversary of the Prince may wear different masks—the woman to whom the swallow is to carry the petition, the lady who asks her lover to plead no more, the "maid" upon the mountain. But all these masks are diaphanous, and serve only to expose Ida and the type of resistance she is still marshaling against the Prince. The indirections are multiple, but they are transparent, not enriched for their own sake the way the children and the warriors are. In the lyric "O Swallow, Swallow" (IV, 75–98) the Prince gives direct vent to male impatience: he pleads with the swallow to intervene with the woman. "O Swallow, Swallow" preserves a strangely charming blend of pastoral simplicity and human insight. In the lover's imagination of cheeping and twittering "twenty million loves" (IV, 83) Tennyson captures the innocent view of nature that underlies all pastoral myth. But "gilded eaves" and "golden woods" (IV, 76, 96) also combine in a single mounting impression of light and dark, sun and moon, composing harmoniously in the outer eye of the poet and the lover's inner eye. The duality of the phrases adds to the sense of competing forces—"bright and fierce and fickle"; "dark and true and tender" (IV, 79–80)— and expresses the expected and desired contraries that make any marriage possible.

Psychological indirection becomes most explicit when Ida, torn between a mistaken sense of freedom and love for Psyche and the Prince, begins to shape the ambiguous tumult of her heart into wit and wordplay: "that / Which kills me with myself" (VI, 287–288); "Ah false but dear, / Dear traitor, too much loved" (VI, 274–275). The sharp chiasmus, or repetition of terms in reverse, and the matching forms stress the proximity of love and hate. No longer constrained by outmoded attitudes toward sex, Tennyson elicits in that rueful mixture of feeling a profound human truth. Yet, oppressed by her "weight of gratitude" (VI, 281), the Princess can still not see how two lives may be shared without being sacrificed or wholly merged.

The woman in the next song, "Ask me no more" (VI, 364 ff.), though resisting love, is also dying of love. She repeats the words "Ask me no more," not to tranquilize, but to charge the phrase with more and more feeling. The content of the phrase changes from threat of refusal in the first stanza to uncertainty in stanza 2 to imminent surrender at the end. The surprising force of the lyric comes partly from metrical bareness and partly from the swift progression in intimacy, focused in the change of epithets: "fond," "friend," "dear love" (ll. 4, 8, 14). Until the surrender of the last stanza, question and petition—"when have I answered thee? / Ask me no more" (ll. 4–5); "Ask me no more: what answer should I give?" (l. 6)—continue to echo and re-echo in finely distinct shadings. There is a blend of tones gentle and wondering, ironic and profound.

An insistent indirection marks the growth of Ida's love. When Ida sees that Psyche, the woman she most admires, is in love with Cyril, she wants a lover for herself (VII, 63–66).[26] But Ida is unwilling to acknowledge her desire. The immediate effect of her clinging more tenaciously than ever to her ideology is to make the Prince desire her more ardently. Starting from a premise of mockery, *The Princess* insinuates the folly of passion with the lightest of touches. But its delicate innuendoes imply no more disrespect for the grand manner of loving than the mock-heroic poems of Dryden and Pope imply for Virgil and Homer. We have shared Tennyson's delight in the absurdities of passion. Now, in

26. The most searching study of the imitative nature of desire in literature is René Girard's "Triangular Desire," in *Deceit, Desire, and the Novel* (Baltimore, 1965), pp. 1–52. "The great novelists reveal the imitative nature of desire. In our days its nature is hard to perceive because the most fervent imitation is the most vigorously denied" (pp. 14–15).

the Prince's dreamlike invocation to Ida (VII, 130–135), we discover that indirection has a more important function. The Prince's invocation is consecrated by hope, yet distanced by hypothesis: "If you be, what I think you" (l. 130); "if a dream" (l. 133). A product of subjunctive moods—"I would but ask" (l. 131)—and of verbs of illusion—"seem to kiss" (l. 135)—the indirections make it hard to surpass Tennyson in the ceremonial adornment of love, in the perception and refinement of desire.

The two concluding lyrics in *The Princess* confirm Ida in her new love. In "Now sleeps the crimson petal" (VII, 161–174) the lover becomes more a seer than a painter of landscape, and under his eye a marvelous transformation takes place. In an unbroken, chainlike process of visual mergings, the beloved, the meteor, and the stars join together in cosmic space, with the lover as one of the marveling participants. But the true marvel comes with the merging of objects, when the blending becomes so complete that the lily is lost entirely in the lake. In the penetration of the male form by the lily, Tennyson appropriately transforms the physical union, reversing the sexual metaphor. Though the vivid images are contrastive, they are placed in positions of symmetry, reinforced by parity of rhythm, alliteration, assonance, and anaphora (the repetition of "Now" and "Nor" at the beginning of successive clauses).

Now sleeps the crimson petal	now the white
Nor waves the cypress	Nor winks the gold fin
Now lies the Earth	Now slides the silent meteor

Since the natural tendency of symmetrical placement is to equate the items listed, the contrasts become less oppositional, until the man and the woman, the stars and the earth, the lily and the lake become mirror images of paradoxical identity, lost in each other. To add psychological indirection, the receiving element is first equated with the woman—"the Earth all Danaë" (l. 167) to the shower of stars—and then with the man, "the bosom of the lake" that enfolds the lily (l. 172). The reversals help make solid things fluid. Fish and peacocks are made insubstantial by shimmering verbs: "winks" and "glimmers" (ll. 163, 166). Meteors slide down to earth, and earth itself is ploughed into "A shining furrow" (l. 170) gleaming fitfully across a nighttime sky. By the end of the lyric, opposites no longer consciously embrace but slip into each other, lost in a coupling of pronouns—"my dearest, thou" (l. 173)—a grammatical identity of persons. The iterative syntax moves words of similar form but of contrary sense into positions of prominence. The repetition of the verbs "wakens: waken," "folds" and "fold" in slightly altered form is meant to minimize the shift from the indicative to the imperative mood by introducing superficial affinities: simple juxtaposition in the first case ("The fire-fly wakens: waken thou with me" [l. 164]), and inversion of verb and subject in the second case ("Now folds the lily . . . / So fold thyself" [ll. 171, 173]). By disguising the grammatical difference between the indicative verb, followed by an impersonal subject, and the imperative verb followed by a personal reflexive pronoun—"fold *thyself*" (my italics)—the hyperbaton, or dislocation of the normal word order, allows the lover to petition with sleight of hand. His appeal is over before we register the change. Yet the climax goes far beyond original expectations in its blend of metaphor and fact. The photographic details of the opening stanza—the microscopic charm of the winking "fin" and "fire-fly" (VII, 163–164)—are now beautifully fused in images that join heaven and earth and approximate in words a water-lily painting by Monet.

The poem's concluding lyric, "Come down, O maid" (VII, 177–207) alternates predictably between the perverse unloveliness of a kind of northern purity and various impressions of pastoral warmth. The shocked sense of frightening powers in nature is mythological seeing in its purest form. The "white ravine" and "firths of ice" (VII, 190–191) are as terrifying as Wordsworth's "spots of time" in *The Prelude*. There is even a suggestion that the woman who seems anxious, like the frigid mountain, to keep men at a distance may lead them to suppose she feels the necessity. But Tennyson tries to balance the desolation of the Jungfrau against reassuring impressions of pastoral community. Large pic-

torial effects of "height and cold" are happily combined with
images of richly packed luxuriance, with "murmuring . . . bees"
(VII, 207) and vineyards. Semibiblical repetition and echo (VII,
183–184) carry the surge and ebb of sounds to the climactic
petition of the children, the shepherd, and the pillars of the
hearth. Soon a pattern of climax builds up (VII, 201–203) that
anticipates the triumphal passages in *Maud*. Such is the indirection, however, that we continue to feel the mountain peak's sublimity and power. Approbation, we are reminded, is for the
typical, for what is common, like shepherd pipes and hearths, and
therefore uninteresting. But the Prince does not love Ida because
he approves. His love is the passionate attempt to find himself in
another. And oneself, like the Jungfrau, is unique.

Christopher Ricks believes that the psychological indirections
of *The Princess* are "directed . . . to a therapy of evasion."[27]
But the Lawrentian themes of "freedom in otherness" and the
transformation of sexual roles are dangerous themes for an early
Victorian to explore. As G. M. Young observes, "Collision of the
Two Spheres is a Late-Victorian theme, almost a Late-Victorian
revolution: in Mid-Victorian England only the first mutterings
of the revolution can be heard."[28] It is difficult to see how Tennyson in 1847 could have been more direct. The psychological truths
keep intruding more insistently, until the Prince comes to realize
that romantic courtship tends to be immoral, for it is the instinctive deference of the lover to the pleasure of one being. In the
sequence of events that transforms the "fair college" into a "hos-

27. *Tennyson,* p. 190. D. H. Lawrence's classic statement of these themes
appears in chapter xix of *Women in Love* (New York, 1948), p. 290:
"There was another way, the way of freedom. There was the paradisal
entry into pure, single being, the individual soul taking precedence over
love and desire for union, stronger than any pangs of emotion, a lovely
state of free proud singleness, which accepted the obligation of the
permanent connection with others, and with the other, submits to the yoke
and leash of love, but never forfeits its own proud individual singleness,
even while it loves and yields."
28. *Victorian England,* p. 92.

pital," Ida, too, discovers that, while the overthrow of her college is a form of defeat, retreat into her soul's immutable core—if it has a core—can hardly be amiable, and is also a defeat. The oxymorons of the lyric "Tears, idle tears" are a microcosm of the whole process. They are to the paradoxical form of *The Princess*[29] what the synecdoche of the shell is to the transforming power of the mind in *Maud*. The inability in "Tears, idle tears" to unite a public with a private past also reflects the larger failure to join history with myth, social narrative with dream romance, in the rest of the poem. But Ida and the Prince do not merely react to their discoveries; they respond. Such response is creative. The change is a form of "summer tempest," like the rebirth depicted in the song "Home they brought her warrior dead" (ll. 15–16), or like the resurgence of life in "The Revival" section of "The Day-Dream." The Prince's change is marked by an illness, and Ida's by atonement and remorse.

The Princess first tricks out the dream romance of love and freedom with the pageantry of conflicting political states. Ida's refusal of the Prince even brings two countries to war. Then, through the lyrics and the Prince's seizures, Tennyson slowly lets the reader see that the whole pretentious enterprise of war and empire is unsubstantial—a dream. To discredit ordinary, social judgments of love and freedom Tennyson introduces characters like the Prince's blustering father and the dim-witted Arac to defend the family cause with obvious inadequacy. Just when everything is becoming exaggerated and distorted, Tennyson brings Ida and the Prince back in a flash to where the lovers in the lyrics started, to simple longing and desire.

29. The mock-heroic formula to which *The Princess* points is S is P and P is S. Commitment is betrayal and betrayal is commitment. The comic is serious and the serious comic. The failure of the college is a discovery for Ida, and her attainment of freedom a human defeat. The formula also applies to minor characters such as Sir Walter. Though "the great broad-shouldered genial Englishman" is a generous host, he is also Matthew Arnold's prototype of the flattered barbarian. Arnold quotes this description from *The Princess* in chapter iii of *Culture and Anarchy*.

At first there are no real objects of sexual desire in *The Princess,* and it is natural that the Prince should turn to Florian, and Ida to Psyche. The transition from these ennobling but crippling friendships to love between the Princess and the Prince is the kind of transition that occurs in the symbolic dream of *In Memoriam* (CIII). The transformation in *The Princess* becomes more and more expressive of the change that takes place in Tennyson's life after Hallam's death and Tennyson's marriage to Emily Sellwood. The poetry of *The Princess* is splendidly enriched by such a growth in love. To be sure, Tennyson does not show how the marvelous transformation of the Prince and his beloved—an exercise in lyric ostentation—might be expected to bear fruit in the ordinary world of Vivian-place. If he tried to envision their married life together, he would not want to imagine another Arthur and Guinevere. Since Ida will share with the Prince a common province of intelligence and sympathy, her fulfillment will not be wholly sexual, intellectual, or even moral, but simply human in the fullest sense. The failure to dramatize this vision represents a weakness, not in the poem, I think, but in the world beyond the poem, in the resonances set up in that world by the consecration of love in some of the most eloquent lyrics ever written. The events or developments that follow the poem's transforming encounter are not to be found within *The Princess* itself. They take place beyond the poem—and perhaps beyond any poem. We may interpret this absence of a dramatized outcome as a final indirection—or as a failure to imagine what a completed encounter might be like. But if the lyrics in *The Princess* are merely visions in a dream, they remain visions of surpassing beauty whose perception and refinement of desire have seldom been equaled in an English poem.

After the laconic compressions of "Ulysses" the florid expansions of *The Princess* come as an enormous ballooning. The increased dimensions of the poem allow Tennyson to combine a narrative structure with the sensuous and fantastic qualities of his lyric style, and to produce as a result the characteristic impression of a dream. After his apprenticeship in *The Princess,* where he learns to combine dream romance and the indirection of a mock-heroic style with the discipline of organizing and extending his inventions, Tennyson has only to add the universal significance of themes already explored in the classical monologues to achieve new and subtler combinations in his two most successful poems, *In Memoriam* and *Maud.*

4

The Autobiography of
a Mourner: *In Memoriam*

For the ornateness of *The Princess, In Memoriam* (1850) substitutes the plainness of epitaphs. With their lapidary concision and severity of self-demand, the spare quatrains ensure that the depth of the mourner's grief is equaled only by the perfect control of what he feels. T. S. Eliot compares the hundred and thirty-one sections of *In Memoriam* to entries in a diary.[1] These entries have all the urgent economy of a psychotherapist's report, cramped into private jottings. The attenuated stanzas have a way of turning into memorials, pointed and durable as gravestone inscriptions. As we pass from one stone to another, certain familiar landmarks of pastoral elegy emerge: the mourner's grief, his visions of the dead man, the restoration of the dead man to permanent life, the retrospective vistas of the mourner, and his eventual return to the world. But in *In Memoriam* these familiar landmarks commemorate more than just Hallam. They are signposts on the poet's interior journey. *In Memoriam*'s chief generic innovation is a fusion of disparate features. The result is an unlikely combination of expansiveness and economy. Individual sections have the concision of gravestone inscriptions, but the poem as a whole is digressive. It has the amplitude of spiritual autobiography. It combines the cathartic power of Milton's

1. "In Memoriam," in *Selected Essays* (London, 1932), pp. 333–334: "It is unique: it is a long poem made by putting together lyrics, which have only the unity and continuity of a diary, the concentrated diary of a man confessing himself. It is a diary of which we have to read every word."

Lycidas with the range and reflective reach of Wordsworth's *The Prelude*.

The Rhetoric of Confession

Since *In Memoriam* has as much in common with Augustine's *Confessions*, John Bunyan's *Grace Abounding*, and John Henry Newman's *Apologia pro Vita Sua* as it has with *Lycidas* or Pope's *An Essay on Man*, a brief consideration of what defines confessional writing should provide a helpful context for interpreting the poem.[2] In the first place, the confession, as its name implies, presents the personal, and often private, experience of the author. But by admitting us to his private world, the author hopes to convince us of the truth of his discoveries. Though private and inward, it explores ideas that it wants us to share; it is therefore, ultimately, pragmatic or rhetorical in aim. That is to say, the authors of confessions, from Augustine to Joyce, want to persuade the reader of some truth, but they realize that they can introduce only such public "professions" of this truth as their private "confessions" will sustain.

Another characteristic of the confession is its tendency to view the speaker's life as a re-enactment of some prototypic experience or event. Augustine and Bunyan use biblical situations to give order to their present experience. In the same way that Dante uses the history of Israel as a figure of his own pilgrimage in *The Divine Comedy*, Tennyson keeps referring his personal experience in *In Memoriam* to Hallam's life, death, and afterlife as a kind of continuing Bible or paradigm of his own spiritual history.

A third characteristic of the confession is its use of a second person, or a "mediator," who helps make accessible to the

2. For a more detailed explanation of the defining features see my article "*In Memoriam* and the Rhetoric of Confession," *Journal of English Literary History* (1971) XXXVIII, 80–103. Graham Hough, in "The Natural Theology of *In Memoriam*," *Review of English Studies* (1947), XXIII, 244–256, also sees the virtues of *In Memoriam* as "essentially those of a personal confession." For a somewhat different account see M. H. Abrams, "Wordsworth's *Prelude* and the Crisis-Autobiography," in *Natural Supernaturalism* (New York, 1971), pp. 73–140, especially pp. 80–83.

speaker the truths or values he is trying to reach. Hallam, as
mediator, enables Tennyson to accept a spiritual principle of
revelation throught withdrawal. In Geoffrey Hartman's phrase,
Hallam teaches Tennyson that "consciousness is always OF
death"; only "a confrontation of the self with a buried self" can
raise the energies of consciousness to their highest pitch.[3] We find
a similar pattern in confessional forms such as John Stuart Mill's
Autobiography, Thomas Carlyle's *Sartor Resartus,* and John
Henry Newman's *Apologia pro Vita Sua.* Wordsworth as mediator enables Mill to discover the value of "states of feeling, and of
thought colored by feeling," which were previously inaccessible
to him.[4] Mediators like Goethe and Fichte help Carlyle affirm the
value of ethical and spiritual truths, and mentors like John Keble
and Richard Whately render intelligible intellectual and religious truths for Newman.

A fourth feature of the confession is its pattern of conversion.
When the author becomes fully conscious for the first time of the
truth that the mediator makes available, he undergoes a kind of
conversion, a discovery or revelation that produces a break with
his past life. The conversion may be explicitly religious, as is
Newman's conversion to Catholicism, or only implicitly so, as in
the use of religious analogies to present Carlyle's experience of the
Everlasting Yea or Tennyson's climactic spiritual experience in
Section XCV of *In Memoriam.*

The confession tends, in the fifth place, to be "circular" in
form; that is to say, it ends where it begins. The final resolutions
of the author's problems are usually evident, at least by analogy
(or in embryonic and symbolic ways), at a very early stage of the
confession. A trivial example is Newman's youthful practice of
crossing himself when entering a darkened room. The significance
of the gesture is clear to Newman only in retrospect, after his
conversion to Catholicism; one feature of the confession is pre-

3. *Wordsworth's Poetry: 1787–1814* (New Haven, 1964), p. 22. See "The
Boy of Winander," pp. 19–22.
4. J. S. Mill, *Autobiography,* ed. Currin V. Shields (New York, 1957),
ch. v, p. 96.

cisely this use of the "trivial" episode as a key to the critical event. Sometimes the very words that the author uses at the beginning of his confession express disguised analogies of crucial principles, whose significance becomes apparent to him only at the moment of conversion. Thus, as Kenneth Burke observes, Augustine finds unsuspected relations between rhetorical words and the theological Word.[5] And Tennyson discovers in the very language he must use verbal analogues of a key principle: the truth of the self-concealing word, the protective though desolating truth that all truths are private truths.[6] The principle of the "lucid veil," of a spirit that "half reveal[s]" and "half conceal[s]" itself (V, 3–4), makes indirection part of the poem's epistemology. Tennyson's theory of knowledge means that all the indirections of the genre enact the truth about the truth to be professed.

Since the conclusion seems the natural outcome of the opening, the circular structure gives to the conclusion what Frank Kermode has called "the sense of an ending."[7] But the confessional form has a sixth property: despite this sense of an ending it is also "open-ended." The progressive disclosure of truths that are all along implicit never predetermines the confession's outcome. Perhaps the best evidence of In Memoriam's open form is its apparent instability. Granted that Tennyson has a unified vision of the world, his vision is the most expressive that Victorian poetry can offer, and In Memoriam is its most complete expression. But its design is visibly strained beyond the point of unity; fragmentation lurks in every section. The peril of generic experiment, the restless search after vision, the vagrant asides, the uncertainty of logic—all these are expressed as powerfully by the broken forms of In Memoriam as if the poem were another cry of suffering from the grave, like "Break, break, break." But beneath the agile play of intellect, the spiderwork of logic and analogy, and even beneath the grief, a pathos of self-distrust lies buried in the poem.

5. Kenneth Burke, The Rhetoric of Religion (Boston, 1961), pp. 49–51.
6. Cf. F. H. Bradley, aphorism 44, in Aphorisms (Oxford, 1930).
7. The Sense of an Ending: Studies in the Theory of Fiction (New York, 1967).

A terror lurks in the spare quatrains, hidden in the skeletal forms
as their final secret. The epitaph-like inscriptions, the slow advance against obstacles, the hesitant ascent toward Hallam—none
of these ever allows us to forget that, in contrast to elegies more
securely founded, the aspiring soul alone supports the vaulting
ribs of the edifice.

A seventh feature of the confession is its tendency to bring the
author to forms of self-knowledge and understanding that he did
not possess at the beginning. Thus, though the confession is circular, and restates at the end what is all along implicit, its formu-
lations are not simply tautological. By reformulating old truths in
new ways, the confession may communicate additional knowledge. The "profession" of belief in which a confession like the
Apologia culminates is implicit in Newman's initial perceptions.
The dogma of original sin is implicit in the contradictions of
man's estate, and the principle of infallibility in the pride of human intellect. The confession must first discredit the force of
outmoded dogmas—whether the dogmas of science in *In Memoriam,* the myths of secular liberalism in the *Apologia,* or the de-
terministic creed of Utilitarians in *Sartor Resartus.* The transfer
of the reader's allegiance from one set of "truths" to another set is
more than an emotive transfer. Since it changes our beliefs and
records a process of internalizing truth, of appropriating intellectual systems as part of our own experience, the transfer may
be construed as a genuine gain in knowledge.

Another feature of the confession, and one closely allied to
control of the reader's sympathies, is its retention of oral and
polemical qualities. The privacy of "confession" is never far removed from the publicity of "profession"; the confessor is often
the advocate in disguise. Even when his hortatory or forensic
appeals are indirect, as they are in *In Memoriam,* the polemical
cast of the confession is still apparent. It survives in Tennyson's
disputations with imaginary opponents, and in the importance
assumed by the spoken word, both in the talking breeze of Section
XCV and in the formal qualities of the poetry, which for full appreciation, like the rhetoric of *Sartor Resartus* or Newman's

Apologia, must be read aloud. The confessional form, with its oral cast, accommodates more readily than other genres the kind of oracular truth that Father Ong has analyzed in *The Presence of the Word,*[8] and that such diverse types of confession as *In Memoriam* and *Sartor Resartus* try to restore when opposing the too exclusive claims of science or Utilitarianism.

A final characteristic of the confession is its formal duplication of its theme. The use of a "confession" to sustain the "profession" of some truth often reproduces formally the truth to be professed. Thus the addition of affective to intellectual values, of "real" to "notional" assent, or the internal appropriation of external truths (a process which adds the experiential quality of "wisdom" to the objectivity of mere "knowledge") is a theme that appears in confessions as dissimilar as Mill's *Autobiography, Apologia pro Vita Sua,* and *In Memoriam.* In each case, with the addition of "confession" to "profession," or of experience to doctrine, the "what" becomes a "how," as the very manner of the author's "confession" enacts the truths to be professed.

If *In Memoriam* were simply a record of the poet's grief, it would lack general interest. But like most confessions, it is (to use Northrop Frye's terms) both "introverted" and "intellectual."[9] The first half of the poem is a confession of the mourner's grief. The control of that grief, and its eventual purgation in the three climactic visions (Sections LXVII–LXIX, XCV, CIII), are most accurately described as a form of psychotherapy leading to personal catharsis. *In Memoriam,* however, is also "intellectual." In J. H. Buckley's phrase, the poem is a "Victorian *Essay on Man,*"[10] a confession of the mourner's metaphysical despair and doubts, which also epitomize the doubts of his age. These appear sporadically in the first half of the poem, most notably in Sections LIV–LVI. They increasingly dominate the last part of *In Memoriam.*

8. Walter J. Ong, *The Presence of the Word* (New Haven, 1967).

9. *Anatomy of Criticism* (Princeton, 1957), p. 308: "The confession is . . . introverted, but intellectualized in content. . . . Nearly always some theoretical and intellectual interest . . . plays a leading role in the confession."

10. *Tennyson: The Growth of a Poet* (Cambridge, Mass., 1960), p. 108.

Their final resolution is less a form of psychological catharsis than of intellectual and spiritual consolation.

The language of confession is deliberately impoverished and oblique. Since the mourner's grief cannot be told directly, it must be told indirectly. And in the indirection of his verse, in words that "half reveal / And half conceal" what they express (V, 3–4), Tennyson the mourner discovers a principle of spiritual truth. This is the truth of the "lucid veil" (LXVII, 14), the truth that the sacramental breeze and flowers of Section XCV are an adjective of spirit, hiding the face of God even as they reveal his presence. The language of spiritual profession is more revolutionary and direct. It has less in common with the sacramental language of Hopkins or of Newman than it has with the revolutionary proclamation of Wordsworth at the end of *The Prelude* that the mind of man is a thousand times more beautiful than the earth.[11] Like James Ferrier, the advocate of a Victorian philosophy of consciousness, and Robert Chambers, the brilliant amateur of evolutionary science, Tennyson finally tears away the veil from nature. He discloses that there is nothing behind the veil that is not already in front of it. The divine is an amplified echo of the mourner's love; it is the image of his own soul in a nonexistent mirror. Profession of this visionary faith without veneration of the lucid veil would be too audacious. Confession of grief and doubt without profession of this visionary power would be weak and blind. Tennyson's achievement is to hold the cruelty and the beneficence of nature, the passivity and the power of the mind, in balance. He is both revolutionary and traditional, visionary and sacramental, in the same poem.

Consolation and Catharsis

The mourner achieves his personal catharsis in five principal ways. Formal features of the verse, including a movement of expansion and contraction in its stanzaic form, help stabilize his

11. "Instruct them how the mind of man becomes / A thousand times more beautiful than the earth / . . . In beauty exalted, as it is itself / Of quality and fabric more divine" (XIV, 448–454).

grief. He also achieves solace by identifying, first tentatively (in the autumnal calm of Section XI and in the biblical language of Section XX), and then more confidently (in the sacramental landscapes of Sections LXXXVI and XCV) with redemptive powers in nature. Third, by using puns and epigrams to activate his mind, the mourner delivers his grief, which is unstable, over to the intellect, which stabilizes. A fourth source of solace is the poem's generic indirection. The need to hold contradictory things simultaneously in the mind forces the mourner to be active. Finally, as the poet begins to discover in visionary experiences and in dreams that what seems other and greater than himself is partly his own creation, he becomes increasingly aware of his ability to exorcise fear and morbidity and partially to control the world he helps create.

We might think that the form of *In Memoriam,* the autobiography of a mourner, does more to amplify and extend emotion than to contain it. But, strange as it may seem, amplification is also a cathartic device. The vast winds of sadness blowing through *In Memoriam* make Hallam's life tragic in the way that all past events are tragic, simply because they are over. Such sadness trembles on pathos; and pathos, however poignant, draws the sting, the sharpness, of more concentrated pain. We must remember, too, that the mourner does not simply throw his arms wide with a gesture of protest to the universe. There is both an opening and a shutting of the hand, the heart, the mind. A motion of dilation, when grief stretches itself almost to the breaking point in the effort to include the universe, is followed by a contracting motion, when the mourner simply wants to throw his arms around his friend. Grief expands for a while, and then draws in to contain itself. The ability of Tennyson the therapist to provide Tennyson the grief-stricken patient with lyric catharsis[12] is

12. The verbal therapy by means of grief—or the "malady of the way of living" (a translation of Democritus' *nosos biou*)—is a familiar practice in classical antiquity. The best treatment of the subject is Pedro Laín Entralgo, *The Therapy of the Word in Classical Antiquity,* tr. L. J. Rather and J. M. Sharp (New Haven, 1970). The idea is found in many of the

made more fascinating by the way the two middle lines of each stanza contract and stabilize emotion, while the first and fourth lines diffuse it.

> We ceased: a gentler feeling crept
> Upon us: surely rest is meet:
> 'They rest,' we said, 'their sleep is sweet,'
> And silence followed, and we wept.   [XXX, 17–20]

The mourner balances each amplification with the elusive detachment of a psychotherapist's report, "given in outline and no more" (V, 12). He prefers forms that are stripped and bare, reflected in the slowly unfolding tetrameter quatrains. If the mourner had to enunciate his thoughts more quickly, he could not go on. Often the first words of stanzas—"Old Yew" (Section II), "Dark house" (VII), "Fair ship" (IX)—are formulaic devices. Like the mnemonic tags of epic poetry and ballads, they allow the mourner to set up compass points by which to chart his course. Their power to tranquilize and console depends upon ritual repetition—upon a tour de force of single words with changes.

A second form of catharsis is implicitly available in the sacramental landscapes of the poem. But the efficacy of such catharsis depends, as does the sacramental principle of the "lucid veil" (LXVII, 14), on indirection, on the truth that "words, like Nature, half reveal / And half conceal" what they express (V, 3–4). In Section XII, for example, the hovering and indirection of

---

affective theories of poetry in the nineteenth century. It is especially crucial in the Oxford poetry lectures of Tennyson's contemporary the Reverend John Keble, who sees poetry as a personal catharsis capable of curing sorrows and afflictions of a morbid kind. Tennyson owned both volumes of Keble's *De Poeticae Vi Medica: Praelectiones Academicae Oxonii Habitae, Annis 1832–1841* (Oxford, 1844). Both volumes are at the Lincoln archives, but the second volume is largely uncut. In his first lecture Keble defines poetry as "a kind of medicine divinely bestowed upon man: which gives healing relief to secret mental emotion, yet without detriment to modest reserve" (John Keble, *Lectures on Poetry, 1832–1841*, tr. E. K. Francis [2 vols.; Oxford, 1912], I, 22). Keble later identifies poetry's distinguishing characteristic as "its power to relieve breasts surcharged with emotion" (II, 417).

the speaker's birdlike motions match, rhythmically and lyrically, the stalemate between forces in the poem. The first full stop, after the reiterated question "Is this the end?" (l. 16), literally brings to an end the two concurrent patterns—one logical, with its own rhetorical patterns, and one lyrical and formal—that have been competing with each other since the beginning of the section. While the oblique consolations of the biblical imagery, of the ark and the dove, are bringing to the suffering soul the therapy of the healing word, the lyric of loss is animating the consolation by acting out its own indirection in the syntax. The Prologue, in contrast, is too overt. Private truths have become part of a public testament, or at most catchwords. The logical and syntactic patterns coincide too regularly and insistently with the formal patterns. The parade of couplets becomes a liability, contributing to the general vapidness.

The sacramental landscapes of Sections LXXXVI and CXV are a geography of the mourner's soul. Their consolation does not depend on the successful transfer of a quality from landscapes to the mind. This is not true, however, of Section XI, which presents a journey through autumnal landscapes to a new mental state. Just as the pattering sounds of the chestnuts tend toward the symphony of sweeping bowers and bounding main, so green, red, and gold are stretched into a spectrum and finally blended in the truer formulation of silver hues and "Calm . . . still light." The grieving comparisons of past and present in the "Dark house" elegy (VII) have been discarded, and the landscape is now seen with no overtones of misery. Once the nostalgias of elegy have been purified into vision the mourner can see the same qualities of peace and calm in the high wold and great plain that he sees in the faded leaf and gossamers. Tennyson loosely attaches to the principal clause—"Calm is the morn" (l. 1)—the absolute construction of "The chestnut pattering" (l. 4). He introduces a series of freely floating phrases such as "the silvery gossamers," which attaches itself as readily to "the furze" as to the "high wold," functioning either as a direct object of the verb "drench" or as a third object of the preposition "on."

> Calm and deep peace on this high wold,
>   And on these dews that drench the furze,
>   And all the silvery gossamers
> That twinkle into green and gold.   [ll. 5–8]

The loose syntax creates an impression of expansion and diffusion, momentarily unchecked by the microscopic focus of the gossamers. Yet what, we may ask, have the last two lines of stanzas 4 and 5 to do with the aesthetic and geographical progression the reader has been following?

> And in my heart, if calm at all,
> If any calm, a calm despair.   [ll. 15–16]

> And dead calm in that noble breast
> Which heaves but with the heaving deep.   [ll. 19–20]

In the absence of precise analogies, the mourner's "calm despair" and Hallam's consoling nobility become forms of "pseudo-reference," to borrow Yvor Winters' phrase:[13] they affirm a healing power without showing how the poet's words produce the change.

There is no reason why the end of a section cannot make a perfectly independent assertion, as does the last quatrain in Section XI, which is not sustained by the logic the mourner has been following. In Section CXXIII, for example, the last stanza separates itself from what precedes; yet its reversal of attitudes is dramatic, and powerfully effective. The problem in Section XI is that the repetitions of "calm" disguise the separation between nature and mind that Section CXXIII affirms and celebrates. Though parallels between "calm" nature and "calm" heart or "calm" despair affirm an identity, the eleven repetitions of the same word conceal a more crucial and dramatic difference. The mourner's hypothetical clause "if calm at all" concedes that his

13. In his chapter "The Experimental School in American Poetry," in *In Defense of Reason* (Denver, 1947), Winters lists seven forms of "pseudo-reference." Hallam's nobility in *In Memoriam* would be an example of the fourth type: explicit reference to a nonexistent symbolic value. For comparable criticism see R. A. Brower, *The Fields of Light* (New York, 1962), p. 34.

parallels are discontinuous, "diatonic"—to use Hopkins' term.[14]
Yet the elisions of mind and nature set up the deceptive appearance of perfect merging. We seem to rise on an eleven-note scale
of continuous "chromatic" blendings.

No such problem occurs in Section LXXXVI. There is no transition from internal to external states, for nature is now a geography of the mourner's restored state of mind.

> Sweet after showers, ambrosial air,
>> That rollest from the gorgeous gloom
>> Of evening over brake and bloom
> And meadow, slowly breathing bare
>
> The round of space, and rapt below
>> Through all the dewy-tasselled wood,
>> And shadowing down the hornèd flood
> In ripples, fan my brows and blow
>
> The fever from my cheek, and sigh
>> The full new life that feeds thy breath
>> Throughout my frame, till Doubt and Death,
> Ill brethren, let the fancy fly
>
> From belt to belt of crimson seas
>> On leagues of odour streaming far,
>> To where in yonder orient star
> A hundred spirits whisper 'Peace.'   [LXXXVI]

The springtime landscapes bind the soul with obligation and affection. Unlike the bare diction of earlier sections, the language is
grand and ornate, befitting the dignity of a mind that can at last
renew its world. The poet's figurative pattern reinforces the contraction and expansion of his syntactic pattern—7 lines of apostrophe, in apposition to "showers"; 4 lines of principal verbs and

14. "On the Origin of Beauty: A Platonic Dialogue," in *The Journals
and Papers of Gerard Manley Hopkins,* ed. Humphrey House (Oxford,
1959), pp. 104, 106: "Of the many divisions one might make of beautiful
things, I shall consider that there is one . . . I think I would call . . . a
division into *chromatic* and *diatonic* beauty. The diatonic scale, you know,
leaves out, the chromatic puts in, the half-notes. . . . Parallelism . . . we
put under the head of diatonic beauty; under that of chromatic beauty
come emphasis, expression (in the sense it has in Music), tone, intensity,
climax, and so on."

objects; 5 lines of subordinate adverbial clause. His pictures descend from the "gorgeous gloom" of the evening sky to the trees, the meadow, and the "hornèd flood," only to reverse direction in the last quatrain, where the images rise again from the "crimson seas" to the odors of the streaming breezes and the "orient star." The closely huddled alliterating sounds at the beginning of the final adverbial clause—"Doubt and Death"; "fancy fly"; "From belt to belt" (ll. 11–13)—begin to disperse. The last two alliterating pairs appear in lines that directly contradict the despairing substance of "Doubt and Death." The looser rhythm, without pauses we could clearly call caesuras, together with the looser sound patterning and the larger syntactic units, establishes a growing, relaxed movement, leading naturally into the grand simplicities of the hundred spirits whispering "Peace." The attainment of "Peace" is more than an assertion; its consolation is a "heard event," part of the reader's own experience—a goal that Tennyson has syntactically, formally, and phonetically achieved.

A third way to contain emotion is to use an epigram to secure and stabilize a consoling conclusion. The final two lines—" 'Tis better to have loved and lost / Than never to have loved at all" (ll. 15–16)—are a summary in reverse order of Section XXVII as a whole. Line 15 solidly endorses splendor of the heart, even when only briefly attained—a value that the three main agents, the prisoner, the beast, and the unaspiring soul, have never known; and the last line is a reminder of their now discredited attitudes. The epigram is stable, predetermined in form—yet, in its reversal of attitudes, unexpected. In a poem that seems to drift, this epigram is also teleological; its energy is directed toward the termination of the first major section of the poem. Like inscriptions in a graveyard, it helps make sense of the rows of skeletal stones. There may be indirection in the meter, the syntax, the logic of *In Memoriam*. It may seem to be going to pieces, breaking up with grief; but epigrams allow the mourner to consolidate any gains. He can rough out his advance in brief notations, momentarily stabilizing the elusive elements.

A similar way of achieving catharsis is by using a puzzle or a paradox to contain despair and justify the mourner's hope. The metaphysical wit that compares emotional loss to financial loss by punning on "The far-off interest of tears" (I, 8) does less to solve than to extend the puzzle of why Tennyson should make the comparison in the first place. It is more usual for the poet to contain emotion by explicitly presenting the puzzle as such, and then going on to justify it through a paradox. In Section XXXII, for example, we are invited to conceive the single word "Life" in a multiplicity of contexts. At the simplest level, the word is a metonymy: a substitution of the cause of Lazarus' resurrection for the effect itself. But the capitalization also turns the word into the Word, "the Way, the Truth, and the Life." The turn upon "living" and "Life" is surprising. Roving from "the living . . . face" to rest "upon the Life indeed" has epigrammatic force (ll. 7–8). The puzzle and its solution revive both the shock and the consolation of the Incarnation, the validating paradox they attest to and depend on. Tennyson has already demonstrated the theological power of metonymy in the last line of Section XXX, where hope is transformed from a momentary impulse in the speaker into a metonymic attribute of God himself:

> O Father, touch the east, and light
> The light that shone when Hope was born.   [XXX, 31–32]

Christ as a cause of all men's hope is identified with his principal effect. The surprise of seeing a human attribute suddenly transformed into a metonym for God confirms the validity of the reader's momentary experience of the many contexts in which any individual word or line of *In Memoriam* may have to be interpreted. Though such effects are distinguished by their ingenuity, and we may think of them as witty, they are also moving. Like the metaphysical conceits and puns in *In Memoriam*, these little puzzles confine despair: since they suggest an ultimate economy in theological dogma—a resourceful attainment of a foreseen end, deftly and without waste—they are not only ingenious but resonating.

More pervasive than the logical indirection of puns and epigrams is the poem's generic indirection,[15] which seems at first to frustrate catharsis by leaving the mourner without compass points by which to chart his course. The surest way of insulating a reader from the experience of disorder in art is to commit what A. N. Whitehead calls the "fallacy of misplaced concreteness."[16] To treat poetic genres as if they were objective things rather than mental conveniences, and then to proceed on the assumption that a poem is per se a pastoral elegy or a philosophic treatise, is to enjoy the intellectual comfort of a limited but highly artificial order. The values and expectations associated with a different genre—the autobiography or the sonnet sequence, for example—will not apply. Much of *In Memoriam,* in contrast, tries to do self-contradictory things; in controlling grief, it tries *not* to make the reader feel that art is controlled. Instead of supplying a simple or a single coherence, the autobiography of the mourner supplies a sense of different coherences. The reader's emotional experience of trying to resolve disorder by organizing the coherences of pastoral elegy, philosophic treatise, lyric sequence, and autobiographical poem may at first frustrate catharsis. But at least it approximates the mourner's own search for relief as he seeks for new philosophic forms, combinations which will reconcile the indifference of evolution with the historic transmission of faith; the origin of the earth with the existence of God; and the nature of time and space with the fate of the soul.

It is not just generic indirection, but also the reader's need to hold in the mind formal, logical, and syntactic patterns that run simultaneously but not concurrently, that forces him to experience and begin to resolve disorders that the mourner, too, experiences, but can still not resolve in life. At various points in the poem Tennyson simply turns away from the difficult task of holding incompatible things simultaneously in his mind. But even

15. On the subject of generic indirection see F. E. L. Priestley, "The Creation of New Genres," in *Language and Structure in Tennyson's Poetry* (London, 1973), 106–136.
16. "The Century of Genius," in *Science and the Modern World,* ch. iii, (New York, 1925), p. 51.

if there is no final generic reconciliation in *In Memoriam* (and I
know of no study that convincingly demonstrates that there is),
the poem as a whole does manage to achieve the kind of continuity in change that we experience in reading Sections XXXIV–
XXXVII. Because these sections simultaneously adhere to and
remain separate from each other, the reader sees how even the
mourner's darkest fears may clarify and be resolved. More important, by being emotionally and intellectually involved, the
reader *experiences* these resolutions. Even when the mourner is
still too greatly grieved for consolation, the reader, who cannot
expect the critic—any more than the poet—to show him only one
way of looking at these lyrics, is already undergoing a miniature
catharsis in his mind.

> My own dim life should teach me this,
>   That life shall live for evermore,
>   Else earth is darkness at the core,
> And dust and ashes all that is;
>
> This round of green, this orb of flame,
>   Fantastic beauty; such as lurks
>   In some wild Poet, when he works
> Without a conscience or an aim.
>
> What then were God to such as I?
>   'Twere hardly worth my while to choose
>   Of things all mortal, or to use
> A little patience ere I die;
>
> 'Twere best at once to sink to peace,
>   Like birds the charming serpent draws,
>   To drop head-foremost in the jaws
> Of vacant darkness and to cease.   [Section XXXIV]

This section is one of the most desolating. In the midst of "Fantastic beauty," the mind pauses to formulate a hypothetical syl-
logism. If life is not eternal, then all is dust and ashes. But all
cannot be dust and ashes, it urges; therefore life must "live for
evermore" (1. 2). Though denial of the consequent logically allows the speaker to deny the antecedent, there is a material fallacy

in his denial. Faith so seizes on the mind that belief in eternal life
precedes the evidence. Though it must be remembered that belief
in Darwinian evolution is no less a faith—a godsend to the disbe-
lievers in God, that is defended and embraced in advance of total
proof—the speaker, sensing the material fallacy, dwells on the
horrifying alternative. For if death is the end, as Aristotle affirms,
then nature is merely rapacious, like the serpent whose jaws expand into a metaphor for earth and sky, luring man to "darkness." Sinking "to peace" (l. 13) seems to refer to the innocence
of repose, half in love with easeful death. But the rhyme of
"draws" and "jaws" makes the beauty of the serpent, as it con-
spires with dark powers in nature to destroy the bird, hateful
and insidious. "To drop head-foremost" (l. 15) is more appalling
than "to sink to peace" (l. 13). If the serpent, like the bird, is
innocent of evil design, its "vacant darkness" is no less horrifying,
for its rapt and cosmic indifference may signify no design at all.
If God is not malicious, he may not, as Einstein thought, be
subtle either, but simply the "Vast Imbecility" that Hardy fears:[17]
a God who produces minds, but lacks one himself—a monstrous
paradox. The head of this monster-god is the heavens, and its
jaws the abyss; its body, the earth in total panorama. G. M.
Young criticizes *In Memoriam* for its "incapacity to follow any
chain of reasoning which seems likely to result in an unpleasant
conclusion." But the speaker in Section XXXIV is not the
"archangel" of Young's description, "assuring the universe that it
will muddle through."[18] In an orgy of mad fecundity the world
of his vision adorns itself in "Fantastic beauty," but only to dazzle
and allure its children, then obliterate them pitilessly.

In Section XXXV the experience is still one of terror and loneliness. The flow of the "homeless sea" (l. 9) destroys the loving
relationship of man to man. The sea is the "universal cataract"
of Robert Frost "That spends to nothingness."[19] No longer exalted and assigned its great place in the hierarchy of creation, the

17. Thomas Hardy, "Nature's Questioning," l. 13.
18. *Victorian England: Portrait of an Age* (London, 1936), p. 75.
19. "West-Running Brook," ll. 56–57.

mind seems only a curious accident. Charles Lyell's new geology, which pictures nature "sow[ing] / The dust of continents to be" (ll. 11–12), supplants the omnipotence ascribed to God in traditional theology. But unlike God, the earth of scientific vision builds its oceans "swift or slow" and "Draw[s] down" its "Aeonian hills" (l. 11), not out of love or hatred for man, but out of sheer indifference.

Though both the substance and spirit of Section XXXVI begin to follow from what precedes, the need to hold each element in more than one context helps the mind enlarge its vision and assimilate its dread.

> Though truths in manhood darkly join,
>> Deep-seated in our mystic frame,
>> We yield all blessing to the name
> Of Him that made them current coin;
>
> For Wisdom dealt with mortal powers,
>> Where truth in closest words shall fail,
>> When truth embodied in a tale
> Shall enter in at lowly doors.
>
> And so the Word had breath, and wrought
>> With human hands the creed of creeds
>> In loveliness of perfect deeds,
> More strong than all poetic thought;
>
> Which he may read that binds the sheaf,
>> Or builds the house, or digs the grave,
>> And those wild eyes that watch the wave
> In roarings round the coral reef.

At first the links are reinforced by the economic metaphor of line 4—"Of Him that made them current coin"—which answers the earlier question: "what *profits* it to put / An idle case?" (XXXV, 17–18— my italics). The connections are also strengthened by line 12—"More strong than all poetic thought"—which casually picks up the contrast between aesthetics and theology that has been central to the conceit of the "wild Poet," God, working "Without a conscience or an aim" in Section XXXIV (ll. 7–8). But Tennyson wants to go so far with these metaphors

and no further. As Frost says, "All metaphor breaks down somewhere. That is the beauty of it. It is touch and go with the metaphor, and until you have lived with it long enough you don't
know when it is going."[20] In Section XXXVI the reader has to
adapt to a new use of metaphor: he finds that the "Aeonian
hills" (XXXV, 11) and "homeless sea" (XXXV, 9) are now
parts of a "mystic frame" (XXXVI, 2). But no sooner has the
reader adapted to the new use of metaphor than he finds he has
overadapted; the geological imagery is no longer the primary
source of meaning, but it has not completely disappeared either.
The roaring waves "round the coral reef" (XXXVI, 16) are
just as incessant as "The moanings of the homeless sea" (XXXV,
9); the only difference is that the watching eyes can now perceive a design and final cause in nature. The beauty of the reef
is now muted and incidental; Tennyson subordinates it to the
"loveliness of perfect deeds," a theological mystery "More strong
than all poetic thought" (XXXVI, 11–12). He also ascribes the
wildness to a creature beholding God's creation, whereas in
Section XXXIV he attributed it directly to God himself. The
reader never knows how much meaning he can get out of these
metaphors and when they will cease to yield. They are very much
alive. In the midst of death, they are like life itself.

Recoil against primitive terror allows the poet to achieve
momentary catharsis. It takes place in two stages: first as a
theological transformation (XXXVI, 5–12), and then as a
pastoral assimilation of the "homeless sea" to the "native rill"
(XXXVII, 5). In Section XXXVII the aesthetic and theological
motives opposed in Section XXXIV, and momentarily merged in
Section XXXVI, separate again in the conflict between Urania
and Melpomene. The consolations of theology seem to ebb away
in the pastoral flow; actually, they are undergoing a sea change,
and surface at the end in another form. While the act of darkening "sanctities with song" (XXXVII, 24) pertains directly to
Melpomene's "touch of shame" (l. 10), it also returns the reader

20. "Education by Poetry," in *Selected Prose of Robert Frost*, ed. H.
Cox and E. Lathem (New York, 1968), p. 41.

to Urania's "darkened brow." This phrase had itself grown out of a theological context of truths that "darkly join." The darkness does not simply violate theology. Like the ravishing elusiveness of the Holy Grail or the "lucid veil" of Section LXVII (l. 14), it reminds the mourner that indirection is a principle of truth itself. As Browning's Pope affirms, a limited aperture may "soothe the eye made blind by blaze,— / Better the very clarity of heaven."[21]

A final source of consolation is the soul's discovery of its own visionary power. It may be terrifying to think that in the end the soul is alone. But the mourner is consoled by more than para-lipsis, by more than the rhetorical satisfaction of insinuating his loss while pretending to pass over what sorrows "blindly drown." For there is also desperate human consolation in the thought that one never tells more than half; in the end perhaps one cannot. Until its final breakdown, the careful alignment of rhetorical and figurative patterns in Section XLIX, for example, keeps the grief firmly under control.

> From art, from nature, from the schools,
>   Let random influences glance,
>   Like light in many a shivered lance
> That breaks about the dappled pools:
>
> The lightest wave of thought shall lisp,
>   The fancy's tenderest eddy wreathe,
>   The slightest air of song shall breathe
> To make the sullen surface crisp.
>
> And look thy look, and go thy way,
>   But blame not thou the winds that make
>   The seeming-wanton ripple break,
> The tender-pencilled shadow play.
>
> Beneath all fancied hopes and fears
>   Ay me, the sorrow deepens down,
>   Whose muffled motions blindly drown
> The bases of my life in tears.

The mourner has a double experience—first of using meter, syn-tax, and logic to stabilize emotion, and then of seeming to go to

21. Robert Browning, *The Ring and the Book*, X, 1640–1641.

pieces, breaking up, as language fails and he can no longer utter what he feels. The final retreat into the inner recesses of the soul brings the astonishing discovery—in Sections LXVII–LXIX, XCV, and CIII—that the visionary world of the "mystic glory," of the talking breeze, and of the statue of the veiled Hallam is partly a creation of the mourner's own unconscious mind.

In the first actual vision (Section LXVII), which is a product of the mourner's consciousness as he lies awake at night, tranquil scenes of moonlit gravestones, of lucid veils and ghosts, begin to vibrate strangely, as if the mourner were hallucinating.

> When on my bed the moonlight falls,
>   I know that in thy place of rest
>   By that broad water of the west,
> There comes a glory on the walls;
>
> Thy marble bright in dark appears,
>   As slowly steals a silver flame
>   Along the letters of thy name,
> And o'er the number of thy years.
>
> The mystic glory swims away;
>   From off my bed the moonlight dies;
>   And closing eaves of wearied eyes
> I sleep till dusk is dipt in gray:
>
> And then I know the mist is drawn
>   A lucid veil from coast to coast,
>   And in the dark church like a ghost
> Thy tablet glimmers to the dawn.

In the first eight lines the visions take place in spacious syntactic units: in the first stanza a one-line adverbial clause is followed by a half-line principal clause and then by a two-and-a-half-line noun clause; in the second stanza a one-line principle clause is followed by a three-line adverbial clause. In contrast to these expanding units, the syntax in the third stanza diminishes dramatically into two one-line principal clauses followed by a two-line unit consisting of a participial phrase in the first line and a principal clause in the second. Only in the fourth stanza, where a half-line principal clause is followed by a noun clause of three and a half

lines, does the syntax once again expand. The transition from
visions in spacious syntactic units (ll. 1–8) to visions in diminished
ones (ll. 9–12) has the effect of narrowing the reader's vision,
just as the drawing of the veil of mist obscures the land from
"coast to coast" (l. 14). The two contradictory senses of the
curtain-like "drawing" of the mist (both *from* and *over* the
land) concentrate the contradictory motives of the "lucid veil" in
a simultaneous veiling and unveiling.

In Section LXIX, which combines the expansive effect of
Section LXIII with the diminishing effect of Section LXVII, the
mourner achieves another elusive vision.

> I dreamed there would be Spring no more,
>   That Nature's ancient power was lost:
>   The streets were black with smoke and frost,
> They chattered trifles at the door:
>
> I wandered from the noisy town,
>   I found a wood with thorny boughs:
>   I took the thorns to bind my brows,
> I wore them like a civic crown:
>
> I met with scoffs, I met with scorns
>   From youth and babe and hoary hairs:
>   They called me in the public squares
> The fool that wears a crown of thorns:
>
> They called me fool, they called me child:
>   I found an angel of the night;
>   The voice was low, the look was bright;
> He looked upon my crown and smiled:
>
> He reached the glory of a hand,
>   That seemed to touch it into leaf:
>   The voice was not the voice of grief,
> The words were hard to understand.

Upon the logical division of the lyrics (the first thirteen lines of
desolation and rejection, the last seven lines of Hallam's annuncia-
tion), the poet imposes a diminishing and then augmenting syntactic pattern. The first stanza's two-line principal clause beginning with "I" contracts in stanza 2 into four one-line clauses, then

contracts still further at the beginning of stanza 3 into two half-line units: "I met with scoffs, I met with scorns" (l. 9). In the last seven lines the syntactic units begin to grow larger. From the two half-line units in line 15 they expand into a one-line clause and then into a two-line unit: "He reached the glory of a hand, / That seemed to touch it into leaf" (ll. 17–18). Complementing the syntax is a pattern of contracting and expanding exemplifying units (two lines devoted to the dream; one line each to the blackness of the streets, their sounds, the exodus from the town, the wood; and then seven lines each devoted to the crown of thorns and the angel's advent). Both the syntactic and the exemplifying patterns have an initial imprisoning effect, appropriate to the mourner's passage from a dream of desolation into the physical confines of the noisy town. But then the patterns reverse themselves. They produce an effect of liberation, as the "angel of the night" extends toward the mourner "the glory of a hand" (ll. 14, 17). The combination in this last phrase of the definite and indefinite articles poises the vision ambiguously between material and numinous worlds. In preceding stanzas the indefinite articles suggest that the strange nature of "*a* glory" or "*a* silver flame" is beyond the mourner's grasp; later, as he assimilates their meaning, the articles become definite. A fine comment on Tennyson's grammar comes from Alan Sinfield, who describes the effect of shifting from the indefinite to the definite form of the article: "When the poet has absorbed the experience and taken it into his personality, then he can write, '*The* mystic glory swims away.' Tennyson uses the smallest particles of language at first to bring out the contrast between material things and the numinous, and then, by switching articles, to suggest that the mystical has become as real to him as the physical."[22] The final fusion of the two forms in a single phrase, "the glory of a hand," accurately portrays the mourner's tremors of nuance and his fine sense of wavering: he knows the angel's voice is "not the voice of grief,"

22. "Matter-Moulded Forms of Speech," in *The Major Victorian Poets: Reconsiderations,* ed. Isobel Armstrong (Lincoln, Neb., 1969), p. 57.

but "The words," he says, are "hard to understand" (LXIX, 19–20).

In the mourner's first visions the boundaries between self and not-self remain distinct. The mourner simply discovers that these boundaries divide the ego from the alter ego. The second vision, which takes place in Section XCV, carries the process one stage further. By blurring the boundaries of self and not-self, the mourner turns nature from the fixed glare of a death mask into something evasive and animate. As the firmament flares, absorbed into a volatile world, startling and evanescent as the gusts of wind, oracular as its words, nature acquires the elusiveness of a living person. We have already seen in this second vision how Tennyson moves from natural observation to prophetic vision so unobtrusively that we scarcely notice what has happened.[23] Tenor and vehicle have already reversed themselves before we register the change. The merging of life and death, at first clearly metaphorical, becomes strangely real as the timeless infinitive "To broaden" (l. 64) hovers over an argument for immortality without actually making it. The transformations come as an immense relief, for they release thoughts about immortality that become, not reflections on the scene, but actors in it. It takes little effort to find that in the end God is inscrutable. It is easy to perceive that any vision of him, being indirect, is in a sense fallacious. These truths are within everyone's reach, but they are not the truth of Tennyson's poem. It is against both mistakes, the view that the real sits apart and does not descend into phenomena and the view that the real is immanent in all its appearances, that the paradox of his "lucid veil" is directed. All nature, as an adjective of spirit, veils the face of God; but his mind shines lucidly through the world in different degrees and with diverse values. This double truth stands at the center of *In Memoriam*. The philosophic attempt to describe the flaring firmament of the northern night in terms of spirit, and the spirit of the talking wind and "boundless day" in terms of nature, then to make of both the

23. See above, pp. 47–49.

final unity, coincides with Frost's description of "the height of all poetic thinking" as the "attempt to say matter in terms of spirit and spirit in terms of matter."[24] The mourner, no longer lost in his world, has found a summarizing metaphor and vision to throw it into shape and order. He may subside into doubt, but he is no longer a soul without hope.

From his summit of unspeakable emotion the mourner descends in the simile of the next section as though he were Moses descending from Mount Sinai. Armed now with his tablets, with what one critic calls "a new charter for his time."[25] the mourner is in a position to pass to a final consolation in his third dream.

In Section CIII the veiled statue of Hallam, as it appears on the deck of a ship, invites the mourner to bring on board the maidens. This vision represents the kind of inclusive love that supplements love for Hallam after Tennyson's marriage to Emily Sellwood. Now the love of women takes its rightful place, and the mourner completes his personal catharsis.

The Lucid Veil

Until his final visionary encounter with Hallam the mourner is mainly concerned with expressing and purging his personal grief. But as the autobiography of a mourner, *In Memoriam* is both "introverted" and "intellectual." In the rest of the poem Tennyson is increasingly preoccupied with exploring the metaphysical and spiritual problems of his age. At times he implies that in sacramental nature spirit can find its adequate embodiment. But the nature that is a *"lucid* veil" to the sacramentalist is a "lucid *veil"* to the visionary; it is a sensuous curtain, hiding God from view. In astrotheologies (CXXIV, 5) and nebular hypotheses (CXVIII, 9–12) nature obscures its own final cause. And Hallam's pantheistic diffusion through "the rolling air" and "waters" (CXXX, 1–2) so attenuates the divine that spirit threatens to dissolve altogether, lost in "the general Soul" (XLVII, 4) posited by the Averroists, those medieval Aristotelians who be-

24. "Education by Poetry," p. 41.
25. Alan Sinfield, *The Language of Tennyson's "In Memoriam"* (New York, 1971), p. 138.

lieved that the intellect survives bodily death, but not as a personal, individual existent. If "Eternal form" is still to "divide /
The eternal soul from all beside" (XLVII, 6–7), as Tennyson
insists it must, then the soul must persist and be celebrated, in
exaltation and sublimity, above all its inadequate natural embodi-
ments.

This reciprocal inadequacy of nature and spirit prevents the
mourner's veneration of sacramental landscapes from degen-
erating into mere idolatry. It is the source of the soul's aspiration
and disquiet, of its exaltation and unrest, and is most clearly
defined in the great antiphony of faith and doubt in Sections
LIV and LV. Here human love is an analogy of divine love, and
seems to validate the principle. Yet what appears to be greater
than the soul is partly its own creation. The question "Derives it
not from what we have / The likest God within the soul?" (LV,
3–4) seems to change its drift in mid-course. Is divine love only
an anthropomorphic projection of a human attribute? And even
if love were a divine principle, would unrequited love not be
enough to destroy faith in the principle? Within an "odious scene
of violence and tyranny," as Mill calls it,[26] there runs a counter-
current of grandeur. The two-way meanings mirror an indirection
in nature's language, an irony of immensity and indifference, of
sublimity and inhumanity. The soul postulates a divine principle
by which it is judged—but if there is nothing behind the veil but
an amplified echo of its own love, by what is it judged? These
subversive thoughts may be "evil dreams" (l. 6). But are we to
suppose that nightmares are any less "real" than other visions?
From empirical knowledge, facts he can clutch in his "hands"
(l. 17), the mourner advances to the transcendental "larger
hope" (l. 20) through the diplomatic mediation of the phrases
"lame hands" (l. 17) and "faintly trust" (l. 20), which look two
ways at once. "Lame" and "faintly" are primarily figurative descriptions, but in their secondary meaning they describe physical
swooning on the staircase. Taken figuratively, the words strictly
limit the faltering "I's" communion with God. But the literal

26. "Nature," in *Three Essays on Religion,* in *Collected Works of John
Stuart Mill,* ed. J. M. Robson, X (Toronto, 1969), p. 398.

gesture of groping and the fear of actually fainting never eliminate the possibility of a gradual move "through darkness" (l. 16)
up the stair. A word like "lame" or "faintly" is likely to shift from
one context to another. The reader's mind is constantly required
to adjust.

In Section LVI, the series of subordinate clauses modifying
"Man" (l. 9), which remains suspended for three stanzas without
a verb, produces one of the most desperate moments in *In
Memoriam*.

> 'So careful of the type?' but no.
>   From scarpèd cliff and quarried stone
>   She cries, 'A thousand types are gone:
> I care for nothing, all shall go.
>
> 'Thou makest thine appeal to me:
>   I bring to life, I bring to death:
>   The spirit does but mean the breath:
> I know no more.' And he, shall he,
>
> Man, her last work, who seemed so fair,
>   Such splendid purpose in his eyes,
>   Who rolled the psalm to wintry skies,
> Who built him fanes of fruitless prayer,
>
> Who trusted God was love indeed
>   And love Creation's final law—
>   Though Nature, red in tooth and claw
> With ravine, shrieked against his creed—
>
> Who loved, who suffered countless ills,
>   Who battled for the True, the Just,
>   Be blown about the desert dust,
> Or sealed within the iron hills?
>
> No more? A monster then, a dream,
>   A discord. Dragons of the prime,
>   That tare each other in their slime,
> Were mellow music matched with him.
>
> O life as futile, then, as frail!
>   O for thy voice to soothe and bless!
>   What hope of answer, or redress?
> Behind the veil, behind the veil.

The repetitive contrasts, accumulative doubts, and hysterical predicate of the sentence beginning "And he, shall he, / Man," mount in a crescendo of fear which betrays the origin of the final question (ll. 19–20). In the midst of the anguish—"What hope of answer, or redress?"—we may doubt the materialization of any form "Behind the veil" (ll. 27–28). The anxious insistence of the subordinate clauses brings the tempting slip into a frantic acceleration and tripling of the relative pronoun: "Who rolled . . . / Who built . . . / Who trusted" (ll. 11–13); "Who loved, who suffered . . . / Who battled . . ." (ll. 17–18). The final fearful decline into fragments without verbs—"No more? A monster then, a dream, / A discord . . ." (ll. 21–22)—wrecks the harmony of the "mellow music" (l. 24). Do dreams of cosmic harmony, as Thomas Hardy believes, tragically unfit man for life and love in a warring world, the world of "Nature, red in tooth and claw" (l. 15)? The section ends in a cacophony of disintegration, subsiding in the final breathless phrases "Behind the veil, behind the veil" to a momentary stasis of chord and discord, expectation and distress. Such an experience lies at the heart of certain modes of atheist existentialism. Just as an immobile face may lead one to suspect that its owner is entranced or dead, so here the conviction may grow that there is nothing behind the mask for the mourner to unveil.

Despair and disbelief, however, represent a necessary stage in the mourner's development. They are antidotes to idolatry. Tennyson has to renounce the superb solidness of the world before he can see that there is nothing behind its mask that is not already in front of it. Far from being an object he can clutch in his hands, faith is self-produced. It is what Kant would call a postulate of the Practical Reason, a regulative truth that makes life intelligible, but not a concept that the understanding can directly apprehend.[27] To avoid idolatry the mourner must explore the teleology

27. Browning presents a similar theory of knowledge in *La Saisiaz,* where he affirms that man has immediate knowledge of himself and God. All other knowledge is a construction of the mind—the work of "fancy" or "surmise." Though such "surmises" granted as "facts" make life intel-

of the spiritual world in its own medium, renouncing the veil of nature as something transient and fugitive. While Lyell and Darwin are grounding the bold paradoxes of Heraclitus in a science of universal flux, the deathly magnificence of the earth's decline is slowly liberating the mourner's soul from veneration of a dissolving world. While the sun is running down through endless time out of infinite space, the soul sees the hills pass by like shadows in time-lapse photography, drifting across the plains into the sea, with which the Alps were level aeons ago. But even when "earth's dark forehead flings athwart the heavens / Her shadow crowned with stars" ("The Ancient Sage," ll. 200–201), the hard brilliance of her diadem can never obscure the dignity of her dispossessed children. For a poet who hears always the melancholy chime of mutability, who sees solid land melt into mist and flow away beneath his feet, only one form abides to sanctify and to console. This is the mind's image of itself, the image of its self-creating light, seen for the first time, as the veil is torn away, without the aid of nature.

Like one of Wordsworth's violations of nature, when the spirit of place rises up in revenge,[28] the mind's act of glimpsing behind an insubstantial veil an image of itself is an exhilarating but frightening experience. Its supreme expression is Section CXXIII.

---

ligible, the philosophic or religious worth of these surmises is also a matter of aesthetic appeal. The daring notion that spirit is immanent in all creation, so that "earth changes like a human face" (*Paracelsus*, V, 654), the notion that the analogue of human love is the action of the stars, and that in even the smallest "chance-sown plant" man can discover the laws of the spiritual universe—such surmises are quite ennobling, and, taken as analogies, quite valid. But even after surmises of superb daring, analogies in which much of the delight and poetry of existence lies, Browning never allows the reader to forget that the mysteries of life that can be spoken are not the real mysteries. In Kant's terminology, what can be expressed are merely the postulates of the Practical Reason, regulative and self-produced, and not the truths of the Pure Reason.

28. For my interpretation of such violations, which Wordsworth associates with "spots of time," I am indebted to Geoffrey H. Hartman's analysis in *Wordsworth's Poetry: 1787–1814*, pp. 211–219. "The spots of time, then, bring the child closer to confronting the power or mystery of its own imagination" (p. 216).

The long perspective of geological time, which had loomed before the mourner to frighten and appall, now spectacularly liberates the mind, turning it against all phenomenal being as null and evanescent. As the mourner submits to the geological truths, and then participates in them, the dizzying depths of duration are dispelled before his eyes. The soul is left alone in solitude, like a child without its parents, yet invulnerable, at the end, to the grand annihilation.

> There rolls the deep where grew the tree.
>   O earth, what changes hast thou seen!
>   There where the long street roars, hath been
> The stillness of the central sea.
>
> The hills are shadows, and they flow
>   From form to form, and nothing stands;
>   They melt like mist, the solid lands,
> Like clouds they shape themselves and go.
>
> But in my spirit will I dwell,
>   And dream my dream, and hold it true;
>   For though my lips may breathe adieu,
> I cannot think the thing farewell.

The great dread of extinction is made irresistible by the predictable alternation between images of motion or fluidity— "There rolls the deep" (l. 1); "they flow / From form to form" (ll. 5–6)—and solid, stable images: "where grew the tree" (l. 1); "where the long street roars" (l. 3). Despite the regularity, each time an example of change is cited there is a slight adjustment of the fluid and stable elements. The noise of the rolling deep, the unstable element in the first example (l. 1), is transferred to "the long street," the solid element in the second example (ll. 3–4); and the fluid sea becomes silent (l. 4). In addition, the second example ends with the image of the sea that introduced the first example, clamping the illustrations into a chiastic vise: X, Y, Y, X. The confusion of elements that accompanies the emphatic recurrence of logical and syntactic patterns reaches a minor climax in the third example of change (ll. 5–8), where the most fluid and solid elements are paradoxically identified:

"The hills are shadows" (1. 5); "They melt like mist, the solid
lands" (1. 7). Though the original pattern persists, it persists with
an important difference. The fluid, moving pattern is still contrasted with its opposite, but now the subject of the stable and
solid verb "stands" is the shocking and harrowing "nothing."
A perceptive comment on the word order comes from Alan Sinfield. He notes that "the solid lands," instead of coming first, are
"completely engulfed by images of insubstantiality; and 'go' is
made starkly to end the sentence and the stanza so that the solid
lands seem to slide suddenly away into an indefinite void. Tennyson's deployment of word order for emphasis makes the account . . . dramatic and alarming."[29] The continuing antithesis
of splendor and terror reaches its most acute point in the short,
rigid clauses of the central stanza. The imposition of the stern
parataxis—"and they flow," "and nothing stands"—on the yielding lyric similes—"like mist," "Like clouds"—establishes a momentary pathos. But the absolute parity of all the forms, of the
moving and the motionless, of the gentle and the remorseless,
amounts to a sudden collapse in beauty and interest. The pageant
seems about to end in terrifying absurdity, leaving the eye of its
dispossessed spectator cold and glazed, blank and indifferent. Yet
the world's dissolution brings the consoling discovery that every
soul, by birth and by nature, is an artist, an architect, a fashioner
of new and private worlds.

For the journey of the eye is into inner as well as outer space;
and in the privacy of the spirit, where the visual "eye" becomes
the human "I," the lyric refuses to be undone by the deathly
sublimities. There is a flicker of irony in "dream my dream" (1.
10). But the soul's high joking is a desperate way of staving off
its loneliness, its terror of solipsism; and the joking is sustained
without loss of inner seriousness. At the end of the lyric, the great
dread of extinction appears for a final time. But now it is subdued to gentler tones, to the "lips" that softly "breathe adieu"
(1. 11). The soul's reduction of creation to a nameless "thing"
(1. 12) is almost too harrowing. But while we are tempted to

29. *The Language of Tennyson's "In Memoriam,"* p. 84.

grieve for the soul's fragile defense against loneliness and time, the mourner uses two-way grammar; and the tone is also more than poignant. "Thing" refers, not primarily to the eye's outward spectacle, but to the "I's" inward journey, to the privacy of "dream." By converting the most impalpable element, the dream, into the most palpable element, "the thing," the soul can show how the more solitary it becomes, deserted by a dissolving world, the more aware it becomes of its power to survive and create its own enduring worlds. From its vision of homelessness the eye travels much further than anticipated. The lyric ends in private sacrament, in the celebration of a very internal form of mystery. This discovery of the soul's power to create its world finally overcomes the poet's intellectual despair. A visionary faith completes the thinker's metaphysical and spiritual consolation, just as the sacramental nature of Sections XCV and CIII completed the mourner's psychological catharsis earlier in the poem.

By balancing the sacramental and the visionary, a faith in natural benevolence with a more revolutionary faith in a living spirit behind the veil, the mourner learns to avoid both idolatry and skepticism. Since Hallam can be glimpsed through a sensuous curtain, there is always a danger that the mourner will worship him pantheistically, not as something more individual and distinct than nature, but as something less distinct, a mere "voice" upon "the rolling air" (CXXX, 1). In tearing aside the lucid veil, however, and in finding there an image of his own love for Hallam, the mourner is also in danger of falling into the opposite error. Although Love is a concrete universal, a "Lord and King" (CXXVI, 1), a sovereign the poet can both crown and worship, he must not therefore assume that this divine principle is nothing more than an amplified echo of himself. Tennyson is not merely exalting the divinity of man, in the manner of the mystical Wordsworth and the earlier Romantic poets. The heart that stands up and answers "I have felt" (CXXIV, 16) does not know the truth directly, in the way the conceptual understanding knows and interprets the natural world. Yet the necessary indirection of the soul's attempt to know and define its truths absolves it from the need for further squinting, for anxious peering "Behind the veil, behind the veil" (LVI, 28). As the purposeless creator, the indifferent god of evolution, is transformed into a principle of perfectibility, either through the general elevation of mankind or the emergence of a higher moral law, we can see "the ideas of the future," as G. M. Young observes, shaping themselves "lucidly, and with almost mystical clarity . . . in the language of the past; and still set out with something of the romantic urgency of a more pious, a more confident time."[30]

If "Nature" is "like an open book" (Epilogue, l. 132), it is not because Tennyson, as an interpreter of sacramental signs like the rose, the lilies, and the talking breeze (Section XCV), can read all its pages. Nor is it because he can penetrate behind its covers with the X-ray vision of the prophet or the seer. The mourner's heroic renunciation of elusive self-knowledge is his final consolation, his equivalent of Kant's "Copernican revolution" in philosophy. He learns to accept as ultimate and irreducible the distinction between man as he observes himself to be, but really is not, a product of "seeming-random forms" (CXVIII, 10), a "Magnetic mockery" or a "greater ape" (CXX, 3, 11), and man as he really is, but cannot observe himself to be, "the roof and crown of things," as the lotos-eaters proclaim ("The Lotos-Eaters," l. 69)—a being *born* to other things" (CXX, 12), a final cause of the creation.[31]

Though no language can enshrine the mourner's faith, it hinges on the knowledge that man is conscious as nothing else in creation is conscious. Even "in the night of fear," when "faith and form" are sundered (CXXVII, 1–2), the child's consciousness of its father's absence allows the child to know its father's nature and to affirm that he is near (CXXIV, 17–20). The

30. *Victorian England,* pp. 112–113.
31. Cf. F. E. Sparshott, *Looking for Philosophy* (Montreal and London, 1972), p. 127: "The same theme is to be found in all those fairy tales in which the furniture talks and dances while the family is asleep; for the converse of the belief that observation fixes is that non-observation releases. The great appeal of Kant's 'Copernican revolution' in philosophy was that it carried this fairy-tale theme to the highest level."

mourner's God is not the Unknowable God of Sir William
Hamilton[32] and Herbert Spencer.[33] For as Tennyson's contemporary, James Ferrier, argues in his agnoiology, or theory of ignorance, a self-conscious mind cannot be aware of the absence of
"that which is absolutely and necessarily unknowable to all
intelligence."[34] Knowledge of God's absence is proof that God is
in principle knowable. Though man is "a ripple on the boundless
deep," he "Feels that the deep is boundless" ("The Ancient
Sage," ll. 191–192). Despite its stupendous immensity, the universe is denied the supreme gift possessed by the self-conscious
mind. The "Fantastic beauty" (XXXIV, 6) of the universe
shines unseen, and dies away unknown in tropic wastes. "As in
some piece of art," where "toil" is "coöperant to" a well-defined
"end" (CXXVIII, 23–24), the teleology of the "one far-off
divine event" (Epilogue, l. 143) transforms the naïve, self-centered
being of the inanimate world. The final cause of the world, like
the final cause of a work of art, is essentially a mirror of the responsive soul, an appeal to affections and to minds.[35] Consciousness produces what is purposive: it strips the outer world of its

32. Hamilton presents his thesis that the Unconditioned is "incognisable
and inconceivable" in his influential article, "M. Cousin's 'Course of
Philosophy,'" *Edinburgh Review,* L (October, 1829), 194–221.

33. See "The Unknowable," in *First Principles* (New York, 1880), Part
I, pp. 1–103.

34. *Institutes of Metaphysics: Theory of Knowing and Being* (Edinburgh and London, 1854), pp. 407–408.

35. Tennyson's comparison is a familiar idea in German Idealist thought.
In the *Critique of Judgment,* Kant locates aesthetic judgment in the
purposiveness or teleology of its objects. Art is able to assume "a subjective purposiveness" (Immanuel Kant, *Selections,* ed. T. M. Greene [New
York, 1957], p. 412), since it is a human creation addressed to man, "the
only being which has the purpose of its existence in itself [and] who can
determine his purposes by Reason" (p. 404). The mind's ability to re-
duplicate itself, and to find itself mirrored in nature, as it finds itself
mirrored in works of art, is an important theme of Hegel's *Lectures on
Aesthetics.* See G. W. F. Hegel, *On Art, Religion, Philosophy,* ed. J. Glenn
Gray (New York, 1970), p. 126: "Poetry is the universal art of the mind
which has become free in its own nature, and which is not dependent for
its realisation on external sensuous matter."

stubborn foreignness, and enjoys in the shape and fashion of external nature an image of itself.

Though Robert Chambers' *Vestiges of the Natural History of Creation* is often cited as a source of Tennyson's despair in *In Memoriam*, it seems probable that Chambers' book is also a source of *In Memoriam*'s large and renovating truths. Intellectual historians sometimes forget that in trying to reconcile theories of design with theories of descent, and in celebrating the dignity of consciousness as it breaks through the hard rind of nature to the final causes which give the world its meaning,[36] Chambers reveals as much affinity with natural theologians like Bishop William Paley and with Idealist philosophers like James Ferrier as with the evolutionary theorists Darwin and Spencer. Without the soul's anguish and exalted visions, without the sudden gleams that illuminate its landscapes, the world of *In Memoriam* would be an irremediable disaster, its universe a vast absurdity. Like Herbert's "seasoned timber," which "though the whole world turn to coal / Then chiefly lives,"[37] the self-conscious mind, despite its apparent fragility, is durable as "rock" (CXXXI, 3). As "living will that shalt endure" (CXXXI, 1), the soul will survive even the wreck of nature, "When all that seems shall suffer shock"

36. See, for example, the teleological celebration of mind in Robert Chambers, "Mental Constitution of Animals," in *Vestiges of the Natural History of Creation*, ed. Gavin de Beer (Leicester, Eng., 1969), especially pp. 332, 348. "The face of God is reflected in the organization of man, as a little pool reflects the glorious sun" (p. 348). The metaphysical significance of the mind's self-consciousness receives its fullest, most toughly reasoned exposition in the Victorian age in James Ferrier's series of seven articles, entitled "An Introduction to the Philosophy of Consciousness," published in *Blackwood's Magazine* between February, 1838, and March, 1839. See, in particular, Ferrier's eloquent peroration to Part II, *Blackwood's Magazine*, XLIII (April, 1838), 452: "That man should feel and act, and bring about all his operations *without* consciousness, is just what we would naturally and at once expect from the whole analogy of creation, and the wide dominion of the law of cause and effect. . . . But come ye forward and explain to us the true miracle of man's being, how he ever, first of all, escaped therefrom, and how he acts, and feels, and goes through intelligent processes with consciousness, and thus stands alone, a contradiction in nature, the free master and maker of himself."
37. George Herbert, "Virtue," ll. 14–16.

(CXXXI, 2), and the whole of inanimate creation will flow through the void into nothingness. There is still a resistance in the soul—and a power in consciousness to create its world—that save.

From grief so appalling that its record seems a caricature of what human language is forced to portray, the mourner rises through the accumulated weight of his suffering to the psychological catharsis of his three climactic visions. The mourner's encounter with Hallam in Section XCV leads him to consecrate the divine in a sacramental vision of the world, in which the brazen glare of nature's mask, "red in tooth and claw," is shown to veil a living spirit. But elsewhere he is not in a position to add metaphysical and spiritual consolation to his personal catharsis until he tears the veil aside. Only in the last part of *In Memoriam,* beginning in Sections LV and LVI, then culminating in Sections CXXIII and CXXXI, does the mourner rise to a truth more self-evident than the immanence of God. This is the large, consoling premise of Chambers and of Ferrier, of Wordsworth and the Romantic poets: the premise that the soul reveals a greater power—and despite its destitution a greater dignity—than the rest of the created universe. Like Augustine in his *Confessions,* Newman in the *Apologia,* or Wordsworth in *The Prelude,* the mourner transforms official affirmations of his era into experienced truths. In balancing his sacramental vision of the world with his revelation of a living spirit behind the veil—a mirror image of his self-creating soul—the mourner steers a middle course between idolatry and skepticism, between a traditional and a revolutionary theory of the mind. Combining the indirection of his psychological catharsis with his direct profession of belief and faith, the mourner-sage achieves the double focus, "introverted" and "intellectual,"[38] of the most successful autobiographies.

38. Frye, *Anatomy of Criticism,* p. 308.

5

Lightning under
the Stars: *Maud*

Though it is more fragmented and hallucinatory than *In Memoriam,* Tennyson's *Maud* (1855) achieves a wholeness of form rarely surpassed in Victorian poetry and rivaled in Tennyson's canon only by "Lucretius." The poem possesses the authority that comes from the poet's having experienced the fear of madness and of suicidal death, with the complete awareness of what produces these disorders, then of coming out again on the other side. Like repressed material that floats to consciousness under psychoanalysis, or that drifts into view through shifting apertures, these dark forces are glimpsed and then obscured. In their confused lucidity, they are not permanently cut off, but used in the end constructively, to enlarge and renew the speaker. The hero's confrontation with his buried fears allows him to realize the promise of even the most diminished life. In rising above adverse circumstances, he learns to remake and remold himself; he is advanced in the dignity of thinking beings.

Verbal Therapy and Lyric Power

In Memoriam's tour de force of the tetrameter quatrain can hardly embrace the bravado, virtuosity, and volatile irony that Tennyson achieves in the more copious poetry of *Maud.* Having previously limited himself stringently to spare techniques, Tennyson now writes a rapturous love poem, a wild aria of ecstasy and hate. Though inconceivable without the discipline engendered by the other long poems, *Maud* fashions a new style of ostentation and despair, mediating between the unwieldy ornateness of *The Princess* and the attenuated epitaphs of *In Memoriam*. *Maud* is a virtuoso medley of hysteria and catharsis, of breakdown and mental therapy. The speaker is psychologically unstable, and an unreliable narrator who invents roles for himself. But like Tennyson, he is also able to exorcise his fears. His transformation through sacrifice and suffering reconciles him with Maud's brother after the duel, and later with society; the change leads to the kind of reversal and purgation that Aristotle associates with every tragic action. A partly autobiographical poem, *Maud* uses the Reverend John Keble's principles of "analogy" and "parody" to veil the poet's expressive impulse, which surfaces in the germinal lyric expressing Tennyson's love for Hallam (II, 141 ff.). The poem offers an "expedient of shifted responsibility"—to use Keble's phrase.[1] It provides Tennyson with a disguise when he is exposing and purging his own reactions to madness, suicide, and frustrated love.[2] It is no coincidence that *Hamlet*, the least Aristotelian of Shakespeare's tragedies, has often been compared to *Maud*, the most therapeutic of Tennyson's dramatic poems. *Hamlet* is a play

1. *Keble's Lectures on Poetry, 1832–1841*, tr. E. K. Francis (Oxford, 1912), II, 97. Great writers involve the reader in scenes that are remote or fabulous by "a twofold device: either they threw light on the whole scene by the help of some analogy [as did Lucretius, when describing earthquakes in Rome—a catastrophe almost unknown there]; or else they seemed, as if by accident, to bring out some familiar and homey detail, where the best light could fall upon it" (II, 320). See also I, 259: True and primary poetry gives "utterance sparingly, and only under veils and disguises, to the deepest feelings." Tennyson owned both volumes of Keble's *Lectures*, which are now in the Lincoln archives. The only modern scholar to do justice to the originality and range of Keble's aesthetic theories is Stanley Burnshaw, in *The Seamless Web* (New York, 1970), pp. 307–308: "No one, so far as I know, save the much neglected Keble, has regarded a work of art as a conflict-resolved in an act which preserves its maker 'from actual madness,' or has taken such care to explain that if poetry 'reveals the fervent emotions of the mind,' it can do so '*only* under certain veils and disguises.' "

2. The bitter personal experiences that flowed into *Maud* are well summarized by Christopher Ricks at the beginning of his chapter "*Maud*, 1855," in *Tennyson* (New York, 1972), pp. 246–247.

that achieves as much lyric anxiety as tragic catharsis; and *Maud* is a lyric that achieves as much verbal therapy as lyric power.[3]

Maud is closer in form to a movie, made up of separate "shots," than it is to any traditional genre. By "shooting" scenes and incidents, then making different shots collide, Tennyson can avoid the kind of sequential narrative that forces him to link scene to scene in the historical plays. The cinematic technique can either impede or accelerate the flow of the narrative; it makes the action flow in harmony with the hero's inner life, which, however precarious and spasmodic, is perpetually renewing its form. To capture the flow of "sensual thinking"—to use Sergei Eisenstein's term[4]—Tennyson occasionally introduces a flashback, a picture of the hero's father or of Maud as a child; at other times he gives us a close-up of an object like the shell, or a fade-out as the hero waits for Maud in the garden, then appears in the next "frame" as an exile in Brittany.

But if the details were merely to multiply in random disorder, according to principles of simple association, the poem would be condemned to sensual chaos or elemental raving. The pit that brings to mind the father's suicide would merge into pictures of social injustice, which would prompt denunciation by the hero, and so on. To control the flow Tennyson creates a shuttering effect by blocking off the action. In Part I each block contains at least one passionate lyric followed by a reflective passage; and Tennyson marks the blocks off either by ending couplets, as in

3. Compare with Northrop Frye's distinction between Aristotelian and Longinian conceptions in *Anatomy of Criticism* (Princeton, 1957), p. 67: "Just as catharsis is the central conception of the Aristotelian approach to literature, so ecstasis or absorption is the central conception of the Longinian approach. . . . The Longinian conception . . . is more useful for lyrics, just as the Aristotelian one is more useful for plays. Sometimes, however, the normal categories of approach are not the right ones. . . . *Hamlet* is best approached as a tragedy of Angst or of melancholy as a state in itself, rather than purely as an Aristotelian imitation of an action. On the other hand, . . . *Lycidas*, like *Samson Agonistes*, should be read in terms of catharsis with all passion spent."
4. "Film Form: New Problems," in *Film Form: Essays in Film Theory*, ed. and tr. Jay Leyda (New York, 1949), pp. 122–149.

Shakespeare (Part I, section viii, ll. 312–313; I, x, 396–397; I, xiii, 487–488), or else by quatrains, which have the same resolving function as the couplets (I, i, 73–76; I, xvi, 567–570). The combination of order and disorder—of photographic naturalism and directionless proliferation of detail, as though each image had acquired a life of its own—illustrates in a vividly cinematic way the futility of the hero's attempt to exorcise the past. By making all his shots collide, Tennyson creates the impression of a hallucinatory world, broken in pieces. But because the speaker's passions form themselves spontaneously into constellations of flowers, jewels, and animals, stars and colors, every sensory fragment is weirdly and intimately connected with every other fragment. While the hero is operating like the lens of a movie camera, Tennyson himself, as a skilled director and editor, is exercising incredible control over endless details of foreshadowing, connecting, and echoing that all miraculously cohere.

There is an insistent resurgence in *Maud* of talismanic presences: the white of the lily, the red of the rose, the horror of the blood-red hollow. The poem is written in the syntax of inner as distinct from outer speech; it catches the train of the speaker's thoughts and feelings in an excited state. According to Eisenstein, a characteristic of inner speech, the flow and sequence of sensual thinking, is its use of the so-called *pars pro toto* (part for whole).[5] At the beginning of *Maud* there is no unity of part and whole; the "lips" (I, 2) dripping with blood take the place of the wounded body of nature, and they achieve an intensity of impression that could not be achieved by the body itself. When the hero seems to be using metaphor to project a notion of ruin upon the autumn landscape, "the flying gold" of "the woodlands" (I, 12) is also functioning as a metonymy for wealth. The inversion of war and peace, which is really a form of civil war in disguise, introduces a paradox; and from paradox the speaker progresses through the Utopian irony of his taking "the print / Of the golden age" (I, 29–30) to the deeper irony of his pun on "print" and "golden"—his accepting the currency of an age of Mammon

5. "Film Form: New Problems," p. 132.

worship—which justifies the inversion of war and peace in an unexpected way. Normally, no speaker who had subverted the word "golden" would imagine he had thereby established that society had been subverted by the financial power that "golden" stands for. But as soon as we analyze the syntax of inner speech we are exploring a poetry of disconnection in which semilogical constructions are decisive. Obsession with his father's death as a result of financial ruin introduces subversive double meanings that give the hero's language a metonymic, punning quality; and he is constantly steadying the faster, more tempestuous movements of his ranting song with counterlogical elements—like the heavily alliterating maxim "only the ledger lives" (I, 35) or the defiant slogan "better, war! loud war by land and sea" (I, 47).

Even when the hero seems to be arguing logically, he is really playing syllogistic games in which he defines peace as lust for gain and lust for gain as a curse. If peace is a curse, it does not follow that war is a blessing. But in attempting an illogical conversion— denial of the antecedent, peace, does not logically entail denial of its consequent, the curse—the speaker is not simply forgetting that some forms of peace are not warlike; he is using the broad sense of "warlike" to stress unexpected analogies between civil and military plunder.

> When a Mammonite mother kills her babe for a burial fee,
> And Timour-Mammon grins on a pile of children's bones,
> Is it peace or war? better, war! loud war by land and by sea,
> War with a thousand battles, and shaking a hundred thrones.
> [ll. 45–48]

Slow stunned movements of shock and despair culminate in a momentary vision of apocalyptic war, an ultimate battle between good and evil, a confrontation in which the "children's bones" and the "hundred thrones" (I, 46, 48), like close-ups in a movie, make a huge sensational impression. The technique consists in replacing the whole (the bodies and the empires) with parts (the bones and the thrones); it recalls the use of the surgeon's pince-nez in *Potemkin*, which, as Eisenstein observes, makes a much greater impact than the reappearance of the surgeon by himself could make.

The forms of sensual thinking are familiar to the poet of *In Memoriam*, where they appear sporadically as states of aberration like hallucination and nightmare. But the mind's reluctant return to life balances the chaos; and Tennyson instinctively registers the slow overcoming of obstacles in the tempo and feeling of his verse. Though a violent subsurface energy is constantly distorting and destroying the meaning of *Maud*, the reader senses from the beginning the undercurrent of renewal that finally distinguishes the highest artistic achievements from other states of sensual thinking that are produced as a result of hysteria, hypnosis, and schizophrenia. The first passage in which ranting turns to outright celebration is the lyric recounting the childhood memories of Maud (I, i, 69–72). It is a lyric of unobtrusive metaphor whose meanings are as much embodied in the increased number of anapaestic feet and the buoyant tone as in the ideas or images. The placid surface of the next section (ll. 77–87), barely rippled like Maud's perfect face, comes as a pleasant surprise after the harsh declamations. But the hero immediately betrays himself by denying that he is "broken"; and his defiant insult asserting that Maud "has neither savour nor salt" (I, 78) builds up irony in tone, rhythm, and image that grows into irony of another kind. At first he mocks Maud's "Dead perfection," but he does so playfully, and mainly through rhythm:

Faultily / faultless, / icily / regular, / splendidly null   [I, 82]

The falling dactyls and trochees stress each of the oxymoronic elements, as if parodying the perfection they mock. The further irony that the placidity is really the torpor of resignation, and that the hero is already Maud's slave, develops through contradictory pictures. The lover keeps up a protective game of banter in the playful heaping of adjectives: "least little delicate aquiline curve" (I, 86). But sensual thinking has its own laws; and the oblique joking about Maud's defects, about the ripeness of the underlip and the curve of the nose, can hardly conceal the lover's enslave-

ment. His protective fiction of indifference to Maud represents a
miniature version inside the poem of Tennyson's own disguises.
The poet has suppressed his far more vituperative original versions, in which the specter of Rosa Baring, the woman Tennyson
loved in vain, is painfully present. He buries his love for Hallam
and for Rosa Baring, as he buries his fears of madness and of
suicidal death, deep beneath an elaborate array of narrative
masks.

Section ii (I, 77–87) is a lull in the storm. At first it sustains
the kindling of passion by its deliberately serene and static quality.
But as the expanding and contracting action of Maud's beauty
"grows and fades and grows" with the ebb and flow of the lover's
pulse, his tone, no longer half-mocking, and no longer detached
like that of an easy observer, becomes first inquisitorial and then
feverish and tormented, edged with panic. Ironically, the lover
pleads that he has wronged Maud's beauty only "in thought" (as
if her revenge and the reason for it—the "slanderous" compliment that in fact betrays his enslavement to her—both conspire
to bring him to the same delirious pitch). He tries to fortify himself by going from the house to the "dark garden" to listen to the
wind and tide, as if bracing for disaster. His histrionics blend with
an eerie resonance of open vowels ("broad," "roar," "Orion,"
"low"), and with auroral impressions of whiteness glimmering in
"wintry wind" (I, 100), which suggest that there may now be
alternatives to loneliness and terror. Maud has been transformed
into a cosmic principle; her evocation has become an exercise of
the tormented lover in ironic attitudes, shading from the hypnosis
of the "clear-cut face" (I, 88) to apocalyptic terror in the garden.

The hero finds himself in an Edenic grove of weird opulence
and perfumed warmth, curiously reminiscent of the nocturnal
setting of Tennyson's exhilarating midsummer vision in *In Memoriam* (Section XCV). Verse and meaning rise to a crescendo
that meets and goes beyond expectation in its blend of metaphor
and fact. "The shining daffodil dead" (I, 101) is a precisely
etched flower, seen against "the ghastly glimmer" with daylight
accuracy. The dead flower, like the later "daffodil sky" (I, 859),

is a surrealistic object; it is the essence of the wintry scene itself, a kind of northern nowhere connected with the eerie beauty of the northern lights.[6] Reversing metaphors make light, colors, and forms flow together in a merging of cosmic and human elements. Orion "low in his grave" is also the poet's father; and the dead flower is the sky. The wail of the hero's father merges with the "scream" of a "maddened beach" (I, 99); and the auroral light is the cold and luminous beauty of Maud, now coterminous with the lover's universe. The impressionistic blendings, which are just as often rhythmic as visual or aural, and the lack of strong pauses, increase marvelously the sense of flow and of pulsating growth. The rise and fall of the ghastly light accompanies the surge of the hero's blood; and the series of magnificent rhythmic curves plunge downward and then upward, before culminating in the half-stormy sweep of

The shí / ning dáff / odil déad, / / and Orí / on lów / in his gráve
[I, 101]

The recurrence of the same words and sounds, especially long arcs of adjectives of about the same size and shape—"passionless, pale, cold face" (I, 91); "Luminous, gemlike, ghostlike, death-like" (I, 95); "broad-flung, shipwrecking roar" (I, 98)—increases the sense of circling flow.

The speaker first worships Maud because she is immaculate light free from the grossness of the blood-red wood. But he also recognizes the equivalence of such worship with desire for death. When Maud is fully detached, "a silent lightning under the stars" (III, 9), she is dead; and a chill descends on the poem whenever the hero alludes to Maud's cold beauty in one of those flaring symbols, like the auroral light draping the Holy Grail, that Tennyson values for their ravishing elusiveness. While the movement is mainly toward darkness and terror, there is also a merging of human and cosmic processes, which prepares for later sacra-

6. For a fuller treatment of the auroral references in *Maud* see W. David Shaw and Carl W. Gartlein, "The Aurora: A Spiritual Metaphor in Tennyson," *Victorian Poetry,* III (1965), 213–222.

mental and demonic visions. The revelation in the garden is followed by a grand but slightly amused suggestion of a sacramental marriage of the "sapphire-spangled" land and sea (I, 107). The speaker hints, too, of an apocalyptic marvel in "A million emeralds [breaking] from the . . . lime" (I, 102). But he glances tentatively at these marvelous possibilities; after the strain of apocalypse he yearns for a less demanding natural world, as if reminding himself that he is now too far removed from his nocturnal vision to be transformed by it.

Like "Locksley Hall," the following sections of *Maud* dramatize a subtle but important gap between what is happening to the lover and what the lover tells himself is happening. The yearning for "a philosopher's life" (I, 150) is only a game, not a lived doctrine. The lover's animus is curiously out of keeping with his professed detachment as a stoic philosopher; and his sententiousness is felt in the almost mechanical exactness of the meter. Lines end as they do merely because of the didactic or metrical paradigm—not, as in the later lyrics, for reasons of music, phrase, or gesture. A nobler way of writing and living is set forth, reluctantly and tentatively, in the "martial song" of the "voice by the cedar tree" (I, 162), which is a kind of trumpet call to action.

The important transitions in *Maud* are not simply to different moods, rhythms, or events, but to sharply opposed qualities. Maud's "beautiful voice" (I, 180) breaks upon the speaker with a freedom of form that literally explodes the long, inflexible lines of the preceding section. The passing from quality to quality presents the same going out of himself, the same ecstasy, that the lover feels whenever he is drawn into Maud's magnetic field. Maud becomes a disembodied hieroglyph for something beyond her; he wants "Not her, not her, but a voice" (I, 189). The mock epithalamium of the sixth section is a new leap into opposition; it tells us something about the passing of ecstasy. The speaker is now a male Mariana, a neurotic lover whose nerves are set on edge by the "shrieking rush of the wainscot mouse" (I, 260). He is also uneasy about Maud's dandified brother, who appears with his "glassy smile" (I, 238)—the mirror of the vanity in which he continues to worship and adore his own splendid foppery. The preposterous break in rhythm after "dandy-despot"—"What if that dandy-despot, he, / That jewelled mass of millinery" (I, 231–232)—prepares for a parody of eastern and baroque styles, which is also a tribute to the hero's native English sense. The "oiled and curled Assyrian Bull" (I, 233) has the bourgeois soul of Arnold's Philistines; he is a merchant who retails desire, and who would barter his sister's heart for a vote in the next election (I, 243–245). The confusion of love and politics debases the marriage arrangements of the parents. The banality extends to the dull shape of the stanzas, which barely rise above the level of doggerel. Like most assured poets, Tennyson is never constrained to maintain a dazzling succession of lyric high points; his doggerel is an accurate projection of his hero's mood at the moment.

The next transition is not a leap into opposition but a leap into a new quality of despair. Slow and knell-like, the monosyllabic iambs, ponderously stressed, drain all life from the verse as they drain all hope from the lover: "Then returns the dark / With no more hope of light" (I, 328–329). After looking in vain for a new kind of hero, now that Maud seems lost, the lover moves with swift jumps and turns to a conclusion that is as right as it is surprising. Tennyson's own memory of Hallam breaks in with poignant and unexpected power: "And ah for a man to arise in me, / That the man I am may cease to be!" (I, 396–397). We hear the sudden resurgence from "Break, break, break": "But O for the touch of a vanished hand / And the sound of a voice that is still!"[7] The evocation of Hallam is beautifully right; lover and poet can momentarily speak together in a new accent of awe that is perfectly in harmony with the quest for a hero that has been developing since the beginning of the fourth stanza. Tortured at the very center of his faith, the speaker, by his alternation of tones—insolent, demagogic, eloquently intimate—expresses him-

7. "Break, break, break," ll. 11–12. Humbert Wolfe was the first critic to identify the rhythmic allusion. See his monograph *Tennyson* (London, 1930), pp. 36–37.

self in a confusion of tongues. He finds a way at last largely because Tennyson comes to his aid, introducing a fragment in which we can hear Eliot's "first voice of poetry" speaking through the "third voice"—a fragment that unites the lover's dramatic voice with the lyric voice of the poet. The victory is of a very special kind, and though the next section almost reluctantly breaks into a cadence of renewal, we know the victory can be only temporary.

In a cry for love and sanity, the lyric impulse that has long been on the verge of expression at last breaks forth in what one interpreter finely calls a language of exalted and "transfigured platitudes."[8] Though the meter catches the excited beat of hope and expectation, it is also charged with prophetic power, which gives the feeling of larger relevance. The surprising force of the love lyrics comes in part from their metrical bareness. The starkness of "Maud, Maud, Maud, Maud, / They were crying and calling" (I, 414–415) keeps the feeling of rapture generalized. The piercing cry of the birds and the speaker's replies (I, 415–416, 430–431) echo in one tone, ecstatically and wonderingly; but in another less hopeful tone, they strike a note of terror and gloom. By inducing a mood between rapture and lament, Tennyson exalts and transfigures his great platitudes of feeling. He combines the ecstatic leap "out of oneself" with the earlier leaps into opposition. For the first time he makes the two forms of ecstasy spring concurrently from the center of his poem.

Before celebrating his own rapture in "Go not, happy day" (I, xvii, 571–598), the hero must first overcome the reader's natural resistance. He meets a possible objection to his wild conceits by stating the charge himself: "The fancy flattered my mind, / And again seemed overbold" (I, 511–512). To forestall mistaken responses to his love for Maud he grounds them in "the gross mud-honey" (I, 541) of her brother's lust. A victim of private but horrifying tricks of identification, the lover confuses sleep with

8. A. S. Byatt, "The Lyric Structure of Tennyson's *Maud*," in *The Major Victorian Poets: Reconsiderations,* ed. Isobel Armstrong (London, 1969), p. 73.

death. He uses the seemingly artless ballad form to conjure from
the "curtain" in Maud's window, which "meant but sleep," a
"death-white" horror (I, 525). The surprise and terror have
seldom been surpassed, even by Wordsworth in his Lucy poems.
The passage from such horror to the rapture of "Go not, happy
day"[9] tells us a great deal about the experience of going outside
oneself, about ecstasy. The almost incoherent joy expresses the
heavy weight that has been lifted from the lover; yet he does not
so much articulate his feeling as allow the reader to infer the
whole range of mood released by self-forgetful joy. The simplicity
of the lyric flamboyantly calls attention to itself. Just as the
declarative sentence is the simplest grammatical figure, so tautology is the simplest rhetorical form, and Tennyson deliberately
uses both to make the language infantile. Maud's real qualities
never emerge from the rush of the truncated trochaic line or from
the dazzle of the blurring images. No genuine metaphors cross
the bridge of tautology between the Indian dance and the cedar
tree, or between the glowing ships and Maud. The one word
"rose" (I, xvii, 595–598) is made to assume all the work of
praise and vision.

In contrast, the climactic song "I have led her home, my love,
my only friend" defines and evaluates the multitude of rosy
metaphors which, in proclaiming the lover's ecstasy, show a
stubborn unwillingness to refine that ecstasy or to progress to
lucid understanding of it.[10] "I have led her home" combines the

9. Humbert Wolfe, in *Tennyson,* p. 39, calls this lyric "the worst poem
in *Maud.*" But his comments suggest that the breakdown is a deliberate
"illustrative failure," for "neither the poet nor the cadence have given
themselves time to think, and scarcely time to breathe."

10. Hence, as Wordsworth insisted, half a century earlier, all poets
must refract their "powerful feelings" through reflection and memory
(Preface to the second edition of *Lyrical Ballads* [1800]). For a brilliant
criticism of the fallacy of imitative form see Ivor Winters' discussion of
pseudoexperimental poetry in the chapter "Poetic Convention," in *In
Defense of Reason* (Denver, 1947). According to Winters, the sound procedure is to make a lucid and controlled statement about being uncontrolled, a procedure which requires that the poet understand the nature of
the uncontrolled, not that he *be* uncontrolled.

lyric joy of "Go not, happy day" with the marveling judgments
of a psalmlike prayer. The rapture is restrained by strong rhetorical patterns, in which the same ideas keep returning in simple
variations of surpassing dignity and ease: "Full to the banks" (I,
604); "thy limbs have here increased" (I, 616); "And made my
life a perfumed altar-flame" (I, 622). Within such chantlike
measures Tennyson introduces controlled changes of lyric tone,
giving reiterated values to the same word or phrase: "There is
none like her, none" (I, 600). The banks are brimming and
tumescent, and the pulses play with an erotic fullness of the
blood, which "never yet so warmly ran . . . / And sweetly" (I,
601–602). Though Maud's whiteness is now bridal, associated
with the nakedness of "snow-limbed Eve" (I, 626), the lover's
sexual paradox of "dying" to live (I, 664) is also a biblical paradox of losing life to save it (I Cor. 15:36); and he supplants the
"mud-honey of town" (I, 541) with celestial gifts of "honeyed
rain" (I, 619). The "pattering talk" of the laurels (I, 606) and
the opulent biblical images introduce a cosmic dimension; without strain, even the decease of "summers" (I, 612) comes to
mark the passing of whole geological periods.

With perfect adjustment between feeling and landscape, Tennyson creates from the sway of "limbs" (I, 616) and the "pastoral slope" (I, 617) a garden of Eden, whose dangerous per-
fumes, guarded by a jealous sultan, heighten both the sensuous
and religious ecstasy. So integral are the "delicate air" (I, 619),
the streaming breezes (I, 614), and the "starry head" (I, 620) to
a woman, a landscape, and a biblical idea that without any
straining for effect the lover can link a chain of grand renewals;
in his simple description of a cedar of Lebanon much that pertains to sensuous and spiritual mystery is conveyed.

> O, art thou sighing for Lebanon
> In the long breeze that streams to thy delicious East,
> Sighing for Lebanon,
> Dark cedar, though thy limbs have here increased,
> Upon a pastoral slope as fair,
> And looking to the South, and fed
> With honeyed rain and delicate air,

> And haunted by the starry head
> Of her whose gentle will has changed my fate,
> And made my life a perfumed altar-flame;
> And over whom thy darkness must have spread
> With such delight as theirs of old, thy great
> Forefathers of the thornless garden, there
> Shadowing the snow-limbed Eve from whom she came.
>   [I, 613–626]

The reader hears a reverent voice, still vibrant after the crude ecstasy of the preceding lyric, but now evaluative and analytic, cutting across the soaring tones and easy song. The anapaestic runs of the long lines settle into a pattern of strong rhymes— "East," "increased" (I, 614–616); "fair," "air" (I, 617–619)— broken only by marveling apostrophes: "O, art thou sighing for Lebanon" (I, 613); "Sighing for Lebanon, / Dark cedar" (I, 615). Tennyson presents the odd arrest and flow of an appreciative growth in wonder—an effect that requires more relaxed rhythms in order to balance the claims of both reflective speech and rising song. We are now spectators of a religious drama, a rite of love that moves from powerful lamentation for Lebanon to relaxed and more subdued demand for spiritual union with Maud. The lover prays in the language of litany; his sensual imagination is strictly sacramental, enumerating the sensuous features of the landscape in eternal biblical symbols of fruition and constancy. The "merry play" (I, 629) of the erotic stars, as they move "in and out" among the swaying limbs, introduces a stroke of broad parody across the solemnity of man's creation in the "thornless garden" (I, 625). But instead of only burning like "Cold fires" (I, 637), the stars also form a bridal crown for Maud, who is both Eve and Mary the second Eve, the virgin of the *hortus conclusus* in the Song of Songs.

Though the lover seems to discover in his transforming vision "The countercharm of space and hollow sky" (I, 641), he immediately begins to question the central Romantic faith, what Wallace Stevens calls belief in the "analogy between nature and the imagination," and in "the acute intelligence of the imagination, the illimitable resources of its memory."[11] The inevitable fall from vision terrifies the lover; it confronts him with the horror of a scientific universe, an iron brand that burns into man reminders of "His nothingness" (I, 638). As Christopher Ricks observes, "It seems that I am happy" (I, 648) is "a desolating way" of affirming joy.[12] A moment later the fall from grace generates a quality of indescribable gusto and pathos: "O, why should Love, like men in drinking-songs, / Spice his fair banquet with the dust of death?" (I, 653–654). As the lover passes from enchanted contemplation of the sea to the gentle plainness of "Dear heart, I feel with thee the drowsy spell" (I, 670), the rhythmic current turns again with ease. But the beating of the "happy stars, timing with things below" (I, 679), has an effect of breathlessness, and of hurrying toward pauses. The haste imitates the lover's own impatience; its expression immediately falls into a meter that hints at panic. The fall from assurance is felt in the balance so finely held between hope and peril, and in the premonition of "some dark undercurrent woe" (I, 681).

Since the lover still values his apocalyptic vision, he defines the word "dream" so that its strongly charged emotive meaning, as a "dream of bliss" (I, 686), will coincide with his new descriptive meaning, as a vision that moves constantly in the direction of the credible: "I have walked awake with Truth" (I, 687). The less responsible kinds of dreaming are now dramatized in reminiscing reveries, whose mocking feminine rhymes lumber on the edge of flat prose: "For nothing can be sweeter / Than maiden Maud in either" (I, 807–808). The hero seems to be parodying the Sultan, who cannot sustain an inspiring thought for long. Though the very flatness (I, 824) provides a kind of self-consoling satisfaction, it also makes possible, after the important mediating and preparatory Section XXI, the culminating leap into the next great lyric, "Come into the garden, Maud."

As tempo and feeling increase, the poetry moves with surprising

11. *The Necessary Angel: Essays on Reality and the Imagination* (New York, 1942), pp. 118, 61.
12. *Tennyson,* p. 257.

force and with quiet eagerness of emotion to the lover's climactic vision of Maud in "the valleys of Paradise" (I, 893). Strange as it seems, Tennyson achieves a delicate poising of whimsey and ardor—though these qualities, like the innocence and bitterness of "Aylmer's Field," usually exist in inverse ratios. He is not afraid to experiment with the popular polka measure, extending the music of "flute, violin, bassoon" (I, 863) until the meter catches the whirling rise and fall of the lover's hopes. The rose and lily are invested with personality in a pseudo-Oriental manner, and belong to a world where "daffodil" and "sky" are fused and where even cosmic and sexual climaxes are merged: "To faint in the light of the sun she loves, / To faint in his light, and to die" (I, 860–861). Though it is easy to hear a call to lament in some of the refrains—"All night have the roses heard" (I, 862); "There has fallen a splendid tear" (I, 908)—the excited expectation shows how strongly the speaker feels a contrary impulse. Tennyson builds a rhythm perfectly apt for his poising of hope and fear. The rose becomes a purely external symbol of the lover's hopes. The debate form, the sinister premonitions, and the insistent, obsessive repetitions—"She is near, she is near" (I, 912); "I hear, I hear" (I, 914)—resist any tendency toward overeasy song.

The moods waver: the speaker inclines at first toward fable; he even risks bantering in doggerel, and dares to introduce a looking-glass world of talking flowers. The playful shifts are partly a psychological defense, a stay against confusion. His rhythmic form embraces and molds even the most graceless rhymes: "I said to the rose, 'The brief night goes . . .'" (I, 876). All the singsong lines are pulled into the increasing speed of the rhythm; they are wrenched from wistfulness or plaintiveness by the antiphony of floral voices, which rapidly shift the pace of the verse and do not allow us to linger over any one fragment. The lover tries to make peace with the night by going through grotesque and half-magical routines with the flowers. But like everything else he does, his routines are inadequate. Instead of tranquilizing him, the repetitions charge the flowers with more and more feeling. Even the full stops are signals to go ahead; the momentum of the verse carries the lover from the fantasy of the floral dialogue, to the imagined ecstasy and consecration of reunion with Maud, to the sheer horror of trembling "under her feet / . . . in an earthy bed" (I, 919, 922). The corpse's "blossom[ing] in purple and red" (I, 923) combines flower impression and the half-formed thought to create out of two depictable objects the representation of a third thing that is graphically undepictable. Tennyson has fused separate shots of the "red-ribbed" hollow (I, 3) and the blood-dripping "passion-flower" (I, 909) into the visual representation of a psychological idea. Out of two separate hieroglyphs he has created an ideogram —or the montage of cinema; he has given to the blood and the flower the terror of the lover's darkest imaginings.

The Ostentation of Our Love

Tennyson opens the second part of *Maud* with a chaotic close-up of the duel. He represents the lover's frenzy as a chaos of impressions. As the scene of the father's suicide, the "red-ribbed" hollow has always been a place of terror. But now it merges with the lover's homicidal act, with "the Christless code" of "life for a blow" (II, 26–27); and the brother's charitable acceptance of blame (II, 1) intensifies a horror that recalls the most nightmarish moments in Wordsworth. At the beginning Tennyson uses narrative exposition. But when Maud's "ghastly Wraith," wailing its "passionate cry / . . . for a brother's blood" (II, 32–34) looms menacingly on the scene, its shocking revelation replaces Tennyson's narrative method with progression through images. Tennyson's whole method of exposing the action accomplishes its own leap, to parallel the lover's: a leap from dimension to dimension—and also from quality to quality. For, surprisingly, the falling of "a gentle rain" (II, 41) is full of redemptive possibilities. It presents Maud, like the veiled statue of Hallam in *In Memoriam*, transfigured and larger than life (CIII), not as a demonic presence, but as an instrument of higher truth. Her re-

moval may even be necessary if the lover, having overcome his
fear of love, is to recover his own soul.

Tennyson can best represent the transition to a new quality in
the lover by interrupting the action. After the opulent mode of
the love lyrics, the meditation on the shell (II, 49–78) fashions
a new aesthetic of the spare and the eccentric. Like the slow
motion of a film, it allows Tennyson to explore a conflict between
the short duration of an event and its momentous human impact.
Since fastidious obsession with the details of the shell is a stay
against confusion, Tennyson can link the shell's astonishing design
with the mind's concentrating power by referring to the two
phenomena in metrically identical lines.

> Strange / that the mind / when fraught . . .   [II, 106]

> Frail, / but a work / divine . . .   [II, 52]

The lover is an exhausted observer, using the bare skeleton of
language to resist the seductions of metaphor, trying desperately
to find the right names for what he sees:

> What is it? a learned man
> Could give it a clumsy name.
> Let him name it who can,
> The beauty would be the same.   [II, 57–60]

Even in such bareness of statement, Tennyson, as usual, manages
artifice. The three sentences, though flat, and weighted with
monotony, are in different moods (interrogative, declarative, and
subjunctive); and the variations that follow are anything but
casual. The syntax becomes more and more primitive, with all the
urgency and flatness of hurried jottings. Stanza 4 drops its verbs,
and the series of adjectives—"Slight," "Small," "Frail"—cramp
the rhetoric into simple labeling. To keep from lapsing into
nightmare, the lover tries to sketch his relation to the shell in
brief notations. The meditation is described in a kind of puzzle-
poem; and despite the strict severity of means, the shell is
systematically transformed in several stages. At first, as a beautiful

curiosity, the shell is totally detached from the speaker: "What is it?" (II, 57); then, in its fragile hardihood, it is totally identi- fied with him: "Courage, poor heart of stone!" (II, 132). In between, despite the simply factual tone and the deliberate im- poverishment of metaphor, the shell is constantly being redefined. Like the exiled lover, the shell is another wrecked hulk on the Breton shore; and, like the ten stanzas in which it appears, the shell is also a "miracle of design," a microcosm of creation— God's, the poet's, the lover's. Finally, as an explosive cell of an embryo, like the individual frame in a movie—which Eisenstein, in fact, calls a "montage *cell*"[13]—the shell resembles the seminal lyric to Hallam in *Maud* (II, 141–144), the germ of creation around which the rest of the poem fashions itself in whorl-like design.

After the close-up of the shell—a combination of atrophy and hypersensitive perception, of unnatural intensity, painfully lucid, and of utter blur—Tennyson presents in a long shot the speaker's aimless odyssey through "drifts of lurid smoke" (II, 206). Though there is a spatial leap, as well as a leap from the natural to the supernatural, there is no change in tempo: Maud's "hard mechanic ghost" (II, 82) displays the same dogged rigor in scrutinizing the speaker as he himself has displayed in scrutiniz- ing the shell. But now the terror comes out in the Miltonic iciness of "That abiding phantom cold"[14]—a horror that is made to seem more terrible by the shade's omnipresence and by the artful in- adequacy of the speaker's psychological theory, by his attempt to dismiss the nightmare as "a juggle . . . of the brain" (II, 90). Finally, in the scene in the madhouse, the tempo speeds up: the speaker's fantasy of hearing the wheels above his head after he is buried imitates the earlier wheeling movements of the dance, the beating hooves of the brother's horses, and the quickened tempo of the speaker's pulse. Though he thinks he is dead, he still longs

13. Sergei Eisenstein, "The Cinematographic Principle and the Ideo- gram," in *Film Form: Essays in Film Theory*, p. 37.

14. Miltonic, because of the placing of the noun between two adjectives, a mannerism also common in Keats and Arnold.

for death, as Tithonus does; and his longing is endlessly thwarted.
Now the thoughts move forward in rushes, and the speaker's voice
keeps lapsing into rhyming fits of hysteria—fits that shape themselves into chainlike fragments: "Driving, hurrying, marrying,
burying" (II, 250) and multiple rhymes:

> For I thought the dead had peace, but it is not so;
>
> . . . . .
>
> But up and down and to and fro,
> Ever about me the dead men go.   [II, 253, 255–256]

Like Lady Macbeth's sleepwalking speech, the culminating
nightmare recalls and confuses earlier events. At first the lover
simply confuses the time references, blurring details of the father's
suicide and brother's death. Recalling opulent biblical and eastern
modes, the banal lyricism of the "music and flutes" (II, 314) and
"Sultan of brutes" (II, 319) sustains a rhythm of dreamlike confusion. But as the speaker blends images of red and white, sweet
scent and lips, which he had used earlier for both Maud and her
brother (I, 452), he discovers he can no longer keep his feelings
separate. Though the hallucinatory vision of roses as blood adds
to the horror and confusion, it also dramatizes an exchange between love and hatred, venegeance and compassion. Now the
hero replaces his taunts against Maud's father, "that gray old
wolf" (II, 291), with a finer, more searching irony: "For what
will the old man say / When he comes to the second corpse in the
pit?" (II, 325–326). Instead of denouncing the "wolf's" malig-
nity, the speaker feels sorry for the old man, and is moved to forgive him. The reversal represents that shocked condition, that
turning point in the poem, when love casts out fear and changes
horror into awe. There is a gentle lucidity in the hero's disordered
thoughts; his descent into madness is now propelled by an as-
cending leap from hate to love, vengeance to compassion, by a
new and unexpected power to feel pity.

When Maud appears to the lover in a last flash of beauty, "like
a silent lightning under the stars" (III, 9), her shadow no longer
pursues and torments him; the speaker is now in control of the

terror, no longer its victim. Such a change at the end of a long train of partial changes justifies everything that precedes. The lover, as if resentful of his own credulity in believing madness more real than sanity, despair more real than hope, reverts passionately to the great love visions that transformed his life. He learns a respect, at the end, for all versions of experience: for the claims of history and the claims of vision, for the harsh pressure of time resisting the pressure of man's longing for another world, for a volatile beauty of "lightning under the stars," beyond earth altogether.

Other poets might have decided that there is nowhere now for the hero to go. But the hero's vision of himself, standing on the "giant deck" of a ship (III, 34), has the same function as the appearance of Hallam's veiled statue in *In Memoriam*. In both cases Tennyson is trying to imagine what the hero will do with the rest of his life. The speaker's "belief" in war is melodramatic and defiant, the impulse of a moment—his exhortation to action is a strain to create new extremes of love and hate. Though he half mocks his own sensationalism, his cryptic reference to "a hope for the world" (III, 11) and his fabulous pursuit of some "dreary phantom . . . / Far into the North" (III, 36–37) are clearly millennial; the "giant liar" (III, 45) sounds like some apocalyptic beast, "Horrible, hateful, monstrous" (III, 41). Tennyson's efforts to render these transforming images as narrative action are clearly inadequate. The speaker tries to translate his despair into heroism, his fury into eloquence, the chaos of war into new forms of order; but like the speaker in "Locksley Hall," he is just inventing roles. The truth is that whatever happens after the transforming moments in the madhouse takes place beyond the poem we have, and probably beyond most poems. Literature provides few examples of completed encounters; the end of most discoveries is not expressible.

The poem's three visionary encounters—the ambiguous auroral vision (I, 88–101), the divine apparitions of Maud in the garden (I, 571–684), and the transforming nightmare in the madhouse (II, 151–342)—comprise a grand triadic sequence, analogous to

Carlyle's Everlasting No, Centre of Indifference, and Everlasting Yea. Like the three visionary encounters in *In Memoriam* (Sections LXVII–LXVIII, XCV, CIII), they bring the hero from a suicidal state, through reliance on a deliverer, to an extraordinary comprehension that love, philosophy, and politics are all concerned to fashion self-sufficiency—a free-standing spirit that can exorcise fear and morbidity. But beyond this bleak discovery lies a further vision, an appalling vision, one that is responsible for the hero's brutality as well as his compassion. Just as Hallam's death had seemed to Tennyson the suicide of God, so Maud's death throws the hero into a meaningless world, where anarchy is asserted with an ever enlarging incoherence. From the riot of social protest he passes through sensual riot to the perfect riot—or revelry—of madness. Originally, social injustice is identified with Maud's family, which provides the hero with a scapegoat. But once the brother behaves magnanimously the hero needs a new scapegoat; without a sustaining fiction, there is no longer any "order" to disorder, and he goes insane. In extravagant, exalted, terror-ridden rhetoric, the speaker is made to experience the essential anguish of man in time—the suffering from which the world tries in vain to tear each man away. Humbert Wolfe believes that *Maud* should dispel forever the myth that Tennyson is merely "the muffled poet of domestic horizons."[15] I believe we must go further. It is not enough to speak merely of Tennyson's wildness or ferocity; it is rather a matter of his sheer terror in the poem, his overriding fear of suicidal death—the fear which blackened the Somersby rectory—the fear of being deranged like his brother Septimus or of being driven literally insane like his brother Edward. T. S. Eliot complains that "the real feelings of Tennyson, profound and tumultuous as they are, never arrive at expression" in *Maud*. But the brilliant mixture of lyric and dramatic modes, which Eliot dismisses as "a fundamental error of form,"[16] provides Tennyson with just the right mixture of involve-

15. *Tennyson*, p. 55.
16. T. S. Eliot, "In Memoriam," in *Selected Essays* (London, 1932), pp. 332–333.

ment and detachment. Without the transforming, expressive power of lyric poetry and the cathartic power of drama, Tennyson would break down completely; it is difficult to see how he could write the poem at all.

The madhouse scene offers a glimpse into the terrifying universe in which the phantasmagoria, the whirl of events and images in *Maud,* is always on the point of being engulfed. Madness, however, has its own cathartic devices; one means of controlling events is the hero's sense of being possessed by the phantom. His feeling that the nightmare world is not his own world allows him to stay partly detached. Madness also makes possible that moment of renewal, that profound and moving turning point in the poem, when the hero learns to identify, like Lear, with the distress of other people. And if *Maud* has the cathartic power of tragic drama, it also has the transforming power of great lyric poetry. This power is implicit in the speaker's love for Maud; in his celebration of this love, largeness of diction and sanity become precious characteristics of an imaginative power that is in essence an empire—the empire of a sultan in some eastern paradise. Hence the grand adornment of his passion in the gorgeous language of the Song of Songs. The great lyrics are what Shakespeare in *Antony and Cleopatra* calls "the ostentation of our love,"[17] the opulent adornment of love and empire. In presenting the instinctive integrations of normal love and normal beauty, which are a feat of great imagination in the midst of much that is abnormal, no celebration can be too noble or too grand. Only after Tennyson has elevated love into forms of imperial and cosmic "ostentation," can he afford to reverse direction by dramatizing Maud's cry for vengeance and the hero's consignment to a madhouse. Insanity seems to be the dreadful price exacted for snatching beauty from the higher world. But even when Tennyson annihilates the grand illusion, he cannot undo its splendor.

17. III, vi, 52. Compare Tennyson's adornment of love with Shakespeare's "exercise in ostentation," particularly as analyzed by Kenneth Burke in "Shakespearean Persuasion: Antony and Cleopatra," in *Language as Symbolic Action* (Berkeley, Calif., 1968), pp. 101–114.

The hero discovers that if the ostentatious visions of the great love lyrics are illusions, they are illusions of transforming beauty that ennobles him. It is as if the insanity and violence that conspire against the marvelous visions at the center of *Maud* express the hero's own tragic fears about the vast pretentiousness of these visions, and so purge the fears and preserve the poem's transforming power intact.

6

Terror and Innocence:
Idylls of the King

It is no wonder that Tennyson can never weave *Maud*'s transforming visions into the fabric of time and human history. Nor can we expect him to bring the romantic ideals of Ida and the Prince into meaningful alignment with the social world of Vivianplace. Such ideals are inexpressible and point beyond the poems that Tennyson wrote, and perhaps beyond any poem. But having explored the conflict between thought and feeling, facts and values, in a variety of short poems, Tennyson is now prepared to turn more fully to panorama and to accept the severe and more harassing demands of a historical portrayal. With psychological insight worthy of *Maud* and *In Memoriam, Idylls of the King* first hides its darkest fears deep beneath decorative veils of Arthurian romance. But instead of doubling back into repression, or skipping out indefinitely into a wide array of disguises, these fears are finally forced to the surface and assimilated. Gareth's unmasking of the pasteboard giants of Night and Day is what Kenneth Burke would call the "representative anecdote," or "ideal synecdoche" of the *Idylls.*[1] The more terrifying each knight appears, the less formidable he proves when finally unmasked. Like the mourner in *In Memoriam,* the poet discovers that there is nothing behind the "lucid veil" that is not already in front of it. Just as the mourner finds himself reflected in the dead Hallam, so in *Idylls of the King* the mind finds mirrored in each of its adversar-

1. *"A Grammar of Motives"* and *"A Rhetoric of Motives"* (Cleveland, 1962), pp. 59–61, 508.

ies an image of itself. The mind is able to re-create itself, not by cutting off any impulses, but by constantly extending them. Instead of abandoning hope in order to be free from fear, *Idylls of the King* tries to bring into an active, if perilous, unity of terror and innocence, of nature and spirit, the many resources of the human person.

The Panoramic Stage

Idylls of the King is the saddest of all Tennyson's poems. The reader wants it to succeed completely, to achieve on the panoramic stage[2] of Arthurian romance what Tennyson was trying to achieve in the more personal poetry of *In Memoriam* and *Maud*—and in short poems such as "Lucretius," where a brilliant, though unsuccessful, attempt is made to hold facts and values together. Tennyson wants to believe that the highest ideal is most human, too, and that the hero can have power in the world, consolidating the kinds of universal value sought by Newman in religion, by Arnold in culture, and by Ruskin in art. *Idylls of the King* contains some of Tennyson's most ravishing lines, and some of his most austere and desolate poetry. But unable to resolve the double focus of history and vision, except momentarily in two idylls, the poem is the victim of its own duality. The anatomy of the saint and the soldier, the skeptic and the dupe, the sensualist and the stoic starts to decompose the poem, until its heroic ideal breaks down because of sheer inclusiveness and range.

Tennyson is most successful in restoring the sundered fragments, and in achieving the final unity of nature and spirit, in two idylls: "The Holy Grail" and "The Passing of Arthur." To evaluate their achievement we must briefly trace the process of sundering, which begins as early as the opening idyll. According

2. Any panoramic view or theory of unified development in the *Idylls* is partly qualified, however, by the thirty-year composition of the work and by the fragmentary publication. On the other hand, the eighteen-year composition of *In Memorian* has not prevented studies of that poem from finding in it a coherent development. On unifying devices in the *Idylls* see, in the Bibliographical Essay, below, pp. 328–329.

to Whitehead, religion is "something which is real, and yet waiting to be realised; . . . something that gives meaning to all that
passes, and yet eludes apprehension."[3] Conceived as real, but
waiting to be realized, Arthur's mission is an *imitatio Christi:* a
mandate to marry spirit to the world, to make eternal values
dwell in time and history. But as the narrator's lofty speculations
about Arthur's status yield to the violence of war, the opening
ease of narrative—"made a realm, and reigned" (l. 19)—is never
recovered. Without the aid of "Powers who walk the world" (l.
106) Arthur, like Spenser's Redcrosse Knight, is lost in "throes
and agonies" (l. 75). The extremes of human frailty subject the
Romantic-Pelagian myth, the doctrine of the innate goodness of
man, to the same scrutiny to which the Augustinian rigor of
Spenser's Puritanism subjects the more gracious and accom-
modating theology of Richard Hooker.

As skeptical scrutiny increases, not even the fancifully charming
marriage of the mighty Sun to the white bride of May (ll. 481,
496) is safe from questioning. When the marriage figure is extended to include the alliance of "The heathen hordes" (l. 518)
under the conquering war lord, loving union is confused with despotism and with the prostitution of Rome, "the slowly fading
mistress" (l. 504). The very idea of marriage seems headed for
ruin. The fullest shock comes with the discovery that there is a
worse terror in the poem than defeat in war. Arthur's fear that his
union of mind and nature is still only a willed union, not a necessary and intrinsic one, alerts him to a potential solipsism in the
operations of his mind, and to a sense of being alone in a solitude,
a feeling of desertion nothing can relieve. The idealist's view may
be bracing, but it can ignore essential detail; as "The Holy
Grail" shows, it can also fasten too exclusively on distant objects.
As the tenuous union of heaven and earth, equivocally affirmed
at the wedding and briefly glimpsed in Merlin's riddle and
Leodogran's dream, is slowly lost to view, the way is opened in
the rest of the *Idylls* to a vision resembling Yeats's vision of center-

3. A. N. Whitehead, "Religion and Science," in *Science and the Modern
World,* ch. xii (New York, 1925), pp. 191–192.

less proliferation: "Things fall apart; the centre will not hold; /
Mere anarchy is loosed upon the world" (Yeats, "The Second
Coming," ll. 3–4).

As Arthur's heroism is refracted in successive idylls through the
idealism of Gareth and Balin and the innocence of Enid and
Elaine, the double focus of nature and spirit, terror and innocence, begins to tilt further and further out of balance. There is an
increasing emphasis on the darkening human foreground, the
Hegelian "slaughter-bench" of history.[4] In "Gareth and Lynette"
terror is no longer a contrived effect—the product of a waxwork
museum of Gothic horrors, peopled by monsters like the primordial Earl Doorm. The greatest threat to Arthur's ideal is now not
the world's but the mind's defects: the private horrors of a mind
diseased. The worst form of terror is Frost's shocking truth: "I
have it in me so much nearer home / To scare myself with my
own desert places" ("Desert Places," ll. 15–16). Gareth is still
the Chaplinesque victim of great hoaxes and absurd reversals.
But in later idylls Tennyson can no longer jokingly mute the
horror, as Frost does, nor can he mask the terror as he does in
"Gareth and Lynette" or, with less discreet irony, in the near
tragedy of Enid. One by one, as the betrayers of Arthur emerge,
their qualities are immortalized as potentialities of every heart
and mind. Guinevere, Vivien, and Lancelot are forces that range
the world, familiar and untamed, unpredictable and many
faceted. They elicit that rueful reaction of recognition and revulsion, pity and fear, which, without abolishing moral judgment,
creates powerful sympathy for them.

This mixture of identification and revulsion makes "Balin and
Balan," the next idyll, though the last to be written (1872–1873),
one of the most unforgettable and disquieting. Arthur's attempts
to assuage the isolation of the mind are reflected in the ascetic

4. G. W. F. Hegel, *Introduction to the Philosophy of History*, in *Hegel
Selections*, ed. J. Loewenberg (New York, 1929), p. 365: "But even regarding History as the slaughter-bench at which the happiness of peoples,
the wisdom of States, and the virtue of individuals have been victimised—
the question involuntarily arises—to what principle, to what final aim these
enormous sacrifices have been offered."

Balin's involuntary shudder as he recoils in horror from the rank-
ness of the world. Balin's deathbed defense of the guilty Guinevere,
who he still insists is innocent, is one of the fictions of madness.
Founded on a noble hypothesis, like the grand hallucinations of
the lover in *Maud,* its nakedness and solitude are a parody of the
mind's supremacy, far more horrifying distortions of the truth
than the merely selfish delusions of the raddled Geraint. As the
poem gropes toward exhausted repetition, the repetition without
progress of earlier episodes imitates the dreadful monotony with
which the thoughts of the insane—urgent but shapeless—seem
fated to recur. For example, the two accounts of the enigmatic
spear that was "Shot from behind" and "ran along the ground"
(ll. 318, 369)', are unincremental. The more violent their impingements, the less meaningful they become. The imbalance of a
disordered mind is also reflected in the structural asymmetry between the few lines in which Balin painfully anatomizes private
horrors and the many passages in which he hysterically defends
the Queen. The outbursts of self-contempt become a play on
indefinite pronouns, articles, and tautologies; and in spite of the
general structure of imbalance, a bizarre symmetry occurs between the violently willed refusals to "see . . . what [he] see[s]"
(l. 276) and the deadly accuracy of his self-abuse. Causal patterns are elaborated with insane precision, with symmetries worthy
of a mad logician.

   The horror of discovery is at first too traumatic to permit detachment. It is expressed in fragmented questions—"Queen? subject?" (l. 276); "Damsel and lover?" (l. 277)—which are quickly
distanced by two tautologies. X is not X is the simplest form of
contradiction: the anguished denial of the principle of identity
is an infantile attempt to leave horror unnamed, indefinite, and
obscure. Like Troilus' desperate faith in Cressida's innocence—
"If there be rule in unity itself, / This is not she" (Shakespeare,
Troilus and Cressida, V, ii, 141–142)—the abstractions of logic
are a stay against confusion. The eye refuses to dart closer to the
adulteress in an attempt to define its horror, but retreats into indefinite pronouns and articles: "the things before me" (l. 279);

"A churl, a clown" (l. 281). At first Balin carefully qualifies the epithets of self-abuse with indefinite articles. But as the moments of internal scrutiny began to tilt out of balance, with almost no time given to the horrifying memory of the garden, Balin focuses more and more precisely on his own responsibility, until its relation to his memory becomes grotesquely causal. The reversal of elements—"I have shamed thee so that now thou shamest me" (l. 425)—makes misdirected rationalism culminate in a logic of madness, as unbalanced rhetoric turns into chiastic parody of balance. For Tennyson, as for Samuel Butler, "extremes are alone logical, and they are always absurd."[5] The mean alone is sane, and as a postulate of faith its truth is always more than rational.

Each shift of emphasis, from the niceties of Balin's logic to the despair of madness, from his assumption of moral guilt to the abdication of his humanity, is balanced by a contrary shift in the articles and pronouns describing the Queen. When the first-person pronouns are most precise, the Queen herself retreats from view; Balin addresses her indirectly through a metonymic substitute, her crown royal. But the two motions of Balin's mind, his exaltation of the Queen and his own fearful decline, are mirror images of each other. As first-person pronouns drop away, Guinevere comes into sharp focus for the first time. Only when Balin sinks into indefiniteness, into the rigidities of madness and the tedium of rage, can the "beast whose anger was his lord" (l. 481) bear to substitute for his fragmented questions and metonyms Guinevere's proper name (l. 482). Through the haze of total madness comes his one lucid reference to Lancelot and the Queen.

The true revulsion of the reader comes from the inevitable exhaustion suffered by the mind when it tries to sustain its dignity in defiance of nature. Revolted by the ostentatious lustiness of the world, Balin's mind cannot be assuaged. When Vivien destroys its last protective fictions, its nobility becomes expendable, and

5. Samuel Butler, *The Way of All Flesh* (New York, 1967), pp. 310–311: "This is illogical, but extremes are alone logical, and they are always absurd; the mean is alone practicable and it is always illogical. It is faith and not logic which is the supreme arbiter."

shatters grotesquely in a riot of primitivism. Grinding teeth and
animal yells shockingly repudiate the mind's hypotheses. Balin's
too subtle evasions of the world make unavoidable his maniacal
destruction of the crown royal. But his renunciation is disastrous,
a blunt confrontation of mind and body; and the clashes of emotion allow Balin no trace of dignity. Even his passion for oracular
statement—"Dark my doom was here, and dark / It will be
there" (ll. 612–613)—is disallowed, checked by the irony of his
last sustaining fiction. As the mind turns despairingly on its
visions, and rejects them in disgust, its paeans to purity collapse in
shattered fragments.

Tennyson's vision continues to darken in the sinister intimations and playful vagaries of the next idyll, "Merlin and Vivien"
(1859). Vivien's song to Merlin (ll. 385–396) begins, surprisingly, not as a transparent deception, but as a charming plea for
trust.

> "In Love, if Love be Love, if Love be ours,
> Faith and unfaith can ne'er be equal powers:
> Unfaith in aught is want of faith in all.
>
> "It is the little rift within the lute,
> That by and by will make the music mute,
> And ever widening slowly silence all.
>
> "The little rift within the lover's lute
> Or little pitted speck in garnered fruit,
> That rotting inward slowly moulders all.
>
> "It is not worth the keeping: let it go:
> But shall it? answer, darling, answer, no.
> And trust me not at all or all in all."

Sinister hints are embraced by the querulous phrasing, by the
infectious whirl and giddiness of her insistent rhymes. There is a
touch of biblical logic—or illogic—in her equation of "Unfaith in
aught" with "want of faith in all"; a flicker of humor in the
"little rift"; and a tinge of grossness in the rotting fruit. The
magical, almost incantatory, manipulation of a few charged
words—"Love," "Faith," "rift," and "lute"—rings slight changes

on the argument in each triad. The blurring of grammatical reference in the first word of the last stanza marks a final wavering. It
prepares for the false disjunction of the last line, which hinges on
three grammatical uses of the same word—as intensive ("not at
all"), as adverb ("trust me . . . all [or wholly]"), and as pronoun: ("in all"). Despite the charm of the beginning, there is a
hardness in Vivien's tone. The same rhyme words, and the same
rasping dentals, keep grating on the ear. Though studiously intimate, Vivien is also mercilessly aloof—an icy siren betrayed by the
overpitch of her song.

The lines in "Merlin and Vivien" identified by Christopher
Ricks as "the finest"[6] in the *Idylls* show Tennyson's grammar
struggling delicately with the problem of suspending outcomes:

> So dark a forethought rolled about his brain,
> As on a dull day in an Ocean cave
> The blind wave feeling round his long sea-hall
> In silence. [ll. 228–231]

By twisting the ocean cave against the caverns of the skull the
simile allays the fear of probing the mind's darkest places. The
suspension works on two counts: because the blind groping of the
wave, drifting through spacious rhymes and assonances, allows
the mind's probing to undergo a sea change; and because the
grammar itself leaves its objects drifting. The syntax presents dark
ocean—an impressionistic fusion of blindness, wave, and feeling—
and spaciousness and silence. "Blind wave," we expect, will be
the subject of a principal verb, but the predicate never comes. Instead, the rare sea impressions are left echoing in their ocean
depths, sounding there forever. There is no point in claiming that
the difficulty of the syntax is a result of ellipsis: "When the blind
wave is feeling." The point is simply that Tennyson is fusing his
sense impressions to make sightless liquidity seem tactile and solid.
A principal verb would restore the suspended sea impressions to
the temporal world. In its absence the grammatical fragments
fluctuate before us like deep-sea film shots. The absolute construc-

6. *Tennyson* (New York, 1972), p. 276.

tion, working with the finality of the last phrase—"In silence"—
enacts the sense of endlessly drifting. The simile, like the wave,
dissolves its unity, falling apart into a nominative absolute and
three prepositional phrases. Tennyson allows Merlin to float out
of his cavernous skull on the same flow of fragments that leave
the grammar floating in space, with no syntactic links.

The next idyll, "Lancelot and Elaine" (1859), darkens and
complicates the tragedy of innocence. The product of loneliness
and rejection, Elaine's plaintive melody (ll. 1000–1011) has its
own curious sophistry, its own riddling plainness and self-created
torment. If love is sweet, Elaine urges, then death must be bitter
(l. 1003). The hypothetical form suggests a logical conversion,
which the syntactic device of repeating a word the other way
round locks into a chiastic vise: $X\ Y\ Y\ X$. But Elaine proceeds to
perform the conversion in an invalid mood: a denial of the
antecedent logically entails no denial of the consequent.

> 'Sweet is true love though given in vain, in vain;
> And sweet is death who puts an end to pain:
> I know not which is sweeter, no, not I.
>
> 'Love, art thou sweet? then bitter death must be:
> Love, thou art bitter; sweet is death to me.
> O Love, if death be sweeter, let me die.
>
> 'Sweet love, that seems not made to fade away,
> Sweet death, that seems to make us loveless clay,
> I know not which is sweeter, no, not I.
>
> 'I fain would follow love, if that could be;
> I needs must follow death, who calls for me;
> Call and I follow, I follow! let me die.'   [ll. 1000–1011]

If love is bitter, it does not follow that death, the opposite of love
and life, is inherently less bitter. The illogical patterns, which
subtly confuse the harsh permanence of "loveless clay" with the
endurance of "Sweet love," give the poetry an unsettling coherence, a confused lucidity like that of the mad stanzas in *Maud*.
The recurrence of the hypothetical constructions—"if death be
sweeter"; "if that could be"—maintains the impression that the

song is proceeding as logically as it begins. Even as death begins
to call, and logic breaks down, rhetorical coherence continues in
force. Elaine sees death, not simply as the opposite of love, which
it is, but as a fixity of negative duration, as something that is
sweeter and more permanent than love, too.

Lancelot's wrench of agony does nothing to lessen his victim's
pain, or to make her death less pathetic. But Elaine is the first
victim to involve, not just herself, but her destroyer, also, in
tragedy. The Victorian master of moral ambiguity is Browning.
Unlike the poet of "The Statue and the Bust," Tennyson is
usually too staunch a moralist to criticize, even obliquely, the
moral norms of his age. Yet one feels in reading Tennyson, as one
feels in reading writers as diverse as Henry James and Dante,
that his moral imagination in his poetry is richer and more generous than his moral judgments in life. Nowhere does Tennyson, the
Victorian moralist, balance his understanding with greater charity
or poise of mind than in his portrayal of the two adulterers
Lancelot and Guinevere. A fine example of Tennyson's moral
ambiguity is Arthur's observation at the end of "Lancelot and
Elaine" that Lancelot is, "as I think, / Unbound as yet, and
gentle, as I know" (ll. 1374–1375). Though Lancelot may half
suspect an ironic intent, there is nothing else in Arthur's cordial
address to suggest it. If we take "Unbound" at face value, then
we are denied the melodramatic satisfaction of pitying the heroine
and punishing the villain. What confronts us is something more
absurd and anguished, a tragedy that involves Lancelot just as
deeply as his victim. In his interview with Guinevere it is clear
that Lancelot can never be "bound" to the Queen in the way he
might have been bound to Elaine. Lancelot's concluding soliloquy
makes us fully aware of what Lancelot's betrayal of Arthur has
done to himself ("Mine own name shames me, seeming a re-
proach" [l. 1392]), but it makes us aware as a matter of moral
experience, not of moral judging. The humanity we share with
Lancelot makes us partners in his terror and remorse. Because
Lancelot's love is never bound through service to a wife, part of
his own tragedy is that he never will be free. As the theodicy of

the seer gives way to the anguish of the mad Ophelia, suffering is too oppressively real, too unnecessary and evitable, as Thomas Hardy would insist, even to be explained as unexplainable. Not until "The Holy Grail" (published in 1869) does Tennyson begin to express nature in terms of spirit and spirit in terms of nature, and to make of both elements a final unity.

"The Holy Grail"

This grand poem, which robes itself in the deathly magnificence of the auroras, is Tennyson's most dazzling achievement in visionary writing. The young visionary of "Timbuctoo" resists in vain the undertow of waves that drown his mind in cones of "diamond light" (l. 164). And almost at the end of his career, in "Merlin and the Gleam," the poet pursues an *ignis fatuus* with the same icy glow and recoils from its cruel if gorgeous will-to-change, just as Tithonus recoils from the cold rose shadows of Aurora. As fire, the flickering light is dangerous, and as part of the void, it is cold and terrifying. But changeful light is also innocent. And "The Holy Grail" uses its innocence to allay the terror and to resolve in the light's great gusts and colored sweeps the simultaneous fear and fascination of "the great deep" beyond. In poetry of sublime transformation that forms the radiant center of the *Idylls,* Tennyson creates a volatile world of vertiginous light, alive with mystery, yet deathly, inhuman, weirdly veiled.

To dramatize *In Memoriam*'s truth of the "lucid veil," the truth that the supernatural must half reveal and half conceal its presence, Tennyson places between ourselves and the visions a succession of human filters, ranging from the simple minded Ambrosius, through the more enlightened Percivale, to the visionary genius Sir Galahad himself. In the earlier "Sir Galahad" (September, 1834) the hero hears the "gentle" rustling "sound" which, in the experience of many observers, accompanies the aurora's "awful light" (l. 41).

> When down the stormy crescent goes,
>   A light before me swims,
> Between dark stems the forest glows,
>   I hear a noise of hymns.   [ll. 25–28]

As Galahad receives his vision of three angels bearing the Holy Grail and passing along striped arcs of the display, the "Pure spaces" of the northern sky majestically "clothe" themselves in the "living beams" of an aurora whose rays give the appearance of a large curtain or drapery (ll. 47, 66). In "The Holy Grail," a similar musical sound accompanies the visions of Percivale's sister, who is kept beautifully poised between heaven and earth by the lavish but inhuman "rosy quiverings" (l. 123). The rapid fluctuations of chill, flickering light, even when the gleams are not specifically auroral, help keep Galahad and Lancelot suspended. The movement of both their quests is an uncertain ascent, accompanied by dizzying sweeps and surges of volatile light. When Sir Bors receives his vision, the rosy sparkles of the rayed aurora flicker "like the fingers of a hand" in candlelight (l. 690). Because Lancelot does not understand the limits of human strength, his less distinct vision of the Holy Grail is "palled" like an auroral drapery in "crimson samite" (l. 844). Percivale, in contrast, who preaches the paradox of strength through humility, which he identifies with the mystery of Incarnation, when Christ "made Himself '/ Naked of glory for His mortal change" (ll. 447–448), has a splendid auroral vision of "the spiritual city and all her spires" (l. 526)—a vision that makes us aware of the ordinary but important sense in which an autumn night in England may become a fitting receptacle for the light and fire of heaven.

> and straight beyond the star
> I saw the spiritual city and all her spires
> And gateways in a glory like one pearl—
> No larger, though the goal of all the saints—
> Strike from the sea; and from the star there shot
> A rose-red sparkle to the city, and there
> Dwelt, and I knew it was the Holy Grail,
> Which never eyes on earth again shall see.   [ll. 525–532]

The knight who understands most fully the connection between his "prowess" and his "sins" is Sir Galahad. Though Galahad's motivating energies are pointedly magical and reminiscent of Merlin's, his glistening mail also emphasizes his human powers.

Galahad's courage helps him cross the swamp. Yet the crossing is also supernatural, for once the bridge is behind him it vanishes in fire. And now, to the accompaniment of the thundering heavens and the shouting "sons of God" (l. 509), a crucial change occurs. As Galahad becomes part of the cosmic setting, human effort passes from Galahad to the narrator, Sir Percivale, and also to the reader, who have to work at the height of their powers to keep pace with the vision. Achievement in the past is no guarantee of Galahad's continued advance. In every moment Galahad must begin again and create himself anew. The parity of the demonic lightnings that lick the rotting trunks and the fiery light that bathes Galahad coldly as he flees along the thousand piers prevents even the saint's quest from being clearly one-directional. Until the "rose-red sparkle" finally ascends to the spiritual city the transformations of the fiery light remain deathly and ambiguous. The surrealistic apparition of the blazing heavens and reddening Grail is startling, part of Percivale's terrified response to the volatile fire that imitates in its magnificent coruscations the spiritual change in Galahad.

Percivale opens with a deceptive affirmation of total vision: "and first / At once I saw" (ll. 509–510). But he immediately qualifies the statement with hypothetical clauses and negative constructions: "If boat it were—I saw not whence it came" (l. 515). The sequence of present participles—"Roaring" (l. 517); "Opening" (l. 524)—implies that the miracle is now taking place. Yet the distancing through simile—"like a silver star" (l. 517)—and the uncertainty of the repeated questions—"had he set the sail, or had the boat / Become a living creature?" (ll. 518–519)—continue to veil the outcome for another seven lines. Then the star yields a vision of the spiritual city and the accomplished miracle of the Grail's simultaneous appearance and withdrawal. When the Grail draws near, it does so in the symbols of the sacred. But symbols soon turn into idols, and the Grail must fade—so that the symbols may live.

Though Percivale is narrating past events, his visions center the mind on the present; they do not drift nostalgically back in time, or press prophetically forward. Composed of Tennyson's most congenial subjects—illusion, flux, self-concealment, and withdrawal—the passing of Galahad is a magnificent whorl of pulsating growth and contraction. It is built of vertiginous waves of half-glanced lights and veilings. Visions of "a living creature clad with wings" and of "the least of little stars / Down on the waste" (ll. 519, 524–525) rise and fall on the billows of an antiphonal rhetoric that floods both heaven and earth with tides of grandeur (ll. 516–536).

had he set the sail	or had the boat / Become a living creature
No larger	though the goal of all the saints
it was the Holy Grail	Then fell the floods of heaven
No memory in me lives	but that I touched / The chapel-doors . . . I know;

The splendor of the Holy Grail, solidified like the "gateways" of the New Jerusalem "in a glory like one pearl," but made fluid in form like a "rose-red sparkle," tenuous as a veil and strangely shimmering, is the splendor of Percivale's terrified response as he finds himself caught up in the luminous glow "on the great Sea" (l. 510), absorbed into gusts of light as startling and ephemeral as shooting stars, and of constantly shifting shape. Like the climax of *In Memoriam,* this is the height of all thinking, the height of all poetic thinking: the attempt of the soul, lost in nature, to find a gathering metaphor that will throw into shape and order its broken world.

When Galahad is absorbed into this volatile realm, he is no longer in a position to consider himself a child of light or merely a civilized supporter of Camelot. He is saved from becoming blanched and void, like "the great . . . swamp . . . / Part black, part whitened" (ll. 499–500), both by his own efforts and by grace—the ravishing light of the "spiritual city." "The Holy Grail" ends with a mixed view of the New Jerusalem—part admiring, part critical. The appetite for visions may become more gross than the appetite for nature, because in some knights it may

be more insatiable. Tennyson keeps the appetites for heaven and
earth "corrected": their interaction is, above all, balanced. The
end deliberately approaches tautology on two occasions: "I saw /
That which I saw" (ll. 847–848); "Ye have seen what ye have
seen" (l. 915). But in each case Tennyson qualifies that simplest
of rhetorical figures: first, by introducing the hypothetical "me-
thought I saw" (l. 843) and by adding that the vision is "veiled"
(l. 848); and, then, by prefacing the final tautology with a whole
series of formulaic rejections of tautology: earth is not earth,
light is not light, air is not air, but vision.

> and many a time they come,
> Until this earth he walks on seems not earth,
> This light that strikes his eyeball is not light,
> This air that smites his forehead is not air
> But vision—yea, his very hand and foot—
> In moments when he feels he cannot die,
> And knows himself no vision to himself,
> Nor the high God a vision, nor that One
> Who rose again.   [ll. 907–915]

"Until" is a conjunction of implicit futurity. But Arthur presents his conjectures about the future, first as a hypothesis—
"seems not earth"—and then as a series of eternal truths narrated
as a timeless event in the present. Though hidden from most
knights, the vision of "the high God" is scaled to the cosmos. It
is bigger than history, and as relevant to the future as it is to the
past. When Arthur's mind recognizes its own supremacy, then it
can confidently assert its right to refer to X, Y, and Z, not as X,
Y, and Z, but as A, where A equals the mind itself and its visionary power. The daring equation does not produce solipsism, for
the mind has now left behind its pathetic fallacies and illusions.
Proclaiming that the mind's visions participate in the power of
"the high God" and "One / Who rose again" (ll. 914–915), the
statements become grandly assertive for the first time. By introducing "the high God" only after expressing, first tentatively and
then with full assurance, the severe negations about "earth,"
"light" and "air," Arthur can fill out in gradually expanding vi-

sion the shrunken dimensions of life in his "allotted field" (l. 904).
In this way he validates the great assertion of Hegel that outside
of spirit there is not, and cannot be, any reality.

Yet indirection continues in force. Arthur's puzzling summation, "ye have seen what ye have seen" (l. 915), leaves Percivale
mystified. If Arthur is referring merely to the knights' visions of
the Grail, the statement would be redundant, or at best clumsy.
But the phrase is a poetic stroke essential to "the high God's"
appearance (l. 914), not simply as a *deus ex machina,* but as
evidence of the reader's own capacity to see. The phrase "what
ye have seen" extends and complicates the double value of disclosure and disguise by continuing the reader's involvement in
the great enterprise of maintaining faith in the Grail as a sacred
symbol, resisting at the same time the temptation to profane the
sacred, to turn the unknowable into an idolatrous object.

Tennyson's real triumph is not in being unequivocally visionary,
but in finding a tone at once celebratory and restrained, where
the climax is also the assertion of anticlimax: "So spake the
King: I know not all he meant" (l. 916). The celestial climaxes
of Galahad are unsuited to the ironies of earth; and Tennyson
uses the narrators, Ambrosius and Percivale, to tame the visions
into new decorum. The visionary mind must not annihilate the
world but must do to minds of the world as it would be done by,
according to a policy of tolerance and concession. "The Holy
Grail" demands of its heroes a continuous high-wire act of the
mind, as it demands of the reader or of anyone who wants to be,
not in possession of, but possessed by, the truth. Galahad has to
generate a storm within Camelot, welcoming it as the very condition of his life. And Arthur has to prevent the absurdity at the
heart of holiness, at the explosive center of every transformation
by the sacred, from destroying the city. If the heavenly city is
beyond knowing, the corruption of Camelot is beyond belief.
Arthur's "allotted field" may not be heaven, but it is as close to
heaven as any flaring New Jerusalem adored by the visionary.
Idylls of the King is at once torn and animated by the imponder-
able pressure of two great forces: an early Victorian faith in

progress, which imagines a New Jerusalem on earth; and evangelical theology's profound apprehension of the soul's worthless-
ness before God. But, momentarily, "The Holy Grail's" austere
and ravishing visions resolve the double focus of terror and hope.
They reconcile Galahad's mandate as a knight of the infinite
with the sanctions of Arthur, which are those of earthly heroism.
If the attempt to make the final unity cannot be sustained, it is
still, as Frost declares, "the greatest attempt that ever failed. We
stop just short there. But it is the height of poetry."[7]

One of the profoundest conflicts in early Victorian culture, and
one of the profoundest puzzles in *The Faerie Queene,* the great
Arthurian poem by Spenser, is the claim on man of nature and
grace, of the earthly and heavenly cities. When Arthur helps God
in his struggle, even when he knows the end will be God's defeat,
he rises to an extreme of human heroism. With this lowering of
God, his religion seems to have been heightened. Is Mill, then,
right? Must we admit the imperfection of God in order to save
religion?[8] Tennyson knows that the demand for theoretical consistency mutilates the substance of religion. He shows that in the
exaltation of Galahad, religion also provides the satisfying assurance that God is good. It is simply not true that with the lowering
of God religion has been heightened. Galahad's God belittles
Camelot, and Arthur's stress on the practical struggle opens a

7. "Education by Poetry," in *Selected Prose of Robert Frost,* ed. H. Cox
and E. Lathem (New York, 1968), p. 41.

8. John Stuart Mill, "Nature," in *Three Essays on Religion,* in *Collected
Works of John Stuart Mill,* ed. J. M. Robson, X (Toronto, 1969), 389–
390: "Not even on the most distorted and contracted theory of good which
ever was framed by religious or philosophical fanaticism, can the govern-
ment of Nature be made to resemble the work of a being at once good and
omnipotent. . . . The only admissible moral theory of Creation is that
the Principle of Good CANNOT at once and altogether subdue the powers
of evil, either physical or moral. . . . There is no subject on which men's
practical belief is more incorrectly indicated by the words they use to
express it, than religion. . . . But those who have been strengthened in
goodness by relying on the sympathizing support of a powerful and good
Governor of the world, have, I am satisfied, never really believed that
Governor to be, in the strict sense of the term, omnipotent. They have
always saved his goodness at the expense of his power."

dualism by which the universe is in principle torn apart. Whereas blind devotion to theoretical consistency involves either greater inconsistency, or else the mutilation of religion, the contradictory attitudes of "The Holy Grail" provide a useful mythology. Unless religion is to lose large realms of what is beautiful and sublime, it must, like Tennyson, generously balance the rival claims of Arthur and Galahad. It must explore all sides, without indignity to any attitude, with charity—and yet with the same "rigorous logic," the same "eternal microscope" that evangelical theology used, in G. M. Young's phrase, to pursue "its argument into the recesses of the heart."[9] As the terror of destructive fire and the innocence of changeful light finally blend, absorbed into transforming flame, Tennyson celebrates in poetry of sublime vision, beyond tragic fear and pity, the heroic ideals of both Arthur and Galahad.

Recantation and Renewal

But Tennyson cannot rest in sublimity, and in the following idyll, "Pelleas and Ettarre" (1869), the mind of the idealist turns upon itself in cruel reflexiveness. Pelleas' inability to dominate the violence of nature anticipates Arthur's great recantation at the end of the *Idylls*. The mind's supremacy can no longer assert itself, but confronts the terror "so fearfully yet exactly described in the Apostle's words," as Newman records, " 'having no hope and without God in the world.' "[10] Pelleas' broken syntax and asides—"hiss, snake—I saw you there— / Let the fox bark, let the wolf yell" (ll. 462–463)—evoke the psychological horror of being surprised on all sides. In the loathings of Pelleas' diction, violence is done to language by hysterical apostrophes, fragmented questions, and disordered catalogues, all jumbled together in a sexual flinching and intense revulsion from the body. Tennyson invites the reader to contemplate in Pelleas a terrible potentiality of all human love: "I loathe her, as I loved her to my

9. *Victorian England: Portrait of an Age* (London, 1936), p. 2.
10. John Henry Newman, *Apologia pro Vita Sua*, ed. David J. DeLaura (New York, 1968), ch. v, p. 187.

shame" (l. 474). The use of like-sounding words close together—
"loved," "looked," "lusted"—disintegrates the syntax by locking
words of opposite sense into parallel positions. The knight's emotions are the potentialities and disappointments of all human feeling, not just of lust, corrupt passion, or disintegrating minds.

When we compare "The Last Tournament" (written from
1869 to 1872) with more successful idylls such as "The Holy
Grail" or "The Passing of Arthur," we see that the partial failure
of "The Last Tournament" is a failure to use enough indirection.
The idyll discloses a ravaged nobility, the solitude and majesty of
an immense ruin. The gravely alliterated doubling—"gloom and
gleam," "shower and shorn plume" (l. 155)—is a familiar feature of Tennyson's style. The trouble is that "contrived" is a more
accurate description of the idyll than it ought to be. The last
tournament is a secularized doomsday, but instead of fulfilling our
expectations in arresting ways, its doom is predetermined, foreseen from the start. The constant use of similes predictably dis-
tances the last tournament, presenting it archaeologically in
another country—in the bleak luster of a dying feudal rite. The
energies of repudiation are seldom more clearly willed than in the
terrifying motions of the twisting snakes or the surrealist swoops
of the birds of prey, dehumanized through simile into vultures of
remorse, circling and shrieking round Lancelot's head. Malice is
protracted by present participles into horrors of "swording,"
"Whitening," "flying" and "glooming down" (ll. 472, 464, 139,
215). Metonymies brutally butcher language, chopping bodies
into naked throats and sensual lips, into ungainly crane legs and
a hanged man's swinging neck. As we might expect, the syntax
even parodies the Miltonic device of framing a noun between two
heroic attributes. Crushing the proper noun "Mordred" between
two debased phrases—"vermin in its hole" and "narrow face"
(ll. 165–166)—the appositions swallow up his ugly evocation in
a surge of disgust. Tristram, the chief villain of "The Last
Tournament," wants to enact the heroic, the dignified, the complete. But in the rhetorician's hand he becomes a mere puppet,
forced to enact the melodramatic, the absurd, the incomplete.

Crude, elliptical jottings render Tristram primordial and idiotic: "Whom Lancelot knew, had held sometime with pain / His own against him" (ll. 178–179). Who is the subject of the principal verb, "had held," Lancelot or Tristram? The momentary confusion is the result of a Latinism, based on the relative pronoun *quem*, for which the English accusative "him" is an inadequate substitute. With the blurring of references, even the grammar becomes barbarous; and the fatuous iteration of the proper name— "Sir Tristram of the Woods" (l. 177)—mocks predictably his dull conceit.

With temporary indirection, Tennyson presents Arthur's moment of truth, not in the grand, elegiac style of "The Passing," but in the short, piercing style of the Fool's riddles. Though the Fool's mockery has its gentler side, and allows for new nostalgia, his short, pregnant outbursts are cruel and stringent—the bare, fatal shorthand of necessity. Unfortunately, from the barrenness of ruin Tennyson, the eloquent rhetorician, is lulled into describing the glittering beauties of ruin. To blunt the terror, he forgets the Fool's truths, and wraps the bare style in debilitated grandeur. Whether the Victorian moralist is describing the spectacular murder of Tristram or the opulence of barbarous surfeit, of fountains running blood instead of wine, his efforts to discredit the hedonist, Tristram, are frantically willed. In "Aylmer's Field" the solemn gravities of ruin work more obliquely. Like the obliterating triumphs of Pope's Ceres (*Moral Essays*, "Epistle IV: To Richard Boyle, Earl of Burlington," ll. 175–176), they wisely leave moral judgment to the reader. Pope's "Deep Harvests," like Sir Aylmer's "open field," compose a noble epitaph triumphantly mocking aristocratic waste. But in "The Last Tournament" the moral never seems to run itself, nor does it carry the poet away with it. Instead of unfolding by surprise as it goes, Tennyson's moral is imposed. And the more portentous he sounds, the less assured he seems. The rhetorician is trying to put a manageable mask on the void. He is trying to throttle terror by turning tragedy into melodrama, giving decay a meretricious glow.

Tennyson is more successful in the penultimate idyll, "Guine-

vere" (1859), where he dramatizes the last vanquished energies
of love and faith, now exhausted in a depleted marriage. Confining the narrative to Arthur's point of view would encourage
melodrama. It would invite the reader to celebrate Arthur's
virtue and detest Guinevere's villainy, as he detests Tristram's.
But because the story is told from Guinevere's point of view
nothing either Arthur or Guinevere can say is able to neutralize
the morally unintelligible nature of their suffering. Arthur's light
is pitiless, showing Guinevere to herself as she is, not as she wants
to be considered. But are we to blame Guinevere, in her protective twilight, for not falling in love with the sun? The same
capacity to see events from two points of view informs Guinevere's
dual eulogy of Lancelot and Arthur, which is remarkable for its
ability to hold conflicting values in balance. Without any sense of
contradiction, the Queen brings out elements of strength in both
men—capacities for confidence, nobility, and graciousness to
women (ll. 325–334). Guinevere clearly apprehends and keeps
in poise the two moral perspectives, "the fruit / Of loyal nature,
and of noble mind" (ll. 333–334), largely because of her parallel
syntax and her repetition of the clause "Forebore his own advantage" (ll. 329, 331). But by giving identical predicates to
very dissimilar men—Lancelot and Arthur—the poetry also introduces moral indirection. Knowledge of Lancelot and Arthur
is not so much historical knowledge as a continuous form of
mental and moral exercise in which each character must engage.
Change the point of view and see Arthur through the eyes of the
Queen, or Lancelot through Arthur's eyes, and the whole meaning of each history changes. Tennyson rejects the idea that
Arthur's aloofness and purity are responsible for his tragedy. But
susceptibility to imperfection in others is itself part of the charm
of Guinevere's character. Even our awareness of the ease with
which she combines duty, profit, and pleasure symmetrically in a
moral formula—

> It was my duty to have loved the highest:
> It surely was my profit had I known:
> It would have been my pleasure had I seen.   [ll. 652–654]

—is ironically qualified by our knowledge that as long as Guinevere lives she will love men, not because of what they are, but because of what she herself is. Guinevere's clearest consciousness of Arthur's authority comes as an internal perception, and only at the moment he goes, only when he leaves her life forever.

Tennyson's shifts in point of view extend as well to unexpected shifts in his syntax. After delaying a threatened outcome, the hesitating syntax may dissolve it altogether. Grammar wavers, uncertain for a moment which of two paths to take.

> And from the sun there swiftly made at her
> A ghastly something, and its shadow flew
> Before it, till it touched her, and she turned—
> When lo! her own, that broadening from her feet,
> And blackening, swallowed all the land, and in it
> Far cities burnt, and with a cry she woke.
>   ["Guinevere," ll. 77–82]

In these lines describing the fearful growth of the shadow in Guinevere's dream, the narrator uses short principal clauses and two participles to make a small syntactical model of a quite large and cataclysmic series of events. The polysyndeton of the first three lines, with their repetition in rapid succession of the coordinate conjunction—"And from the sun," "and its shadow flew," "and she turned"—conveys the fearful encroachment of the "ghastly something" and its dreadful shadow. The concluding lines move much more slowly. We drift from narrative into psychological time on two present participles, "broadening" and "blackening," which loosen the syntactical links just as the shadow is loosening order in the land. At first we are likely to construe as a conjunction—as a relative pronoun modifying "own"—the word "that" in the pivotal construction, "her own, that broadening from her feet." If so, the use of the relative pronoun as the subject of the principal verb "swallowed" sets up the expectation of a further principal clause, enclosing "swallowed," to serve as a predicate for the subject "own." Instead, the grammar provides not just one but two enclosures, and both different from what we expect. If the word "own" is not to be left suspended, the coordinate clause "and in it / Far cities burnt" forces us to reconstrue the hinge word "that." We must parse it, not as a relative pronoun, but as an ellipsis: "that [one]"—in apposition to "her own." But just when the grammatical suspension is itself suspended and disaster seems all too real, Tennyson shifts his frame for a second time. The use of the phrase "and . . . she woke" to frame the earlier enclosure "and . . . / Far cities burnt" suspends the threatening outcome in a surprising way. The expectation of suspension has not been raised so that it may then be frustrated. It is fulfilled by the poet's showing that the earlier frames are windows opening, not on a vast historical canvas of decline and fall, but on the private terrors of a mind diseased. These windows expose the mind's darkest places.

The breadth and generosity of Tennyson's mind are nowhere more apparent than in his last idyll, "The Passing of Arthur" (1869). Arthur's heroic plainness, as he stoically scrutinizes his own bareness, suppresses none of the attitudes evident in the other idylls: neither the sublimity of "The Holy Grail" nor the disillusion and ruin of "The Last Tournament," neither the elegiac dignity of "Lancelot and Elaine" nor the revulsion and indignity of "Pelleas and Ettarre." Not yet resigned to failure yet charting the pathos of his decline, Arthur is made vividly aware of the fearful toll that heroism exacts. A victim of isolation, of utter personal, moral, and historical aloneness, Arthur withdraws in horror from the unimaginable ruin, the wreckage of his hopes. In a poetry of bleak grandeur, which anticipates the elegies of Tennyson's old age, Arthur records the barrenness of nature, seen now without human power to change. In barely enunciated phrases—"O me!"; "And hollow, hollow, hollow" (l. 37)— Arthur's dream expresses the nameless weight of depression, a desiccation worse than the ruin that has overtaken Camelot itself. The perfection of "moonlit haze among the hills," like "the lonely city sacked by night" (ll. 42–43), is undone by the misery of the wandering wind, by the whirlings of the birds that "wail their way / From cloud to cloud" (ll. 39–40). These are the whimpers of the king's own voice, the ultimate chill, stupor, and then the letting-go.

The formula for affirmation in the *Idylls* is earth is not earth, light is not light, air is not air, but vision. At the beginning of "The Passing of Arthur" the king reverses the formula: God is in the stars, God is in the fields, but God is not to be found in his ways with men, where we should most expect to find him.

> I found Him in the shining of the stars,
> I marked Him in the flowering of His fields,
> But in His ways with men I find Him not. [ll. 9–11]

As the inversion of the earlier formula indicates, Arthur's despair parodies his grand discovery in "The Holy Grail" that God and nature are expressions of his own visionary power, displayed, not in a mirror, but with the aid of the mind's self-creating lamp. To express the divinity of his visionary power Arthur had used a new majesty of tone. In a Jehovah-like assertion, he had pronounced himself no vision to himself ("vision" in the sense of illusion, as distinct from the higher sense of "vision"—as a synonym for spirit —that he also exalts); and he had concluded his celebration with an oracular tautology: "ye have seen what ye have seen" (compare "I am that I am"). The disturbing corollary of Arthur's Romantic celebration, reminiscent of Wordsworth's celebration at the end of *The Prelude* of a mind that is "A thousand times more beautiful than the earth / . . . In beauty exalted, as it is itself / Of quality and fabric more divine,"[11] is the discovery that this godlike mind can turn upon itself in cruel reflexiveness, recanting its creed, a parody of Christian faith, as a perpetual delusion. Arthur, the godlike visionary, may not live on earth but in a dream of earth, like Gawain: "I am blown along a wandering wind / And hollow, hollow, hollow all delight'" (ll. 36–37). The interchange between the spiritual and secular cities is now no longer a genuine giving and taking. It is not a marriage at all, but the solipsism of a vain and hollow narcissist, staring blankly at the void. If X is not X and Y is not Y, it is because both are now zero, the mirror in nature of the empty mind, the Lockean *tabula rasa*.

11. William Wordsworth, *The Prelude*, XIV, 449, 453–454.

If Arthur were simply a soldier, saint, and seer, possessed of some extraordinary qualities, we should expect the cause of his failure to be morally or psychologically intelligible: we should look for personal shortcomings to explain his fall. But Tennyson invites the reader to do something more interesting and difficult: to participate in a tragedy that is never completely understandable. Tennyson is trying to explore an ironic truth about authority: to exercise authority, to resist chaos, takes a dreadful toll. Far from being a remote paragon, immune to the frailties most men feel, Arthur realizes that power involves responsibility and hard work; and he refuses to put his trust in magic. If we think of Arthur as a character in a novel or a play, it is natural to evaluate his personality as cold and aloof. But Arthur's long declarations in "Guinevere" and "The Passing of Arthur" are significant, not as expressions of individual psychology, but as formal declarations of principle. Arthur is saying that without courage any position of power is an empty office; a firm and confident resistance to danger is essential to the courage and integrity of any man who exercises power. Yet authority should be obeyed, not because it is based on threats or force, but because it is embodied judgment and wisdom—a light that all civilized men must love and live by. The principles that Arthur defends—the claims of spiritual authority, the origin and maintenance of values, the grounds of moral obligation—can always be challenged, but they cannot be superseded along with other Victorian teachings about ethics or religion, which may now seem outdated. They remain crucial concepts in any man's definition of his world or himself.

Indeed, Tennyson's final homage is not to extraordinary qualities in Arthur but to the virtues of Bedivere, whose daily routine is celebrated as the actual grandeur of the commonplace. The coda lends elevation to Bedivere's repetitive routine, which is ordinary and humane. The deadened statements resemble the simple eulogy on an epitaph. They are the hesitating, minimal urgings of the kind of heroism average people can achieve.

> Thereat once more he moved about, and clomb
> Even to the highest he could climb.   [ll. 462–463]

The view is double: on this Pisgah height the illumined expanse of Arthur's miraculous vanishing "into light" (l. 468) and Bedivere's hesitation and strain in tracking "the speck that bare the King" (l. 465) exist together in reciprocal dignity. The commonplace and the mysterious, the large and the small, are all plainly present, none denying the others, as Bedivere on his peak confronts two worlds at once.

In a poem that puzzles over nature and fortune, on the small scale of daily living and on the large scale of civilizations and history, it is an unexpected affirmation to have the simple rising of the sun reveal the advent of a new order. There is no idealizing in the coda. Tennyson immediately qualifies the certitude of "saw" by the provisional "Or thought he saw" (ll. 463, 465); and even the sun that "rose bringing the new year" (l. 469) is the neutral sun of the Sermon on the Mount, which God "maketh . . . to arise on the evil and on the good" alike (Matthew 5:45). The cautious advance and retreat are gravely barren. They must be distinguished from the earlier hovering elusiveness, from the piling up of appositions and qualifiers in "The Lotos-Eaters" and "Tithonus" to evoke the mind's pathetic fallacies. The motions backward to the real and the observed from the temptations of the visionary now give an impression of tremendous honesty. The insistent couplings of "clomb" and "climb," "saw" and "saw," the passing "on and on," then going from "less to less" before dissolving, show Bedivere looking harder and harder at the object. Yet the indefinite protraction of three present participles—"Straining," "opening," "bringing" (ll. 464, 466, 469)—as Bedivere stares endlessly into space, seem to suspend the action forever between real and visionary worlds. Arthur's humiliation and defeat, like their medium, the mist and night, may be dispelled by sunrise. But Tennyson's formula does not dispel, as the mythological dawn of "The Vision of Sin" would have dispelled, Arthur's reason for feeling humiliation and dismay. In his dedication "To the Queen" the narrator makes clear that men must learn to live, like Arthur—or like Bedivere on his Pisgah peak—in a time that is neither the eternal now of their visionary moments nor the miserable, infernal time of the last tournament. It is a double time which, amid misery, contains the promise of happiness and which makes beauty rise out of ugliness—a penultimate moment which both fails to realize "the goal of this great world" ("To the Queen," l. 59) and tends toward it.

Many of the elements contributing to strong effects of closure are present in "The Passing of Arthur." Even when the concluding lines are not strictly enjambed, the syntax propels us forward, without full pauses, so that there is no rest until the last two lines: "From less to less and vanish into light. / And the new sun rose bringing the new year" (ll. 468–469). The penultimate line affirms the completion of a pattern; and, like an alexandrine at the end of a Spenserian stanza, the last line signals closure by stepping up the number of accents from five to six. An impressive emphasis results, as in Hopkins' use of sprung rhythm, from the huddling together of all the accents, with only one break between the fourth and fifth stresses. In addition, by separating itself from the rest of the poem the last line makes a stable comment from outside, like the frame around a picture. But countering the terminal features of night, autumn, passing on and on, and vanishing are the rising of the sun and the advent of another year. The closing words are not—significantly—words of decline and dissolution, but words that break out of closure.

In the epilogue, "To the Queen," by using a second closure to enclose his first closure, Tennyson sets up a regress of closures. By recalling that the defeat and death of Arthur are the subject of an "old imperfect tale" (l. 36), a mere fiction taken out "Of Geoffrey's book, or . . . Malleor's" (l. 42), Tennyson hopes to master his own fears. A simple closure would be merely elegiac; but the affective qualities here are biblical or sacred. Like the Queen's Prince Consort, over whose "grave" the *Idylls* are written (l. 35) and to whom the poem is dedicated, "all of high and holy" seems to die "away" (l. 66). Before Tennyson can mute the force of all human as of all poetic closures, he must move beyond time and history altogether, making Arthur, not "that gray king" of legend (l. 39), but a timeless figure, a symbol of "Ideal manhood closed in real man" (l. 38). The only way Tennyson can attain the philosophic attitude that conquers death in *Idylls of the King* is by passing like Arthur into other worlds or frames.

The ravishing visions of "The Holy Grail" form the radiant center of the *Idylls*. The identity of lowliness and grandeur, of gloom and exaltation, is a celestial phenomenon that Tennyson accurately portrays in the glorious transformation of earth and nighttime sky. As the great gusts of auroral light are pressed into doctrinal service, the heroic values of saint, seer, and soldier effortlessly fuse in volatile displays of ethereal caprice and earthly power. But celestial ease is eclipsed by "wandering wind[s]" ("The Passing of Arthur," 1, 36); and when the radiant unities recede, dualities of hope and despair, credulity and distrust, continue to spread. In the *Idylls* as a whole, Tennyson even duplicates the careers of his knights—double figures like Gareth and Pelleas, and the brothers Balin and Balan; and he multiplies the main action, the character, and the career of Arthur, who turns out to be a double in himself, a split personality. From the volatile splendor of "The Holy Grail" and the glittering ruin of "The Last Tournament," *Idylls of the King* passes to the somber interrogations of the dying Arthur. In his elusive and modest way, Tennyson seems ignorant of Spenserian allegory: he seldom explicitly relates his Arthurian matter to historical examples and moral precepts. The supernatural occurrences are all things to all men; and we come to feel that the truth is forever hidden, wrapped in "lucid veils" like the Holy Grail, or like Hallam's ghost in *In Memoriam*. The cryptic songs and riddles are to the self-concealing truth of the *Idylls* what the synecdoche of the shell is to the hero's self-regenerating power in *Maud*. An allegorist would show mainly aversion to characters like Guinevere and Lancelot; but by making them extensions of ourselves, Tennyson repudiates the allegorical intelligence, as he would repudiate the intelligence of St. Simeon's God. The God who fulfills himself in many ways does not hate any man, but like Spinoza's God, he does not seem to love any man either. Arthur's secret fear, disclosed in "The Passing of Arthur," that "some lesser god had made the world" (l. 14) alerts the reader to terrors that confirm the unstable nature of the world, always verging on fragmentation and nightmare. Even as Arthur civilizes nature, his failures tell of the failure of man's existence and the failure of his power to exist.

So relentlessly does Tennyson expose, in the *Idylls,* the contradictions in all religion, that we begin to feel the truth of F. H. Bradley's comment: "The man who has passed, however little, behind the scenes of the religious life, must have had his moments of revolt."[12] We are repelled by Pellam's empty religious devotions, in which we witness the birth of monstrous hypocrisy; and in the fitful piety of the Grail questers, we see how the moral life may be idly dreamed away. The religion of courtly love that ennobles Lancelot by lifting him above the moral law also seduces him into blatant perversions. If Galahad's religion is in danger of dissolving in inanities, Arthur's religion is in danger of collapsing into bare morality. When Camelot falls, it is not enough that Arthur has done his best; swollen with private sentiment, such morality would justify the emptiest self-will. Arthur believes in divine providence, but, because his faith is practical, he acts as if he does not believe in it, too. If taken seriously, the irreligious element in Arthur's creed—man's self-sufficiency—destroys the religious element—awareness of man's impotence without God. Though nothing in the end falls outside God, it is safer to pretend he is a finite being, a goal the knights must struggle to reach. If perfect union ever were achieved, God would be lost, and religion with him. Baffled by his failure, Arthur acknowledges that it may even be his moral duty not to be moral. Goodness and badness do not depend wholly on himself; moral duty can survive only as an element of higher truth. His life affirms the austere sentence of F. H. Bradley, the greatest of the Idealists: "There is [much] in the universe, I am sure, beyond mere morality; and I have yet to learn that, even in the moral world, the highest law is justice."[13]

12. *Appearance and Reality: A Metaphysical Essay* (Oxford, 1930), p. 393.

13. *Appearance and Reality,* p. 450.

Like Bradley's *Appearance and Reality,* the *Idylls* have the variety and iridescence of life itself, and its indirection, too.[14] Both works move among opposites and rejoice in contradictions, but founder on the same paradox: "What seems to us sheer waste is, to a very large extent, the way of the universe."[15] But because Tennyson honestly confronts this paradox, he is able to achieve at the end a powerful consolation. The discovery of the dying Arthur is neither the consolation of the optimist—in this best of all possible worlds, everything is a necessary evil—nor is it the consolation of the pessimist—where everything is bad, it must be good to know the worst. "The Passing of Arthur" combines present despair with distant hope. The saddest and most brooding of Tennyson's endings, it charts the Virgilian abyss, the tears in things. Yet the *Idylls,* as Harold Bloom has finely said of Keats's "Ode to Autumn," end "in an acceptance of process beyond the possibility of grief."[16] Though Arthur learns to fathom, in isolation and among the ruins of time, the fear of oblivion—that powerful undertow of terror flowing deep beneath the surface of every human life—his celebration of death, if rightly understood and pondered, becomes a consecration of remembering. It is precisely this kind of subdued elation that Tennyson achieves in the classical monologues and in *In Memoriam*—indeed, in all his best verse, which is always elegiac, even in prophecy and passion. At such moments, glancing down "cliffs of fall / Frightful, sheer, no-man-fathomed" (Gerard Manley Hopkins, "No worst, there is none," ll. 9–10), Tennyson reflects on the dissolving past. From his crumbling foothold in time he has glimpses of hope, but never loses his fear of quick, precipitate descent. The great enemy for

14. Such elusiveness and indirection are seldom absent from Tennyson's highest poetry. They are precisely the qualities that elude my earlier study " 'Idylls of the King': A Dialectical Reading," *Victorian Poetry,* VII (1969), 175–190. Tennyson possesses a ranging and communicative mind. But there are many fugitive phenomena, many metaphysical outcasts in the *Idylls.* The attempt to impose intellectual coherence spawns too many categories, too many schema, which batten parasitically, draining off life from the poem.

15. *Appearance and Reality,* p. 450.

16. *The Visionary Company* (New York, 1961), p. 456.

Arthur is not a computer programmed to achieve his annihilation. It is despair, a force that is all the more insidious for being internal and self-generated. But as Arthur masters his despair, he affirms his belief in a power above the doomsday machine: a grace that sanctifies and pre-empts from the forces of darkness the judgment of the last great battle. Arthur's distant hopes owe something to the play of his mind on ultimate abstractions such as virtue and justice, qualities already embodied in his life, which flow into the world from the energies of a mind that can exorcise its fears and morbidity, realizing like the mourner of *In Memoriam* and like the poet of the late elegies the promise of even the most diminished life.

By incorporating in a long poem the pathetic enigmas of "The Lady of Shalott" with the rituals of "Morte d'Arthur" and "Sir Galahad," the glittering ruin of "The Vision of Sin" with the solemn wonder of "St. Agnes' Eve," the gravities of "The Ancient Sage" with the hysterias of "St. Simeon Stylites," the *Idylls* are, in their wide embrace of styles, Tennyson's most ambitious attempt to resolve the growing conflict between facts and values in post-Romantic culture. Unfortunately, the resolutions of the *Idylls* are too often contrived resolutions, like Guinevere's easy combination of duty, profit, and pleasure, and Arthur's faith that "More things are wrought by prayer / Than this world dreams of" ("The Passing of Arthur," ll. 415–416).[17] Such oracular assurance is wrong only because it cannot be content without

17. It is possible, of course, that Tennyson never intended to resolve the discrepant features of his poem. Nor is such a possibility incompatible with Tennyson's Idealism. On the contrary, it may even be required by it. For where there is no "ought" there is no morality or religion, and where there is no discrepancy there is no "ought," no imperative to resolve the discrepancy in a continuing search for truth. The unreduced opposites of *Idylls of the King* may impair the poem's unity. But they are also the Idealist's way of reflecting relative untruths, which veer between rival claims. To seize and hold the truth, if truth were really attained, would destroy morality and religion as we know them. For, as Browning understood, it would destroy the desire for truth. A satisfied desire is inconsistent with itself: if it is entirely satisfied, it is not a desire, and if it remains a desire, it is only partly satisfied.

thinking it is right. Arthur sees too clearly to succumb to the rela-
tivist's fallacy that every truth is so true that any truth must be
false. But though his creedal innocence denies mortal terror, it
cannot eliminate it. For a more successful resolution of the conflict between facts and values we must turn in the next chapter to
Tennyson's poetry of reflection. And for more complete joinings
of elation and despair we must turn ultimately to the quieter perfection of "Demeter and Persephone" and the late elegies. In
these poems of his old age Tennyson's effort to assimilate terror
and innocence, though less dazzling, is also more sustained than
in the *Idylls*.

✿✿✿ 7

The Sage and the Seer:
The Poet of Reflection

Tennyson the poet of dissolving roles longs all his life for stable forms. The poet of sensation wants to write reflectively, as a sage and a seer, just as Browning, the artist of roles, wants to write what he was born to write, "R. B.—a poem," a work in which he can drop his masks and address his audience directly, speaking in Eliot's "second voice" of poetry. In his major poems Tennyson is the Prospero of an insubstantial pageant. He expresses the melancholy, amounting at times to panic, that also afflicts Keats in his odes—and perhaps any poet of genius who knows the transience, and hence the seriousness, of beauty. The solid lands and hills of *In Memoriam* melt into mist, and the dream romance of *The Princess,* though an illusion of surpassing charm, fades into thin air, like one more phantom in the Prince's brain. In *Maud,* insanity and death are the dreadful price exacted for snatching beauty from a higher world. In *Idylls of the King* the cloud-capped towers of Camelot, like Prospero's "great globe itself," dissolve as if in a dream. Beyond the fading pageant, Tennyson looks for stable truths. He hopes to find them by writing three types of poems: poems of politics and state, theological and visionary poems which seek to identify unchanging attributes of God, and poems exploring various elements of Idealist thought, including Idealism's Oriental counterpart, Taoism. As a reflective sage and seer, can Tennyson discover for himself and for his age what Matthew Arnold sought, some joys "whose grounds are true?" (Arnold, "Obermann Once More," l. 238). When the rest of the globe, and "all which it inherit" (Shakespeare, *The Tempest*, IV, i, 154), shall have melted into air, and like Prospero's "insubstantial pageant faded," left "not a rack behind," will there be any vision of God or of the state, any goal of this great world, that remains secure, invulnerable at the end to the grand annihilation?

Qualified Political Assertion

Tennyson's poems of politics and state seem to be among his most stable productions. To glorify a heroic patriot such as Wellington the poet laureate has only to celebrate the strict discipline of doing one's duty. The heroism of a Wellington or Queen Victoria is not extraordinary: its formula can be laid out quite flatly, almost as mechanically as a recipe. Nevertheless, it is surprising to discover how full the political poems are of unstable grammar and qualified assertion.

> Oh yet, if Nature's evil star
>> Drive men in manhood, as in youth,
>> To follow flying steps of Truth
> Across the brazen bridge of war . . .
>
> Not yet the wise of heart would cease
>> To hold his hope through shame and guilt. . . .
>
> Not less, though dogs of Faction bay,
>> Would serve his kind in deed and word,
>> Certain, if knowledge bring the sword,
> That knowledge takes the sword away—
>
> Would love the gleams of good that broke
>> From either side, nor veil his eye:
>> And if some dreadful need should rise
> Would strike, and firmly, and one stroke.   [ll. 73–92]

These concluding stanzas from "Love Thou Thy Land" (1832–1834) present a program for action, not a description of action—but a program in which the hypothetical constructions are eventually almost forgotten. To give the illusion that his speculations are more than wishful thinking, Tennyson progresses from subjunctive to indicative moods: from the hypothetical clause "if knowledge bring the sword" to the unconditional assertion "knowledge takes the sword away." He also leads the reader from the hypothetical "if Nature's evil star / Drive men," and the conditional verb "would cease," to two tenseless infinitives: "To follow . . . Truth" and "To hold his hope," which render timeless actions. As the poem draws to its close Tennyson succeeds in obliterating, in branching clusters of "Would's" and more subordinate clauses, the long-forgotten protasis of the sentence: the advent of "Nature's evil star." Though he builds the long, concluding sentence on his fear of war, Tennyson's political hopes all but bury that fear. The conditional grammar is muted by the urgent imperatives with which the poem ends and by the timeless quality of the repeated auxiliary—"Would pace," "Would serve," "Would love," "Would strike" (ll. 84, 86, 89, 92)—which changes from a future conditional to an imperfect indicative tense.

The illusion of progress in "Love Thou Thy Land," born of an early Victorian pride in human capacity, and not yet exalted by the vision of empire, issues in a momentary triumph of hope over history. Some twenty years later, in *Ode on the Death of the Duke of Wellington* (1852), the self-assurance, though similarly qualified, works in the opposite way. Reduced from an aspiration to a formula, the sententious identification of "The path of duty" with the "way of glory" (l. 210) cannot quite disguise oddities in the account. Certain lines waver, expressing the lapse into doubt. And submerged metaphors of darkness, death, and gloom increasingly obsess Tennyson. The probability of God's accepting Wellington, and of Christ's receiving him, depends on the preceding hypothesis that the duke is "Something far advanced in State" (l. 275). The spectral amorphousness of "Something" is far from reassuring. But whenever Tennyson tries to be more assertive, he can imagine nothing more inspiring than a heavenly Bentham and an apotheosis of machine-like simplicity and practical capacity: "There must be other nobler work to do / Than when he fought at Waterloo, / And Victor he must ever be" (ll. 256–258). As Tennyson begins to appropriate the prescriptive form of "must," then switches to the interrogative mood of half-stated enthymemes (syllogisms with suppressed premises)—"What know we greater than the soul?" (l. 265)—and to qualified statements of obligation and belief—"On God and Godlike men we build our trust" (l. 266)—there is a willed wrenching of the style. A curious mixture of strain and conviction results. The great vistas of geological and astronomical time weigh upon Tennyson; and it is as if the shift from military to spiritual battle takes him by surprise. Wellington's transformation from a political to a spiritual "State" strongly asserts Tennyson's skepticism about the eternity of Wellington's "honour" (ll. 149–150)—a word whose fivefold repetition in two lines betrays a failure in conviction. The play on "State" shows how skeptical, how playfully subversive, Tennyson remains, willing to change a premise as soon as he entertains it. None of the pathetic attempts at self-conviction, the impulse to dictate to God, or the final honesty could exist without the qualifications and two-way meanings. These require constant shifts of grammatical mood and a changing sense of the subject.

There is always a danger that poems of politics and state will simply equate heroism with the large and the communal. But a war, a funeral, or a royal marriage, however large, cannot satisfy that hunger of the imagination, which, as Dr. Johnson saw, is always simplifying its desires into specific wants, then finding them insubstantial and fugitive. The second thoughts and reservations which abound in the ceremonial poems are evidence of Tennyson's unwillingness to falsify belief. Two further examples must suffice. Halfway through "A Welcome to Her Royal Highness Marie Alexandrovna" (1874) the glories of state suddenly strike the poet as too overwhelming. Though he feels the grand fulfillment of history in the marriage ceremony, he somberly reflects that history's "thrones and peoples are as waifs that swing, / And float or fall, in endless ebb and flow" (ll. 26–27). A proper reading of the ode must realize the support the princess receives from "Fair empires branching, both, in lusty life" (l. 21) and the support that the two empires Britain and Russia, recently enemies in the Crimean War, must hope to receive from a Messiah, a princess who can "Breathe through the world and change the hearts of men" (l. 44). The questions in the first half of the last stanza disclose Tennyson's reluctance to assert the possibility of even an equivocal peace, whether now or in the future. Social progress remains a hypothesis, not a truth; and Tennyson seems to dispute the hypothesis, first by turning, as Carlyle had done, from normal political remedies to a Messiah, and, then, after the second question, by introducing his qualifying "But" and closing optative: "And peace be yours." As the last filaments of Utopian light sputter out, speculation and question finally collapse in the very private night of lovers, "soul in soul." At the end of the poem only Duke Alfred and his bride seem secure, no longer buffeted by their rolling world nor whirled by its "ebb and flow."

Another example of unstable assertion is "Ode on the Jubilee of Queen Victoria" (1887), a poem which qualifies the empty indicatives of official faith with fearful interrogatives and prayerful optatives of hope. The flexible use of quantity, stress, and alliteration achieves at best a vigorous dignity, though one that just succeeds in carrying the sentiments of the first ten stanzas over the brink of banality. In contrast, the last six lines, allegedly added at Victoria's request, change Tennyson's whole direction and attitude, acknowledging the inadequacy of his earlier praise. They begin with two fearful questions—"Are there thunders moaning in the distance? / Are there spectres moving in the darkness?" (ll. 66–67)—then try to veil the fear by slipping into a religious exhortation: "Trust the Hand of Light will lead her people" (l. 68). The verb "will lead" hovers between a present subjunctive and a simple future tense. Tennyson is clearly trying to turn the fulfillment of a wish into a statement of fact, but since every future is also a fiction, he is compelled to return to "thunders" and "spectres" in the next line. As he comes to grip with these fears, Tennyson shifts without warning from the subjunctive "pass" and "vanish" to two present indicatives—"And the Light is Victor, and the darkness / Dawns"—as if to imply that desire has at last found its object. But the unstable grammar is like the quicksand of empire and alerts us to the possibility of being deceived about the coming dawn. "Till," followed by two present tenses, is really a future in disguise. The grammar can imply either the endless present of celestial time or a visionary hope that may never be realized—a qualification on which Tennyson relies. Looking forward to Victoria's death, his appeal to the Second Coming, when the darkness will dawn "into the Jubilee of the Ages" (l. 71), rejects the terms on which the whole ode has been constructed. Such a rejection is common enough in satirical verse such as Pope's "Epistle to Augustus," which values the monarch George II only when his "suns of glory" will have "set." But in Tennyson's case the nominal subject of his ode—the greatness of secular empire—has changed to imperial gloom, with the result that the poem we think we are reading turns into something else.

Tennyson's reverence for the English constitution, like his reverence for Camelot, is inspired by a Burkean vision of civilized order, a contract between the living, the dead, and those yet unborn[1]—a view of history and society that would have been intelligible to Aquinas and Hooker, as it was to their nineteenth-century counterparts Coleridge and Matthew Arnold. But with his Burkean faith in civilized order Tennyson combines a Godwinian doctrine of progress. Founded on a belief that human nature is perfectible, the political philosophy of Godwin and Shelley developed into the official Victorian creed that social truth will spread. Though Tennyson endorses the creed, he comes to view it, particularly in later years, as a triumph of hope over expectation. As theories of progress give way in nineteenth-century thought to theories of random process, Tennyson fears that society may develop haphazardly. His political poetry is therefore of two kinds: a poetry of official apology, written from a sense of belonging to an elect people, and a poetry of foreboding which disengages itself from the partisanship of empire and party in a way Matthew Arnold would approve. In the first kind of verse

1. Tennyson owned eight volumes of an edition of Edmund Burke's works published in London in 1801. They are now housed in the Tennyson Archives at Lincoln.

the laureate is writing as the friend of Gladstone, Queen Victoria, and imperialists such as the Marquis of Dufferin and General Charles George (Chinese) Gordon. But in the second kind of verse, in the disturbing prophecies of the second "Locksley Hall," which his old friend Gladstone deeply resented,[2] Tennyson discloses that he has less in common with the liberal camp than with Hardy and Henry Adams, thinkers who are distressed by the non-teleological implications of Darwin. For the aging Tennyson the evolutionary escalator is no longer a smoothly rising "altar-stairs / That slope through darkness up to God" (*In Memoriam*, LV, 15–16) but a wild, careening roller coaster, doubtfully teleological and frightening to contemplate.

Visions of God

Though Tennyson finds political life less and less stable, perhaps he can still find stable identity as a visionary poet and a seer. One of the seer's earliest attempts to prolong and stabilize a supernatural vision occurs at the beginning of "The Vision of Sin" (1842). The merit of comparing hedonistic energy to a progress of orgiastic melodies is not simply that there are links between hedonism and "nerve-dissolving" music (l. 44). There is also a much larger range of specialized terminology connected with music and the dance than there is with hedonism. The "Low voluptuous music," the kernel of the first sentence, in addition to winding and trembling, is heavily qualified by the participles that come before and after it: "Narrowing in to where they sat assembled / Low voluptuous music winding trembled, / Woven in circles" (ll. 16–18). Like Latin syntax, the self-embedding grammar is a logical means for writing about temporal sequence. But

2. Charles Tennyson, *Alfred Tennyson* (New York, 1949), p. 494: The poem "seemed to be a deliberate repudiation of all the social and economic progress of the last half-century. Mr. Gladstone felt it deeply and took up the challenge with an elaborately deferential article in *The Nineteenth Century* for January, 1887. In this he gave an impressive catalogue of the reforms adopted by Parliament since 1842, and expressed the fear that Tennyson's poem might be taken for 'a deliberate authoritative estimate of the time.'"

the crushing of the single noun "music" between two adjectives
and three participles is not primarily logical in its effect. The
density of the inflections—"Narrowing . . . assembled . . .
trembled, / Woven"—active as well as passive, and the two
adjectives and present participle—"Low voluptuous . . . winding"—that operate inside this general pastness resemble a dance
of bees around a flower. The jostling together of participles,
which might be thought would speed the outcome, slows it down
and keeps the syntax hovering instead. The absence of normal
syntax makes it easier to hark back and pick up any element in a
series of appositions. Such writing is less suited to going forward
than it is to turning round and pivoting. In the rest of the description (ll. 23–45) each item of syntax—the quick succession of
principal verbs, the cluster of participles, the simile of the nightingales—opens another window in the dreamer's head.

> Then the music touched the gates and died;
> Rose again from where it seemed to fail,
> Stormed in orbs of song, a growing gale;
> Till thronging in and in, to where they waited,
> As 'twere a hundred-throated nightingale,
> The strong tempestuous treble throbbed and palpitated;
> Ran into its giddiest whirl of sound,
> Caught the sparkles, and in circles,
> Purple gauzes, golden hazes, liquid mazes,
> Flung the torrent rainbow round:
> Then they started from their places,
> Moved with violence, changed in hue,
> Caught each other with wild grimaces,
> Half-invisible to the view,
> Wheeling with precipitate paces
> To the melody, till they flew,
> Hair, and eyes, and limbs, and faces,
> Twisted hard in fierce embraces,
> Like to Furies, like to Graces,
> Dashed together in blinding dew:
> Till, killed with some luxurious agony,
> The nerve-dissolving melody
> Fluttered headlong from the sky.   [ll. 23–45]

Unable to move to another comparison fast enough, the self-inwoven syntax jumps to vaguer, more exotic notions of its subject. By the time the "nerve-dissolving" music has "Flung . . . the rainbow round," and has throbbed, wheeled, whirled, and finally fluttered "from the sky," we may have forgotten what its casual beginning was. By framing the music in a window (the dreamer's vision), which is itself seen through a nearer window (the poem), Tennyson emphasizes the cinematic quality of the flow. Like backgrounds in a surrealist movie, each aperture in the story flow exposes the sharply etched detail of what is hardly describable at all, though impressionistically sketched in Tennyson's poem with unusual clarity and power. There is no reason why the music should be compared to a nightingale, and even less reason why the nightingale should be followed by a sparkle, a circle, or by colors in a rainbow. Their value lies in a window-opening or perspective effect. From the urgency of the clustered participles Tennyson moves to the static window-framing of the colorful triad: "Purple gauzes, golden hazes, liquid mazes," until the principal verb "Flung" dissolves him again in the orgiastic flow. From the flux of moving pictures to vivid still shots, then back again, the grammar acts as the lens of a camera. Even in punctuating the dream, it keeps the music moving and prolongs the vision.

In the rest of the poem the seer approaches the divine through demonic impressions. The demonic proliferation is to be seen in the spawning of bodily parts. The personification, "Freedom" (l. 136), turns out to be a live monster, dragging in its hand a severed "head" and slaking its thirst on human blood. Phrases like Freedom's "sweetest meal" (l. 145) and the "Hollow hearts and empty heads" of the citizens (l. 174) are poised at first between figurative and literal meanings. But they have a habit of developing the most starkly literal possibilities. Freedom's "sweetest meal" turns out to be the feast of a cannibal upon her "first-born" sons, and the "Hollow hearts and empty heads" are cavities in a corpse. One defense against chaos is irony: the jauntiness of the speaker's tone is an escape, a hurried look away from the depleted energies of hedonism. Another device is the retreat into epigram. Sententious formulas abound, but they are little more than platitudes, last-minute attempts to ascribe everyday understanding to a nightmare. Most reassuring, perhaps, is the discovery that the demonic is also "daemonic." Inscrutable evil attests to equally inscrutable divinity. The coda's two-way syntax allows a phrase like "far withdrawn" to reach back, innocuously, to "the glimmering limit" (l. 223), but also to reach forward, daringly, to darken into a *deus absconditus* the face of God, who makes both out of himself and for himself "an awful rose of dawn" (l. 224). The backtracking in sense and pattern enacts a circling movement; the syntax seems to pause and turn on itself, as if in terror of discovering, not a benevolent principle, but a God of desolation or indifference. The "awful rose of dawn" forces the reader to participate in the seer's insight by trying to construct the connecting links between words not usually found in each other's presence. If all words betray, words about the Absolute betray absolutely. And the rolling echoes of the answer from the summit, like the inhuman, rosy quiverings of the Holy Grail, present God obliquely, in a "tongue no man could understand" (l. 222). Though the seer enlarges his meaning by showing how the energies of disorder make the forces of order kinetic and more ample, the ways of the universe seem, in the end, to be darker, more oblique than either.

To find stability at "the still point" of T. S. Eliot's "turning world" ("Burnt Norton," *Four Quartets,* II, 16), Tennyson the seer must experiment with forms of grammar that allow him to evoke "The point of intersection of the timeless / With time" ("The Dry Salvages," *Four Quartets,* V, 18–19). He discovers that often he cannot describe such points directly, nor can he evoke them by analogy and image. Instead, he must transmute them directly into the grammar of his poems. In a fascinating discussion of grammar in his treatise on logic, Coleridge speaks of the infinitive as the *punctum indifferentiae,* the indifference of substantive and verb. Since the infinitive can function as either part of speech, it is, Coleridge says, "the Homo Androgynous," abstracted from the senses "at each extreme of Action and Being."[3] In trying to evoke a "point of intersection of the timeless / With time" at the climax of *In Memoriam,* Tennyson uses the substantives "breeze" and "breath" to define God's essence. To define God's action in the world Tennyson uses a series of principal verbs describing the operations of the "breeze": "Rocked," "swung," "flung," and "said" (XCV, 58–60). Suspended between the extremes of action and being, between the verbs and substantives, are the points of intersection, the infinitive phrases: "to tremble," "[to] fluctuate," "To broaden" (XCV, 54, 56, 64). These phrases are examples of Coleridge's *punctum indifferentiae.* Timeless-temporal words, poised like "East and West" and "life and death" between opposing worlds, they grow out of finite verbal forms, but expand before the poet into timeless truths.

Tennyson uses a similar array of substantives, verbs, and infinitive forms when trying to evoke the points of intersection in "Tithonus." The essence of Aurora's divine nature is provided by a constellation of luminous nouns and adjectives: "mysterious glimmer" (l. 34); "glimmering thresholds" (l. 69); "rosy shadows" (l. 66); and their action is portrayed in time by a succession of verbs and adverbs: "Glow" (l. 56); "brighten slowly" (l. 38); "crimsoned all" (l. 56). The most obvious *punctum indifferentiae,* poised like the deity herself between eternity and time, is the simple infinitive form: "to redden through the gloom" (l. 37). But in a line such as "Glow with the glow that slowly crimsoned all" (l. 56) Tennyson uses a subtler device. To show how the deity may be understood to exist through herself, and to derive

3. Egerton MS. 2825, folio 31, British Museum. Coleridge introduces the idea of the *punctum indifferentiae* on folio 28. He includes the following diagram:

"A = Point of Identity. A is Verb and Substantive in one and as one, or Both at the Same Time. Such in grammar is the Infinitive.
B = Being (in grammer, Substantive); C = Action (in grammar, Verb)."

her existence as the dawn from her luminous essence, Tennyson
combines the verb "Glow" with its cognate noun. This grammatical form ("Glow with the glow") is first recommended by St.
Anselm in the *Monologion*.[4] Although Anselm anticipates Coleridge, and observes that the accurate infinitive statement may
describe God substantially, he thinks it best to conceive of God by
means of cognates, the way Tennyson does—as light that is
lucent, through and from itself.

"Tithonus" uses fewer infinitives than the passage from *In
Memoriam;* their place is taken by a larger number of present
participles. The transformation of the verbs into participles is
best seen in the second, intermediate use of the verb "to beat."
Its first use, in the simple past tense, is savagely temporal, the
hammering polysyndeton of "beat me down and marred and
wasted me" (l. 19). Its third use, though finite in grammatical
form, is infinite in effect: "And beat the twilight into flakes of
fire" (l. 42). Tithonus uses the beating of fire to airy thinness to
temper the earlier savageness. "Shaking" and "beating" are
violent, but "flakes of fire" are ethereal and light. Momentarily,
the stallions' shaking of the "darkness" and the proud tossing of
their "loosened manes" (l. 41) are seen as a marvel of strength
controlled by will. For a spacious moment, as Tithonus identifies
with the stallions, Tennyson invokes a point of intersection, which
allows the earlier roles of beaten victim and fire-beating vanquisher to change position. Poised between the first and third uses
of the verb is its intermediate use as a present participle: "And
bosom beating with a heart renewed" (l. 36). No longer cruelly
temporal, nor contriving, on the other hand, a false apotheosis,
the intransitive participle suspends Aurora between eternity and
time. Though warm and passionate, like most things temporal,
Aurora's heart is always "renewed" and her "bosom" always
beating, for like the lovers on Keats's Grecian urn she is "All
breathing human passion far above" ("Ode on a Grecian Urn,"

4. For a fuller discussion see Marcia L. Colish, *The Mirror of Language: A Study in the Medieval Theory of Knowledge* (New Haven,
1968), especially the analysis of "Grammatical Theology," pp. 137 ff.

l. 28). The intransitive participle has the same function as Tennyson's infinitive statements in *In Memoriam,* which hover between action in time (in their finite verbal form) and eternal being (functioning as nouns).

In "Merlin and the Gleam," where Tennyson defines a more elusive form of vision, infinitive phrases drop out altogether. Examples of Coleridge's *punctum indifferentiae,* poised between verbs such as "Flitted," "Slided," "Flickered" (ll. 48, 61, 70), and the substantives "Gleam" and "wintry glimmer" (l. 3) are a sequence of present participles: "slowly brightening" (l. 88); "slowly moving" (l. 90); "flying onward" (l. 96). Though the participles are appropriately less stable than infinitive phrases, the adverbial qualifications and the doubling of units—"streaming and shining on" (l. 51)—protract the vision endlessly. The old Tennyson has dwindled to one of his cold ghosts, the dying Merlin. But, surprisingly, even in the bleakness of age Tennyson is buoyant and jaunty. Instead of absorbing the seer into its total colorlessness, the supernatural's icy glow, with its flippant indirection, continues to elude him, half coy and teasing. The seer is never rarefied into Emerson's transparent eyeball: his mind is an enchanted glass and continues to admit light fitfully through shifting apertures. As a visionary poet and a seer Tennyson is liveliest when he accepts the responsibility of making forays into unknown territory. The critic's interest is also likely to be liveliest at exactly those points where he sees the possibility of making forays of his own —where, therefore, as in any study of the grammar of visionary poetry, poised between eternity and time, substantive and verb, the critic's methods and his terminology, like Coleridge's discussion of the *punctum indifferentiae,* are also likely to be most tentative and most experimental.

Through a Glass Darkly

Though Tennyson cannot find stable identity as a political or a visionary poet, we might expect he can still find it as an Idealist philosopher and mystic. Yet the more we understand Tennyson's affinities with Victorian Idealism and Oriental mysticism,[5] the more we understand the necessary imbalance in his poetry between a world of unstable appearance and a fading reality beyond appearance. For an Idealist like Tennyson there is a fundamental indirection in the way the mind arrives at truth; and this indirection qualifies the logic of Tennyson's best discursive poems. In F. H. Bradley's terms, the predicate of a judgment can never be equivalent to its subject. The indirection of all grammar and logic arises from the fact that in no judgment are the subject (the reality language is trying to define) and the predicate (the statement about reality) ever the same. If there is no sundering of the two, there is no judgment; and if there is no judgment there is no thought. Logic is indirect and relational; if it ceases to be thus, it commits suicide. But if it remains indirect how can it describe direct experience? Thought, to be satisfied, would have to become one with immediate reality; but in reaching it, thought would lose its distinctive character. Because all logic betrays dissection and the knife, the rationalist's assumption that thought can di-

5. The large number of books on Oriental thought in Tennyson's library, now in the Lincoln archives, testifies to the poet's abiding interest in the subject. Particularly relevant are: William Brockie, *Indian Thought: A Popular Essay* (Sunderland, privately printed, 1876); Eugène Burnouf, *Introduction à l'histoire du Buddhisme Indien* (Paris, 1844), I; [Chao Plya Thipakon], *The Modern Buddhist: Being the Views of a Siamese Minister of State on His Own and Other Religions,* tr. Henry Alabaster (London, 1870); Gidumal Dayaram, *The Life and Work of Behramji M. Malabari* (Bombay, 1881); Marquis Marie Jean Léon d'Hervey-Saint-Denys, *Poésies de l'époque des Thang,* translations, with a study of the art of Chinese poetry (Paris, 1862); Kesavachandra Sena, *Lectures and Tracts: First and Second Series,* ed. Sophia Dobson (London, 1870); Mahabharata, *The Song Celestial; or, Bhagavad-Gita,* tr. Edwin Arnold (3d ed.; London and Trubner, 1886); and Saddharmapundarika, *Le Lotus de la bonne loi,* tr. from Sanskrit by E. Burnouf (Paris, 1852). Also relevant are the translations of Indian hymns in the Orientalist Sir William Jones's *Works,* ed. Anna Maria Jones (6 vols; London, 1799). See, in particular, "Hymn to Bhaváni," VI, 334; "A Hymn to Surya," VI, 354; and "A Hymn to Náráyena," VI, 373. Also influential in the popularizing of Indian thought and culture was the energetic Victorian scholar Max Müller, editor of the *Rig-Veda,* and subject of a biography by Nira C. Chaudhuri: *Scholar Extraordinary: The Life of Professor the Rt. Hon. Friedrich Max Müller, P.C.* (Oxford, 1975).

rectly contain experience takes him, instead, straight to the
suicide of thought.

Both "The Two Voices" and "The Ancient Sage" reveal that
religious beliefs lie beyond discursive reason. But the speakers
must find that out by means of reason itself. With amused irony,
Tennyson uses logic and debate to disqualify themselves: to
illustrate that, like knowledge, "the swallow on the lake," discursive arguments are the most capricious and evanescent of all the
forms of imagining.

> For Knowledge is the swallow on the lake
> That sees and stirs the surface-shadow there
> But never yet hath dipt into the abysm,
> The Abysm of all Abysms.   ["The Ancient Sage," ll. 37–40]

The debater's first principles are "real assents,"[6] primary and unconditional. They are subject, not to logical inference, but to the
sanctions of Newman's illative sense, that active, inner principle,
that power of perfectly judging and concluding, which is both a
hallmark of the mind and its chief mystery. Throughout "The
Two Voices" (1833) Tennyson introduces indeterminate meanings to alert us, indirectly, to the truth of the coda: that life is
always more than thought. The true metaphysician, like the true
critic, finds fact nowhere and approximation always. His truths
are truths of experience, partial and fragmentary. Man's whole
duty is to serve both God *and* his adversary, for the voices of both
are interpretations of the world, and have to be reinterpreted by
every thinking mind and by every era. The power that most
readers have felt in the arguments of despair—man's chronic dis-
satisfaction, his frailty and pride—is due to the way they are
partly generated by the reader's own energies and values. Despair
associates even suicide with heroic motivation and choice (ll.
103–108). Still, impressive as the arguments of despair may
be, Tennyson seldom misses an opportunity to discredit them.
"Go, vexed Spirit, sleep in trust; / The right ear, that is filled
with dust, / Hears little of the false or just" (ll. 115–117). Despair's contrast between "false or just," instead of "false or true,"

6. John Henry Newman, "Real Assents," in *An Essay in Aid of a
Grammar of Assent* (Garden City, N.Y., 1955), pp. 76–86.

seems to be a logical disordering created by the demands of Tennyson's rhyme scheme.[7] "Just" also connotes "divine judgment," however; and in the context of the dust-filled corpse the word clearly harbors an eschatological irony at the speaker's expense, which the more logical "true" would not provide.

Despair's main technique is to reduce the spiritual strength affirmed by the "I", his opponent in the debate, to its physical origins. Despair argues that even St. Stephen, who imagines he acts as a free agent, is a human puppet, swayed by impulses of which he knows nothing, and dancing to ancestral tunes: "The sullen answer slid betwixt: / 'Not that the ground of hope were fixed, / The elements were kindlier mixed' " (ll. 226–228). "Betwixt" may seem at first to be a pseudopoetic concession to the demands of Tennyson's rhyme scheme. Would it not be more natural to say "interposed," or at least "slid between"? But the adjustment of the meaning to the sound pattern undermines the logic. The sound pattern links the "sullen" sliding to the closed "i" and to the harsh dental consonants in "betwixt," "fixed," and "mixed." If the "I's" faith is only a biological accident, as despair argues, what is his own doubt? Just as despair links the faith of the saint *logically,* so Tennyson links despair's own "sullen" sliding *phonetically,* to "the mixing" (l. 228) of elements. As the syntax turns upon key words—"dream it was a dream" (l. 213); "show the dead are dead" (l. 267)—the mind is forced to turn over different possibilities, considering both visionary experience and death in an altered sense.

If despair's doubt is simply an accident of physiology or dreams, the "I's" rhetoric is also arbitrary. Though the "I" could have

7. The most complete treatment of logical disordering in poetry is J. C. Ransom's discussion of "ontological theory" in *The New Criticism* (Norfolk, Conn., 1941). According to Ransom, the argument of a poem is exactly determined by its own logical laws, but is "un-determined" by the meter. Conversely, the metrical pattern of a poem is partly "un-determined" by the argument it proposes to embody. The presence of "indeterminate meaning" and "indeterminate sound-patterns" sets poetry aside from conceptual discourse (pp. 299, 317). Ransom's theory seems to work best for argumentative poetry, verse for which we can supply a logical paraphrase in order to see how the logical disordering occurs.

chosen a word like "there" to rhyme with "where" and "declare,"
the near-rhyme of "here" introduces an indeterminate element:
"Of something felt, like something here; / Of something done, I
know not where; / Such as no language may declare" (ll. 382–
384). The indeterminate rhymes reinforce the logical indeterminacy of contrasting in parallel syntactic units "felt" and "done"
instead of the more logical "felt" and "thought"; and "here" and
"where" instead of "here" and "there." In the context, both kinds
of indeterminacy—logical and phonetic—are appropriate, for
what better way has the "I" of trying to express what "no language may declare"? Tennyson increases the indeterminacy by
moving phrases of opposite sense into parallel positions at the end
of successive lines. "Like something here" affirms the validity of
an analogical process: X is as Y. But the parallel phrase "I know
not where" rejects analogy: X may not be Y or Z, or anything
else the mind can conceive. As Christopher Ricks has shown, the
"I's" active grammar ("To flatter me that I may die" [l. 204])
and punning diction (forging "That heat of inward evidence"
[ll. 283–284]—both in the sense of shaping metal and of counter-
feiting) make all his arguments equivocal.[8] No logic can exhibit
the cloud of particulars which determine the apparent indirection
of actual events. Rhetoric leaves each debater at the end with a
remote and colorless extract of ideas, resting everywhere on dissection—a result which cannot, if life is real, be anything but
unreal. The arguments in "The Two Voices" are based on assumptions about what is worth living and dying for. These are
rooted in the imagination and the moral sense, and only experience—not logic—can nourish them.

The major indirection in "The Ancient Sage" (1885) is the
necessary indirection of any epistemology which seeks to know
and define the nature of God. Since the sage's knowledge is first
assumed, and not proved, it is guaranteed in advance. The logical
objection is that *petitio principii* (begging the question) assumes
in the major premise what it proves in the conclusion. The poetic
objection is that, like any tautology, the logical fallacy creates

8. *Tennyson* (New York, 1972), pp. 105–106.

predictably obvious effects. Tennyson avoids the obviousness by showing why contact with God is necessarily oblique. It takes place through limited apertures. Everything beyond we feel burningly in one small focus. If God is "the Nameless" (l. 57), who never can be proved, it might be thought he is the Kantian Thing-in-Itself, or the Unknowable God of Sir William Hamilton, Herbert Spencer, or of Dean Henry Mansel's *The Limits of Religious Thought* (1858). But Tennyson believes, with Aquinas, that, though God cannot be known directly or univocally, knowledge of him is more than just equivocal. Analogy can provide the human mind with likely similitudes about God. The chief absurdity of the skeptical argument is that if God were unknowable, we could never know he is unknowable. As Ferrier and F. H. Bradley argue, there is no reconciling our knowledge of the truth of this doctrine with the general condition which exists if it is true. Yet thought about God cannot satisfy us that God falls wholly within its limits. The best it can do is to provide the ancient sage with analogies, sensibly derived intellectual signs like the broken shell of the egg (l. 154), the gates of light (l. 174), or the ripple on the boundless deep (ll. 191–192), which is consciousness itself. The most probable similitude of God is the last of these analogies. For a thing has contexts, but only a consciousness has perspectives. And in contemplating his proper name, the word that symbolizes his consciousness, the ancient sage discovers that the edges of his identity are ragged in such a way as to imply another existence, the Nameless, from which he has been torn, and without which neither he nor the world really exists. The sage's repetition of his name operates like a mantra, and resembles a mystical technique practiced by Tennyson since early boyhood. He records that, as he silently repeats his name, the mirror of nature fades and dissolves, until the finite mind in front of the mirror flows into the boundless mind on the other side.[9]

There is a danger that a mystic like the ancient sage, or like Tennyson, will defy the truth of indirection—the truth of the limited aperture—by trying to spread out his window until all is

9. Hallam Tennyson, *Tennyson: A Memoir*, I (London, 1897), 320.

transparent, until all frames in his landscape disappear. Tennyson resists this tendency by forcing the sage to allow self-fulfillment to each of his frames: to the parables of the egg and the chrysalis, for example, through which we are invited to glimpse the evolution of bird and butterfly—and "gleams . . . / Of more than mortal things" (ll. 129–130, 154, 210–211, 214–215). To prevent the world from dissolving into the cold and imageless void, "The Abysm of all Abysms" (l. 40), the night in which, in Hegel's acid phrase, all cows are black, Tennyson has the skeptic remind the sage that the mind must do to the world as the mind would be done by. It is easy for the mind's pathetic fallacies to do violence to the rose tree and the lily, the seascape and the clouds, by arranging them according to its private will. But when the skeptic grants nature its own composition, he also unmasks its cruelties and horrors. The dust of the beloved that is greening in the rose tree's leaf, and her blood, reddening in the bloom, expose the secret terror lurking behind all pathetic fallacies.

> O rosetree planted in my grief,
>   And growing, on her tomb,
> Her dust is greening in your leaf,
>   Her blood is in your bloom.
> O slender lily waving there,
>   And laughing back the light,
> In vain you tell me "Earth is fair"
>   When all is dark as night.   [ll. 163–170]

The sage's final vision, not prearranged, and therefore not subversively rearranged by the skeptic, abstracts from both nature's composition and the mind's (ll. 200–201). At night the earth's forehead chooses to adorn itself in black, but only as a setting for its "shadow crowned with stars" (ll. 200–201). The sage knows the skeptic's fear of being swallowed up like the stars in an impersonal universe. But the sage's metaphor admits the fear, and uses it to enlarge and renew his meaning. The terror of his metaphor is inseparable from its chill beauty, from the regality and pathos of the earthly crown. The truth of analogy is consummated in the deathly magnificence of the glittering diadem. Its severity assimilates both terror and innocence, allowing the mind to be faithful to the bare surfaces of its world while pouring on their poverty a transfiguring light.

Because the predicates of logic, the words which are the symbols of our thought, lack the sensible and compulsory detail of their subjects, they remain "shadows." God himself is "unshadowable" (l. 238), because as soon as he enters into our predicates, he is infected with the indirection of our logic and our grammar. The mind that breaks "into 'Thens' and 'Whens' the Eternal Now" (l. 104) cannot exhaust its subject. As Philip Wheelwright observes, "The noble warning with which the *Tao Teh Ching* opens—'The Tao that can be spoken is not the real Tao'—stands as the oldest clearest expression of this . . . semantic insight on record."[10] Whereas "The Two Voices" establishes the meaninglessness of debate in the traditional Socratic form, "The Ancient Sage" destroys the genre by removing from it even the conventional elements of drama and climax. Its indirection is such that it encircles and subsumes, rather than directly repudiates, the skeptic. Similitudes about God are not heuristic. No predicate, whether logical or analogical, tells the mind anything about the subject it does not already know. The metaphors and analogies of the human mind, these "shadows of a shadow-world" (l. 239), are a species of intellectual faith. The indirection of the signs is never so extreme that they become "equivocal" in Aquinas' sense, trapping the knower within his own mind. "The Passion of the Past" (l. 219) reveals to the mind a great deal more about the universe than an insistent empiricism would lead one to suspect. Signs are analogical, true as far as they go. But the knower is capable of judging that signs do not go the whole way. Though God may be partly the same as our mental construction of him, in the end he diverges. Since any human logic or epistemology must reach its truth by indirection, God, like any other subject, is always being driven beyond limits by the failure of our predicates to include and exhaust his content. Such indirection is necessary. It forces Tennyson to turn from debate's simplistic faith in logic to forms in which he can explore more obliquely than in the tradi-

10. *Metaphor and Reality* (Bloomington, Ind., 1962), p. 22.

tional *psychomachia* (a poem of conflict between personified virtue and vice) the mind's efforts to establish contact with God through limited apertures.

In other Idealist poems such as "The Higher Pantheism" (1867) and "De Profundis" (1880)—poems which are in danger of turning into doctrinal exhortations—Tennyson sees God through one small window, and sees him inadequately in one poor focus, like the optical effect of refraction, which makes the "straight staff" look "bent" in water ("The Higher Pantheism," l. 16). But the fixity of a window frame, like the inadequacy of a metaphor, has no existence in God, but only in the rigidity of the perceiving mind. The prayers redefine their subject, usually by shifting the logic or by switching the metaphors.

One of the most striking of these shifts occurs at the beginning of "The Higher Pantheism." Tennyson has been praising "The sun, the moon, the stars" as "the Vision of Him who reigns" (ll. 1–2). Logically, "of Him" is a subjective genitive; but Tennyson is not satisfied with an aloof God—with a monarch surveying his realm from a throne. Because God is also immanent in creation, Tennyson turns the genitive from the subjective to objective form, and writes, "Is not the Vision He?" (l. 3). If the world is the object of God's vision, how can the world itself be the envisioning God? And if God is defined as everything that lacks the power to feel "I am I," how can God also be defined as a "Spirit" with whom "Spirit can meet?" (l. 11). The ever present alternatives to any single conception come from Tennyson's conviction that God's vision is not his own, and that each renewed insight will disclose deeper problems regarding God. Though wise men may insist that "God is law" (l. 13), it is almost inevitable that God will have a different definition in mind. In Spinoza's biting phrase, a community of triangles would worship a triangular God; and Tennyson bends his mind to imagining what a better definition might be.

Completed in 1880, in the intellectuality of old age, "De Profundis" illustrates both a successful application and a disastrous repudiation of the indirection that necessarily accompanies any epistemology that seeks to know and define the nature of God. In the coda Tennyson is too close to his emotions; and a hymn to "Infinite Ideality! / Immeasurable Reality! / Infinite Personality!" (ll. 58–60) that moved the poet to tears fails to move us at all. But a study of the main part of the poem in the Harvard manuscript reveals how repeatedly Tennyson kept rewriting in order to introduce more indirection.[11] In revising his affirmation of the soul's return to the spirit world, Tennyson makes the movement from "life to life" (a phrase in the Harvard manuscript) far from certain. If we marvel at "Sun, sun, and sun, through finite-infinite space / In finite-infinite Time" (ll. 45–46), it is because the cosmic immensities already exist in "this main-miracle" (l. 55), the infant soul, which comprehending all, is all, and represents the seer's final image of perfection. With remarkable precision, oxymorons about the "divisible-indivisible," "the numerable-innumerable" (ll. 43–44) correct the overeasy faith of the early version by registering Tennyson's conviction that God's nature is profoundly hidden, "unconceivably" itself (l. 48). Except for the coda, where Tennyson defines God's attributes too directly, forgetting that God may be known analogically but not univocally, his prayer is never self-satisfied acceptance of something given. It is an act of growing comprehension, of seeing God more clearly through limited apertures.[12]

Tennyson's most sustained examination of the imbalance be-

11. In Harvard MS. 44 Tennyson makes a number of marginal notations: "go return to us"; "Godlike to know us"; "on my spirit." In place of the final version of ll. 30 ff., he has written several alternative versions, none of which seems to satisfy him.

12. Versions of Tennyson's "limited aperture" appear in the poetry of Browning and the philosophy of F. H. Bradley. Browning, like Tennyson, can see God clearly only by using St. John's "optic glass" or the focusing "artifice" of "Mandeville" in *The Parleyings*. There is a striking similarity between "Mandeville," ll. 300–303—"Thus moaned / Man till Prometheus helped him,—as we learn,— / Offered an artifice whereby he drew / Sun's rays into a focus"—and F. H. Bradley's metaphor of the burning glass: "Our immediate interchange and transfluence takes place through one small opening. Everything beyond, though not less real, is an expansion of the common essence which we feel burningly in this one focus" (*Appearance and Reality: A Metaphysical Essay* [Oxford, 1930], p. 229).

tween an unstable world of dissolving forms and an elusive reality
beyond the forms is his monologue "Lucretius." Though we have
studied the poem in an earlier context, we must touch on it here,
for it puts the Idealist's dilemma into sharpest focus. Initially,
"Lucretius" is designed to discredit all logical systems which
babble in the tradition of a senile empiricism, or contort themselves in the atomism of some fractured metaphysic. Because
Lucretius is logically more consistent than Newton, who con-
secrates the Lucretian void as the sensorium of God,[13] the Roman
philosopher admits there is no room for theology in his system.
In an ironic simile, in which Tennyson dramatizes the fatal implications of an empirical epistemology, Lucretius compares the
tumult of sense impressions to an angry mob that during an insur-
rection throngs in rags into the council chamber of the soul.

> How should the mind, except it loved them, clasp
> These idols to herself? or do they fly
> Now thinner, and now thicker, like the flakes
> In a fall of snow, and so press in, perforce
> Of multitude, as crowds that in an hour
> Of civic tumult jam the doors, and bear
> The keepers down, and throng, their rags and they
> The basest, far into that council-hall
> Where sit the best and stateliest of the land? [ll. 164–172]

Tennyson believes that anarchy is naïve epistemology. Though
Hume in his *Treatise of Human Nature* may disclose a darkness
that is as much internal as external, Tennyson insists that the
mind is a lamp. It has to light its world, then furnish, select, and
organize its materials. He uses Lucretius' positivism to show that
a scientific philosophy can never provide the motives for action.
For all its celebration of facts, positivism is the philosophy that

13. To the "General Scholium" of the third edition of the *Principia*
(London, 1725–1726), Newton adds the sentences: "Every soul that has
perception is, though in different times and different organs of sense and
motion, still the same indivisible person. . . . Every man, so far as he is
a thing that has perception, is one and the same man during his whole life,
in all and each of his organs of sense. God is the same God, always and
everywhere" (*Mathematical Principles of Natural Philosophy*, ed. F.
Cajori [Berkeley, Calif., 1934], II, 545).

can least bear confrontation with facts. Unless the mind itself furnishes the essential ingredients of its knowledge, as in Cambridge Platonism and British Idealism, everything that happens must be ascribed to mere chance. Even if Hume is right and it is impossible for any thinker to argue from the darkness and solipsism of his mind to one metaphysical view rather than another, Tennyson concludes with Hume that the reasons for philosophic belief are of another order. They are in a sense prolegomena to faith, as they are for Aquinas, for Newman, and for many of the British Idealists.[14]

For Tennyson's monologue is more than just an attack upon the positivists. As a skeptic and cosmologist, Lucretius is torn between facts and values, as J. S. Mill is torn in his essays on Bentham and Coleridge and as many Idealists—most notably Coleridge and F. H. Bradley—are also torn. Like Plato, the poet-philosopher who banishes poets, Lucretius fascinates the Victorians because of his apparent inconsistencies. Contemporaries of Tennyson such as the Reverend John Keble[15] devise many ingenious arguments, based on analogy and parody, to account for the incongruity of this eloquent materialist, this Santayana of the ancient world. Another contemporary, J. A. Symonds, believes "Lucretius stood at the same point of ignorance" as the Victorians themselves, torn between science and religion "after the labours of Darwin and of Spencer, of Helmholtz and of Huxley."[16] Lucretius is groping toward some synthesizing form, a version of

14. On the affinities of Hume and Newman see J. M. Cameron, "Newman and Empiricism," in *The Night Battle* (London, 1962), especially p. 236.

15. See *Keble's Lectures on Poetry, 1832–1841*, tr. E. K. Francis (Oxford, 1912), II, 350: "And, in truth, you will not easily find any one among the poets who lacked the enlightenment of revealed Truth, who affords so many splendid lines [as Lucretius] which, as it were spontaneously, cast their testimony in favour of sound and sincere piety. Not one of them has left more numerous passages which any one, perhaps changing here and there a word or two, but yet maintaining the general tenor of the whole, can quote on the side of goodness and righteousness. Such a method of quotation is technically called a 'parody.' "

16. "Lucretius," *Fortnightly Review*, XXIII (January, 1875), 58.

Arnold's "imaginative reason" or Newman's illative sense. As a
poet he is appalled by the notion that existence can be the same
as his logical understanding of it. His logic leaves the poet in him
as cold and ghostlike as the dogmas of positivism leave Tennyson,
or as the dreariest materialism strikes the most profound Victorian logician, F. H. Bradley. In sundering the subject from its
logical predicates, the necessary indirection of all abstract thinking
produces, not the delights and pains of the flesh, but the colorless
movement of Lucretius' atoms, "some spectral woof of impalpable
abstractions"—in Bradley's phrase—"or unearthly ballet of
bloodless categories." The ultimate indirection of Tennyson's
rhetoric is the indirection of thought itself. "Though dragged to
such conclusions," as Bradley says, "we cannot embrace them.
Our [logical] principles may be true, but they are not reality.
They no more MAKE that whole which commands our devotion,
than some shredded dissection of human tatters IS that warm and
breathing beauty of flesh which our heart found delightful."[17]
Elation and terror belong to perfect thought, or they do not. If
they do not, there is an aspect of existence beyond Lucretius' atoms.
If they do belong, then thought is different from the atomist's abstractions. To include the warm and breathing beauty of life,
thought must be transformed. It must make of the subject's
final reunion with its sundered predicates—the goal of all logic—
something fuller and more nuanced than either.

   "The intolerable use of abstractions," says A. N. Whitehead, "is
the major vice of the intellect."[18] With the sundering of the subject from its logical predicates, atomic categories, like a "shredded
dissection of human tatters,"[19] threaten to swallow up Lucretius'
world. How is he to account for the delights and pains of his
flesh, for the agonies and raptures of his soul—these unexpected
meteors falling through his void? There lurks a further irony in
the fact that Lucretius, the systematizer, devises a system that

   17. F. H. Bradley, *The Principles of Logic* (London, 1883), p. 533.
   18. "The Origins of Modern Science," in *Science and the Modern
World* (New York, 1925), p. 18.
   19. F. H. Bradley, *The Principles of Logic,* p. 533.

destroys all system. In an atomic universe in which the paths of
the atoms are derived from no necessities of their natures, the only
law that Lucretius can affirm is that there is no law. Similarly, the
only law that the Idealist Bradley can formulate about relational
thought is the law that it cannot be "real." Lucretius is left with
the spectacle of a phantom universe, the same specter that confronts Tennyson in *In Memoriam*.

> . . . and I saw the flaring atom-streams
> And torrents of her myriad universe,
> Ruining along the illimitable inane,
> Fly on to clash together again, and make
> Another and another frame of things
> For ever. ["Lucretius," ll. 38–43]

In opposition to modern wave theories of the atom, Lucretius
affirms that the fate of a particular particle has nothing to do with
the nature of the particle.[20] Thus there is no justification for posit-
ing, as Newton does, a First Cause that imposes mechanical laws.
In a universe of clashing atoms there is no room for an indwelling eros that urges the soul toward attainment. Lucretius the poet
and cosmologist is therefore logically inconsistent when he invokes
the teleological principle identified with Venus in his prayer. As
an intimate critic of logical process, like his fellow Idealist Bradley, Tennyson uses mental breakdown to remind the rationalist
that he is never more rational than when acknowleding the limits
of his reason. "The intellect of man," says Yeats, "is forced to
choose / Perfection of the life, or of the work" ("The Choice,"
ll. 1–2). If we are to avoid the insanity of Lucretius, who makes
logic his passion, or the fanaticism of those misguided idealists
Pelleas and Balin, who exclude middle terms, we may have to
"choose / Perfection of the life" by embracing more inclusive
forms of vision. The dissolution of logic, though a brilliant dramatic device, is also the Idealist's way of establishing the essential
sanity of the seer, who knows how to control his reason, and the
madness of all merely rational minds. As F. H. Bradley concludes,

20. Compare with A. N. Whitehead, "Cosmologies," in *Adventures of
Ideas* (New York, 1955), especially pp. 135–139.

"the philosopher's reason" may share the fate of "the sculptor who moulded the lion. When in the reason's philosophy, the rational appears dominant and sole possessor of the world, we can only wonder what place would be left to it, if the element excluded might break through the charm of the magic circle, and . . . find expression."[21] The dissolution of logic wakes the rationalist from the pleasant delusion of the madman. It lets the lion rear, roar rampant, walk in time.

> . . . him I proved impossible;
> Twy-natured is no nature: yet he draws
> Nearer and nearer, and I scan him now
> Beastlier than any phantom of his kind
> That ever butted his rough brother-brute.   [ll. 193–197]

As the caged beast breaks through the magic circle, the rationalist discovers, too late, that the shades nowhere speak without blood, and that the ghosts of abstraction accept no substitute. According to Bradley's aphorism, "they reveal themselves only to that victim whose life they have drained, and to converse with shadows" the rationalist must himself "become a shade."[22]

In a world in which all intellectual systems dissolve, in which all political institutions and visions of God are found to be unstable, the aging Tennyson discovers stable identity in only one kind of poem. Drawn into the dismal fellowship of the dead, he comes to write most eloquently of the one thing that does not change: unpredictable decay, the brutal shock of change itself. The problem that baffles the seer and the sage, the impossibility of finding stable forms, now becomes the subject of elegies in which an old man's refinement culminates in love plainly speaking, in which urbanity and grace temper grief for his friends.

21. *The Principles of Logic*, p. 533.
22. F. H. Bradley, aphorism 98, in *Aphorisms* (Oxford, 1930).

The Farther Shore:
The Late Elegies

Except for the gorgeous amplitude of "Demeter and Perse-phone" (finished in May, 1887) and the ceremonial richness of "Frater Ave atque Vale" (1883) and "To Virgil" (1882), the elegies of Tennyson's old age are brutally honest poems, severe and unadorned. When Tennyson the bereaved father is indicting God in "Demeter and Persephone," he still seeks the safety of a dramatic mask. But otherwise he no longer feels the need to hide behind the decorative veils of Arthurian romance or the narrative disguises of *Maud.* Everything comes to the patient man who waits—among other things, death. And Tennyson is too old now to be patient, too old to play with masks. The terror of the void, a subject which age makes more urgent than ever, is a topic that Tennyson still treats obliquely, but with more confidence now and more authority. In some of his barest experiments since *In Memoriam,* in poems stripped of color, metaphor, and ornate language, Tennyson examines the contours of diminished life. Three of his plainest, but still most oblique, elegies, "In the Garden at Swainston" (1870), "To Edward Fitzgerald" (1885), and "To the Marquis of Dufferin and Ava" (1889), are desperately impoverished poems. They begin in a toneless language of exhaustion, and seem barely capable of overcoming the despair and grief that motivate them. Nevertheless, one of the most unexpected turns in Tennyson's late development is the rebirth recorded in "Demeter and Persephone." In autumn, Tennyson rediscovers spring; and burdened with age, he writes a sublime poetry of millennial hope and new beginnings.

Ceremonial Richness

Born of the anguish of Tennyson's old age, after his son Lionel's death in 1886, "Demeter and Persephone" offers the poet vicarious relief. When the goddess Demeter is first reunited with her daughter, she must revive painful memories of the rape, so that in their pastoral paradise the countervailing reflections of hell, like repressed materials under psychoanalysis, may be brought into focus and dispelled. Driven to distraction by her child's loss, just as Tennyson is by the loss of his son, the great earth mother nurses "ailing infants in the night" (l. 55). The death of nature becomes, in M. H. Abrams' phrase, "a theodicy of [her] private life."[1]

> I climbed on all the cliffs of all the seas,
> And asked the waves that moan about the world
> 'Where? do ye make your moaning for my child?'
> And round from all the world the voices came
> 'We know not, and we know not why we moan.' [ll. 62–66]

There is a final unaccountableness in creation. As the ancient sage realizes, intelligent men can do no more than perceive the profundity of the abyss. It is as if an indifferent and amoral energy produced the universe or, as Spinoza declared, a God whose thoughts are not like our thoughts. By speaking through the goddess, the grieving father can subject even God himself to criticism. Through a double indirection—psychological and dramatic—Tennyson learns to use his energies constructively. A union of strong feeling, accurate vision, and true thought remains one of the permanent achievements of classical myth. In "Demeter and Persephone" it allows the bereaved father to master subversive thoughts—thoughts he could not have borne to reach out and assimilate directly. But so authoritative is Tennyson's sense of what produces the quarrel of life with the conditions of life itself, and so powerful is the catharsis he achieves, that after finishing the monologue, only a short poem, we feel we might be at the end of a tragedy or epic.

Though "Demeter and Persephone" is a simpler poem than

1. *Natural Supernaturalism* (New York, 1971), p. 95.

the classical monologues of the eighteen-thirties—"Ulysses" and "Tithonus"—it reveals a comparable division in the speaker's mind. Is death really dreadful, or is it, in Wallace Stevens' phrase, "the mother of beauty"?[2] The wavering is clearest toward the end of the poem. Though "the harvest hymns of Earth" (l. 146) strike a note of festive celebration, they convey the same slowing down of life that we find in "Tithonus": a sense of richness and repose, but also of withdrawal, or recession and decline. The cycles of frustrated work and torture—the repetition without progress of rolling "The Stone" or turning "the Wheel"—are infernal and terrifying. But the undulating music of "dimly-glimmering," "fires," "glide," and "silent field" hovers with uncertainty over thin vowels, harsh gutturals, and soft alliterations. Its tremors of nuance capture that perishable quality in beauty which makes the death of nature, however dreadful, both subtle and enchanting.

These fluctuations are most apparent in Tennyson's revision of the last few lines.

and see no more

> The Stone, the Wheel, the dimly-glimmering lawns
> Of that Elysium, all the hateful fires
> Of torment, and the shadowy warrior glide
> Along the silent field of Asphodel.   [ll. 147–151]

In the first of four versions preserved in Harvard notebook 53, Tennyson celebrates as "The Demigods of Earth" the "souls of men" who "made themselves as Gods." But in revising, he drops the reference to the "Demigods" and makes the cadences themselves heroic. The thin vowel music of "sinful fires" turns into a resonant indictment of "hateful fires," but the harshness is qualified by a melodious evocation of Achilles, who instead of *"fleeting"* along "the *noiseless* field," *glides*, more gently and lightly now, "Along the *silent* field" (my italics). A final music, varied and intense, replaces the simple majesty of prophecy and the rigors of lament. As the coda focuses, with full pathos, on "the Stone," "the Wheel," and the "field of Asphodel," the prophetic certitude

2. "Sunday Morning," V, 3.

of "see no more" is quietly discarded. The eye registers the undulations, phrase by phrase, waiting to locate Sisyphus and Achilles in their twilight world, until Demeter's prophecy of obliterating that world is all but forgotten. Achilles moves softly in the last great lines, and twilight descends in the way in which a man might hope to die. As each phrase subsides, knowing its inevitable direction but pausing and hovering before descent, prophetic assurance is replaced by a natural dignity of movement that precludes lament.

As majestic and austere as "Demeter and Persephone," the jewel among the late poems, are two of Tennyson's classically inspired elegies, "Frater Ave atque Vale" (1883) and "To Virgil" (1882). Through the exquisite melody of "Frater Ave atque Vale" throbs the personal grief of the aging Tennyson, whose favorite brother had died the year before. The balancing of salutation and farewell in the title extends to every detail of the elegy: its blend of enchantment and despair, conplacency and muted protest. At first Tennyson seems to swoon in a passivity of sound and sense, as he surrenders to the lulling accords of "all-but-island, olive-silvery Sirmio" (l. 9). But the charm of Sirmio, he implies, correcting the first delighted response, is inseparable from Catullus' poem on Sirmio, an elegy for his dead brother, which reminds Tennyson of the hitherto neglected elements of memory and intellect. Beauty is not simply a datum, something given, but—as Catullus understood—something that the memory contributes to the senses; it is a *comprehensum,* like the poignant greeting "Frater Ave atque Vale," which links the present with a world beyond and which, like other familiar and untranslatable lines, is at once the least explicit and the most explicit in the poem.

Though the landscape expresses subtle dualities that allow the mind to allay its grief, the poem is also designed to disappoint the speaker by pairing each item of potential joy—the purple flowers, the tenderness, the Lydian laughter—with a negation of joy: the Roman ruin, the hopeless woe, the distanced prospect of merely "Gazing" (l. 8). The last line is a meditation on that moment of ripeness which verges on dissolution. By conveying, imperceptibly, a moment of transition between excess and decay the speaker refuses to indulge the devious logic of hope that "Tithonus" and "Demeter and Persephone" indulge: the illusory wish that the self-forgetful ripeness of nature might endure.

"To Virgil," which Douglas Bush calls "the briefest and finest appreciation" of the classical poet "ever written,"[3] exists, like "Frater Ave atque Vale," in a state of reversible equilibrium. The triumphal beginning soon becomes the vision of "Ilion falling, Rome arising" (l. 2), which prepares in turn for the decline of all civilizations, and Tennyson's personal, scrutinizing vision of the world itself as a "phantom shore" (l. 13).

> Light among the vanished ages; star that gildest yet this
> phantom shore;
> Golden branch amid the shadows, kings and realms that pass
> to rise no more. [ll. 13–14]

The tribute to Virgil begins with the ceremony of epic, the rich simplicity of pastoral, the prophecy of eclogue. It makes very little difference where Virgil finds his themes; the "Landscape-lover, lord of language" (l. 3) alchemizes all his elements into gold; in the midst of grief, he celebrates the power of "Universal Mind" (l. 11). Giving mysterious access to a world beyond, he shines like his epic's "Golden branch amid the shadows" (l. 14). Tennyson does not try to resolve the celebration and despair. Rather, he permits contradictory reactions to take place. Examination of the Harvard manuscript discloses that when Tennyson revises, he consistently balances his first impressions of Virgil's opulence and ease with pictures of brooding and gloom.[4] Understandably, the

3. *Mythology and the Romantic Tradition in English Poetry* (Cambridge, Mass., 1937), p. 226.
4. The original version of the poem appears in Harvard notebook 66. The only lines that Tennyson has completely discarded, in substance as well as in form, are the following: "Quoted in the halls of Council, spoken yet in every schoolboys home / Only living [Imperator left?] of all thine own imperial Rome." The original version of the fifth stanza, the last to be composed, was: "Thou that in thy Pollio chantest unlaborious earth and oarless sea, / Summers of the snakeless meadow, glories of the balsam-bearing tree." The germ of the famous sixth stanza, which otherwise does not appear in the Harvard manuscript, is the discarded line: "Thou that findest mind and soul in Sun and Moon and Star and Earth and Sea."

germ of the poem is the marvelous phrase "Landscape-lover, lord
of language." But as Tennyson revises, he subordinates the landscape painter, the celebrant of "balsambearing" trees, to the sage
"majestic" in his "sadness" (l. 12). The poet who sees "Universal
Nature" is no longer the authority quoted in council halls, as he
was in the first version. Nor does he see "Universal Mind" in an
exotic catalogue of "Sun and Moon and Star and Earth and
Sea." Virgil now broods over "the doubtful doom of human
kind" in the gravest line of the poem, and in—significantly—the
last stanza to be written.

> Thou that seëst Universal Nature moved by Universal Mind;
> Thou majestic in thy sadness at the doubtful doom of human
> kind. [ll. 11–12]

The inveterate human tendency to idealize experience is nowhere more beautifully resisted than in Tennyson's tribute to
Virgil. During the repetitive and enchanting review of Virgil's
achievement, many painful truths become clear. To pay formal
tribute to Rome is not to deify it; to praise a landscape is not to
worship it. Virgil's love is inseparable from his disenchantment;
his prayers are suffused with an inconsolable grief, the product of
a temperamental melancholy, a brooding sense of what has passed.
The glimpse into "Universal Mind" is also a glimpse into the
abyss, "the doubtful doom of human kind" (l. 12)—a vision of
chaos that has as much power to frighten and appall the poet as
to soothe and console him.

The lines to Virgil raise the issue of how sight is related to insight, and the envisaged to the perceived. After the opening vision
of the fall and rise of great civilizations, the pastoral ease of the
mere "Landscape-lover" is never left unchallenged. The world
of "wheat and woodland, tilth and vineyard" (l. 5) may seem too
ripe for gloom. But "the doubtful doom of human kind" is foreshadowed by the claims the poet makes about the pastoral paradise: "Summers of the snakeless meadow, unlaborious earth and
oarless sea" (l. 10). Tennyson's praise is all put in negative terms.
As in lotos land, the warmth and ease emerge from the heavy toll

of the mariners' disasters, from serpent-like coilings at the heart's core. The knell-like cycle of "kings and realms" that mount and shine, then fall "to rise no more" (l. 14), inspires in Tennyson the somber elation of Virgil and Arnold: the paradox of majesty in grief, the truth of the elegist who has brooded on ruin, on "Glooms that enhance and glorify this earth" (Matthew Arnold, "To a Gipsy Child by the Sea-Shore," l. 20).

The Plain Style

More characteristic of Tennyson's late phase than the ceremonial richness of the classical pieces is the plain style of his lines "To The Marquis of Dufferin and Ava" (1889), "In the Garden at Swainston" (1870), and "Crossing the Bar" (1889). Set in desolate scenes, unremittingly stark and minimal, these late elegies use a deliberately impoverished but oblique style, first perfected in two early elegies written shortly after Hallam's death: "Break, break, break" (probably 1834) and "On a Mourner" (1833).

"On a Mourner" uses three different forms of the plain style: descriptive, allegorical, and mythic. There is nothing in the opening plainness of description to transport the mourner's heart beyond the "purple lilac" of spring or the "airy hill" (ll. 7–8). But with the coming of night the pageant of "Hope," "Memory," "Faith" instructs the mourner's heart in other mysteries. The eye, still in love with light, yearns for the beauty of an unseen world. Corresponding to a gradual enlargement of the figurative pattern in the last three stanzas are the progressively larger syntactical units: in stanza 5, a two-line subordinate clause followed by a three-line principal clause; and in stanzas 6 and 7, a two-line subordinate clause followed by an expansive eight-line principal clause, spanning the break between stanzas with a spacious simile.

5

And when the zoning eve has died
    Where yon dark valleys wind forlorn,
Come Hope and Memory, spouse and bride,
    From out the borders of the morn,
    With that fair child betwixt them born.

6

> And when no mortal motion jars
>   The blackness round the tombing sod,
> Through silence and the trembling stars
>   Comes Faith from tracts no feet have trod,
>   And Virtue, like a household god

7

> Promising empire; such as those
>   Once heard at dead of night to greet
> Troy's wandering prince, so that he rose
>   With sacrifice, while all the fleet
>   Had rest by stony hills of Crete.   [ll. 21-35]

Tennyson uses a similar technique in *In Memoriam*, where the expansion of figurative and exemplary units in Section L, for example, is auxiliary to the speaker's increasingly expansive statements, culminating in "The twilight of eternal day" (L, 16). The increasing size of the exemplifying units and the grammatical dependence of the two concluding objects—"the term" and "The twilight" (L, 14, 16)—on a tenseless infinitive "To point" (L, 14), which directs our gaze beyond time, give direct support to the speaker's final statement, as do the suspended participle "Promising" (l. 31) and the timeless infinitive "to greet" (l. 32) in "On a Mourner." The tremendous authority and bareness of the lyric's ending recall the grand austerities of the great elegy. Like the seventh-syllable caesuras in Section XLII of *In Memoriam* (ll. 7, 11)—

> A lord of large experience, train
> To riper growth the mind and will.   [ll. 7-8]

> When one that loves but knows not, reaps
> A truth from one that loves and knows?   [ll. 11-12]

—the run-over at the end of the sixth stanza and the fifth-syllable caesura in the next line beautifully prepare for the poet's inclusion in a larger truth. Standing out in craggy relief against the "stony hills," whose bleakness is audible, as Ricks observes, "in the con-

cluding hard-edged rhyme,"[5] Aeneas hears voices that urge him
beyond Crete to a promised empire on some farther shore. The
plain style's mixture of description, pageant, and Virgilian myth
is so contrived that the poet grandly, in Aeneas' prophetic vision;
incidentally, in allegorical fragments; and pictorially, in the simple analogies between God and nature, discovers powerful consolations.

In "Break, break, break" Tennyson forgoes even the simplicities
of myth. Though written in the same decade as "Ulysses" and
"Tithonus," the poem renounces the grand harmonies of those
monologues for the spare obliquity of Tennyson's late elegies. As
in *In Memoriam,* Tennyson begins by discounting the power of
words to say explicitly what he feels. Instead he seeks distraction
in the innocent pleasures of "the fisherman's boy" (l. 5), the
carefree toil of the "sailor lad" (l. 7), and the progress of the
ships. Each pair of lines stands like an epitaph, in strict grammatical autonomy; and the final pair, the most desolate of them,
is an epitaph for the mourner:

> But the tender grace of a day that is dead
> Will never come back to me.   [ll. 15–16]

The silence of the grave finds the poet mocked by the change of
contour, as the desolate scene seems to yield more buoyant impressions at the center. The final stanza repeats the opening line; and
weighted with monotony, it discovers the same loss everywhere.
Still, despite the flat negation, "The tender grace of a day that is
dead" is curiously alive. The "voice that is still" and the "vanished
hand" (ll. 4, 3) come to life with an expressed tone of regard
that Tennyson could not have realized before Hallam's death,
and that his "tongue" could not begin to "utter" (l. 3) when he
started the poem.

In its oblique simplicity, the perfection of "Break, break, break"
is inseparable from the powerful barrenness of *In Memoriam.* If
the mourner's grief can be given only "in outline and no more,"
as it is in *In Memoriam* (V, 12), then it is impossible to realize

5. Christopher Ricks, *Tennyson* (New York, 1972), p. 120.

the particular nature—and so the particular limits—of that grief; it is already on the way to becoming a "divine despair" (*The Princess*, IV, 22). But if the elegist is not to be trapped in ineffectual gestures of mourning, which like the dove in Section XII have a habit of circling round and round a topic without advancing, his suffering will have to draw support from the faith that "men may rise on stepping-stones / Of their dead selves to higher things" (I, 3–4). Though "Break, break, break" has its burden of "immedicable woes," of what Frost has called "woes that nothing can be done for—woes flat and final,"[6] one of the best commentators on the elegy notes that "the destructive element [is] twice described as 'Thy' stones, 'Thy' crags."[7] Even as the worth of life seems to fade away forever, the "sea becomes a symbol . . . of a principle behind both life and death"[8] that gives the mourner another way to feel. Just as crucial to the poem's success as the suffering, the pain immediately felt, are the elegist's faith in such a principle and the paradox of elation in grief. The poignant life of "a day that is dead" (l. 15) hovers just beyond language; the truth about its life—and death—is something unsayable that the elegist can never quite put into words.

These early "steps toward the great thoughts, grave thoughts, thoughts lasting to the end,"[9] anticipate the stark elegies of Tennyson's later years. The deaths of Sir John Simeon in 1870, Edward Fitzgerald in 1883, and Tennyson's son Lionel in 1886 overwhelm the poet with a sense of the barren emptiness of the world. If he cannot discern some finer quality beyond the emptiness, the world will seem to be a passing shadow and insignificance the final fact.

6. Robert Frost, Preface to E. A. Robinson's *King Jasper*, in *Selected Prose of Robert Frost*, eds. H. Cox and E. Lathem (New York, 1968), p. 67.

7. F. E. L. Priestley, *Language and Structure in Tennyson's Poetry* (London, 1973), p. 146.

8. *Ibid.*

9. Robert Frost, "Education by Poetry" (1931), in *Selected Prose*, ed. Cox and Lathem, p. 42.

"In the Garden at Swainston" uses the barest tokens, the most meager signs, of what Tennyson wants to convey. From the simplest indications—a nightingale, the shadows of three dead men, and a coffin—he composes, not only the whole decay of nature, but also an implicit defiance of ruin, refusing like the nightingales to be undone by the lifelessness he sees. Tennyson has to retell his experience three times before he can discover why his neighbor's death moves him so deeply. Simeon, after all, was an acquaintance, not an intimate friend. Why should Tennyson have been found on the day of Simeon's funeral stretched out on the floor, immobilized by grief? Though successive stanzas seem at first to add few clues, the redundancy is apparent, not real; for each time the experience is described it is altered. Tennyson's first account is impersonal; the warbling of the nightingales is as prominent as the weeping indoors, and we are not told how the "Shadows" of the "three dead men" affect him. The second stanza gives an equally generalized view, but what is universalized now is the brevity of all life, pondered as a permanent truth. Though Tennyson is concerned with Simeon's finer qualities, his tribute to "the Prince of courtesy" (1. 10) is courtly but restrained. The only words keeping him in touch with despair are the ominous "far away," "lasts but a day," and the ceremonial starkness of "coffin" (ll. 7, 9–10).

The last stanza returns to the deaths of Hallam and Henry Lushington, a gifted Cambridge Apostle, mentioned at the opening; but instead of being remote "Shadows," the dead men are now motions of the poet's soul. Some remnant of Tennyson's claims on life exists in these voices from the grave; their claims, tenacious in memory, have not at all melted away, though they no longer flood his soul with the elation of remembered passion and grief, as they did in the great stanzas of "Tithonus" and "Ulysses." The gravities of resignation belong now to a seer who has given up elation, and whose grieving measured tones are quite subdued.

> Two dead men have I known
> In courtesy like to thee:

> Two dead men have I loved
> With a love that ever will be:
> Three dead men have I loved and thou art last of the three.
>
> [ll. 11–15]

The stark simplicity of the stanza recalls the many sections of *In Memoriam* where Tennyson uses the bare skeleton of language. Even the potential triteness of "a love that ever will be" powerfully reverses, in its context, the "passion that lasts but a day" (l. 9). Like the banality of "How good! how kind! and he is gone" in *In Memoriam* (XX, 20), which illustrates the failure of language to express what the mourner feels, the elegist's commonplace diction is required and justified by his shrunken commentary. In redefining, with increasing approximation to the truth, what Simeon's death means to Tennyson, the plain style demonstrates his absolute willingness to say how things are, to choose the accurate tribute, and to follow the truth of his feeling without forcing feeling too soon. The closing cadences are corpselike; for this aging voice all elation and love are distanced in the remote and remembered pathos of a much greater loss than Simeon's— in the cry of profound sadness and bewilderment that had overtaken Tennyson many years earlier when the person he most loved in life had died.

In the elegy "To Edward Fitzgerald," another poem of Tennyson's old age, originally appended as a postscript to the monologue "Tiresias," life offers an ending that surprises even Tennyson. Most generic indirection is a result of design. But here it is a result of accident, though of accident that Tennyson uses with design. In June of 1883, Tennyson had composed a verse epistle for his friend Fitzgerald, which was to accompany and introduce a copy of "Tiresias," a monologue of pagan sacrifice written in 1833, some fifty years earlier. Before Tennyson could send the monologue and the prefatory epistle, Fitzgerald died. For the conclusion to "Tiresias" that Tennyson had planned, death had written a more powerful ending. There is nothing oblique about a verse epistle to a friend. But not even Tennyson could have anticipated the indirection of its sequel. As the postscript to a monologue that urges us to face death bravely, the elegy for Fitzgerald tests even Tennyson. Its indirection is affecting, for it is dictated, not by art, but by life; and in meeting life's test Tennyson fulfills his design in an unforgettable way.

One might have thought that the coda of "Tiresias," which rings throughout with the finality of death, had well exhausted the subject. In the elegiac postscript, however, Tennyson unexpectedly turns from the incantatory "tolling" of Fitzgerald's "funeral bell" (l. 63) to a chilling envoy that sweeps the poet himself, the friend of "so many dead, / And him the last" (ll. 82–83), into the dismal fellowship of mortality. Though blunted by repeated references to the underworld in the "Pagan Paradise" (l. 64) of "Tiresias," death's sting is sharpened once again in the postscript. By speaking, not simply of his own futile march toward the grave, but of *"Our* living out" (l. 80) and *"our* poor . . . dawn"* (l. 77—my italics), Tennyson revives the piercing truth of Donne: "Ask not for whom the bell tolls; it tolls for thee." The poet has made Fitzgerald's death our own.

For those readers to whom the problems raised in the monologue are more compelling than Tiresias' answers, the postscript is a more effective resolution than the monologue. In focusing on Tennyson himself, as the frame at the end of *Lycidas* focuses on Milton, the elegy relates death to personal motives. Mortality may be "an event by which a wise man can never be surprised," as the sage says in Samuel Johnson's *Rasselas,* for it is always at hand and should be expected when it comes. But the emotion of the postscript is more affecting than such cold certitudes. The source of its power is a sense of grief barely under control, always at the point of overwhelming Tennyson and bringing his verse to a stop. If Tennyson had to write more quickly, he could not go on. But his fears are controlled by the formality of the genre: by the decorative ease with which the verse epistle unfolds its simile of the would-be guest who arrives an hour too late, to find the gate bolted and the master gone. Terror still breaks out in the poet's brooding on darkness and in his repetition, three times, of the dread word "night": "past, in sleep, away / By night, into the

deeper night! / The deeper night?" (ll. 74–76). The rest of the
elegy consists of grammatical fragments, with no syntactical completion until the closing optative. Disintegrating grammar creates
the same effect as the chain of infinitive phrases in Archibald
MacLeish's elegy "You, Andrew Marvell." With no principal
verb, that poem's fragments present the coming on of night,
until all syntax, like all light, fades out in a series of dots. In the
bleak memory of "so many dead, / And him the last" ("To Edward Fitzgerald," ll. 82–83), Tennyson's elegy seems to be going
to pieces, breaking with grief for a final time. But the end of the
poem possesses the authority that comes from having gone
through great disorder, then coming out again on the other side.
The last lines look forward to the poet's own death, and complete
what we understand to be, in every sense, a last farewell.

> What life, so maimed by night, were worth
>   Our living out? Not mine to me
> Remembering all the golden hours
>   Now silent, and so many dead,
> And him the last; and laying flowers,
>   This wreath, above his honoured head,
> And praying that, when I from hence
>   Shall fade with him into the unknown,
> My close of earth's experience
>   May prove as peaceful as his own.   [ll. 79–88]

What surprises the reader is not simply the ingenuity with which
Tennyson has turned one of life's indirections into the indirection
of his poem. It is no longer the shock of Fitzgerald's death that
surprises, but the elegance and ease with which the elegy absorbs
that shock. In an imperfect world, whose disasters befall those we
love best, those who matter most, the perfect control of disaster
is surprising.

The best parts of Tennyson's poem "To the Marquis of Dufferin and Ava" (published in 1889) are always elegiac, even in
gratitude and friendship; they wander, almost casually, as the
poet's thoughts wander. It is as if the thought of his son's death
in India comes only as an afterthought, but as an afterthought too
powerful to turn aside. Memory of the dead son so obsesses the

poet that he seems to change his original plan at the end of the
fourth stanza, just as Robert Gregory intrudes in Yeats's great
elegy:

> I had thought . . .
> . . . to have brought to mind
> All those that manhood tried . . .
> With some appropriate commentary on each;
> . . . but a thought
> Of that late death took all my heart for speech.
> ["In Memory of Major Robert Gregory," ll. 89–96]

Yeats's discovery, as he writes, of the poem's way of unfolding is
beautiful and affecting, as though his provisional conduct of the
poem is the perfect way of expressing the provisional nature of
every life. Similarly, in Tennyson's lines the most moving shift
occurs when the speaker seems to stop in his course, almost bringing the poem to a halt, faltering like his son in his very capacity
to find words.

> Dying, 'Unspeakable' he wrote
> 'Their kindness,' and he wrote no more.   [ll. 35–36]

In recognizing the limits of language—a recognition which con-
stitutes at once a better pride and a better humility than anything
else in the poem—Tennyson, like his dying son, refuses a banal
logic in articulating gratitude in favor of a truer and more
poignant equivocation: "and he wrote no more." The emotional
weight of the words is unbearable; the shift in meaning makes
the brevity shocking, turning the brevity of a letter into a brevity
that is final.

The lines acquire a momentary wildness in their touching on a
subject that must be fulfilled, the "Unspeakable" loss that saves
the whole poem. Though we are stunned by what Emerson calls
"that one wild line out of a private heart," Tennyson barely
touches the subject in passing, so painful is the wound. The reluctance to probe any further is made much clearer in an earlier
version of the poem, now at Harvard, in which the bereaved poet,
not his son, breaks off speaking:

'Unspeakable' he wrote
'Their kindness!' see, I say no more.

But Tennyson wants to say more; he keeps hovering over his son's last words, tearing himself away with difficulty at the end of the poem, as the Harvard manuscript makes clear.

"As kind to me
As if your [Tennyson's] son had been their [the Dufferins']
own."

Few poets understand so well as Tennyson the elusive connection between art and reticence.[10] In the Harvard manuscript the bereaved father is assailed by demonic "shapes, shadows" and "Black decks," and he hears the sound of a "muffled bell."[11] In

10. Reticence allows Tennyson to turn merely "sincere" emotion into "significant" emotion, a truth anticipated by a fascinating little offprint entitled *"Ut Pictura Poesis": An Essay on the Poetic Element* (Dublin, privately printed, 1878) found in Tennyson's library. In propounding a theory of "the poetic mode of dealing with emotion," its anonymous author, who signs himself G. E., denies that even the most expressive forms of art can be "the natural expression of real emotion." If Robert Burns were actually undergoing the agony of soul depicted in his poem "To Mary in Heaven," "he would neither try nor desire to give utterance to his real feelings. . . . The process of. . . . composition was accompanied, not by the acutely painful emotions so powerfully drawn, but by others of a very different kind" (pp. 34–35). We can see G. E. groping toward that elusive connection between the aesthetic and the impersonal, understood so well by Tennyson, which forty years later, T. S. Eliot, in his essay "Tradition and the Individual Talent," would formulate as his famous distinction between "sincere" and "significant" emotion. Though the pseudonym G. E. was used by Edward G. Bulwer-Lytton, he died before the offprint appeared. Since the work was printed in Dublin, its anonymous author is probably the same G. E. who contributed articles to the *Dublin Review* for April, 1898 and April, 1900. *The Wellesley Index to Victorian Periodicals* (Toronto, 1966) has not identified the contributor.

11. The early versions of the poem appear in Harvard notebook 55. Stanza 11 originally read: "But sounds, shapes, shadows, trouble me / Black decks, sea-[whirl?], muffled bell / And that which in the coffin fell, / Fell, and flash'd into the Red Sea." Other variations are "hair's-breadth" for "side-path" in l. 28; and "disastrous Indian air" for "jungle-poisoned air" in l. 31. The original version of the last two lines was: "I mix his memory and his name / With love for you, my friend, and yours." Above these lines appear the words "Of you and yours . . . 'As kind to me / As if your son had been their own.' "

revising the poem Tennyson discards these nightmare impressions; he discovers that he can reveal much more by saying much less. The meaning of Lionel's death is a mystery not to be declared by Tennyson, though it is wonderfully intimated by the charged subtext, by the all but uncontrolled emotion of the words behind the words. Yet as the original version of line 48 emphasizes, with its hesitating motion—and halting pause before the dash—the questioning of fate is "Vain, vain! and—I may meet him soon." Trying to disguise his frustration, Tennyson introduces a sequence of infinitives, syntactically independent, which create a timeless state, just as the "hard Arabian moon / And alien stars" (ll. 45–46) expand the poem spatially: "Not there to bid my boy farewell" (l. 42); " . . . To question, why" (l. 46). Because Tennyson provides no resolution of the infinitive phrases, which simply look forward to the "hueless gray" (l. 50) of his declining years, the phrases allow him to escape, momentarily, the final questions. "I may meet him soon" (l. 48) introduces the uncertainty of knowledge, and makes possible Tennyson's retreat from the unsayable meanings, hovering just beyond the poem, to the loves and memories of his last years.

The poem uses the same stanzaic form as *In Memoriam;* and in fragmented form and substance it recalls the dismal eastern setting of Section XXVI:

> Then might I find, ere yet the morn
>   Breaks hither over Indian seas,
>   That Shadow waiting with the keys,
> To shroud me from my proper scorn.   [XXVI, 13–16]

The rhythm in Section XXVI becomes increasingly agitated as the theological intellect intrudes to correct the inaccuracy of "eye foresee" (XXVI, 9) and to worry over its uneasy chiasmus: "In more of life true life no more" (XXVI, 11). After the imaginative leaps and the theological enigma of God's foreknowledge—a mystery presented in broken syntax, like Tennyson's questioning of God in the lines to Dufferin—the "Shadow" comes almost as a relief. Similarly, as Tennyson forces himself to watch his son's coffin fall and flash in the Red Sea, as the unnamable form "within" passes forever from the mind's eye, he all but welcomes the horror, preferring the harsh truth to nebulous terror, to remote "rites I have not seen" and "one drear sound I have not heard" (ll. 39–40). Though the sentiment of the sage—"I may meet him soon" (l. 48)—is more serene than the bereaved father's anguish, the expression of anguish is more precise and irreplaceable. The tenuous efforts to place some penultimate distractions between himself and the void cannot disguise the fact that Tennyson is not celebrating imperial rule, administering a blow to fate, or even writing a letter of thanks to his son's hosts. He is engaging in a colloquy with himself; in facing bleak, funereal finalities, he renounces consolation. Composing a blank, final music, Tennyson communicates most when willing to affirm nothing.

In its somber destitution, "Crossing the Bar" composes a poetry of the austere and the minimal, a farewell stubbornly resisting its own pathos. It renounces the horror expressed so starkly in the lines to Dufferin, and the need to sanctify through Virgilian consecration or through Demeter's harvest hymns of earth. On the threshold of death, Tennyson, like Ulysses, rediscovers life, and writes an exalted poetry of new beginnings. But its four stanzas carry Tennyson well beyond the naked majesty of the old Ulysses: whereas Ulysses still places heroic adventures between himself and death, Tennyson finally accepts and celebrates his "end"—both his final cause and his death—in a poem whose perfection of form first gives shape to the hugeness and confusion shading away into darkness, then dissolves into the "boundless deep" as it "Turns again home."

Tennyson's provisional way of unfolding his meaning in "Crossing the Bar" has led to charges of confusion and obscurity. But there are few finer examples of Tennyson's ability to discover his meaning as he writes, allowing alternative versions to stand. Instead of being swept away, Tennyson's putting "out to sea" is an act of volition; he is the tide's master, not its victim. Even as his life drains into the "boundless deep" (l. 7), he uses his departure to assimilate terror and innocence and to reaffirm, in a startling and unexpected way, his residual convictions that he will survive the crossing and that a divine providence is in charge.

To pass through the harbor mouth is to see the face of God. But to see and love God, Tennyson thinks, is first to have been seen and loved by God. Instead of ratifying the logic of his original conception, Tennyson changes God from the goal to the guide. If we do not intuit the "natural" ending, we cannot see how Tennyson has made it "supernatural," how he has refused a conventional logic in favor of a deeper mystery. God is the guide as well as the goal, for without his Incarnation as the "Pilot" at the outset of the voyage there would be no immortality on the farther shore. Tennyson turns round, like the tide, and writes "Pilot"—indwelling God or Logos—instead of transcendent "Father" or "Maker," ending in a tone of both greater confidence and greater humility. Though he knows he will not make the journey by using his own navigating skills, his humility is also a form of confidence: a trust in his Pilot's presence, like Milton's trust in "The pilot of the Galilean lake" (*Lycidas,* l. 109), which strengthens the tentative force of "hope." The surprising re-enactment of St. Paul's metaphor "For now we see through a glass darkly, but then face to face" (I Cor. 13:12) is not simply an exercise in theological precision; it is primarily an exercise in the affections, producing in the poet a complex tolerance of his own hopes and fears.

Like the other late elegies, "Crossing the Bar" is modeled on the oblique simplicities of *In Memoriam,* especially Section XVII, where Tennyson awaits the arrival of Hallam's body on the ship.

> Week after week: the days go by:
> Come quick, thou bringest all I love.   [XVII, 7–8]

At first, in Section XVII, the short syntactic units create a sense of urgency, as do the first and third stanzas of "Crossing the Bar," which suggest that Tennyson is impatient to embark. But the pent-up emotion is released in the heartfelt confession "thou bringest all I love" (XVII, 8) and in the reassuring "Henceforth" (XVII, 9), which evaluates the arrival of the ship from a new perspective.

> So kind an office hath been done,
> Such precious relics brought by thee.   [XVII, 17–18]

Like these large benefactions in *In Memoriam,* the spacious movements and vigorous new tone of the second and fourth stanzas in
"Crossing the Bar" are amply earned by the poem's double line of
action: the beneficent external action of the tide and the powerful
internal action of the prayers. "Too full for sound," the tide is
linked by sacramental analogy to the "boundless deep" (ll. 6, 7)
of the spirit world, just as, in *In Memoriam,* "the whisper of an
air" (XVII, 3) is linked to the gracious breeze. In neither poem,
of course, can the visionary elegist prevail completely, for to describe the "Pilot face to face" ("Crossing the Bar," l. 15) or to
capture the *totum simul* of "boundless day" is to render a non-
artistic experience. It is to give the whole of reality, which by
definition no poem, as a highly ordered segment of life, can ever
give.

On the contrary, with the repeated optative—"may there be
no moaning" (l. 3); "may there be no sadness" (l. 11)—and the
final "hope" (l. 15), Tennyson is committed at the end to nothing
but a wish. As if to emphasize that he allows himself no false
hopes, he leaves the first half of the opening and penultimate
stanzas grammatically independent.

> Sunset and evening star,
> And one clear call for me!   [ll. 1–2]

> Twilight and evening bell,
> And after that the dark!   [ll. 9–10]

These are the only unconditional truths in the poem; all else is
construction and surmise, possible ways of relating to the "dark,"
still to be tried, and thus completely tentative. Far from binding
Tennyson to the farther shore, the network of possibilities (the
repeated "may there be"; the phrases "may bear me far" [l. 14]
and "seems asleep" [l. 5]) makes the whole voyage tenuous. The
hypothetical forms create a spiderweb—a fragile threadwork—on
which Tennyson keeps putting out faint feelers, fastidious prob-

ings of the deep. Yet his crossing is so contrived that, even as he
senses the full horror of concluding, the great dread of extinction,
he is able to summon up gestures of assertion. Like the Virgilian
dead whom Charon refuses to ferry to their final abode, Tennyson, the dispossessed heir of *In Memoriam*, the traveler in a universe he once thought purposeless, hesitantly stretches forth his
hands in love of the farther shore.[12]

Tendebantque manus ripae ulterioris amore.
[*Aeneid*, VI, 314]

(And they stretched forth their hands, through love of the
farther shore.)

Whether it ebbs away in grief in the lines to Dufferin, or
mounts to subdued elation in "Tithonus" and "To Virgil," Tennyson's poetry is essentially elegiac, a *meditatio mortis*. Though
Tennyson has prepared all his life for death, he has tended to hide
its terror behind the decorative veils of Arthurian romance or
dramatic masks like *Maud*. Now, in the last poems, Tennyson is
too old to be nostalgic and too honest to equivocate. Like *In
Memoriam*, Tennyson's late elegies are bleak testaments to internal necessity, memorials to very private acts of heroism. Each
begins in grief or exhaustion, then pulls itself together with immense effort to assert the life, not the extinction, of heroic effort.
The impoverished figures in the late elegies suggests the poverty of
earth once night and winter come. Tennyson may still use an
ornate style in the classical pieces, but elsewhere the attenuated
diction is appropriate to the imminence of death. In an imperfect
world the imagination must find its own paradise, as it does in
In Memoriam, absorbing the barrenness of nature. It is true that
as a "lord of language" ("To Virgil," l. 3), Tennyson will be remembered, not for his plain style, but for his celebrated refinement and artifice, for the majestic threnodies that contend in his

12. One recalls Matthew Arnold's final comment on Marcus Aurelius:
"We see him wise, just, self-governed, tender, thankful, blameless; yet, with
all this, agitated, stretching out his arms for something beyond,—*ten-
dentemque manus ripae ulterioris amore*" (R. H. Super, ed., *The Complete
Prose Works of Matthew Arnold*, III [Ann Arbor, Mich., 1962], 157).

greatest poems with the severe refinements of the stoic, with those moods of reticence that create the charged subtexts of "Tithonus" and "Ulysses." Yet there is still a tremendous and intense compression in the late elegies, a powerful indirection in the lines to Dufferin and the verses on Simeon. The grand austerity of style and thought helps the aged Tennyson control his grief. It allows him to retain composure while recording, not the moments of surpassing vision, but a plain version of diminished life, in a poetry of skeletal inscription and epitaph, an hour before the end.

Conclusion:
Achievements of the Style

T. S. Eliot observes that Tennyson combines "three qualities which are seldom found together except in the greatest poets: abundance, variety, and complete competence."[1] The sheer abundance and variety make it difficult to generalize, for Tennyson has many styles. After the choiring verses of "The Lotos-Eaters," derived from the ravishing harmonies of Spenser, the young Tennyson fashions a new spareness of language. In "Ulysses" and "Tithonus" he writes his first great poems of large and nuanced meaning. Heroic in its language, but also elegiac and reflective, "Ulysses" unites the simplicity of the "Mariana" poems with the nostalgia of "Oenone." In "Tithonus" Tennyson tames his love of grandeur to a new mood of reticence, and writes a poetry of "earth in earth"—"simple," "severe," and truly "grand."[2] The increased expanse of *The Princess* releases Tennyson into an easy variety of styles and genres, a beautiful equilibrium of heroic and mock-heroic manners, ceremoniously adorned by the consecration of love in some of the most eloquent lyrics ever written. After limiting himself to spare techniques in *In Memoriam,* a tour de force in its use of the tetrameter quatrain, Tennyson's more copious style in *Maud* allows him to fashion a poetry of ostentation and despair. Bravado, virtuosity, and volatile irony mediate between the unwieldly ornateness of *The Princess* and the attenuated epitaphs of *In Memoriam.* By incorporating in

1. "In Memoriam," in *Selected Essays* (London, 1932), p. 328.
2. The adjectives are Matthew Arnold's, taken from "On Translating Homer: Last Words," in *The Complete Prose Works of Matthew Arnold,* ed. R. H. Super (Ann Arbor, Mich., 1960), I, 190.

a long poem the pathetic enigmas of "The Lady of Shalott" with the rituals of "Morte d'Arthur" and "Sir Galahad," the glittering ruin of "The Vision of Sin" with the solemn wonder of "St. Agnes' Eve," the gravities of "The Ancient Sage" with the hysterias of "St. Simeon Stylites," *Idylls of the King*, in its wide embrace of styles, tries to consolidate the kinds of universal value sought by Newman in religion, by Arnold in culture, and by Ruskin in art. The *Idylls* contain some of Tennyson's most ravishing lines, and some of his most austere and desolate poetry. But they are the victims of their own duality; and for more complete joinings of elation and despair we must turn to the quieter perfection of "Demeter and Persephone" and the late elegies. Among his barest experiments, Tennyson's late elegies, poems stripped of color, metaphor, and ornate language, return to *In Memoriam*'s style of skeletal inscription and epitaph, examining the contours of diminished life an hour before the end. As Douglas Bush observes, Tennyson's "poems are diverse objects made, as it were, by a whole corps of different craftsmen."[3] No other poet of the nineteenth century commands such a wide range of styles and themes. In order to assess Tennyson's achievement I shall try to draw recurrent elements of the style together. We must remember, however, that besides their stylistic excellence, Tennyson's poems continue to minister to the largest, most compelling human needs. A full, compassionate sense of the variety of man's needs and motives gives the poems their dignity, their consistent relevance.

3. "Alfred, Lord Tennyson," in *Major British Writers*, II (New York, 1959), p. 376. The Victorian who comments most perceptively on the variety of Tennyson's styles, and whose distinction between "mind" and "soul" in art anticipates my comments on Tennyson's combination of "epiphoric" and "diaphoric" elements in metaphor, is Walter Pater. See, in particular, "Style," the introductory essay in *Appreciations* (1889), originally published in *Fortnightly Review*, December 1, 1888, and reprinted in C. F. Harrold and W. D. Templeman, eds., *English Prose of the Victorian Era* (New York, 1938), p. 1429: "How illustrative of monosyllabic effect, of sonorous Latin, of the phraseology of science, of metaphysics, of colloquialism even, are the writings of Tennyson; yet with what a fine, fastidious scholarship throughout!"

Features of the Style

Most pervasive is Tennyson's habit of repetition. His iterative syntax, especially his use of schemes like $X\ Y\ Y\ X$ (chiasmus)' and $X\ Y\ X$ to "frame" recurrent elements, his elaborate patterns of sound, and his slowly unfolding cadences all make his poetry circle back on itself in a self-retarding movement. Reinforcing each of these devices are a number of grammatical features. They include the use of tenseless infinitives in "The Lotos-Eaters"—"to fall and pause and fall did seem" (1. 9)—which arrest the falling stream in midflight, and the recurrence of the same adjective with certain nouns. Thus Maud and Aurora are always luminous, Hallam always noble. The unalterable descriptions seem to be defining "real" or Platonic essences, like the stock epithets of epic poetry. A high degree of order may also be imposed on wayward feelings by a repetitive trope like chiasmus, as in this virtuoso piece from "The Lotos-Eaters": "Give us long rest or death, dark death, or dreamful ease" (1. 98). In the coda of "Ulysses," Tennyson's iterative syntax takes the form of isocolon, or parison: the figure of repetition primarily concerned with rhythm. The use of phrases or clauses of equal length and of corresponding structure passes the Greek original through a rhetorical crucible. The result is hightly sententious and intellectualized, like Pope's translation of Homer, though well suited to grand emotion and oratory. Most interesting are the repetitions that originate in Tennyson's view of the world, a view that he shares with other Victorian Idealists. Like James Ferrier, the author of *The Institutes of Metaphysics* (1854), whose books the poet owned,[4] Tennyson believes that energy flows onto nature from the self-conscious mind. It may flow from the individual mind of the observer, and be reflected from the mirror of nature, or it may flow from an infinite mind behind the mirror. When the ancient sage "revolve[s]

4. Charles Tennyson, *Alfred Tennyson* (New York, 1949), p. 279: "He also began to study metaphysics, the works of Spinoza, Berkeley, Kant, Schlegel, Fichte, Hegel and Ferrier being among the books added to his library."

in [him]self / The word that is the symbol of [him]self," Tennyson is using repetition as a mantra. A student of Oriental philosophy, Tennyson records that from early boyhood "a kind of
waking trance I have frequently had . . . , when I have been all
alone. This has generally come upon me thro' repeating my own
name two or three times to myself, silently, till . . . the individ-
uality itself seemed to dissolve and fade away into boundless
being."[5] *In Memoriam* uses repetitions to invoke a "boundless
being" behind the veil, a being that is imperceivable by the senses,
but which Tennyson explains to Mrs. Marian Bradley, wife of
the Dean of Westminster, "is the only true and real part of
[him]."[6] His grammar builds up a mask of appositions (LVI, 9–
28), lets us peep briefly behind them, then to divert the horror of
what is seen—"A monster then, a dream, / A discord" (LVI, ll.
21–22)—directs attention back to the mask. But despite this
anxious masking, the repetitions are constantly raising hopes.
When shall we get another glimpse "Behind the veil, behind the
veil"? (LVI, 28).

Tennyson's language assumes an Idealist theory of mind, a
philosophy of innate ideas. But his mind only intermittently pene-
trates the veil of nature, and casts into darkness only faint shafts
of light. The technique is to draw our attention away from a
vision on the far side of nature, one we are curious to see. The
repetitions keep raising expectations that the masking disappoints.
At the climax of *In Memoriam* the repeating elements "dawn,"
"dim," "lights," "life," "death," "boundless day" (XCV, 61–64)
finally suspend the "curse of time" by substituting for the irreversible flow of history the reversible flow of paradisal time. In
visionary moments, as time turns back upon itself in reversing
patterns of $X Y X$ and chiasmus ($Y X X Y$), energy flows from
the mind onto nature. In *In Memoriam,* Tennyson even approaches F. H. Bradley's—and Wordsworth's—discovery: "For
the truth I come back always to the doctrine of Hegel, that 'there
is nothing behind the curtain other than that which is in front of

5. Hallam Tennyson, *Tennyson: A Memoir,* I (London, 1897), 320.
6. Quoted by Charles Tennyson in *Alfred Tennyson,* p. 385.

it.' "[7] Like all experienced visionaries, Tennyson knows how to repeat himself. The repetition of key words and whole lines in *In Memoriam* serves to woo back some value, fix it more lastingly in the mind. The overall brevity and compression of the tetrameter quatrains, whose very economies can be lavish, lend relief to these values, by turns poignant and obsessive. Yet the repeating elements must not subjugate the senses, as they do in Shelley's poetry, which Tennyson complains is "too much in the clouds."[8] When recurrent adjectives and nouns freeze the cold beauty of Maud into stable attributes—"Faultily faultless, icily regular, splendidly null" (I, 82)—Tennyson mocks the mind's despotism. These epithets harbor their own irony, for they continue in force long after the senses have triumphed, long after the "Cold and clear-cut face" (I, 88) has clearly melted the speaker's heart.

A second feature of Tennyson's poetry is its resourceful hovering. It is circular rather than dialectical. The elements that Tennyson repeats do not blend into each other, as they do in Swinburne's and Shelley's poetry. Nor do they advance, as in Browning, from a lower sensual to a higher ethical or religious awareness. The parallel elements are disjunct, rather than continuous. To use Hopkins' important distinction, Tennyson's poetry is "diatonic," not "chromatic."[9] In music the diatonic scale omits the half notes. Instead of advancing in a continuous chain-like process of visual mergings, Tennyson's poetry usually severs its links. Seldom smoothly transitional, it abounds in broken parallels and antitheses, like the discontinuous planes of Pre-

---

7. F. H. Bradley, *Essays on Truth and Reality* (Oxford, 1914), p. 218. Bradley says he believes them to be Hegel's words, but cannot give any reference for them. He notes that almost the same words will, however, be found in Hegel's *Phenomenology of Mind*. See the translation by J. B. Baillie (New York, 1964), p. 212: "It is manifest that behind the so-called curtain, which is to hide the inner world, there is nothing to be seen unless we ourselves go behind there, as much in order that we may thereby see, as that there may be something behind there which can be seen."

8. Hallam Tennyson, *Tennyson: A Memoir*, II, 285.

9. "On the Origin of Beauty: A Platonic Dialogue," in *The Journals and Papers of Gerard Manley Hopkins*, ed. Humphrey House (Oxford, 1959), pp. 104, 106. For a fuller explanation see above, Ch. 4, n. 14.

Raphaelite painting. Often Tennyson's parallel syntax, instead of mastering an opposition, makes it sound more vibrantly. Tithonus gives like-sounding syntactical forms—"morn by morn," "earth in earth" (ll. 74–75)—to the opposing concepts of Aurora's eternal beauty and his own mortality. Instead of resolving their conflict, he makes it clash more resonantly. Alan Sinfield has analyzed a similar device in *In Memoriam*.[10] In Section LXVII the syntactical inversions which push the adverbial phrases (ll. 1–2) to the beginning of their clauses force the reader to note first the similarity, and then the dissimilarity. Hallam's "place of rest" resonates more piercingly because, despite its similarity to the mourner's place of rest, it is also Hallam's grave. In syntax "diatonism" is also a structural principle inviting language to become its own subject. In a poem such as "The Hesperides" Tennyson breaks his syntax into discontinuous phrases, each of which exists in isolation, like the oracular fragments of Symbolist poetry.

Tennyson's resourceful hovering is most apparent in his monologues. Unlike Browning's "A Toccata of Galuppi's," "Cleon," or "Caliban upon Setebos," few of Tennyson's dramatic monologues advance beyond their original point of view. By presenting actions that are not yet over, monologues as diverse as "Mariana," "Ulysses," "Tithonus," and "The Lotos-Eaters" allow Tennyson to give dignity to widely different motives and hopes. The fact that the final outcome of the action, which takes place in the world beyond the poems, differs from the speakers' expectations reproduces the drama of life, a drama which is rarely neat in the answers it provides. The uncertainty is most affecting at the close of the monologue "Tiresias," which brings to an end, not just the twilight of a pagan paradise, but also the life of Edward Fitzgerald, the friend to whom the prefatory epistle is dedicated. After a pause in the epistle that merely seems final (l. 56), the true finality of death occurs. Tennyson circles back to the last line of "Tiresias," adding a postscript to his epistle in the grieving, measured tones of elegy. Because the urbane but tender language

10. *The Language of Tennyson's "In Memoriam"* (New York, 1971), p. 86.

of the formal epistle manages to absorb the shock, and keep the grief just under control, the elegist fulfills our expectation of decorum in this genre, though in unexpected and quite touching ways.

In most of Tennyson's monologues, the apparent finality of the conclusions disguises Tennyson's own uncertainty. The monologues use formal parallelism, monosyllabic diction, and oracular assertion to secure strong effects of closure. But in "Ulysses" so simple a necessity as ending the poem qualifies the timelessness of the closing infinitives staring off into space. "And not to yield" is a resolution not to pause, not to end. Yet these are the last words of the poem. A moment later the monologue, for all its defiance of ends, is over. In "St. Simeon Stylites" the speaker even wills his poem to end: "The end! the end! / Surely the end!" (ll. 198–199). But as hysterical fiats mount to new crescendos of commotion, his upsurge of hope destroys the repose the reader anticipates in a coda. Despite the repetitions, the assertion of ultimate verities, and the use of other terminal devices such as closural allusion, Simeon lags "Superfluous . . . on the stage," like Johnson's veteran in the quotation,[11] for another twenty lines.

Whereas Tennyson's monologues end where they begin, and the finality of their conclusions betrays a real uncertainty, the apparent uncertainty at the end of "Cleon" and "Caliban upon Setebos" only thinly disguises Browning's own beliefs. Except in the *Dramatic Idyls,* or in inferior monologues like "Count Gismond," readers have seldom any doubt where Browning stands. It is no wonder, on the other hand, that critics have disagreed when trying to decide whether Tennyson preferred Ulysses or Telemachus, Galahad or Arthur. Tennyson's poetry is designed *not* to permit an easy preference, but to make us see the sanctions and motives on each side. Though Tennyson's resourceful hovering does not lend itself readily to dialectical advance, it is admirably suited to reflection. Diatonism is a principle of meditation that expends the same energy on the same matter. Tennyson's circular

11. Samuel Johnson, "The Vanity of Human Wishes," l. 308: "Superfluous lags the veteran on the stage."

"over-and-overing" of ideas is not a defect of thought, but a method—one brilliantly employed and defended by Heidegger: "Ordinary understanding demands that this circle be avoided because it violates logic. [But] we are compelled to follow the circle. This is neither a makeshift nor a defect. To enter upon this path is the strength of thought, to continue on it is the feast of thought."[12]

A third important feature of Tennyson's style is its inventive use of appositional grammar and two-way syntax. Though the parallel units are often discontinuous, the active grammar makes them interact. They are seldom merely detached and isolated, seldom merely "fanciful" in Coleridge's sense. The appositional grammar of "The Lotos-Eaters" does not freeze its meanings but leaves them fluid: "A land of streams! some, like a downward smoke / Slow-dropping veils of thinnest lawn, did go" (ll. 10–11). Are the "Slow-dropping veils" in apposition to "smoke"? Or is "Slow," despite its adjectival form, really an adverb, and "dropping" a participle modifying "smoke," instead of an adjective modifying "veils"? The tenuous grammar confuses the senses, and gives a wavering impression of seeing the water through a light haze. The suspension of the need for active decision about the grammar, though it blurs conceptual clarity, has the effect of thickening textures. The liquid "streams" materialize into tangible "veils of thinnest lawn," then curl into "downward smoke" we can smell and breathe. Combined with the appositional grammar wavering between adjectival and verbal forms, the synesthesia achieves a sense, not merely of how the stream looks from the shore, but of how it actually feels to be part of the stream.

In poetry of active grammar and two-way syntax a great many very precise meanings are free to dispose themselves in a variety of ways. In contrast to the univocal meanings of scientific prose and factual discourse, which are a stabilizing force, in *In Memoriam* a question such as "Derives it not from what we have / The likest God within the soul?" (LV, 3–4) changes it meanings in

12. Martin Heidegger, *Poetry, Language, and Thought,* tr. Albert Hofstadter (New York, 1971), p. 18.

mid-course. With quick fusions and divisions in the syntax, stable words become unstable, as if to secure tamped-down finality. In the rest of this section words of different etymologies— "falter," "falling," "faintly" (ll. 13, 14, 20)—but not of different senses, move in two directions at once. Their harmony of sound and sense appears at first to qualify "firmly," "faith," and "feel" (ll. 13, 17, 19), the other words they sound like. But as well as limiting the quality of the "trust," the adverb "faintly" literally describes the swooning on the stairs.

> I stretch lame hands of faith, and grope,
> And gather dust and chaff, and call
> To what I feel is Lord of all,
> And faintly trust the larger hope. [LV, 17–20]

Just as "lame," a physical attribute of the "hands," qualifies the tenor of the metaphor (the mourner's faith), so his faith in God, which he inwardly "feel[s]," is qualified by a stretching of hands that physically feel and grope. As the alliterating sounds are modulated in a restless zigzag through Section LV, the complex of doubt and faith is caught in the form of an elaborate turn upon the "great world's . . . stairs" (LV, 15–16). Sudden fleeting affinities of hope and dismay run like a shadow down the altar of providence, where the pilgrim, stranded in space, still hourly marks an instability in nature's ascent.

> I falter where I firmly trod,
> And falling with my weight of cares
> Upon the great world's altar-stairs
> That slope through darkness up to God. [LV, 13–16]

The turn on "falter," "falling"—like-sounding words close together—and the attenuated pun on "faintly" (l. 20) make the harmonies of sense slender and precarious. Two-way meanings register an immense and indifferent irony in the system of God's mysteries. The escalator may be going down. It may as readily plunge the mourner into darkness as lift him up to God.

What operates at the level of grammar as an active, two-way syntax operates at the generic level as a series of apertures in the story flow. In *Maud* and "The Holy Grail" the apertures, or frames, control the narrative. In "The Coming of Arthur" they operate like backgrounds in surrealist painting. The window-opening or perspective effect satisfies a Victorian desire to look through magic windows into a world more real than our own. The shifting frames of Merlin's riddles and Leodogran's dream achieve the "perspective by incongruity"[13] familiar to Victorian viewers of stereoscopes and dioramas. A change in point of view is a change of subject. See Arthur through Guinevere, or Lancelot through the king, and the whole meaning of their history changes. More effective than a simple pronouncement about adultery is the shift in point of view that allows Tennyson to discover complex truths about two adulterers. The more he writes about Arthur, Lancelot, and Guinevere, the more he learns to balance all three perspectives with charity and poise of mind. The grammatical equivalent of these shifting frames is parataxis and apposition: the use of two-way syntax to provide the reader with other windows for viewing the same event. These magic windows are the "successive equivalents" described by Alan Sinfield, which "redefine an experience in other terms so we may appreciate its nature through a process of analogy."[14]

A fourth, and equally important, feature of Tennyson's style is its skillful navigation between closed and open, or stable and unstable, use of language. Tennyson does not venerate superstitiously the univocal stability of words, but neither does he licentiously pursue equivocal meanings. A poetry of two-way syntax, by loosening the bonds of grammatical connection, might seem to produce only poetry of madness or ecstasy, like parts of "Lucretius" and *Maud*. Mental disintegration gives Lucretius license to drop his words in any order he chooses.

> although his fire is on my face
> Blinding, he sees not. [ll. 144–145]

13. Kenneth Burke, *Perspectives by Incongruity* (Bloomington, Ind., 1964), pp. 94–99.
14. *The Language of Tennyson's "In Memoriam,"* p. 214.

> And twisted shapes of lust, unspeakable
> Abominable, strangers at my hearth
> Not welcome, harpies miring every dish.   [ll. 157–159]

Does "Blinding" modify "fire" or "face," and what blinds the blinder, who "sees not"? Similar doubts arise about "unspeakable" and "Abominable" and about "Not welcome," which attaches itself to "harpies" and "shapes" as readily as to the more logical antecedent "strangers." But the loose syntax is exactly right for the disintegrating mind. As C. S. Lewis observes of Milton's syntax, "The very crumbling of consciousness is before us and the fringe of syntactical mystery helps rather than hinders the effect."[15]

More often the active syntax creates merely a temporary impression of being open. At first an "underdetermined" grammar invites us to relate elements X and Y in more than one way. But then a third element, Z, forces us to reorder our thinking about the syntax. We have to reject as inappropriate some of the patterns in which the grammar is free to dispose itself. At the climax of *In Memoriam,* for example, syntax begins to work in several ways at once. It allows Tennyson to exercise his extraordinary talent for indirection and for two-way meaning:

> And gathering freshlier overhead,
>   Rocked the full-foliaged elms, and swung
>   The heavy-folded rose, and flung
> The lilies to and fro, and said . . .   [XCV, 57–60]

Although, grammatically, the four principal verbs go with the "breeze" of the preceding stanza, the effect of the syntax is to suggest that "Rocked" and "swung" are intransitive verbs. Since it would surely take more than an ordinary breeze—a hurricane or a tempest—to rock a field of trees, it seems for a moment, through hyperbaton, through an inversion of the verbs and their subjects, that the rocking is being done by "the full-foliaged elms" and the swinging by "The . . . rose." Yet the final elliptical clauses—"and [the breeze] flung," "and [the breeze] said"—make

15. *A Preface to "Paradise Lost"* (London, 1949), p. 46.

clear that logic is being violated by an implicit, deeper logic. The verbs are transitive, as we orginally supposed; and the wind, now no ordinary breeze, but the Holy Spirit itself, is the agent. The temporary confusions of the open grammar dramatize the miraculous animation of nature and the interaction of elements. Though the final elliptical clauses force us to reorder our thinking about the two-way grammar, which is not as open as we thought, the indirection encourages an easy exchange between the predicates and the subjects, between nature and supernature, and cushions the shock of one of *In Memoriam*'s most startling transformations.

Tennyson's syntax wavers, but it seldom actually takes two paths at once. The syntactical fluidity of *In Memoriam* more often flickers with hesitation, uncertain for a moment which of several paths to take. By wavering unsteadily, Section CXXI is able to awaken both elation and grief in the mind.

> Sad Hesper o'er the buried sun
> And ready, thou, to die with him,
> Thou watchest all things ever dim
> And dimmer, and a glory done.   [CXXI, 1–4]

Gerard Manley Hopkins, a reluctant admirer of Tennyson, who dismissed *Idylls of the King* as medieval charades, declared of these lines: "The maturest judgment will never be fooled out of saying that this is divine, terribly beautiful."[16] Grammatical instability, I think, contributes to their power. Is "o'er the buried sun," for example, a geographical direction, or does the phrase modify the adjective "sad"—does it give the reason for Hesper's grief? Are the words "ever dim / And dimmer" another phrase in apposition to the subject? Are they an ellipsis for the implied predicate, "grow ever dim"? Or is "dim" an infinitive, and is "all things" its subject, the indefinite object of the main verb? If we have opted for the third alternative, the phrase "And dimmer" forces us to reorganize our thinking. And, in retrospect, the first

16. Hopkins to A. W. M. Baillie, September 10, 1864; in *Further Letters of Gerard Manley Hopkins, Including His Correspondence with Coventry Patmore,* ed. Claude Colleer Abbott (London, 1938), p. 72.

alternative seems logically inconsistent with Hesper's continuing to shine after the sun is buried. But the appositional grammar, by encouraging such confusions, can be poignant. And the hesitations are not resolved by our realizing that there are not three paths at all but only one. We return via the ambiguous grammar of the dimming light to the distant shining of "a glory done." "Glorious sunset" would be hackneyed; but the metonymy of "a glory done" is strange for "nightfall." We hear it rhyming with "buried sun," and recognize in its flickering hesitation, wavering in emphasis between "a *glory* done" and "a glory *done*," a final concentration of the other fleeting affinities of hope and despair in the mind. In the one moment of diffused brilliance, as Hesper views the last trembling light, the beauty resides, not merely in the possibility of two-way meaning, but in the possibility of a single figurative inscape of elation and grief. Like Hopkins, Tennyson defines an inner landscape, yet one that becomes less analyzable as its loveliness becomes more perfectly definite but fugitive.

A fifth feature of Tennyson's style is its remarkable ability to combine clarity of sense with a suggestion of truths that are not explicit in its statements. Tennyson's metaphors are not purely associative, like the metaphors of Symbolist poetry; but neither are they austerely diagrammatic, like the metaphors of neoclassical and some metaphysical poetry. Occasionally, as in "The Hesperides" and "The Vision of Sin," Tennyson juxtaposes a number of objects and tries to make his meaning speak through things—through sensory objects instead of analogies. Such "diaphoric" use of metaphor—to use Philip Wheelwright's term[17] —creates an indefinable presence through simple juxtaposition. It is the technique of the Symbolist poet who is conscious of the utterly untranslatable character of each of his statements. Such metaphors, as Wallace Stevens says, "resist the intelligence / Almost successfully."[18] Denying themselves any indulgence in

17. "The Two Ways of Metaphor," in *Metaphor and Reality* (Bloomington, Ind., 1962), ch. iv.
18. "Man Carrying Thing," ll. 1–2.

analogy (A is to B as X is to Y), the elements A, B, C establish
a reality of their own particulars. At the other extreme, in Tennyson's metaphysical conceits, is a form of metaphor that acti-
vates the mind. When Tennyson mingles expressions of grief with
the commercial imagery of "far-off interest" in *In Memoriam* (I,
8), he is developing an extrarational direction in the metaphor.
Instead of moving "through" certain particulars of experience, as
in the diaphoric metaphors of "The Hesperides," he is using
analogies that reach out and extend his meaning. The function of
this diagrammatic, or "epiphoric," use of metaphor, as Wheelwright calls it, is to hint significance, whereas purely associative,
or diaphoric, metaphor creates indefinable presences.

Like all poets who cannot be categorized as classic or romantic,
Tennyson combines the two forms of metaphor. The metaphors
in the elegy "Break, break, break" are typical, for they hint a
significance they do not directly state. At first the shifting impressions of the sea appear to be wholly untranslatable, wholly diaphoric, bringing into being a new conception for which there are
no other words. The sea that breaks on the cold gray stones, the
ships going on to their haven, the waves lapping at the foot of
the crags all serve the diaphoric function of leaving unnamed
and unnamable the "thoughts" no "tongue" could "utter" when
Tennyson started the poem. The loneliness of the sea, the peace
of the ships, the mysterious charm of the singing create a meaning
to be apprehended only through the metaphors—a significance
always just out of sight and just beyond definition. But there is
also a kind of third-dimensional significance, pointing from the
breaking waves to the mourner's breaking heart, and from the sea
that breaks at the foot of the crags to the boundless deep beyond.
By an epiphoric implication cutting across the plane of association
in the metaphors, the carefree fisherman's boy and the singing
youth on the bay define states of joy and liberation. These definitions are supported by other details of the elegy: by the homecoming of the ships as they pass to "their haven under the hill"
(l. 10), and even by the mourner's power to revive "the tender
grace of a day that is dead" (l. 15) and make it live again in his
mind. Since oblique analogies are present in the power of the sea

to mean something more than the words actually say, it is very hard for the reader to express the exact truth about the poem.

It is the rare quality of being elusive yet exact that readers admire in Tennyson. But it is this same quality that makes inexact criticism of the poet so easy, and truth so difficult. All we can say is that Tennyson's sea is the vehicle of a metaphor, the boundless deep, whose tenor concerns the fate of souls, the journey from eternity into time, then back again, as "that which drew from out the boundless deep / Turns again home" ("Crossing the Bar," ll. 3–4). As W. K. Wimsatt asks about the children that "sport upon the shore" in Wordsworth's ode,[19] so we might ask of the fisherman's boy and the sailor's lad in Tennyson: "Why are the children found on the seashore? In what way do they add to the solemnity or mystery of the sea? Or do they at all? The answer is that they are not strictly parts of the . . . vehicle, but of the . . . soul-age-time tenor, attracted over, from tenor to vehicle." The carefree, singing youths show a "strange yet . . . artistic warping . . . of vehicle by tenor."[20] Attracted to the vehicle, they are really images of the soul, as it "Turns again home," like the stately ships that return "To their haven" (l. 10), though their place of rest is invisible, just out of sight. In this way a central meaning is created about homecoming, joy in solitude, the affective power of memory, and the fate of the soul. Take from the lines the stately ships going on to their haven, or the singing youth on the bay, whose relation to the day that is dead is too subtle for the intellect, and you take from them their beauty. The indefinable and yet precise emotions cannot be evoked by any other arrangement of images and sounds. The meaning is the effect not wholly of the metaphor elaborated diaphorically (in a purely associative way, which might remain too private and obscure), but of working on two axes, by logic and analogy as well as by association, in a three-dimensional complexity of form.

Even metaphors that are strongly associative turn out to be

19. William Wordsworth, "Intimations of Immortality from Recollections of Early Childhood," l. 167.
20. W. K. Wimsatt, "The Structure of Romantic Nature Imagery," in *The Verbal Icon* (Lexington, Ky., 1954), p. 115.

the vehicles of unexpressed tenors. In those sections of *In Memoriam* that tend toward the impressionistic syntax of *Maud,* at times to the near abolition of syntax, the real subject is a geography of the soul, for which there is no name and no other description. The "Dark house" and "Doors" of Section VII (ll. 1, 3) are loosely joined to the rest of the lyric by the expedient of turning these bare notations, the most impersonal elements in the scene, into intimate apostrophes. The hand and heart, the unlovely street and drizzling rain begin to flicker disjointedly like film shots in a slow-speed movie; dissolving syntax gives a sense of emptiness and vertigo. As Alan Sinfield has noted, "Tennyson's sentence structure is moving in the direction of NO syntax,"[21] and the dissolution of grammar functions as a metaphor for the dissolution of the mourner's world. By simply recording the mind's sensations without comment, the metaphors in *Maud* elliptically conceal their subject behind dissolving syntax and flickering sentiment.

> Cold and clear-cut face, why come you so cruelly meek
>
> . . . . .
>
> Passionless, pale, cold face, star-sweet on a gloom profound;
> Womanlike, taking revenge too deep for a transient wrong
> Done but in thought to your beauty, and ever as pale as before
> Growing and fading and growing upon me without a sound,
> Luminous, gemlike, ghostlike, deathlike, half the night long
> Growing and fading and growing, till I could bear it no more,
> But arose, and all by myself in my own dark garden ground,
> Listening now to the tide in its broad-flung shipwrecking roar,
> Now to the scream of a maddened beach dragged down by
>   the wave,
> Walked in a wintry wind by a ghastly glimmer, and found
> The shining daffodil dead, and Orion low in his grave.
>
> [Part I, ll. 88–101]

Such a passage is not meant to trace a temporal sequence or to locate a place—"now . . . / Now . . . by in / . . . by" (ll. 98–100)—but to represent some northern nowhere, a region where sea, land, and sky are illogically fused, like backgrounds in surrealist painting. We are not to imagine the lover hearing the roar of the

21. *The Language of Tennyson's "In Memoriam,"* p. 105.

sea, then looking at the shining flower before gazing forlornly at the sinking star. We are meant to receive instead, in a single mounting impression, something like "seabeachmadness, wintrygleam, daffodil-stardeath." *Maud*'s impressionistic syntax anticipates the synesthesia of Joyce and Hopkins, as Tennyson composes in sensory wholes that oppose the need to arrange his words in logical sequence. The syntax presents a parataxis of impressions: terrifying beauty, focused in the phrase "cruelly meek"; heavenly splendor; fear converting wonder into self-defense; the beautiful avenger transformed into ghostlike apparition. The chains of epithets, made remorseless by the repeated suffix ("gemlike, ghostlike, deathlike" [l. 95]), enact the pulsating glow, until growing and fading lights begin to fluctuate in space like long-distance film shots. The impressionistic syntax is poignant: the ghastly face drifts into "star-sweet" grandeur with no syntactic link; the reader drifts beyond earth toward auroral vision on the surge of pulsing participles—"Growing and fading and growing"—and is brought back sharply with the earthly lament "till I could bear it no more." Does the unbearable "it" refer to the face, the star, or the auroral light? The loose syntax allows the lover to run up and down the scale of marveling: his two-way meanings slide effortlessly between heaven and earth. The hesitations form another member of a central pattern of flowing and ebbing, of growing and fading, a wavering between elation and grief. The shifting frames, though strongly associative, hint a significance beyond what any of the elements actually say. The point of the metaphors is the loss of self in the mysterious lure of beauty, and the wan isolation after torment and ecstasy. But like most of Tennyson's metaphors, they combine suggestive association with clarity of stated sense and of comparison. Tennyson can convey his meaning in this poem in no other way.

A sixth and final feature of Tennyson's style is its combination of directness and indirectness. Despite Arthur Hallam's judgment, based only on the early poems, that Tennyson was a poet of sensation, Tennyson is a poet of reflection—not simply because he meditates and broods, but because like Henry James he "reflects" his world by means of mirrors. Even when Tennyson writes as a poet of sensation, his perceptions are refined and many faceted. He presents them obliquely, broken into half-lights and shades. Like the appositional grammar and two-way syntax, the use of language as a refracting medium follows from Tennyson's belief that reality is perspectival. As F. H. Bradley insists, "Contact with reality is through a limited aperture. For [we] cannot get at it directly except through . . . one small opening."[22] Because of its perspectival character the ultimate nature of the world is necessarily hidden from any finite mind. It is the tragedy of the poet's vocation, as it is the tragedy of the philosopher's and the theologian's, that every comment he makes on reality is an oblique one, every description a travesty, every definition a mutilation. In "Timbuctoo," *In Memoriam,* and "The Holy Grail," Tennyson must substitute for the noble visions of his ode "The Poet," which expresses a messianic confidence a little too directly, the indirection of a "lucid veil." One of the simplest ways to indicate indirection is to make a statement about it; this is what Tennyson does in *In Memoriam* when he says that "words, like Nature, half reveal / And half conceal" what they express (V, 3–4). To be seen at all, the truth must be glimpsed through F. H. Bradley's "limited apertures," or through the "optic glass," described by Browning's St. John, which reduces eternal truths to "plain historic fact, / Diminished into clearness, proved a point" ("A Death in the Desert," ll. 236–237). Words, like Browning's optic glass, seldom tell more than half, and ultimately perhaps they cannot. All truths are private truths: in its greatest elations, as in its deepest griefs, the soul in the end is alone.

Given Tennyson's conviction, it is not surprising that his striving to communicate more than can be said should compel him to write indirectly as well as directly. Nor is it surprising that his directness and his indirectness often coexist in the same lines. Nothing that Tithonus affirms directly about Aurora's "balmy

22. *Appearance and Reality: A Metaphysical Essay* (Oxford, 1930), p. 229.

kisses" ("Tithonus," 1. 59) and nothing that Demeter predicts oracularly about the death of "Shadow . . . into Light" ("Demeter and Persephone," 1. 136) can equal their splendid codas, which soar above everything else in the two poems. What the codas have in common is their fusion of grandeur and indirection, of stable and wavering vision. Demeter's prophecy of "see[ing] no more" (1. 147) releases touching oxymorons, at once gentle and desperate, which make the "dimly-glimmering lawns" and "silent field of Asphodel" (ll. 148, 151) far more vibrant than the "whole bright year" (1. 137), which the prophetic eye tries to scan too directly. The resonance of "the shadowy warrior" (1. 150) is due to the half lights that resist directness, to the delicate balance of beauty and horror that the unmediated vision, however grand, can never capture. And the very fact that Tithonus' gaze is finally averted from "these empty courts" (1. 75) makes the coda describing the triumphant return of the goddess among the most poignant and enchanting lines Tennyson wrote. "Forget" (1. 75), like "see no more," is an opportunity for the poet to release his full feelings for natural beauty while obliquely affirming the consoling rightness of decline and death. More moving than a predetermined oracular motto—"More things are wrought by prayer / Than this world dreams of" ("The Passing of Arthur," ll. 415–416)—which is more resolutely conclusive than the *Idylls* as a whole will justify, is the conclusion of "Tithonus." Here the complex attitudes toward death, and toward the trap of permanence reflected in immortality, though predestined from the first impulse of the speaker's mood, are also unforeseen. Though nothing seems preconceived, Tennyson is confident enough, as the poem unfolds, to trust the sufficiency of what he finds. His poem "runs a course of lucky events," as Frost would say, and ends in "a clarification of life."[23] It may not be a great clarification, but it is a more profound and valid clarification that any Tennyson could have foreseen when he started the

23. "The Figure a Poem Makes," in *Selected Prose of Robert Frost*, ed. H. Cox and E. Lathem (New York, 1968), p. 18.

poem. He records his discovery with restraint and understatement, in a conclusion that is no more oracular, no more stabilizing, than the scale of his insight will allow.

Psychological Implications

Now that we have traced, through the major poems, some of Tennyson's experiments in style, and have summarized six of the style's recurrent features, is it possible, from the vantage point of a last retrospect, to identify any syndrome that these habits cumulatively represent? One speaks here with less confidence: "All art," Oscar Wilde warns, "is at once surface and symbol," and "those who go beneath the surface do so at their peril."[24] Without psychoanalyzing Tennyson, however, I think we may glimpse behind his habits of syntax and style a soul unable to commit itself, wavering among multiple roles, yet anxious about its indecision, longing for stable identity. Appalled by the violence of an alcoholic father, brutally affronted by the shock of Hallam's death, the young Tennyson is forced to stabilize his world. He learns to multiply his conflicting inner identities through classical monologues and elegies, speaking the language of Ulysses and the lotos-eaters, St. Simeon and Tiresias, living out the contradictory attitudes that they suggest. In a waking dream such as "The Vision of Sin," or a dream romance such as *The Princess,* the poet's various postures need not dissolve the contradictions they contain. Yet the Tennyson of the 1840's, without a profession, too impoverished to marry, becomes increasingly anxious about his inability to commit himself. The characteristically Victorian[25] fear that the power of the poet to improvise roles and identities

24. Preface to *The Picture of Dorian Gray;* reprinted in *Literary Criticism of Oscar Wilde,* ed. Stanley Weintraub (Lincoln, Neb., 1969), p. 230.
25. I say "characteristically Victorian," because the same problem confronts Browning. As a young poet, Browning had lived like Sordello and the lover in *Pauline* in states of dream and torpor, the equivalent of Tennyson's palace of art. In the dramatic monologues Browning, the "semantic stutterer," finds a principle of objectification. He learns to see himself in mirrors, multiplying himself endlessly through other men and women,

may mean that he has no identity of his own is also the fear of being merely a dreamer or escapist, the fear that impels Tennyson to bring the sensuous and fantastic element of his genius into alignment with the narrative and dramatic element. The longing for moral identity, balanced by a horror of entrapment, by a desire to multiply the poet's roles as a way of protecting his "negative capability," his capacity to impersonate anything, is acted out again and again in Tennyson's poems, as it is in the poems and letters of Keats. In the best of Tennyson's poems, in masterpieces such as *In Memoriam* and *Maud*, the poet of sensation also achieves a very powerful moral catharsis. By combining dream and narrative, the poet of negative capability finds a stable identity behind his masks—and behind the mask of nature, too, which is subject to the same unpredictable decay and change as is the artist of dissolving roles.

In Tennyson's major poems a grammar of dependency first substitutes pronouns and metonymies for human agents. It buries action in passives, reflexives, and first-person accusatives. Then, as the soul recovers its self-sufficiency, the impression becomes one of assertiveness and force. In *Maud*, for example, the fears that double back into repression to create anxiety and discontent are faced and eliminated. Hope and despair become more manageable when they are dramatized as the red rose that cries or the

---

speaking their languages and living out the roles that they suggest. Though only a use of multiple masks and self-reflections can protect Browning's identity, he is afraid that like the Keatsian poet of negative capability he may possess no identity of his own. What will the writer of dramatic monologues find when he tears away the final mask? The fear that a void exists at the bottom of his personality explains Browning's desire to write "R. B.—a poem," a work in which "the real" Browning can speak directly in his own voice. As Teufelsdröckh discovers at the end of Carlyle's "Natural Supernaturalism," when he hesitates to strip away the final veil, the problem of personality is also a metaphysical problem. Is there nothing behind the veil of nature that is not already in front of it? And if the poet himself is only a succession of masks, if his identity is only the result of his power to improvise roles, does the poet's discovery of himself behind the mask of nature not mean that the world itself is a lie? Is nature a mask that unveils an empty universe, the "hollow form with empty hands" of *In Memoriam* (III, 12)?

white rose that weeps (*Maud,* I, 912–913). More extreme is the
hallucinatory detachment of the meditation on the shell. The
grammatical features that are missing in the loose ecstasy of the
lyric "Go not, happy day" (I, 571–598) are developed here to an
extraordinary degree, as a way of staving off disaster. The prepositions and conjunctions which disappear in the other lyric, but
which are used here to establish a context for the shell—"close to
my foot"; "pure as a pearl" (II, 50–51)—betray a compulsion
to be alert hypersensitively to every detail. The word heaps of
infantile emotion are replaced by careful parallels and antitheses:
"Small, but a work divine, / Frail, but of force to withstand"
(II, 71–72). And in the analogies between the shell and the ship-
wrecked sailor, and the shell and the soul, the syntactical rules
that organize words into higher units of meaning and larger contexts—features of language that disappear in the ecstasy of the
earlier lyrics—are painstakingly recovered and refined.

In the madhouse scene the speaker still retains normal powers
of substitution and selection. What drop out of his speech are the
conjunctions, pronouns, prepositions that would normally combine the fragments that jostle violently together, yoked only by
dashes. The kernel words—"The fault was mine, the fault was
mine" (II, 30)—are the least destructible. But for these infantile,
four-word utterances, the reader is forced to provide some ex-
planatory context. "That gray old wolf" (II, 291) is Maud's
father; but the unstable reference introduces the powerful irony
of the lover's confusing the enemy, Maud's father, with his own
father. With the loss of context, there comes the impulse on the
hero's part to pity old men, whether they be friends or enemies,
and to forgive them if he can. Finally, the grammatical dependency of the madman on the ghastly shadow, on the impersonal
"It" that leads him blindly, is replaced by a less dependent
grammar. "I know where a garden grows" (II, 310) desperately
affirms the mind's power to control the story flow. The mind can
remake and remold its pictures. First indirectly, and then with
full resurgence, the diffused and luminous beauty of the "shining
daffodil" (III, 6) and "silent lightning" (III, 9) resists the im-

personal grammar that substitutes "It" for Maud and the ghastly
metonymy of blood for roses. Active, value-laden verbs—"hail
once more," "deemed," "embrace the purpose . . . and . . .
doom assigned" (III, 42, 50, 59)—substitute rhetorical acts and
ethical motions for the passivity of earlier verbs. The grammar
has prepared the reader for predicates that require an active subject, no longer dependent on the tormenting "It" of the madhouse, or on god figures such as Maud or Hallam to whom it
can submit.

  Though Tennyson discovers that every man is a creator of
roles—by birth and by nature an artist, an architect, a fashioner
of worlds—an "unchartered freedom" (Wordsworth, "Ode to
Duty," l. 37) to create these roles exhausts Tennyson, as it exhausts
Wordsworth. The aging Tennyson yearns for a "repose that ever
is the same,"[26] for a stable identity of the kind that he celebrates
in his elegy "Ode on the Death of the Duke of Wellington," which
is close in temper to Wordsworth's "Ode to Duty." As a counselor
to Queen Victoria and a friend of Gladstone, Tennyson willingly
assumes the role of patriot and laureate, of sage and seer. But
however impelled he may be to commit himself, to achieve stable
identity, Tennyson is always afraid his identities are a fiction, a
mask, that he is nothing in himself. Even when Tennyson seems
to speak *in propria persona* in a prophetic poem such as "Akbar's
Dream," he is writing on a subject, the unity of all religions, pro-
posed by his friend Benjamin Jowett. The moments of terror in
Tennyson—the weird seizures of the Prince, the madness of the
lover in *Maud,* the disintegration of the dying Lucretius—all express a fear that any single identity the soul may assume is a lie,
a betrayal. Because the Prince is forced into the false role of the
conventional suitor battling for his prize, his weird seizures[27] must

  26. Wordsworth, "Ode to Duty," l. 40.
  27. The same dark principle in other Victorian writers, what Kierkegaard
calls the "wound of the negative," may even destroy the reader's sense of
his own identity. A core of darkness in Browning's poetry, for example, reminds the reader that there is a residue in every self that cannot be reflected into any single role. Why is it disquieting for the reader of *The Inn
Album* to know that a character is continually being interrupted by either

first destroy that role. Only during his recovery in the hospital does the Prince's false identity dissolve like mist in the sun, as his mind wakes to renovating truths. The lover in *Maud* experiments with a number of identities, trying on the mask of the misogynist, the political radical, the Stoic philosopher. Only the ecstasies of his love and the torments of his madness allow the hero to realize that he is more than an actor in an endless series of parts.

There remains a core of darkness in Tennyson—a wound inflicted by Carlyle's fear that life is "the veriest Spectrehunt; [a] howling tumult that made Night hideous."[28] The horror that all life will drain away into the void comes from a conviction that, like the distortions of a face in a hall of broken mirrors, the soul cannot be reflected into any single role. Tennyson's drive toward stable identity, and the endless refraction of such identity through masks and mirrors, make his poems circle back on themselves. In the major poems Tennyson writes as though he were engaged in a struggle for repose and order. But even though he marshals all his forces, he always fails. Behind such failure is a fear of being trapped in any single part. There may even be a suicidal longing, a wish for death. Indeed, in a world where all forms dissolve, and no identity seems real, there is only one identity that Tennyson can honestly assume. He can become an elegist, and make the problem of finding an identity in a world of unpredictable decay and change the subject of his poems. Like James Ferrier, the philosopher of consciousness he studied and admired,

---

the narrator or another actor in the same story? The effect is similar, I think, to Thackeray's removal of the boundaries between art and life in *Vanity Fair*. Thackeray does not merely appear as a character in his own fiction: he also involves the reader by reminding him that there are little chapters in every reader's life. Such exposure of dramatic illusion is disquieting: it suggests that if an actor in a story can be the spectator of some other actor in the same story, then we, their readers and spectators, may also be unreal. Here Tennyson, Browning, and Thackeray all approach the insight of late Victorians like Oscar Wilde, for whom life imitates art because subjective experience is itself a kind of fiction. If every reader is the poet of his own soul, then we all create our lives the way a dramatic poet creates a poem or a play.

28. Thomas Carlyle, "Natural Supernaturalism," in *Sartor Resartus* (New York, 1970), p. 242.

Tennyson the elegist comes to realize that the difference between being a victim of change and being a poet who makes change the basis of a new identity is the difference between the intelligence of an animal, trapped by nature, and the self-consciousness of a human mind, the master of nature. After prolonged self-struggle and despair, the elegist's ability to exorcise fear and morbidity certainly confers enormous dignity on Tennyson. But even though stability may be the "end" of Tennyson's poetry—its goal—it may also be its "end" in another sense; if achieved, it would abolish what is most distinctive about his art. If Tennyson were ever to master the waverings, the swervings, the doublings back upon himself, which refract his poetry and keep it vibrant, he would be courting defeat. But then we should be talking about a different poet. As it is, honest doubts and perplexities persist. While Tennyson, compelled by his need for repose and order, is always trying to find a stable identity behind the mask, his endless proliferation of roles is also generating darker forces. The wound inflicted by his fear that he is spectral, by his fear that the ghost behind his masks cannot be reflected into any single role, looms at times to appall him. But its energy, constructively released by the dissolving forms, allows Tennyson's poetry to be no more stabilizing than the quick decay and change of concrete life permit. The courageous openness to change, which impels Tennyson to enlarge or revise a premise as soon as he establishes it, charges his poetry, making it dynamic and more ample. If the poetry is less stable as a result, it is also more honest; and the honesty is not separate from the poetic art.

Achievements of the Style

My conclusion, then, is not simply that Tennyson is a master of directness and indirectness, of stable identities and dissolving roles, but that in his best verse, in poems such as *Maud, In Memoriam,* and "Lucretius," he has an extraordinary talent for introducing both effects at once. In his subtlest and most powerful writing Tennyson combines the narrative stability of his domestic idylls with the protean, dreamlike qualities of his lyric style. Though he is a puzzled questioner, a victim of terror and dread, his iterative syntax is a way of subduing the terror, of marshaling aid against dark forces, against "The stream of everything that runs away / . . . [that] seriously, sadly, runs away / To fill the abyss' void with emptiness."[29] Though the stability and order that are natural to Tennyson sometimes degenerate into a manner of repeating words, and of giving every verb and noun its appropriate modifier, in his best poems they are a way of mastering powers that would overwhelm and destroy him. More harrowing in *In Memoriam* than the void predicted by the second law of thermodynamics, the state of degraded energy unavailable for any rebuilding of a burned-out universe, is the void much nearer home that entropy reflects. In the most personal passages, the repeating elements combine with the private fears and internal debates of a mind antagonistic to itself, to produce extraordinary poetry.

Though the directness of Tennyson's poetry is occasionally as excessive as indirectness is in many metaphysical and modern poets, I am not contending that Tennyson is never successful when he writes directly. When we remove some lyrics from their contexts in *In Memoriam* and *The Princess* we remove from the lyrics whatever indirectness they may have. These poems, in their direct union of sound, syntax, rhythm, contain some of Tennyson's most perfect passages: lyrics such as "Now sleeps the crimson petal" (*The Princess,* VII, 161–174), which we understand until we try to put our understanding into words. And to do that may betray our own want of understanding. I may seem to have minimized Tennyson's success in employing direct modes of writing. But the critic's craving to express his understanding of such direct and perfect poetry as "Now sleeps the crimson petal" may in the end be mere egoism. Criticism is less helpless, I think, when confronting the lines to Dufferin or the elegies on Simeon and Fitzgerald. Such poems cannot be understood without our reflecting on them, without our taking up where Tennyson leaves off. If I have concentrated on those features of Tennyson's poetry which

29. Robert Frost, "West-Running Brook," ll. 48–49.

qualify the protracted anguish of *In Memoriam*, which qualify the ecstasies of "The Holy Grail" or the grand hysterias of *Maud*, it is because these poems need to be explicated. They are unfinished communications in which there is still something implicit for the critic to explicate, or make explicit. We cannot understand their honesty and power until we study their mixture of directness and restraint, of present despair and distant hope. Then we find in Tennyson a very private but resilient kind of heroism.

The hesitations which keep tempering the remote and exotic elements, subduing the grandeur of *In Memoriam* to plain lament, and touching exaltation with dread in *Maud*, explain why Tennyson's poetry gives the recurrent impression of a problem unresolved, of a mind that suspends judgment on every issue it explores. These swervings and waverings, expressed most clearly in "The Two Voices" and "The Ancient Sage," are ultimately what Tennyson's poetry—its sobriety and savagery, its decorum and despair—is about. Cosmic impressions lend Lucretius and the lover in *Maud* a surrealist power, in which terror alternates with hysteric joy. But in the lucidity of his madness, the lover in *Maud* begins to speak in a new style, in childlike sentences, faltering and entirely gentle. The lover's dream of "lightning under the stars" (III, 9) is a supernatural vision, a dream of another life. There is a measure of holiness as well as torment in the lover's experience; and to evaluate the changes in *Maud* and the *Idylls* it is necessary to chart a drama of suffering and forgiveness that is in a refined sense religious. At the end of both poems the dream of a different life is still a dream. The cruel facts remain unchanged. Yet with full tragic knowledge that the universe is not run on moral principles—in the presence of the truth that Job confronts —Arthur, in proclaiming that God fulfills himself in many ways, passes beyond the heroic ideal of the warrior-king to the godlike heroism of the saint and seer. "The Passing of Arthur" stands alone in its inclusive diversity, spanning the dark terribleness and beauty of *In Memoriam;* the riving of nature, both mental and physical, in the disintegrating grandeur of "Lucretius"; the brilliance and wonder of *Maud*. The quiet authority of "The Passing," in binding together stable and wavering visions, justifies a natural human craving for courage and openness—and also for the embracing of change, an acceptance that has intimidated the imagination of lesser writers.

The drive toward certitude in Tennyson's poetry, the compelling need for order and finality, is constantly being matched and diverted by the doubling back, by the tremors of doubt and indecision. In a verse epistle such as the elegy for Fitzgerald or the lines to Dufferin, an ideal of decorum is not impaired, but enlarged and renewed, by the poet's grief. Decorum is made kinetic and more ample by a style that reflects—that, in a sense, completes and fulfills—general psychological needs. If we were analyzing that style by means of a computer we would find it full of iterative statements or "loops." A unit of syntax appears; it advances by multiplying its elements, or by embedding its kernel word in appositions. Once the operation is performed, there is a pull back, as if to consolidate the advance, before the multiplication or embedding is performed again. Like the "loop" of a computer program, the syntax keeps reaching out, expanding, then returning to the original ground, before expanding further.[30] Renaissance rhetoric has names for these schemes: labels such as antimetabole (the scheme $X\ Y\ Y\ X$), epanalepsis

30. When repeating syntax or a highly determinate verse form like the tetrameter quatrains of *In Memoriam* decides in advance a high percentage of the words a poet must use, redundance will be high and freedom to choose words will be low. Just as it takes longer to state ideas in basic English, when restricted to a vocabulary of some eight hundred words, so repeating syntax and determinate verse forms make *In Memoriam* a more redundant poem than Milton's *Lycidas*. Conversely, when every phrase is a crossword puzzle, a pun, or a metaphysical conceit, as in Joyce's *Finnegans Wake*, words are being used with maximum economy. Tennyson achieves such concision, even in expansive poems such as *In Memoriam*, whenever he uses two-way syntax or puns. Warren Weaver, in *The Mathematical Theory of Communication* (Urbana, Ill., 1964) observes that normal English is about 50 per cent redundant. "A language must have at least fifty percent of real freedom . . . in the choice of letters if one is to be able to construct satisfactory crossword puzzles. . . . Shannon has estimated that if the English language had only about thirty percent redundancy, then it would be possible to construct three-dimensional puzzles" (p. 14).

$(X\ Y\ X)$, and auxesis $(X\ X\ Y\ Y\ )$. Though Tennyson would not have been formally acquainted with these terms, all these schemes are characteristic of Milton's style, the style which most influenced Tennyson, and which he considered "even finer than that of Virgil, 'the lord of language,' "[31] Tennyson's poetry is more genuine because, instead of excluding these turns upon itself, it reaches out and assimilates them. At its best, in *Maud, In Memoriam,* and the late elegies, Tennyson's poetry possesses the authority that comes from having gone through great disorder, with the complete sense of what produces disorder, then coming out on the other side. Tennyson, like Frost, is "one acquainted with the night" (Frost, "Acquainted with the Night," ll. 1, 14). But like Hesper's lament for the "buried sun" in *In Memoriam* (CXXI, 1–4), the night's magnificence allows the mind to be faithful to the bare surfaces of the world, to a "glory done" (CXXI, 4), while pouring on earth's poverty a transfiguring light.

I have identified six recurrent features of Tennyson's style: his repetitions; his resourceful hovering; his inventive use of appositional grammar and two-way syntax; his skillful navigation between closed and open language; his remarkable ability to combine clarity of sense with a suggestion of truths that are not explicit in his statements; and his combination of directness and indirectness. These characteristics of his style derive from three main sources. They originate in his view of the world, in his theory of language, and in his psychological temperament and general needs.

Tennyson solemnly announced to his friends that he was more certain he existed as an eternal spirit than that his hand and foot existed.[32] Yet he differs from other Idealists, most notably from Shelley, in that he insists the mind must not annihilate nature; it must do to the world as the world would be done by, observing a policy of mutual tolerance and concession. Among the nineteenth-century Idealists, Tennyson is closest to F. H. Bradley, the intellectual father of the poet most influenced by Tennyson, T. S.

31. Hallam Tennyson, *Tennyson: A Memoir,* II, 284.
32. Charles Tennyson, *Alfred Tennyson,* p. 385.

Eliot. As Eliot affirms that "human kind / Cannot bear very much reality" ("Burnt Norton," *Four Quartets,* I, 44–45), so Bradley affirms that reality can be held by the finite mind only imperfectly, in one poor focus. Similarly, Tennyson acknowledges that language distorts the divine nature; it has the same effect as refraction, which makes the "straight staff" look "bent" in water ("The Higher Pantheism," l. 16). Tennyson sees God through small apertures. Window after window may be opened, veil after veil drawn back, but the inmost spirit is never revealed. Like Bradley, Tennyson is also the skeptic, the critic of Idealism. In the astonishing conclusion to Bradley's *Principles of Logic* (1883), the "lingering scruple" that forbids the logician to claim that his logic is "real," is a fine example of what Arnold calls "living by ideas" and of that ability of an author to "return upon himself" which always seemed to Arnold "one of the finest things in literature."[33] Tennyson's "over-and-overing" of ideas molds his language into a similar "return upon himself," into an expression of the waverings, the swervings, the doublings back upon himself which accompany his inward doubts and indecisions as their very shadows. *In Memoriam* is like a Gothic cathedral. But its design is visibly strained beyond the point of unity; fragmentation lurks in every section. Its visionary thrust is flung up to heaven, and soars on gaunt ribs of faith. It seems that if the soul falters, God is lost. The whole vast edifice, like one of those grandly aspiring Gothic cathedrals, may come crashing to the ground. The instability of the form is one with Tennyson's ability to turn upon his deepest convictions, enlarging or revising a premise as soon as he establishes it. This habit of turning on himself is well illustrated by his son Hallam's anecdote: "The next morning we wandered about the Abbey for a long time. We climbed up to the chantry, and, while the organ and voices of the choristers were sounding through the cathedral, my father suddenly said: 'It is beautiful, but what empty and awful mockery if there were no God!' "[34]

A second source of Tennyson's stylistic traits is his theory of

33. Matthew Arnold, "The Function of Criticism at the Present Time," in *The Complete Prose Works of Matthew Arnold,* ed. R. H. Super, III, 267.
34. *Tennyson: A Memoir,* II, 275.

language. If the world is a "lucid veil," then the words of the poet must "half reveal / And half conceal" (*In Memoriam,* V, 3–4) what they express. Words are not simply tokens and shadows, as they are for Shelley, but neither can they be direct apprehensions. We encounter in Tennyson a poetic version of the battle over names for God that Victorian metaphysicians were waging. Not wanting to be duped, which is the fate of the idolater, Sir William Hamilton,[35] Dean Mansel,[36] and Herbert Spencer[37] contend that all words for God share only the appropriate replicahood of their labels. They are metaphors rather than analogies— to use the distinction Coleridge makes in *Aids to Reflection.* If they denote anything, it is an emotional attitude in the user, not an attribute of the divine nature. On the other hand, not wanting to be victims of incredulity, which is the wisdom of the fool, neo-Hegelians like the brothers Edward and John Caird argue that names for the Absolute must share with the Absolute certain universal qualities. God is the tenor, and finite minds the vehicles, of a giant metaphor, a "concrete universal."[38] Steering a middle course between the skeptics and the Hegelians, an explorer of analogies like Tennyson tries to know and define the nature of God by seeing him more clearly through limited apertures. The attempt is important both as a subject for theology and as a subject for poetic theory. For as a religious version of the problem of poetic analogy, the difficulty of ascribing attributes to an unconditioned God throws as much light on the way poets use meta-

35. Sir William Hamilton formulates the principles of his philosophy of the unconditioned in an influential review, "M. Cousin's 'Course of Philosophy,'" *Edinburgh Review,* L (October, 1829), 194–221.

36. See Henry Mansel, *The Limits of Religious Thought Examined in Eight Lectures* (London, 1867).

37. See "The Unknowable," in *First Principles* (New York, 1880), Part I.

38. A central idea in the writings of Hegel, in the Preface to *Phenomenology of Mind,* for example (*Hegel Selections,* ed. J. Loewenberg [New York, 1929], pp. 29, 46–51), the concept of the "concrete universal"—of a whole in which the richness and immediacy of the component parts are in direct proportion to the inclusiveness of the whole—is prominent in the writings of many neo-Hegelians. The concept of the "concrete universal" is applied specifically to metaphor by W. K. Wimsatt in his well-known essay "The Concrete Universal," in *The Verbal Icon* (Lexington, Ky., 1954), pp. 79–82.

phor and syntax to define the inexpressible as it throws on theology
or on the theory of knowledge. Occasional lapses into univocal
names for God, as at the end of "De Profundis"—"Infinite Ideality! / Immeasurable Reality! / Infinite Personality" (ll. 58–60)—
and into equivocal names, as in "Lucretius"—"Apollo, Delius, or
of older use / . . . Hyperion—what you will" (ll. 125–126)
—show how difficult it is—in poetic, as well as in theological,
discourse—to steer a proper middle course between idolatry
and skepticism.[39] Tennyson's analogies for the divine are themselves analogies of how he uses indirection in all his best poems.
However incomprehensible his subject may be, Tennyson is never
deterred from refracting that subject into multiple components,
using his appositional grammar to present it in shifting lights.
His multiple points of view require exacting selections. Though
each view falls short, the fluid syntax allows a great many
very precise meanings to dispose themselves in different ways.
Such use of grammar may be exceptional, and perceptible
only to vigilant readers. But it realizes what I. A. Richards identifies as "an important use of words—very frequent," he suggests,
"in poetry—which does not freeze its meanings but leaves them
fluid, which does not fix an assertorial clip upon them in the way
that scientific prose and factual discourse must."[40] The elements
in Tennyson's metaphors that are strongly analogical allow him
to hint significance, to imply something more than his words

39. In "Metaphor and Mistake," *Sewanee Review*, LXVI (1958), 79–99,
Walker Percy identifies "analogy" as a poet's proper middle way between
the idolatry of the modern semanticists, who insist on univocal meanings,
and the skepticism of the behaviorists, who insist that all meanings are
equivocal. Even when the dilemma is not couched in theological terms,
Percy identifies it as the same dilemma I have identified in Victorian metaphysics—a dilemma, he believes, "which has plagued philosophers since
the eighteenth century" (p. 98). "The semanticists, on the one horn, imply
that we know as the angels know, directly and without mediation . . . ;
all that remains is to name what we know and this we do by a semantic
'rule'; . . . The behaviorists, on the other, imply that we do not know at
all but only respond and that even art is a mode of sign-response." Percy
concludes that we apprehend neither univocally nor equivocally but
analogically, "not as the angels know and not as dogs know but as men
who must know one thing through the mirror of another" (p. 99).
40. *Speculative Instruments* (London, 1955), p. 148.

actually say, while the element in metaphor that Wheelwright calls "diaphoric,"[41] and that is essential to Tennyson's appositional method, creates a strong sense of presence. This second element resists "the intelligence / Almost successfully."[42] Even after analogies of superb daring, the untranslatable character of each frame offers us in the end a mystery. As a student of Taoism, Tennyson knows that "The Tao that can be spoken is not the real Tao."[43] The Nameless can be intimated, hinted at, in countless ways. But most of Tennyson's metaphors also represent a constant, resourceful restoration of his ignorance.

Recurrent traits of Tennyson's style derive, in the third place, from his psychological temperament and general needs. The syntax that circles back on itself, hovering over a topic instead of confronting it directly, helps the mourner control his grief. It allows Tennyson to master his fear of suicidal death, his fear of suffering the same fate as his alcoholic father, or his even greater fear of insanity, the affliction of his brothers Edward and Septimus. Arnold's complaint that Tennyson dawdled with the painted shell

41. "The Two Ways of Metaphor," in *Metaphor and Reality,* ch. iv. Other Victorian poets avoid idolatry, not by developing the "diaphoric" elements in metaphor, but by introducing grotesque forms of vision. For example, if Browning's visions are not to be petrified into idolatries and dogmas (the worst form of oblivion), they must be subverted by grotesque elements—all for the sake of perceptibility, of being kept vivid and memorable. Truth is passed through the quirks of language, signs of the mind's intricate turnings and distortions. As Walter Bagehot realizes, the grotesque is the natural mode of a poet like Browning who sees "the ideal struggling with obstacles" and who sees "good elements hidden" incongruously "in horrid accompaniments" (*Literary Studies,* ed. R. H. Hunt, II (London, 1897), p. 375). Art becomes grotesque, as Hegel observes, when the medium betrays the artist; when the infinite, in its mysteriousness and its sublimity, eludes all the forms that try to define it. (See *Aesthetics: Lectures on Fine Art by G. W. F. Hegel,* tr. T. M. Knox, I [Oxford, 1975], p. 77). In Browning's poetry such "reciprocal inadequacy" of form and content is bound to be grotesque. It allows Browning to express a religious vision of the world in which each idol may die so that the truth itself will live. Only in a grotesque universe can Browning find that antidote to idolatry that Balaustion finds in the "master-word" at the close of *Aristophanes' Apology:* "There are no gods, no gods! / Glory to God."
42. Wallace Stevens, "Man Carrying Thing," ll. 1–2.
43. Quoted by Wheelwright in *Metaphor and Reality,* p. 22.

of the universe[44] applies to that fastidiousness in Tennyson's art
which amounts at times to an exhausting compulsion to be awake,
hypersensitively, to every detail. As long as the poet's fears double
back into repression, they create anxiety and discontent: in
Maud, The Princess, and the *Idylls,* they skip out diagonally into
a wide array of masks and disguises. But human nature is able to
remake and remold itself. And this re-creation, instead of cutting
off impulses, as it does in "The Palace of Art," can include them
in broader, more authentic poems. Instead of suppressing or
throttling his fears, Tennyson learns to use his energies constructively. Even in *Maud,* where these energies are most destructive,
they are precious portents of his own powers. William James distinguishes between the "once-born" men who are naturally
assured, and the "second-born," men[45] who attain fulfillment only
precariously. Tennyson's assurance is the attainment of a spirit
"second-born," rising above adverse circumstances. After prolonged self-struggle and despair, he is bent on affirming that the
ultimate forces of love and hate, of sanity and madness, are not
irreconcilable. Such splendor of the heart as is sought by Ulysses
and the lover in *Maud* can never, in man's tragically short life,
be fully realized. But beyond life's terror and its loneliness, and
beyond the tragedy of early death, grief may be mastered, and
darkness turned into transforming vision. Tennyson's ability to
exorcise fear and morbidity and freely evolve his own destiny
gives his poetry enlarged and nuanced meanings. It advances him
in the "intellectual dignity" of men.[46]

44. "Letter to Arthur Hugh Clough," written shortly after December 6,
1847; reprinted in *Poetry and Criticism of Matthew Arnold,* ed. A. Dwight
Culler (Boston, 1961), p. 515.
45. "The Sick Soul" and "The Divided Self," Lectures VI–VIII, in
The Varieties of Religious Experience (New Hyde Park, N.Y., 1963),
especially pp. 157, 165, 166.
46. The idea and the phrase are Dr. Johnson's. To "exempt ourselves
from outward influences," he argues, is to be elevated "to some degree of
intellectual dignity." A "mean flexibility to every impulse, and a patient
submission to the tyranny of casual troubles, is below the dignity of that
mind, which, however . . . weakened, boasts its derivation from a celestial
origin" (*The Rambler,* no. 6, Saturday, 7 April 1750, in *The Yale Edition
of the Works of Samuel Johnson,* III, ed. W. J. Bate and Albrecht B.
Strauss [New Haven and London, 1969], pp. 30–31).

淡淡淡

A Bibliographical Essay

Studies of Tennyson, however precise about particulars, frequently fail in their leaps toward generalization. Some of "the central critical difficulties which make Tennyson a particularly difficult poet to write well about or to assess accurately" are discussed in Kerry McSweeney's review essay, "The State of Tennyson Criticism," *Papers on Language and Literature,* X (1974), 433–446.

The first part of my bibliographical essay examines elements of Tennyson's poetry under five general headings: style and thought; poetic development; Victorian poetic theory; knowledge of rhetoric; generic experiments; and dissociation of sensibility. This part is designed to help the reader see details of individual poems from a wider perspective. The second part is concerned with works of scholarship and criticism devoted to individual poems and categories of poems.

ELEMENTS OF TENNYSON'S POETRY

Style and Thought

An early informative study of Tennyson's language is J. F. A. Pyre's monograph, *The Formation of Tennyson's Style* (Madison, Wis., 1921). More recently, two scholars, Alan Sinfield and F. E. L. Priestley, have related important features of Tennyson's style to his thought. According to Sinfield, Tennyson's syntax exemplifies a pattern of thought which he calls "analogical; it embodies a process of redefinition, thus according with [Tennyson's] opposition to reason and scientific method and his reliance upon subjective experience" (*The Language of Tennyson's "In Memoriam"* [New York, 1971], p. 104). In another important study, Priestley implicitly refutes T. S. Eliot's charge that Tennyson is a poet of reflective, but not of intellectual power, by arguing—with great persuasiveness—that Tennyson's thought is "wide-ranging, penetrating, and profound" (*Language and Structure in Tennyson's Poetry* [London, 1973], p. 181).

Though such scholars as Alan Sinfield have made excellent use of modern linguistic theory, the anticipated alliance of criticism, linguistics, and the analytic philosophies of language is an alliance which exists mainly in the imagination of wishful students like myself. In puzzling over oddities of grammar, over contours of syntax peculiar to a poem, we may still be heartened by the thought that the understanding of poetic language "is not where it was, and can not remain where it is" (F. H. Bradley, *The Principles of Logic* [London, 1883], p. v). And, as F. H. Bradley once remarked of his own field of study, "When one works with the stream a slight effort may bring progress" (*The Principles of Logic,* p. v).

Tennyson's success has sometimes been measured by the degree to which he renounces ideas and cultivates lyric modes. Sir Harold Nicolson's praise of Tennyson's lyric gifts and his condemnation of his rhetoric (*Tennyson: Aspects of His Life, Character and Poetry* [London, 1925]) perpetuates a divorce between emotive and referential meaning familiar to students of I. A. Richards' criticism. It introduces what seems to me a false separation of the intellectual and stylistic satisfactions of poetry. Tennyson's best long poem, *In Memoriam,* is by no means devoid of intellection, and "Lucretius," a masterpiece, is a brilliant fusion of imagination and ideas. If I seem to neglect Tennyson as a thinker, it is not because I accept W. H. Auden's judgment that Tennyson is the stupidest of English poets (*A Selection from the Poems of Alfred, Lord Tennyson* [Garden City, N.Y., 1944]) but because I have chosen to concentrate, not on Tennyson's ideas, but on his style. As for Tennyson's intellectual endowment, there is at least as much truth in the favorable judgment of the late Victorians, best summed up by Charles F. Masterman in *Tennyson as a Religious Teacher* (London, 1900), as there is in Auden's judgment. Though Tennyson's canon lacks the coherence we associate with a poet who is also a systematic thinker like Dante or Milton, awareness of his growing interest in Oriental philosophy, and of his indebtedness to British Idealism, would illuminate many details of his inheritance. Tennyson's idea that we may experience and even choose to love God, but that we can never fully know or understand him, is a familiar idea in Oriental thought, and is perhaps best expressed in Western tradition by the great paradoxes of *The Cloud of Unknowing.* Its principal exponent in the Victorian age is Henry Mansel, the disciple of Sir William Hamilton, who gives an agnostic interpretation to the "regulative truths" of Kant. In *The Limits of Religious Thought* (London, 1867) Mansel argues that it is impossible to know God as he is in himself. The epithets we apply to God must be taken analogically, not idolatrously. We know God only as we experience him, not as he exists in "unconditioned" form. (Compare these ideas with the arguments of Demea in Hume's *Dialogues on Natural Religion* and with Coleridge's distinction between metaphorical and analogical descriptions of deity in *Confessions of an Enquiring Spirit* and *Aids to Reflection*.) Tennyson's indebtedness to British Idealism and to Oriental thought is highly technical, however, and must wait for a more specialized study than the present one.

Poetic Development

The major question concerning Tennyson's development is whether such a system or nonsystem as he embodies is already discernible at the beginning of his career or evolves only gradually. Answers vary from Douglas Bush's view that almost all Tennyson's major themes appear in his early poems, and that there is little subsequent development, to the view of T. S. Eliot that, as Dryden observed of Chaucer in his *Preface to the Fables*, "here is God's plenty." Eliot sees in Tennyson a combination of "three qualities which are seldom found together except in the greatest poets: abundance, variety, and complete competence." In order to "appreciate his work . . . we must read a good deal of it" ("In Memoriam," in *Selected Essays* [London, 1932], p. 328). Douglas Bush, on the other hand, sees a poet of more limited range: "If one allows for the normal mellowing of maturity, Tennyson was at the end what he was at the beginning, an artist who had consummate powers of expression and not very much, except as an emotional poet, to say" (*Mythology and the Romantic Tradition in English Poetry* [Cambridge, Mass., 1937], p. 199). Most readers subscribe now to Eliot's view. As Douglas Bush reminds us, however, the themes themselves are relatively static. Except for Tennyson's growing interest in Oriental philosophy, the subject matter undergoes little extension after 1850.

Victorian Poetic Theory

The most comprehensive study of Victorian theories of poetry and style is Alba H. Warren's *English Poetic Theory, 1825–1865*

(Princeton, 1950). "By means of quotation, paraphrase, and running commentary" (p. v), Warren compares the assumptions of nine Victorian theorists and relates their important observations to criticism written in the age. Warren does not develop his insights by applying the theories to poetic texts. But his excellent summaries clarify the transformation of Romantic theory into the theories of the early and mid-Victorian periods. He also suggests some of the implications of these theories for aesthetes and formalists of a later time. Conceived as a sequel to Warren, and indebted to his format, Marvel Shmiefsky's monograph, *Sense at War with Soul: English Poetics (1865–1900)* (The Hague, 1972) examines nine theorists from Swinburne to A. C. Bradley. Other valuable supplements to Warren's work are Isobel Armstrong's *Victorian Scrutinies: Reviews of Poetry, 1830–1870* (London, 1972); Robert L. Peters' *The Crowns of Apollo: Swinburne's Principles of Literature and Art* (Detroit, 1965); Peters' edition of essays on Victorian aesthetic theory entitled *Victorians on Literature and Art* (New York, 1961); and the fine second edition of *Victorian Poetry and Poetics,* edited by W. E. Houghton and Robert Stange (Boston, 1968). The last two books make important theoretical texts readily available, though editions do not provide the opportunity to generalize about the theoretical assumptions of the age, as Warren's study does.

There still exists no comprehensive study of Victorian poetry that relates it, for example, to the critical traditions of Mill's empiricism, to the idealism of John Grote and James Ferrier, or to the theological impulse behind the new interest in Hegel. What connections exist between Victorian poetics and such intellectual phenomena of the age as Tractarianism (Keble's Tract 89, for example); the Higher Criticism and its theories of myth; the revival of interest in Plato; scientific developments; theories of language and logic? What theories of mind does Tennyson's poetry presuppose? No scholar has done for the Victorian period—perhaps the feat is inimitable—what M. H. Abrams' *Mirror and the Lamp* (New York, 1953) has done so ably for the earlier Romantic age.

Knowledge of Rhetoric

Like most of the handbooks of the eighteenth century, the only manuals on grammar and rhetoric that are likely to have influenced Tennyson make no reference to the many rhetorical schemes that

Tennyson uses in his poems. The two manuals are in the library of Tennyson's father, originally in the rectory at Somersby: the three volumes of Hugh Blair's popular *Lectures on Rhetoric* (London, 1801) and a more obscure monograph by John Foster, *An Essay on the Different Nature of Accent and Quantity* (London, 1820). Instead of painstakingly labeling and arranging the devices of language, Blair comments sensitively on varied effects of shifting the caesura. No other imitator, with the possible exception of Keats, catches so well as Tennyson Milton's majestic use of the sixth-syllable caesura, whose effects of stately locomotion are accurately discerned by Blair.

> Her cheek had lost the rose, and round her neck
> Floated her hair or seemed to float in rest. ["Oenone," ll. 17–18]

The use of a fourth-syllable caesura, as in the second quoted line, is also a technique recommended by Blair, who praises its briskness and vigor. His *Lectures on Rhetoric* go on to observe that "the grace and solemn cadence become still more sensible, when the pause falls after the seventh syllable, which is the nearest place to the end of the line that it can occupy" (Vol. III, lecture xxxviii, p. 101). Blair apparently forgets that eighth-syllable caesuras, though rare, do occasionally occur in pentameter lines, especially in elegies. The brokeness of a poem such as "Tears, Idle Tears" is more than solemn. It is literally the cry of its occasion; in the etymological sense, it is a falling away, an *occasio,* from some unspeakable ecstasy or grief. The elegist falters; he cannot go on, breaking down with emotion before he reaches the final foot. Such is the effect of the late seventh-syllable break in Tennyson's "Dear as remembered kisses after death" (*The Princess,* IV, 36), and of the two eighth-syllable caesuras in the first line of Ben Jonson's elegy "On My First Son": "Farewell, thou child of my right hand, and joy; / My sin was too much hope of thee, loved boy." Despite Blair's oversight, Tennyson must have remembered the advice about late-breaking lines when he came to write "The Kraken." Toward the end of that poem the repeated use of seventh-syllable caesuras produces as powerfully as the closing prophecy in "Oenone" Blair's "slow Alexandrian air, which is finely suited to a close" (III, xxxviii, 101).

Foster's more unorthodox treatise on prosody argues, in opposition to Blair, that the interplay of accent and quantity offers the English poet a rich and varied technical resource. "Metre," he insists, "depends on quantity alone. Rhythm is in its nature more complex, and seems to comprehend accent with quantity" (*An Essay on the Different Nature of Accent and Quantity*, ch. ii, p. 36). Though Foster overstates the case, and treats already familiar material, confining most of his examples to classical meter, he provides Tennyson with an early justification of what was to become a lifelong practice and belief.

Just as Tennyson is unlikely to have studied Renaissance rhetoric in his father's library—and I have no evidence that he was even familiar with George Campbell's eighteenth-century study, *The Philosophy of Rhetoric* (London, 1776)—so it would be oversimple to conclude that his skill in the arts of language is substantially a result of his university studies. In the early nineteenth century, as in the days of Milton, undergraduates at Cambridge were still obliged to perform exercises in disputation, known as acts and opponencies, which are described by D. A. Winstanley in *Early Victorian Cambridge* (Cambridge, Eng., 1955), p. 149. There is no doubt that Tennyson put this rhetorical training to use when he came to write early poems of debate such as "The Two Voices," though this training cannot have inspired the delightful sparring matches in *The Devil and the Lady*, a poem that was written when Tennyson was only fourteen. According to Winstanley, in his classic account of the Cambridge curriculum, it was still possible in Tennyson's day to qualify for an ordinary degree at Cambridge by knowing only the first six books of Euclid, a little arithmetic and algebra, and a smattering of moral and metaphysical philosophy, including Paley (p. 151). Moreover, the schemes that Renaissance rhetoricians labeled and proliferated constitute a tradition that had gradually disappeared. By the early nineteenth century the schemes survived only as a few of the more exciting figures such as syllepsis and paronomasia, figures of ambiguity and punning. Poets and critics had come to distrust the labels of rhetoric and the codifications of grammar, and with good reason. The proliferation of nomenclature had been accomplished by earlier rhetoricians with a certain recklessness and frivolity of purpose. Instead of stirring imaginative insight, they had come to distract and deaden it. It is very unlikely, therefore, that Tennyson would have been able to identify and name most of the rhetorical schemes that occur in his poems. Such awareness of Tennyson's probable lack of knowledge on the scholar's part should make him avoid technical terms unfamiliar to Tennyson. But it must not be allowed to discourage critical investigation, or put an end to further inquiry. According to his son Hallam, Tennyson valued Milton even more than he valued Virgil, his beloved "lord of language" (*Tennyson: A Memoir* [London, 1897], II, 284). Tennyson alludes more often to Milton than to any other classical or English author. It would be strange indeed if Tennyson, one of the most venturesome imitators of Milton, did not incorporate in his poetry some of the rhetorical and grammatical practices of his great predecessor. But the interesting question is surely *not* whether Tennyson is writing as a conscious student of Milton's use of classical rhetoric. The interesting question is what a particular variation from flat writing does for Tennyson's language in a given context. As I. A. Richards reminds us, rhetorical theory is "no more than a somewhat chaotic collection of observations made on the ways of lively, venturesome speech and writing" ("The Places and the Figures," in *Speculative Instruments* [London, 1955], p. 158). More improbable than the thesis that Tennyson acquired firsthand knowledge of rhetorical theory from his classical reading or from his studies at Cambridge is the thesis that Tennyson, one of the liveliest imitators of Virgil and Milton who ever lived, should have had no intuitive grasp at all of their rhetorical schemes and should have assimilated none of these schemes in his poetry.

Generic Experiments

Most attempts in the Victorian period to discuss and analyze poetic genres now seem antiquated. An impulse to create endless categories and meaningless distinctions vitiates the most ambitious of such attempts, those of E. S. Dallas, the author of *Poetics: An Essay on Poetry* (London, 1852) and *The Gay Science* (London, 1886). Even the generic criticism of J. S. Mill ("Thoughts on Poetry and Its Varieties," in *Dissertations and Discussions* [London, 1859], I, 63–94), Robert Browning (*An Essay on Shelley* [London, 1852]), and the Reverend John Keble (*Keble's Lectures on Poetry, 1832–1841,* tr. E. K. Francis [Oxford, 1912]) tends to be so preoccupied with the psychology of the poet or his audience that it provides few clues to the modern critic who wishes to proceed to the formal analysis of texts. Far more helpful than the hints of contemporary Victorians are the principles for generic study laid down in our own time by R. S. Crane and Northrop Frye. In *The Languages of Criticism and the Structure of Poetry* (Toronto, 1953) Crane admirably illustrates some of the generic principles he advocates by applying them, briefly, to Gray's "Elegy," which he calls "an imitative lyric of moral choice," (p. 176) and to the unusual generic mixture in *Macbeth*. More detailed and comprehensive in Frye's "Rhetorical Criticism: A Theory of Genres," chapter IV of *Anatomy of Criticism* (Princeton, 1957). Frye shares with Dallas the schoolmen's impulse to construct elaborate tables. But Dallas' tables obscure more than they reveal. They devise only superficial connections of the kind that eighteenth-century criticism dismissed as "false wit." Dallas throws up a scaffolding, then has to swing and scramble through its pipework. Frye's tables, in contrast, disclose unsuspected combinations that account for more and more of the literary detail. His generic tables become a species of "wit-criticism," in Coleridge's sense of that term; they reveal the diffusion of similarity among literary forms that seem, on first inspection, to be radically different.

The best modern analysis of Tennyson's understanding and use of poetic genres is F. E. L. Priestley's stimulating chapter, "Style and Genre," in *Language and Structure in Tennyson's Poetry*. Priestly demonstrates how the nineteenth-century's "new and freer attitude towards genre" allows Tennyson to "use as selectively or as collectively as he wishes . . . modes of poetry, embodying sets of associations of ideas, of atmosphere, of moods, of emotional tones" (p. 68). The eighteenth century had based its literary tradition on the belief that "kinds" of writing exist apart from the writer, and that they correspond to the objective classifications of taxonomy. Priestley shows how Tennyson, like Wordsworth, "is working, in a sense, in an opposite way from the traditional. . . . [He] is moving back, away from the formal definition to the general idea and associations" (p. 68). William J. Whitla also discusses theories of genre and the efforts of Tennyson and Browning to overcome traditional and rigid views of genre in a suggestive study, "Browning's Lyrics and the Language of Periodical Criticism," *English Studies in Canada*, I (1975), 195–201.

Dissociation of Sensibility

The most searching Victorian analysis of thought and feeling is F. H. Bradley's *Appearance and Reality: A Metaphysical Essay* (Oxford, 1893), pp. 150–151. On the dangers of opposing thought and imagination there are also cogent comments in John Grote's *Exploratio Philosophica* (Cambridge, 1865), p. xlvii, and Roden Noel's "Use of Metaphor and 'Pathetic Fallacy' in Poetry," *Fortnightly Review*, V (August 1, 1866), 672. Bradley's disciple T. S. Eliot is right to demand a "unified sensibility" in poetry. But he is wrong to suppose that Tennyson's sensibility is disunified, and that Tennyson illustrates "the difference between the intellectual poet and the [merely] reflective poet" ("The Metaphysical Poets," in *Selected Essays*, p. 287). A stimulating discussion of Tennyson's awareness of the need for unified sensibility, and of his reluctance to oppose thought and feeling appears in F. E. L. Priestley's chapter "Language and Thought," in *Language and Structure in Tennyson's Poetry*, especially in the comments on pp. 165–166 and in the discussion of the "law of the excluded middle" on pp. 178 ff.

Tennyson's distinction between the wisdom of the seer and the knowledge of the rationalist recalls James Hinton's claim that expository and historical proofs have more positive value than logical proofs (*Man and His Dwelling Place* [London, 1859], especially ch. i, "Of the Work of Science"). A copy of Hinton's work was in Tennyson's library, and is now in the Tennyson Archives, Lincoln, England. Compare Hinton's threefold distinction among expository, historical, and logical proofs with J. Collard's: the truth of propositions must be "grounded either on INTUITION, DEMONSTRATION, or TESTIMONY" (*The Essentials of Logic* [London, 1796], p. 233). The three sources of truth represent the first, second, and third degrees of human evidence, respectively. Collard affirms that error enters only in the formulation of hypotheses, and only in hypotheses grounded on testimony or demonstration. His distrust of logic recalls Tennyson's idea in "The Two Voices," *In Memoriam*, and "The Ancient Sage" that most compelling arguments are rooted in the imagination, and the moral sense, and that only the heart—not the head—can nourish them. Tennyson's distinction between the logical inferences of reason and the unconditional "assents" to truths that cannot be proved—but which are worth living and dying for—is also the distinction Newman makes in his *An Essay in Aid of a Grammar of Assent* (Garden City, N.Y., 1955), originally published in 1870: all assents, whether "real" or "notional," are unconditional, and must be distinguished sharply from the conclusions based on logical demonstrations.

CATEGORIES AND INDIVIDUAL POEMS

Dramatic Monologues

In his dramatic monologues Tennyson is less concerned with different objects, settings, or even philosophic doctrines, than with different responses to these things—responses that may unlock some truth about the speaker. The best treatment of the dramatic monologue in Victorian poetry is Robert Langbaum's influential monograph, *The Poetry of Experience: The Dramatic Monologue in Modern Literary Tradition* (New York, 1957). There are also excellent comments in Park Honan's study, *Browning's Characters* (New Haven, 1961), and in B. W. Fuson's monograph, *Browning and His English Predecessors in the Dramatic Monologue* (Iowa City, 1948). The best observations on Tennyson's classical monologues, and—for that matter—on all his classical verse, are the brief but eloquent comments made by Douglas Bush in *Mythology and the Romantic Tradition*, pp. 202–224.

Theoretically, the dramatic monologues allow Tennyson to be both a lyric poet and a thinker, to combine in a philosopher such as Lucretius the analytic rigor of a David Friedrich Strauss and the visionary power of a Blake or Shelley. But none of Tennyson's contemporaries seems to have recognized the theoretical possibilities of a form that allows the poet to turn pagan martyrdom in "Tiresias" into a prototype of Christian sacrifice, and to cross Demeter's prophetic visions with the subversive speculations of Hardy or Swinburne. Almost every Romantic theorist justifies the use of expressive models. And Victorian theorists such as Sir Henry Taylor, and later Matthew Arnold, urge the poet's "exercise of the intellectual faculties" (Taylor, Preface to *Philip Van Artevelde* [London, 1834]). But few of Tennyson's contemporaries—except for philosophers such as F. H. Bradley, John Grote, and the poet-theorist Roden Noel—understand how, in Coleridge's words, "no man was ever yet a great poet, without being at the same time a profound philosopher" (*Biographia Literaria* [London, 1817], ch. xv). When such Victorians as Alexander Smith identify the fusion of expressive and didactic elements that is characteristic of the most highly developed monologues, they limit poetry to the expressive element alone. (M. H. Abrams—and later *The Wellesley Index to Victorian Periodicals*

(Toronto, 1966)—identify Alexander Smith as the author of the article entitled "The Philosophy of Poetry," in *Blackwood's Magazine*, December 1835.) For a summary of Smith's theories and their affinities with the expressive doctrines of Rudolph Carnap and I. A. Richards see M. H. Abrams, "The Semantics of Expressive Language: Alexander Smith," in *The Mirror and the Lamp*, pp. 148–155. A Victorian such as Smith is still so greatly influenced by the dominant tradition of the Romantic period that he fails to recognize the rhetorical potential of the monologue form. This potential is recognized later by G. B. Shaw when he reminds the Browning Society that "Caliban upon Setebos" is radically "undramatic": Browning endows a primitive savage with the introspective powers of Hamlet and the theology of an evangelical churchman. Instead of granting the intellectual integrity of poetry, Alexander Smith strikingly anticipates I. A. Richards' doctrine of "pseudo-statements" (*Science and Poetry* [London, 1926] and ch. xxxv of *Principles of Literary Criticism* [London, 1925]) by restricting poetry to the expressive or emotive element, consigning ideas to a referential limbo.

Studies of individual dramatic monologues include:

Buckler, William E. "Tennyson's *Lucretius* Bowdlerized?" *Review of English Studies,* N.S., V (1954), 269–271.

Bush, Douglas. "The Personal Note in Tennyson's Classical Poems," *University of Toronto Quarterly,* IV (1934), 201–218.

——. "Tennyson's Ulysses and Hamlet," *Modern Language Review,* XXXVIII (1943), 38.

Chiasson, E. J. "Tennyson's 'Ulysses'—a Re-interpretation," *University of Toronto Quarterly,* XXIII (1954), 402–409.

Donahue, Mary J. "Tennyson's *Hail, Briton!* and *Tithon* in the Heath Manuscript," *PMLA,* LXVII (1952), 572–575.

Fredeman, William E. " 'A Sign betwixt the Meadow and the Cloud': The Ironic Apotheosis of Tennyson's *St. Simeon Stylites,*" *University of Toronto Quarterly,* XXXVIII (1969), 69–83.

Gwynn, Frederick L. "Tennyson's 'Tithon,' 'Tears, Idle Tears,' and 'Tithonus,' " *PMLA,* LXVII (1952), 572–575.

Joseph, Gerhard. "The Idea of Mortality in Tennyson's Classical and Arthurian Poems: 'Honor comes with mystery,' " *Modern Philology,* LXVI (1968), 136–145.

Leggett, B. J. "Dante, Byron, and Tennyson's Ulysses," *Tennessee Studies in Literature,* XV (1970), 143–159.

Mitchell, Charles. "The Undying Will of Tennyson's Ulysses," *Victorian Poetry*, II (1964), 87–95.

Pettigrew, John. "Tennyson's 'Ulysses': A Reconciliation of Opposites," *Victorian Poetry*, I (1963), 27–45.

Ricks, Christopher. "Tennyson's *Lucretius*," *The Library*, XX (1965), 63–64.

Robinns, Tony. "Tennyson's 'Ulysses': The Significance of the Homeric and Dantesque Backgrounds," *Victorian Poetry*, XI (1973), 177–193.

Robson, W. W. "The Dilemma of Tennyson." In *Critical Essays on the Poetry of Tennyson*, ed. John Killham. London, 1960. Pp. 155–163.

Simpson, Arthur L., Jr. "Aurora as Artist: A Reinterpretation of Tennyson's 'Tithonus,' " *Philological Quarterly*, LI (1972), 905–921.

Storch, R. F. "The Fugitive from the Ancestral Hearth: Tennyson's 'Ulysses,' " *Texas Studies in Literature and Language*, XIII (1971), 281–297.

Sundaram, P. S. "Tennyson's 'Ulysses,' " *Rutgers University Studies in English*, V (1971), 11–16.

Turner, Paul. "Some Ancient Light on Tennyson's 'Oenone,' " *Journal of English and Germanic Philology*, LXI (1962), 57–72.

The English Idylls

The English idylls, among the most popular of Tennyson's poems during the Victorian period, have declined more in reputation than any other group of his works. Symptomatic of their eclipse is Douglas Bush's decision to omit the much anthologized *Enoch Arden* from his Modern Library edition, *Selected Poetry of Tennyson* (New York, 1951). More recently, there have been unusually sympathetic appraisals by Christopher Ricks, in his *Tennyson* (New York, 1972), pp. 277–286; by F. E. L. Priestley, in his *Language and Structure in Tennyson's Poetry*, pp. 72–80, 92–105; and by Martin Dodsworth, in his essay "Patterns of Morbidity: Repetition in Tennyson's Poetry," in *The Major Victorian Poets: Reconsiderations*, ed. Isobel Armstrong (Lincoln, Neb., 1969), pp. 9–14. Though by no means great or even exciting works of art, the English idylls—which include "The Gardener's Daughter," "Dora," "The May Queen," an ideology rather than a man. But Tennyson is constantly [...] Ida, as he does Arthur, into conventional social situations. [...] the convergence of idealizing and mimetic conventions ma[...] more human, it also makes her remoteness from muddled [...] feelings of sexual love—a remoteness which would be norm[...] mythological character like Henry James's Isabel Archer [...] *Portrait of a Lady*—much less acceptable.

The conflict between the two views of art—idealizin[...] mimetic—receives its classic Victorian statement in David M[...] essay "Theories of Poetry and a New Poet." The article ap[...] originally in the *North British Review*, August, 1853, and wa[...] included as the ninth chapter of Masson's *Essays Biographic[...] Critical, Chiefly on English Poets* (Cambridge, Eng., 1856). T[...] son's copy of the book is now in the archives at Lincoln, En[...] Masson views the opposition between narrative and myth as a[...] flict between the mimetic theories of Aristotle and the idea[...] theories of Francis Bacon. "Aristotle makes the essence of poe[...] consist in its being imitative and truthful," Masson observes; "E[...] in its being creative and fantastical" (*North British Review*, [...] [1853], 161). Whereas Aristotelians like Ruskin praise the mi[...] power of the poet, Baconians like Newman and Mill believe wr[...] should create idealized romances rather than representational na[...] tives. According to the Baconians, poetry must assimilate the ob[...] tive world to the visions of the poet; its truth does not consist [...] correspondence with history, but in the coherence of the heroic i[...] itself.

The Princess demonstrates how even a profoundly Romantic s[...] sibility like Tennyson's can not only comprehend artifice and e[...] gance, but also feed upon them, be nourished by them, as Pope w[...] Tennyson's grasp of the competing claims of the public and t[...] private realms, of the intellectual and the affective lives, is mirror[...] not only in the subject matter of *The Princess* but also in its sty[...] Using an array of heroic and mock-heroic forms; songs and lyric[...] solemn, comic, and ironic modes—as James R. Kincaid has show[...] in *Tennyson's Major Poems: The Comic and Ironic Patterns* (Ne[...] Haven and London, 1975)—*The Princess* is the work of a poet fo[...] whom the idea of genre is meaningful and precious. Discriminatio[...] among kinds of stylistic behavior in *The Princess* enforces discrim[...] nation among other kinds of behavior; on such discrimination rest[...]

"Lady Clara Vere de Vere," "Aylmer's Field," and *Enoch Arden*—remain instructive generic experiments. To call poems such as *Enoch Arden* and "Aylmer's Field" inspired failures is to pay them a sincere, though fragile, compliment. For the student of Tennyson's renewal of tradition, even such partial failures may be as illuminating as Tennyson's more successful innovations in *The Princess*.

Other studies of special interest include:

Assad, Thomas J. "On the Major Poems of Tennyson's *Enoch Arden* Volume," *Tulane Studies in English*, XIV (1965), 29–56.

Chandler, Alice. "Cousin Clara Vere de Vere," *Victorian Poetry*, V (1967), 55–57.

Drew, Philip. " 'Aylmer's Field': A Problem for Critics," *The Listener*, LXXI (1964).

Frick, Douglas C. "A Study of Myth and Archetype in *Enoch Arden*," *Tennyson Research Bulletin*, II (1974), 106–115.

Hunt, John Dixon. " 'Story Painters and Picture Writers': Tennyson's Idylls and Victorian Painting." In *Writers and Their Background: Tennyson*, ed. D. J. Palmer. Athens, Ohio, 1973. Pp. 180–202.

Norst, Marlene J. "Enoch Arden in the German Alps: A Comparative Study of Tennyson's *Enoch Arden* and Duboc's *Walpra*." In *Affinities: Essays in German and English Literature*, ed. R. W. Last. London, 1971. Pp. 52–67.

Ratchford, Fannie E. "Idylls of the Hearth: Wise's Forgery of 'Enoch Arden,' " *Southwest Review*, XXVI (1941), 317–325.

Scott, P. G. *Tennyson's 'Enoch Arden': A Victorian Best-Seller*. Lincoln, Eng., 1970.

Short, Clarice. "Tennyson and 'The Lover's Tale,' " *PMLA*, LXXXII (1967), 78–84.

Poems of Politics and State

By far the best treatment of Tennyson's political and ceremonial poems is the fifth chapter, "The Laureate's Art," of Valerie Pitt's important study, *Tennyson Laureate* (Toronto, 1962), pp. 189–219. Her shrewd and original comments on Tennyson's patriotic and occasional verse, which too many readers have dismissed as chauvinistic, match in subtlety and good sense the achievement of the poems that she interprets. By means of emphasis and discovery her analysis brings into our world a new and more relevant poe laureate.

Among other studies of interest are:

Hunton, William A. *Tennyson and the Victorian Political Milieu* New York, 1938.

Preyer, Robert. "Alfred Tennyson: The Poetry and Politics of Conservative Vision," *Victorian Studies,* IX (1966), 325–352.

Ricks, Christopher. "A Note on Tennyson's *Ode on the Death of the Duke of Wellington,*" *Studies in Bibliography,* XVIII (1965), 282.

Shannon, Edgar F. "The History of A Poem: Tennyson's *Ode on the Death of the Duke of Wellington,*" *Studies in Bibliography,* XIII (1960), 149–177.

Solimine, Joseph. "The Burkean Idea of the State in Tennyson's Poetry: The Vision in Crisis," *Huntington Library Quarterly,* XXX (1967), 147–165.

Tennyson, Sir Charles. "Tennyson as Poet Laureate." In *Writers and Their Background: Tennyson,* ed. D. J. Palmer. Athens, Ohio, 1973. Pp. 203–225.

———. "Tennyson's Politics." In *Six Tennyson Essays.* London, 1954. Pp. 39–69.

The Plays

Though there is no real body of criticism on Tennyson's plays, J. H. Buckley's chapter "Under the Mask," in his *Tennyson: The Growth of a Poet* (Cambridge, Mass., 1960), pp. 195–215, gives the most just account of the different reasons for the poet's limitations as a playwright. There are also suggestive comments in James Kissane's brief treatment in his monograph for the Twayne series, *Alfred Tennyson* (New York, 1970), pp. 145–153. Tennyson's moral comprehension usually involves dramatic awareness—a sympathetic and intelligent knowledge of the way people act. But he is not totally successful in historical plays such as *Becket* and *Queen Mary,* for the same reason that he is not totally successful in the English idylls. At times, instead of presenting an action, he simply presents a circumstance. At other times he responds more imaginatively to the historical scene, but fails to disengage his dramatic design from factual detail. A lyrical and meditative poet like Tennyson delights to see nature in the mirror of his own mind. He is therefore more at home in a dramatic monologue like "St. Simeon Stylites" than in a

play like *Becket.* Plays are the natural medium of a poet like Shakespeare who delights to see his mind in the mirror of nature, or even of a poet like T. S. Eliot, who uses the chorus in *Murder in t Cathedral,* not to mirror his own mind, but to achieve what Ye calls "the emotion of multitude" ("Emotion of Multitude," in W. Yeats, *Essays and Introductions* [New York, 1961]).

Other studies of special interest include:

Burton, Thomas G. "The Use of Biblical Allusions in Tennys *Harold.*" In *Essays in Memory of Christine Burleson,* ed. Bur Johnson City, Tenn., 1969. Pp. 155–163.

Edison, John O. "The First Performance of Tennyson's *Har New England Quarterly,* XXXVII (1964), 387–390.

———. "The Reception of Tennyson's Plays in America," *Philolo Quarterly,* XXXV (1956), 435–443.

———. "Tennyson's *Becket* on the American Stage," *Emerson S Quarterly,* no. 39 (1965), 15–20.

Grosskurth, Phyllis. "Tennyson, Froude, and Queen Mary," *T son Research Bulletin,* II (1973), 44–54.

Rehak, Louise Rouse. "On the Use of Martyrs: Tennyson and on Thomas Becket," *University of Toronto Quarterly,* X (1963), 43–60.

Solimine, Joseph, Jr. "The Dialectics of Church and State: son's Historical Plays," *The Personalist,* XLVII (1966), 2

Thomson, Peter. "Tennyson's Plays and Their Productic *Writers and Their Background: Tennyson,* ed. D. J. Athens, Ohio, 1973. Pp. 226–254.

The Princess

The best extensive treatments of *The Princess* are I Priestley's indispensable study of Tennyson's generic innov his chapter "Style and Genre" in *Language and Structure nyson's Poetry,* incorporating his earlier "Control of Tone i son's 'The Princess,'" *Proceedings and Transactions of T Society of Canada,* 4th series, I, 295–304; and the fifth of Gerhard Joseph's stimulating book, *Tennysonian Love: Tl Diagonal* (Minneapolis, 1969), pp. 75–101.

Tennyson's achievement in *The Princess* can be better a if we see how he combines mimetic and idealizing views rent in the period. As a mythical figure, Ida is naturally i

Tennyson's ideal of civility, of respect between the sexes, and of true delicacy toward the feelings of other people.

Studies of special importance are:

Assad, Thomas J. "Tennyson's 'Tears, Idle Tears,' " *Tulane Studies in English,* XIII (1963), 71–83.

Bergonzi, Bernard. "Feminism and Femininity in *The Princess.*" In *The Major Victorian Poets,* ed. Isobel Armstrong. Lincoln, Neb., 1969. Pp. 35–50.

Brooks, Cleanth. "The Motivation of Tennyson's Weeper." In *Critical Essays on the Poetry of Tennyson,* ed. John Killham. London, 1960. Pp. 177–185.

Collins, Winston. *"The Princess:* The Education of the Prince," *Victorian Poetry,* XI (1973), 285–294.

Danzig, Allan. "Tennyson's *The Princess:* A Definition of Love," *Victorian Poetry,* IV (1966), 83–89.

Hough, Graham. " 'Tears, Idle Tears,' " *Hopkins Review,* IV (1951), 31–36.

Killham, John. *Tennyson and "The Princess": Reflections of an Age* (London, 1958).

Miller, John A. "Tennyson's Paired Poems." Ph.D. dissertation, McMaster University, 1974. Of special interest is the stimulating discussion of Tennyson's use of covert puns in *The Princess.*

Millhauser, Milton. "Tennyson's *Princess* and *Vestiges,*" *PMLA,* LXIX (1954), 337–343.

Spitzer, Leo. "Tears, Idle Tears Again," *Hopkins Review,* V (1952), 71–80.

Wajid, R. A. "Tennyson's 'Tears, Idle Tears,' " *Rutgers University Studies in English,* V (1971), 31–35.

In Memoriam

While A. C. Bradley's *Commentary* (London, 1901) still remains the indispensable guide to the form of *In Memoriam,* the most helpful full-length study of the poem to appear in recent years is Alan Sinfield's exciting monograph, *The Language of Tennyson's "In Memoriam."* Sinfield's book has the great merit of requiring an alertness on the reader's part to the shifting patterns of Sinfield's analysis, which is analogous to the alertness that *In Memoriam* itself demands. A simplified, less rigorous version of the linguistic instruments that Sinfield devises in the appendix may, in the future, provide critics with a valuable tool for coping with the semantic structure of *In Memoriam*. But, as Sinfield himself recognizes, the poetry of *In Memoriam* is closer than such instruments to the living center of language itself.

Supplementing Sinfield's excellent analysis of circles and bounds in *In Memoriam* (pp. 146 ff.) are Malcolm Ross's suggestive comments on the circular, linear, and spiral movements in the poem, in "Time, the Timeless, and the Timely: Notes on a Victorian Poem," *Transactions of the Royal Society of Canada,* 4th series, LX (1971), 219–234.

Among other studies of special interest are:

August, Eugene R. "Tennyson and Teilhard: The Faith of *In Memoriam,*" *PMLA,* LXXXIV (1969), 217–226.

Bishop, Jonathan. "The Unity of *In Memoriam,*" *Victorian Newsletter,* no. 21 (1962), 9–14.

Boyd, John D. "*In Memoriam* and the 'Logic of Feeling,'" *Victorian Poetry,* X (1972), 95–110.

Burchell, Samuel C. "Tennyson's Dark Night," *South Atlantic Quarterly,* LIV (1955), 75–81.

Edgar, Irving. "The Psychological Sources of Poetic Creative Expression and Tennyson's *In Memoriam.*" In *Essays in English Literature and History.* New York, 1972. Pp. 1–14.

Grant, Stephen Allen. "The Mystical Implications of *In Memoriam,*" *Studies in English Literature,* II (1962), 481–495.

Hunt, John D. "The Symbolist Vision of *In Memoriam,*" *Victorian Poetry,* VIII (1970), 187–198.

Johnson, E. D. H. "'In Memoriam': The Way of a Poet," *Victorian Studies,* II (1958), 139–148.

Kendall, J. L. "A Neglected Theme in Tennyson's *In Memoriam,*" *Modern Language Notes,* LXXVI (1961), 414–420.

Mason, Michael. "*In Memoriam:* The Dramatization of Sorrow," *Victorian Poetry,* X (1972), 161–177.

Mattes, Eleanor B. "*In Memoriam,*" *the Way of a Soul: A Study of Some Influences That Shaped Tennyson's Poem* (New York, 1951).

Mays, J. C. C. "*In Memoriam:* An Aspect of Form," *University of Toronto Quarterly,* XXXV (1965), 22–46.

McSweeney, Kerry. "The Pattern of Natural Consolation in *In Memoriam,*" *Victorian Poetry,* XI (1973), 87–99.

Moore, Carlisle. "Faith, Doubt, and Mystical Experience in *In Memoriam*," *Victorian Studies,* VII (1963), 155–169.

Niermeier, Stuart. *"In Memoriam* and *The Excursion:* A Matter of Comparison," *Victorian Newsletter,* no. 41 (1972), 20–22.

——. "The Problem of the *In Memoriam* Manuscripts," *Harvard Library Bulletin,* XIX (1971), 149–159.

Rosenberg, John D. "The Two Kingdoms of *In Memoriam*," *Journal of English and Germanic Philology,* LVIII (1959), 228–240.

Ryals, Clyde de L. "The 'Heavenly Friend': The 'New Mythus' of *In Memoriam*," *The Personalist,* XLIII (1962), 383–402.

Sendry, Joseph. *"In Memoriam* and *Lycidas*," *PMLA,* LXXXII (1967), 437–443.

——. "The *In Memoriam* Manuscripts: Some Solutions to the Problem," *Harvard Library Bulletin,* XXI (1973), 202–220.

Sinfield, Alan. "Matter-Moulded Forms of Speech: Tennyson's Use of Language in *In Memoriam*." In *The Major Victorian Poets: Reconsiderations,* ed. Isobel Armstrong. Lincoln, Neb., 1969. Pp. 51–67.

Svaglic, Martin J. "A Framework for Tennyson's *In Memoriam*," *Journal of English and Germanic Philology,* LXI (1962), 810–825.

Zuckermann, Joanne P. "Tennyson's *In Memoriam* as Love Poetry," *Dalhousie Review,* LI (1971), 202–217.

Maud

More than most poems, *Maud* has suffered from narrow affective theories of what poetry should be. The great love lyrics in *Maud* were commonly admired by the Victorians, and the rest of the poem dismissed as morbid and diseased. Typical of this Victorian reaction is W. E. Aytoun's review in *Blackwood's Magazine,* LXXVIII (September, 1855), 311–321. Present-day criticism may pride itself on a more just appraisal of *Maud;* but, because it values such qualities as toughness and irony, it has difficulty in accepting "grandeur" and "nobility" in art.

One of the best full-length studies of *Maud* is still the influential monograph by Humbert Wolfe, entitled *Tennyson* (London, 1930). Though part of his study is now out of date, Wolfe was among the first commentators to react against the reaction against Tennyson. Indispensable for its information about the biographical background of the poem is Ralph W. Rader's *Maud: The Biographical Genesis*

(Berkeley, Calif., 1963). Equally suggestive—and often more critical in their approach—are A. S. Byatt's "The Lyric Structure of Tennyson's *Maud*," in *The Major Victorian Poets: Reconsiderations,* ed. Isobel Armstrong, pp. 69–92; J. H. Buckley's "The Intellectual Throne," in *Tennyson: The Growth of a Poet;* E. D. H. Johnson's "The Lily and the Rose: Symbolic Meaning in Tennyson's *Maud*," *PMLA,* LXIV (1949), 1222–1227; F. E. L. Priestley's "The Creation of New Genres," in *Language and Structure in Tennyson's Poetry,* pp. 107–119; Christopher Ricks's "*Maud,* 1855," in *Tennyson,* pp. 246–263.

Other studies of special interest include:

Assad, Thomas J. "Tennyson's 'Courage, Poor Heart of Stone,'" *Tulane Studies in English,* XVII (1970), 73–80.

Chandler, Alice. "Tennyson's *Maud* and the Song of Songs," *Victorian Poetry,* VII (1969), 91–104.

Crawford, John W. "A Unifying Element in Tennyson's *Maud*," *Victorian Poetry,* VII (1969), 64–66.

Drew, Philip. "Tennyson and the Dramatic Monologue: A Study of 'Maud.'" In *Writers and their Background: Tennyson,* ed. D. J. Palmer. Athens, Ohio, 1973. Pp. 115–146.

Harrison, Thomas P., Jr. "Tennyson's *Maud* and Shakespeare," *Shakespeare Association Bulletin,* XVII (1942), 80–85.

Killham, John. "Tennyson's *Maud*—the Function of the Imagery." In *Critical Essays on the Poetry of Tennyson,* ed. John Killham. London, 1960. Pp. 219–235.

Mermin, Dorothy M. "Tennyson's *Maud*: A Thematic Analysis," *Texas Studies in Literature and Language,* XV (1973), 267–278.

Ray, Gordon N. "Tennyson Reads *Maud*." In *Romantic and Victorian: Studies in Memory of William H. Marshall,* ed. W. P. Elledge and R. L. Hoffman. Rutherford, N.J., 1971. Pp. 290–317.

Shannon, Edgar F., Jr. "The Critical Reception of Tennyson's 'Maud,'" *PMLA,* LXVIII (1953), 397–417.

Stokes, Edward. "The Metrics of *Maud*," *Victorian Poetry,* II (1964), 97–110.

Idylls of the King

A review of all the books and articles dealing with the widely varying assessments of *Idylls of the King* would require a small dissertation. We may contrast P. F. Baum's refusal, in *Tennyson Sixty*

Years After (Chapel Hill, N.C., 1948), to see the value of any of the idylls with the more sympathetic reappraisals by F. E. L. Priestley, in "*Idylls of the King*—a Fresh View," in *Critical Essays on the Poetry of Tennyson*, pp. 239–255; by J. H. Buckley, in "The City Built to Music," in *Tennyson*, pp. 171–194; and by John D. Rosenberg, in *The Fall of Camelot: A Study of Tennyson's "Idylls of the King"* (Cambridge, Mass., 1973). Many scholars still have reservations about the poem; and, naturally enough, they have either restricted their commentary, as has Christopher Ricks in his biographical and critical study, or else have tactfully ignored the poem. While their silence must not be construed as approval, we may fairly contrast their skepticism with the civilized intelligence of John D. Rosenberg's commentary, an eloquent book-length study of the poem. The *Idylls* have also won the admiration of such scholars as J. Philip Eggers, in *King Arthur's Laureate: A Study of Tennyson's "Idylls of the King"* (New York, 1971), John R. Reed, in *Perception and Design in Tennyson's "Idylls of the King"* (Athens, Ohio, 1969), and Clyde de L. Ryals, in *From the Great Deep: Essays on "Idylls of the King"* (Athens, Ohio, 1967).

My own position is closer to Rosenberg's and Reed's than to Baum's, although I do not feel that the attempt to see a clear design in the poem should blind us to the indirection of Tennyson's method. Reed is right, I think, to emphasize the simultaneous confinement and freedom, obscurity and clarity, of the *Idylls*. Tennyson sees natural objects as hieroglyphs that his characters can no longer decipher, and speaks of his poem's "parabolic drift" (Hallam Tennyson, *Tennyson: A Memoir*, II, 127). But *Idylls of the King* is not Spenserian allegory. It exists at that transitional moment in literary history when the older traditions are about to turn—but have not yet turned—into the Symbolist tradition of a self-contained poetic world. Unlike most allegories, whose author is present as a superintending god, *Idylls of the King* is also like nature *without* God. Tennyson is the *deus absconditus* who has withdrawn from his creation, leaving the reader to ponder a puzzle whose solution is obscure. The poet celebrates the simple and truthful utterances of an earlier allegorical tradition in complex, broken forms—in riddles, cryptic prophecies and dreams, in poetry of half belief or illusion, and in poetry of madness. Though Tennyson shows that the truth is simple and absolute, he uses distorting reflections of that truth that are

complex and relative; a truth so true that it contains no element of
error Tennyson generally condemns as an idol.

But were Victorian contemporaries such as Longfellow, who believed that in the *Idylls* Tennyson had wrought "rich tapestries
worthy to hang by *The Faerie Queene*" (Hallam Tennyson, *Tennyson: A Memoir*, I, 413), any more mistaken than present-day readers
who study the *Idylls* as a Symbolist poem? The technique of the
Symbolists is aesthetic atomism. The illogical impingements of consciousness which bring the Symbolist to the threshold of inner mystery
recall "the free will" of Epicurus, against which Tennyson directs his
brilliant attack in the monologue "Lucretius." It is fashionable now
to assert the contrary, but in its moral passion, *Idylls of the King* is
still closer in spirit to *The Faerie Queene* than to Baudelaire's *Les
Fleurs du mal*. In its prophetic idealism, it also has more in common with Arnold's *Culture and Anarchy* than with a willed experiment in Symbolist dogma such as T. S. Eliot's *The Waste Land*.

Scholars have analyzed a number of the poem's repetitive devices
and symbolic designs. Especially illuminating is John D. Rosenberg's
view: "The narrative is a sequence of symbols protracted in time,
the symbolism a kind of condensed narration. The story functions
like the melody in a game of musical chairs, with the dramatis per-
sonae exchanging roles as they move from one position to the next"
(*The Fall of Camelot*, p. 137). In *"Idylls of the King—a Fresh
View,"* pp. 239–255, Priestley divides the poem into three groups of
four idylls. Moving from stories with happy endings through idylls of
disenchantment and catastrophe to the tragic denouement of the last
four idylls, the poem corresponds in its divisions to a three-act play.
In *Tennyson: The Growth of a Poet*, J. H. Buckley shows how the
"sequence . . . follows the cycle of the year" (p. 273). Tennyson
himself draws attention to the seasonal symbolism in a manuscript
note cited by Hallam Tennyson in *Tennyson: A Memoir*, II, 133.
Marshall McLuhan's study *From Cliché to Archetype* (New York,
1970) discusses an astrological pattern: "The twelve idylls follow the
cycle of the zodiac, each book corresponding faithfully to the traditional character of the twelve 'houses' of the zodiac" (p. 95). A
highly probable source of Tennyson's symbolic design, not previously
observed, is the ingenious parallel drawn by Gerard de Lairesse between the five acts of a drama and the various divisions of the day
and year. A copy of Lairesse's book, *The Art of Painting in All Its
Branches*, tr. John Frederick Fritsch (London, 1778), was in the

library at the Somersby rectory. In chapter xix, p. 82, the author comments: "The division of the drama into five acts is not without reason, from the example of the sun's course; which begins with daybreak; secondly, ascends all the morning; thirdly, has a median-altitude; fourthly, declines in the afternoon; lastly, sets in the evening. . . . By *time* we understand either the past, present, or to come; and therein, a division into night, morning, noon, and evening; also into spring, summer, autumn and winter."

Only by cultivating a variety of historical and critical approaches can commentators present *Idylls of the King* in its true character and judge its true value—neither encumbering the poem with the fictitious wealth of allegory nor burying it in a barren formalism.

Studies of special importance include:

Adler, Thomas P. "The Uses of Knowledge in Tennyson's *Merlin and Vivien,*" *Texas Studies in Literature and Language,* XI (1970), 1397–1403.

Brashear, William R. "Tennyson's Tragic Vitalism: *Idylls of the King,*" *Victorian Poetry,* VI (1968), 29–49.

Burchell, S. C. "Tennyson's 'Allegory in the Distance,' " *PMLA* LXVIII (1953), 418–424.

Engelberg, Edward. "The Beast Image in Tennyson's *Idylls of the King,*" *English Literary History,* XXII (1955), 287–292.

Grattan, Robert M. " 'Men From Beasts': A View on Conversion in Tennyson's *Idylls of the King,*" *West Virginia University Philological Papers,* XIX (1972), 29–40.

Gray, J. M. "The Creation of Excalibur: An Apparent Inconsistency in the *Idylls,*" *Victorian Poetry,* VI (1968), 68–69.

———. "Fact, Form and Fiction in Tennyson's *Balin and Balan,*" *Renaissance and Modern Studies,* XII (1968), 90–107.

———. *Man and Myth in Victorian England: Tennyson's "The Coming of Arthur."* Lincoln, Eng., 1969.

———. "An Origin for Tennyson's Characterization of Percivale in *The Holy Grail,*" *Notes and Queries,* XVIII (1971), 416–417.

———. "The Purpose of an Epic List in 'The Coming of Arthur,' " *Victorian Poetry,* VIII (1970), 339–341.

———. "Source and Symbol in 'Geraint and Enid': Tennyson's Doorm and Limours," *Victorian Poetry,* IV (1966), 131–132.

Gridley, Roy. "Confusion of the Seasons in Tennyson's 'The Last Tournament,' " *Victorian Newsletter,* no. 22 (1962), 14–16.

Kaplan, Fred. "Woven Paces and Weaving Hands: Tennyson's Merlin as Fallen Artist," *Victorian Poetry*, VII (1969), 285–298.

Kincaid, James R. "Tennyson's 'Gareth and Lynette,'" *Texas Studies in Literature and Language*, XIII (1972), 663–671.

Kozicki, Henry. "Tennyson's *Idylls of the King* as Tragic Drama," *Victorian Poetry*, IV (1966), 15–20.

Legris, Maurice. "Structure and Allegory in Tennyson's *Idylls of the King*," *Humanities Association Bulletin*, XVI (1965), 37–44.

Litzinger, Boyd. "The Structure of Tennyson's 'The Last Tournament,'" *Victorian Poetry*, I (1963), 53–60.

Poston, Laurence, III. " 'Pelleas and Ettarre': Tennyson's 'Troilus,'" *Victorian Poetry*, IV (1966), 199–204.

——. "The Two Provinces of Tennyson's *Idylls*," *Criticism*, IX (1967), 372–382.

Ryals, Clyde de L. *"Idylls of the King:* Tennyson's New Realism," *Victorian Newsletter*, no. 31 (1967), 5–7.

——. "The Moral Paradox of the Hero in *The Idylls of the King*," *English Literary History*, XXX (1963), 53–69.

——. "Percivale, Ambrosius, and the Method of Narration in 'The Holy Grail,'" *Die Neueren Sprachen*, XII (1963), 533–543.

Slinn, E. Warwick. "Deception and Artifice in *Idylls of the King*," *Victorian Poetry*, XI (1973), 1–14.

Solomon, Stanley J. "Tennyson's Paradoxical King," *Victorian Poetry*, I (1963), 258–271.

Wilkenfield, R. B. "Tennyson's Camelot: The Kingdom of Folly," *University of Toronto Quarterly*, XXXVII (1968), 281–294.

The Late Elegies

On Tennyson's art of reticence and obliquity, his "sense of the inadequacy of language as a medium" (p. 139), see the excellent comments in Priestley, *Language and Structure*, especially chapter v, " 'Meanings Ambushed,' " pp. 137–163. The subject of Tennyson's late elegies is his lifelong preoccupation with death, a theme most eloquently explored by James Kissane and Douglas Bush. See Kissane's fine essay, "Tennyson: The Passion of the Past and the Curse of Time," *Journal of English Literary History*, XXXII (1965), 85–109; and Bush's memorable observations in *Mythology and the Romantic Tradition*, especially pp. 227–228. Tennyson's brooding on death is not just a morbid indulgence; death forces Tennyson to hold fast to all that he most values in life. His "Passion of the Past" ("The

Ancient Sage," l. 219) is no less crucial than his future death, for it impels him to repeat a heroic past, not just in the sense of doing the same thing, but in the sense of achieving spiritual autonomy, as he does in *In Memoriam*, or of responding like Ulysses to unrealized possibilities. Few elegists better illustrate the truth of George Santayana's observation: "By becoming the spectator and confessor of his own death and of universal mutation, [the idealist] has identified himself with what is spiritual in all spirit, and masterful in all apprehension; and so conceiving himself, he may truly feel and know that he is eternal" (*The Life of Reason* [New York, 1954], p. 297).

Studies of special importance include:

Assad, Thomas J. "Analogy in Tennyson's 'Crossing the Bar,' " *Tulane Studies in English*, VIII (1958), 153–163.

Baum, Paull F. "Crossing the Bar," *English Language Notes*, I (1963), 115–116.

Crossett, John. "Tennyson and Catullus," *Classic Journal*, II (1958), 313–314.

Dahl, Curtis. "A Double Frame for Tennyson's Demeter?" *Victorian Studies*, I (1958), 356–362.

Elliott, Philip L., Jr. "Tennyson's 'To Virgil,' " *Notes and Queries*, VI (1959), 147–148.

Ferguson, John. "Catullus and Tennyson," *English Studies in Africa* (Johannesburg), XII (1969), 41–58.

Gerhard, Joseph. "Tennyson's Death in Life in Lyric Myth: 'Tears, Idle Tears' and 'Demeter and Persephone,' " *Victorian Newsletter*, no. 34 (1968), 13–18.

Kincaid, James R. "Tennyson's 'Crossing the Bar': A Poem of Frustration," *Victorian Poetry*, III (1965), 57–61.

Kramer, Dale. "Metaphor and Meaning in 'Crossing the Bar,' " *Ball State University Forum*, X (1969), 44–47.

Millhauser, Milton. "Structure and Symbol in 'Crossing the Bar,' " *Victorian Poetry*, IV (1966), 34–39.

Perrine, Laurence, "When Does Hope Mean Doubt? The Tone of 'Crossing the Bar,' " *Victorian Poetry*, IV (1966), 127–131.

Ricks, Christopher. "Tennyson's 'To E. Fitzgerald,' " *The Library*, XXV (1970), 156.

Sonstroem, David. " 'Crossing the Bar' as Last Word," *Victorian Poetry*, VIII (1970), 55–60.

Stange, G. Robert. "Tennyson's Mythology: A Study of *Demeter and Persephone*," *English Literary History*, XXI (1954), 67–80.

Index

Numerals in italic type indicate the main discussions.

Tennyson's Style

Designed by R. E. Rosenbaum.
Composed by York Composition Company, Inc.,
in 11 point Intertype Baskerville, 2 points leaded,
with display lines in Baskerville.
Printed letterpress from type by York Composition Company
on Warren's Number 66 text, 50 pound basis.
Bound by John H. Dekker & Sons, Inc.
in Columbia book cloth
and stamped in All Purpose foil.

Library of Congress Cataloging in Publication Data
(For library cataloging purposes only)

Shaw, William David.
   Tennyson's style.

   Bibliography: p.
   Includes index.
   1. Tennyson, Alfred Tennyson, Baron, 1809–1892—Style. I. Title.
PR5594.S5   821'.8   76–12814
ISBN 0–8014–1021–5

100935

DATE DUE

MAR 31 '77			
DEC 7 '78			
NOV 20 '85			
DEC 23 1987			
APR 19 1999			

821.81
T312Sh
1976
Shaw, William David
Tennyson's style.

Ohio Dominican College Library
1216 Sunbury Road
Columbus, Ohio 43219

DEMCO